GREGG

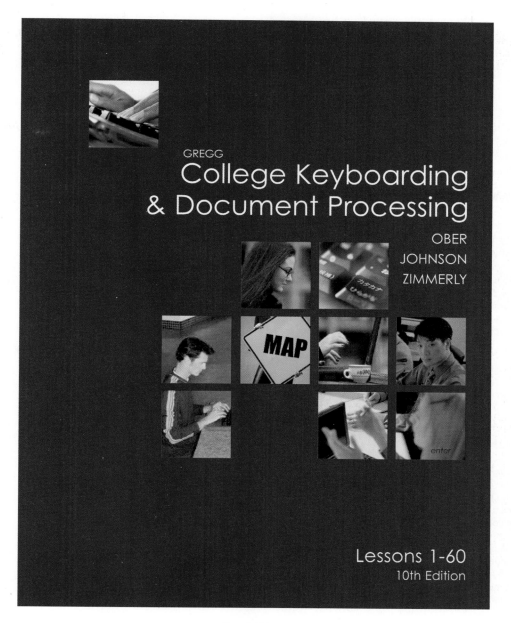

College Keyboarding & Document Processing

OBER
JOHNSON
ZIMMERLY

Lessons 1-60

10th Edition

Scot Ober
Ball State University

Jack E. Johnson
State University of West Georgia

Arlene Zimmerly
Los Angeles City College

Visit the *College Keyboarding* Web site at **www.mhhe.com/g[illegible]**

Boston Burr Ridge, IL Dubuque, IA Madison, WI New York San Francisco St. Louis
Bangkok Bogotá Caracas Kuala Lumpur Lisbon London Madrid Mexico City
Milan Montreal New Delhi Santiago Seoul Singapore Sydney Taipei Toronto

The ***McGraw-Hill*** *Companies*

GREGG COLLEGE KEYBOARDING & DOCUMENT PROCESSING, LESSONS 1-60
Published by McGraw-Hill/Irwin, a business unit of The McGraw-Hill Companies, Inc., 1221 Avenue of the Americas, New York, NY, 10020.

This book is printed on acid-free paper.

1 2 3 4 5 6 7 8 9 0 QPD/QPD 0 9 8 7 6 5 4

ISBN 0-07-296341-7

Editorial director: *John E. Biernat*
Publisher: *Linda Schreiber*
Sponsoring editor: *Doug Hughes*
Developmental editor: *Tammy Higham*
Developmental editor: *Megan Gates*
Marketing manager: *Keari Bedford*
Lead producer, Media technology: *Victoria Bryant*
Lead project manager: *Pat Frederickson*
Freelance project manager: *Rich Wright*
Senior production supervisor: *Michael R. McCormick*
Lead designer: *Matthew Baldwin*
Photo research coordinator: *Lori Kramer*
Senior supplement producer: *Susan Lombardi*
Senior digital content specialist: *Brian Nacik*
Cover design: *Subtle Intensity*
Interior design: *Matthew Baldwin*
Typeface: *11/12 Times Roman*
Compositor: *Seven Worldwide Publishing Solutions*
Printer: *Quebecor World Dubuque Inc.*

www.mhhe.com

CONTENTS

PART ONE: The Alphabet, Number, and Symbol Keys

PART TWO Basic Business Documents

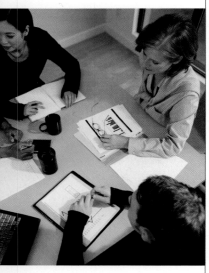

PART THREE: Reports, Correspond- ence, and Employment Documents

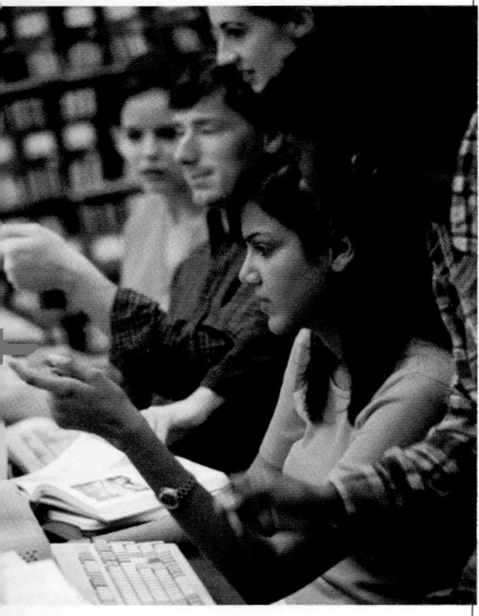

PREFACE

Gregg College Keyboarding & Document Processing Lessons 1–120, 10th Edition, is a multi-component instructional program designed to give the student and the instructor a high degree of flexibility and a high degree of success in meeting their respective goals. For student and instructor convenience, the core components of this instructional system are available in either a kit format or a book format. *Gregg College Keyboarding Lessons 1–20, 10th Edition,* is also available for the development of touch-typing skills for use in shorter computer keyboarding classes.

The Kit Format

Gregg College Keyboarding & Document Processing Lessons 1–120, 10th Edition, provides a complete kit of materials for both courses in the keyboarding curriculum generally offered by colleges. Each kit, which is briefly described below, contains a softcover textbook and a student word processing manual.

Kit 1: Lessons 1–60. This kit provides the text and word processing manual for the first course. Since this kit is designed for the beginning student, its major objectives are to develop touch control of the keyboard and proper typing techniques, to build basic speed and accuracy, and to provide practice in applying those basic skills to the formatting of reports, letters, memos, tables, and other kinds of personal and business communications.

Kit 2: Lessons 61–120. This kit provides the text and word processing manual for the second course. This course continues developing of basic typing skills and emphasizes the formatting of various kinds of business correspondence, reports, tables, electronic forms, and desktop publishing projects from arranged, unarranged, and rough-draft sources.

The Book Format

For the convenience of those who wish to obtain the core instructional materials in separate volumes, *Gregg College Keyboarding & Document Processing Lessons 1–120, 10th Edition,* offers textbooks for the first course: *Gregg College Keyboarding & Document Processing Lessons 1–60, 10th Edition,* or *Gregg College Keyboarding Lessons 1–20, 10th Edition.* For the second course, *Gregg College Document Processing Lessons 61–120* is offered, and for the two-semester course, *Gregg College Keyboarding & Document Processing Lessons 1–120* is available. In each instance, the content of the textbooks is identical to that of the corresponding textbooks in kit format. Third semester instruction is available in *Gregg College Document Processing Lessons 121–180.*

Supporting Materials

Gregg College Keyboarding & Document Processing Lessons 1–120, 10th Edition, includes the following additional components:

Instructional Materials. Supporting materials are provided for instructor use with either the kits or the textbooks. The special Instructor Wraparound Edition (IWE) offers lesson plans and reduced-size student pages to enhance classroom instruction. Distance-learning tips, instructional methodology, adult learner strategies, and special needs features are also included in this wraparound edition. Solution keys for all of the formatting exercises in Lessons 1–180 are contained in separate booklets used with this program. Finally, test booklets are available with the objective tests and alternative document processing tests for each part.

Computer Software. PC-compatible computer software is available for the entire program. The computer software provides complete lesson-by-lesson instruction for the entire 120 lessons.

Structure

Gregg College Keyboarding & Document Processing, 10th Edition, opens with a two-page part opener that introduces students to the focus of the instruction. Objectives are presented, and opportunities within career clusters are highlighted. The unit opener familiarizes students with the lesson content to be presented in the five lessons in the unit.

Every lesson begins with a Warmup that should be typed as soon as students are settled at the keyboard. In the New Keys Section, all alphabet, number, and symbol keys are introduced in the first 20 lessons. Drill lines in this section provide the practice necessary to achieve keyboarding skills.

An easily identifiable Skillbuilding section can be found in every lesson. Each drill presents to the student a variety of different activities designed to improve speed and accuracy. Skillbuilding exercises include Technique Timings, Diagnostic Practice, Paced Practice, Progressive Practice, MAP (Misstroke Analysis and Prescription), and Timed Writings, which progress from 1 to 5 minutes in length.

Many of the Skillbuilding sections also include a Pretest/Practice/Posttest routine. This routine is designed to build speed and accuracy skills as well as confidence. The Pretest helps identify speed and accuracy needs. The Practice activities consist of a variety of intensive enrichment drills. Finally, the Posttest measures improvement.

Part 1

The Alphabet, Number, and Symbol Keys

Keyboarding in Arts, Audio, Video Technology, and Communications Services

Occupations in this cluster deal with organizing and communicating information to the public in various forms and media. This cluster includes jobs in radio and television broadcasting, journalism, motion pictures, the recording industry, the performing arts, multimedia publishing, and the entertainment services. Book editors, computer artists, technical writers, radio announcers, news correspondents, and camera operators are just a few jobs within this cluster.

Qualifications and Skills

Strong oral and written communication skills and technical skills are necessary for anyone in communications and media. Without a doubt, competent keyboarding skill is extremely advantageous.

Working in the media requires creativity, talent, and accurate use of language. In journalism, being observant, thinking clearly, and seeing the significance of events are all of utmost importance. Announcers must have exceptional voices, excellent speaking skills, and a unique style. The ability to work under pressure is important in all areas of media.

Objectives

KEYBOARDING

- Operate by touch the letter, number, and symbol keys.
- Demonstrate proper typing technique.
- Use the correct spacing with punctuation.
- Type at least 28 words per minute on a 2-minute timed writing with no more than 5 errors.

TECHNICAL

- Answer correctly at least 90 percent of the questions on an objective test.

1

INTRODUCTION TO THE STUDENT

Goals

- Type at least 30wpm/3'/5e
- Format one-page business reports

Starting a Lesson

Each lesson begins with the goals for that lesson. Read the goals carefully so that you understand the purpose of your practice. In the example at the left (from Lesson 26), the goals for the lesson are to type 30wpm (words per minute) on a 3-minute timed writing with no more than 5 errors and to format one-page business reports.

Building Straight-Copy Skill

Warmups. Each lesson begins with a Warmup that reinforces learned alphabet, number, and/or symbol keys.

Skillbuilding. The Skillbuilding portion of each lesson includes a variety of drills to individualize your keyboarding speed and accuracy development. Instructions for completing the drills are always provided beside each activity.

Additional Skillbuilding drills are included in the back of the textbook. These drills are intended to help you meet your individual goals.

Measuring Straight-Copy Skill

Straight-copy skill is measured in wpm. All timed writings are the exact length needed to meet the speed goal for the lesson. If you finish a timed writing before time is up, you have automatically reached your speed goal for the lesson.

Counting Errors. Specific criteria are used for counting errors. Count an error when:

1. Any stroke is incorrect.
2. Any punctuation after a word is incorrect or omitted. Count the word before the punctuation as incorrect.
3. The spacing after a word or after its punctuation is incorrect. Count the word as incorrect.
4. A letter or word is omitted.
5. A letter or word is repeated.
6. A direction about spacing, indenting, and so on, is violated.
7. Words are transposed.

(**Note:** Only one error is counted for each word, no matter how many errors it may contain.)

Determining Speed. Typing speed is measured in wpm. To compute wpm, count every 5 strokes, including spaces, as 1 "word." Horizontal word scales below an activity divide lines into 5-stroke words. Vertical word scales beside an activity show the number of words in each line cumulatively totaled. For example, in the illustration below, if you complete a line, you have typed 8 words. If you complete 2 lines, you have typed 16 words. Use the bottom word scale to determine the word count of a partial line. Add that number to the cumulative total for the last complete line.

```
Ada lost her letter; Dee lost her card.         8
Dave sold some of the food to a market.        16
Alva asked Walt for three more matches.        24
Dale asked Seth to watch the last show.        32
| 1  | 2  | 3  | 4  | 5  | 6  | 7  | 8  |
```

Correcting Errors

As you learn to type, you will probably make some errors. To correct an error, press BACKSPACE (shown as ← on some keyboards) to delete the incorrect character. Then type the correct character.

If you notice an error on a different line, use the up, down, left, or right arrows to move the insertion point immediately to the left or right of the error. Press BACKSPACE to delete a character to the left of the insertion point, or DELETE to delete a character to the right of the insertion point. Error-correction settings in the GDP software determine whether you can correct errors in timed writings and drills. Consult your instructor for error-correction guidelines.

Typing Technique

Correct position at the keyboard enables you to type with greater speed and accuracy and with less fatigue. When typing for a long period, rest your eyes occasionally by looking away from the screen. Change position, walk around, or stretch when your muscles feel tired. Making such movements and adjustments may help prevent your body from becoming too tired. In addition, long-term bodily damage, such as carpal tunnel syndrome, can be prevented.

If possible, adjust your workstation as follows:

Chair. Adjust the height so that your upper and lower legs form a 90-degree angle and your lower back is supported by the back of the chair.
Keyboard. Center your body opposite the J key, and lean forward slightly. Keep your forearms horizontal to the keyboard.
Screen. Position the monitor so that the top of the screen is just below eye level and about 18 to 26 inches away.
Text. Position your textbook or other copy on either side of the monitor as close to it as vertically and horizontally possible to minimize head and eye movement and to avoid neck strain.

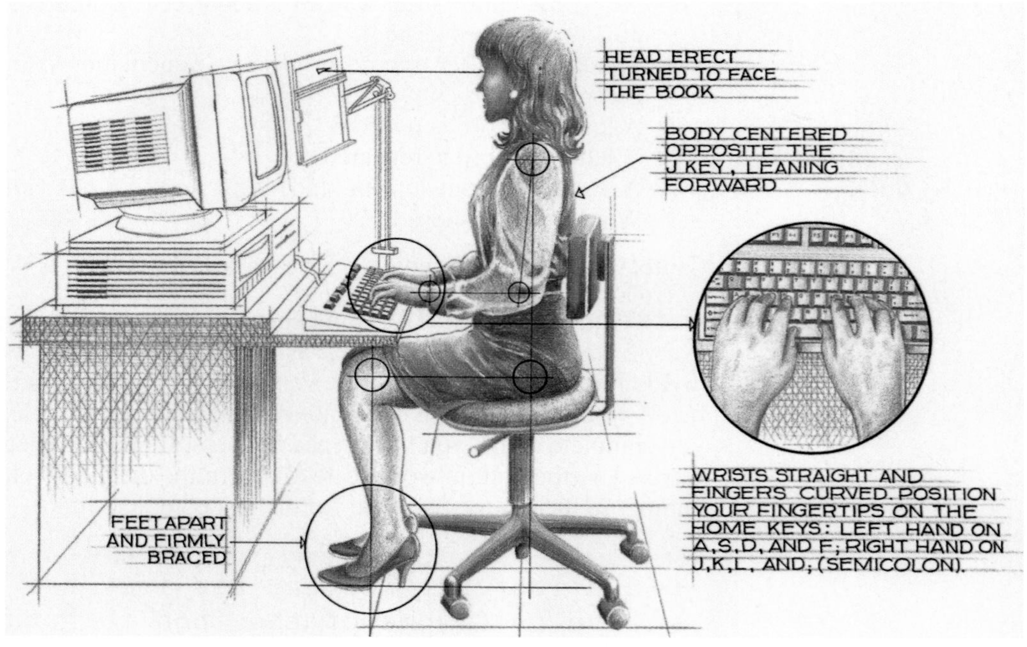

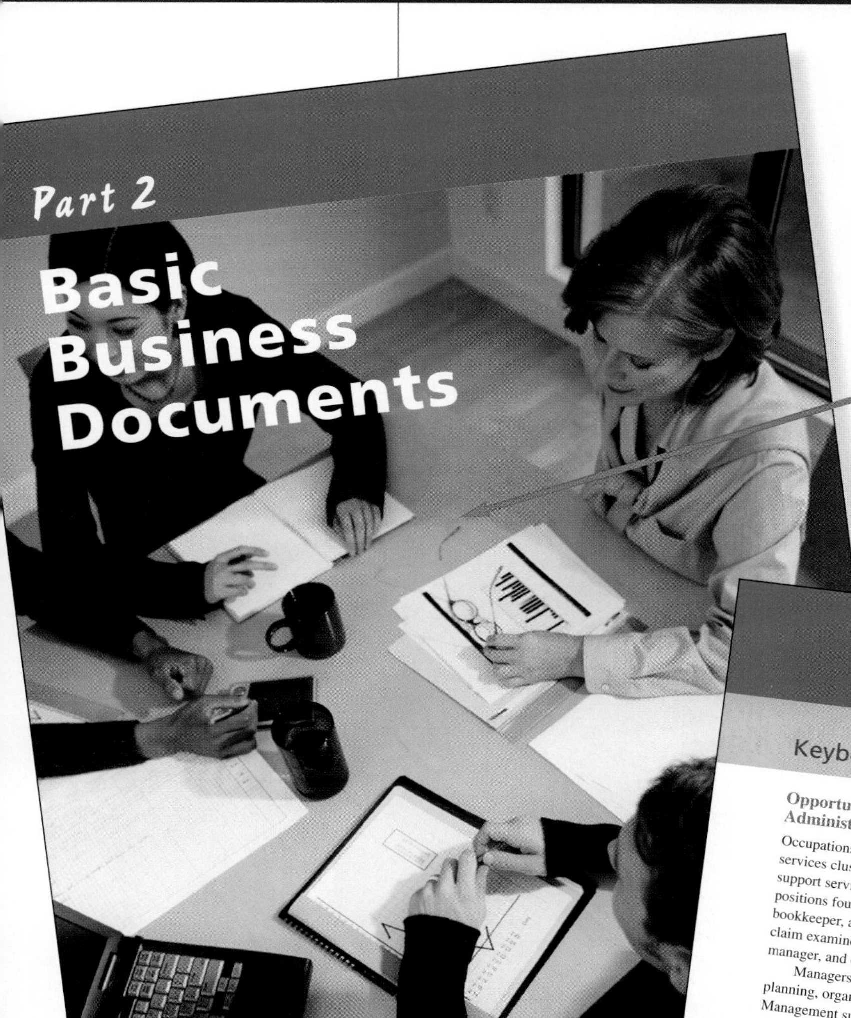

Each **Part Opener** is a two-page spread that provides a list of the part objectives and a special feature that focuses on the use of your keyboarding skills in various career clusters.

Keyboarding in Business and Administrative Services

Opportunities in Business and Administrative Careers

Occupations in the business and administrative services cluster focus on providing management and support services for various companies. The many positions found in this cluster include receptionist, bookkeeper, administrative professional or assistant, claim examiner, accountant, word processor, office manager, and chief executive officer.

Managers and administrators are in charge of planning, organizing, and controlling businesses. Management support workers gather and analyze data to help company executives make decisions. Administrative support workers perform a variety of tasks, such as recordkeeping, operating office equipment, managing their own projects and assignments, and developing high-level integrated software skills as well as Internet research skills. Ideally, everyone in business should be patient, detail-oriented, and cooperative. Excellent written and oral communication skills are definitely an asset as well.

Many companies have been revolutionized by advances in computer technology. As a result, keyboarding skill provides a definite advantage for those who work in business and administrative services. Now, more than ever, success in the business world is dependent upon adaptability and education.

Objectives

KEYBOARDING

- Operate the keyboard by touch.
- Type at least 36 words per minute on a 3-minute timed writing with no more than 4 errors.

LANGUAGE ARTS

- Develop proofreading skills and correctly use proofreaders' marks.
- Use capitals, commas, and apostrophes correctly.
- Develop composing and spelling skills.

WORD PROCESSING

- Use the word processing commands necessary to complete the document processing activities.

DOCUMENT PROCESSING

- Format e-mail, business and academic reports, business letters in block style, envelopes, memos, and tables.

TECHNICAL

- Answer at least 90 percent of the questions correctly on an objective test.

49

Unit 1
Keyboarding: The Alphabet
LESSON 1
A S D F J K L ;
ENTER SPACE BAR
LESSON 2
H E O R
LESSON 3
M T P C
LESSON 4
RIGHT SHIFT V . W
LESSON 5
Review
New Keys
Lesson 4
Goals
Touch-type the RIGHT SHIFT, V, period, and W keys
Count errors
Type at least 13wpm/1′/3e
A. Type 2 times.
A. WARMUP
the farmer asked her to feed the mares;
the late callers came to mop the floor;
NEW KEYS
B. Type each line 2 times.
B. THE RIGHT SHIFT KEY
To capitalize letters on the left half of the keyboard:
1. With the J finger at home, press and hold down the RIGHT SHIFT key with the Sem finger.
2. Press the letter key.
3. Release the RIGHT SHIFT key and return fingers to home position.
UNIT 1 Lesson 4
9

The **Unit Opener** helps you organize your study of unit concepts. The listing of the lessons clearly previews what will be taught in the unit.

Color Coding is used in the early lessons to help you differentiate which finger is used. On the keyboard chart shown at the beginning of each new-key lesson, new keys are highlighted, previously learned keys are labeled but not highlighted, and unlearned keys are blank. You will have a sense of progress as you move through the 20 new-key lessons.

Handwritten examples are used to make lessons more realistic since many letters, reports, and so on, are originally prepared with pen and paper. Including handwritten manuscript also enhances your ability to accurately read and type at the same time.

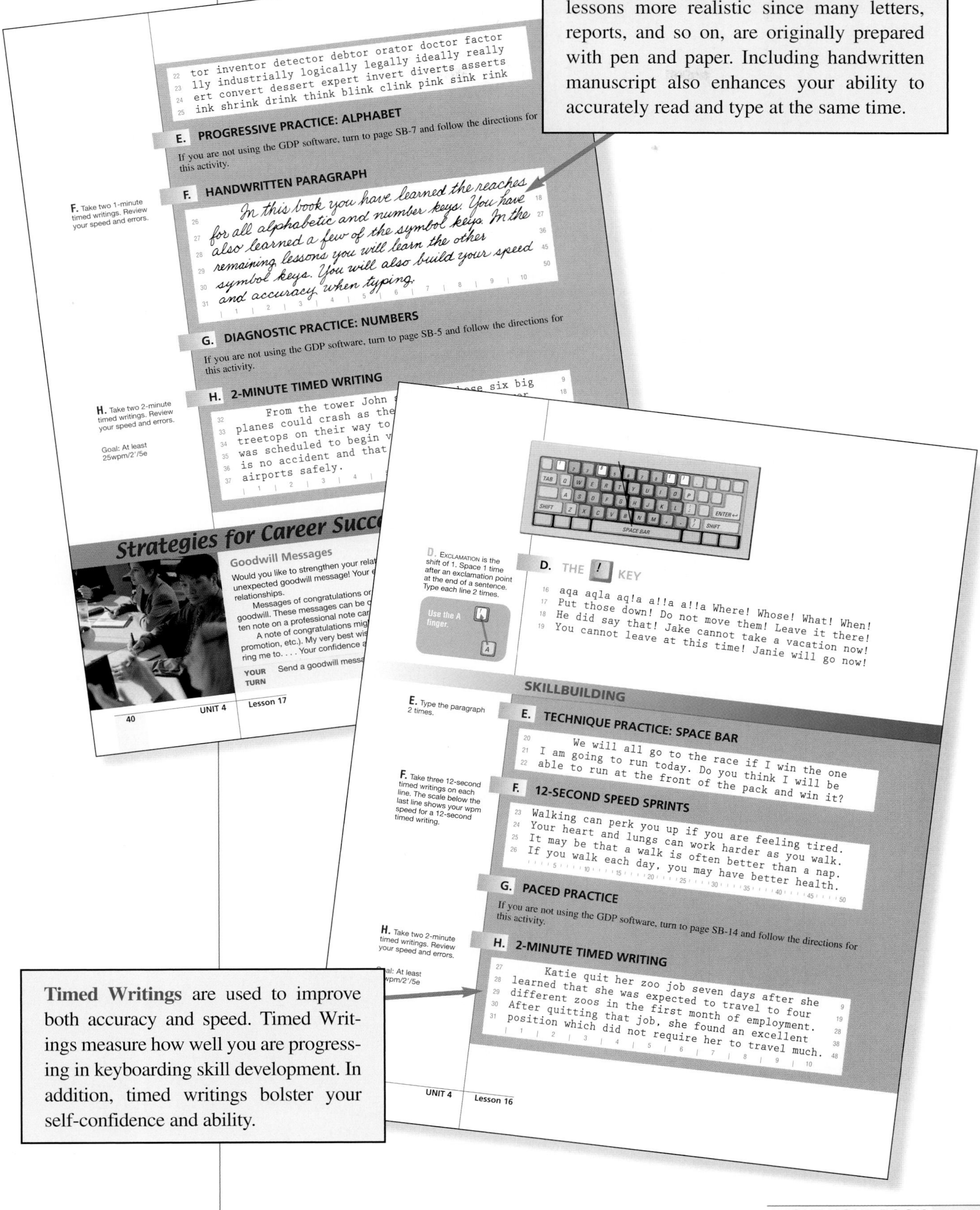

tor inventor detector debtor orator doctor factor
lly industrially logically legally ideally really
ert convert dessert expert invert diverts asserts
ink shrink drink think blink clink pink sink rink

E. PROGRESSIVE PRACTICE: ALPHABET

If you are not using the GDP software, turn to page SB-7 and follow the directions for this activity.

F. HANDWRITTEN PARAGRAPH

F. Take two 1-minute timed writings. Review your speed and errors.

In this book you have learned the reaches for all alphabetic and number keys. You have also learned a few of the symbol keys. In the remaining lessons you will learn the other symbol keys. You will also build your speed and accuracy when typing.

G. DIAGNOSTIC PRACTICE: NUMBERS

If you are not using the GDP software, turn to page SB-5 and follow the directions for this activity.

H. 2-MINUTE TIMED WRITING

H. Take two 2-minute timed writings. Review your speed and errors.

Goal: At least 25wpm/2'/5e

From the tower John s ... se six big planes could crash as the ... treetops on their way to ... was scheduled to begin v ... is no accident and that ... airports safely.

Strategies for Career Succ...

Goodwill Messages

Would you like to strengthen your relat... unexpected goodwill message! Your e... relationships.

Messages of congratulations or ... goodwill. These messages can be c... ten note on a professional note car...

A note of congratulations mig... promotion, etc.). My very best wis... ring me to. . . . Your confidence a...

YOUR TURN Send a goodwill messa...

40 UNIT 4 Lesson 17

D. Exclamation is the shift of 1. Space 1 time after an exclamation point at the end of a sentence. Type each line 2 times.

Use the A finger.

D. THE ! KEY

aqa aqla aq!a a!!a a!!a Where! Whose! What! When!
Put those down! Do not move them! Leave it there!
He did say that! Jake cannot take a vacation now!
You cannot leave at this time! Janie will go now!

SKILLBUILDING

E. TECHNIQUE PRACTICE: SPACE BAR

E. Type the paragraph 2 times.

We will all go to the race if I win the one I am going to run today. Do you think I will be able to run at the front of the pack and win it?

F. 12-SECOND SPEED SPRINTS

F. Take three 12-second timed writings on each line. The scale below the last line shows your wpm speed for a 12-second timed writing.

Walking can perk you up if you are feeling tired.
Your heart and lungs can work harder as you walk.
It may be that a walk is often better than a nap.
If you walk each day, you may have better health.

G. PACED PRACTICE

If you are not using the GDP software, turn to page SB-14 and follow the directions for this activity.

H. 2-MINUTE TIMED WRITING

H. Take two 2-minute timed writings. Review your speed and errors.

Katie quit her zoo job seven days after she learned that she was expected to travel to four different zoos in the first month of employment. After quitting that job, she found an excellent position which did not require her to travel much.

UNIT 4 Lesson 16

Timed Writings are used to improve both accuracy and speed. Timed Writings measure how well you are progressing in keyboarding skill development. In addition, timed writings bolster your self-confidence and ability.

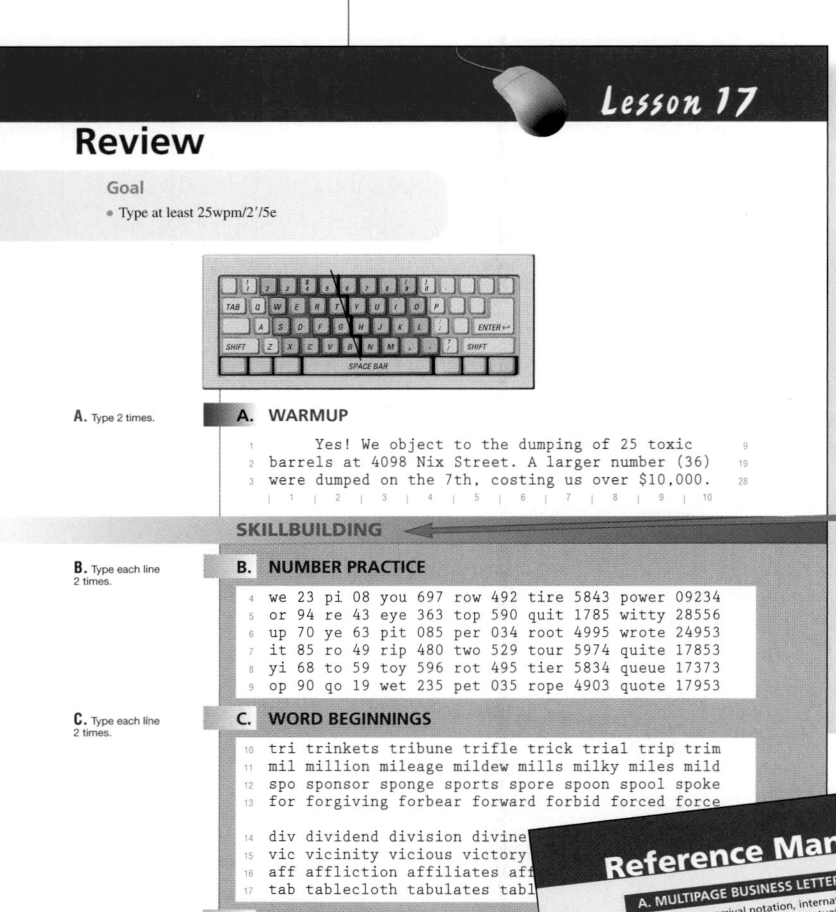

Skillbuilding practice in every lesson offers an individualized plan for speed and accuracy development. A variety of skill-building exercises, including Technique Practice, Pretest/Practice/Posttest, Sustained Practice, 12-Second Speed Sprints, Diagnostic Practice, Progressive Practice, Paced Practice, and Number Practice, provide the foundation for progress in your skill development.

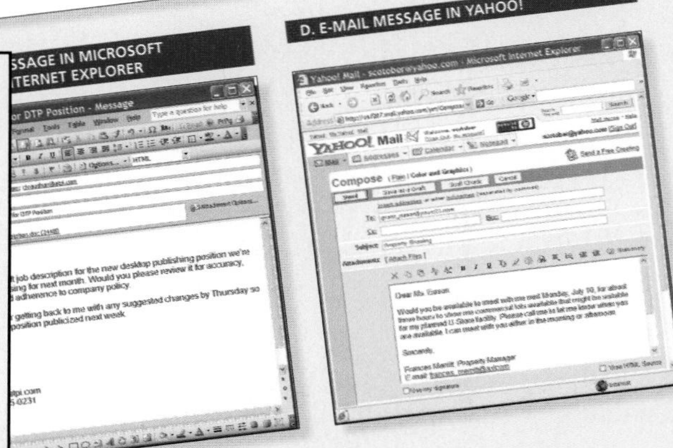

The Reference Manual material found in the front of the book and in the Word manual enables you to easily locate information regarding the proper way to format business letters, reports, e-mail messages, memoranda, and other forms of written communication. Elements such as line spacing and the placement of letterhead and body text are all illustrated in detail for your instructional support. In addition, 50 "must-know" rules for language arts in business contexts are included with examples in the Reference Manual to help improve writing skills.

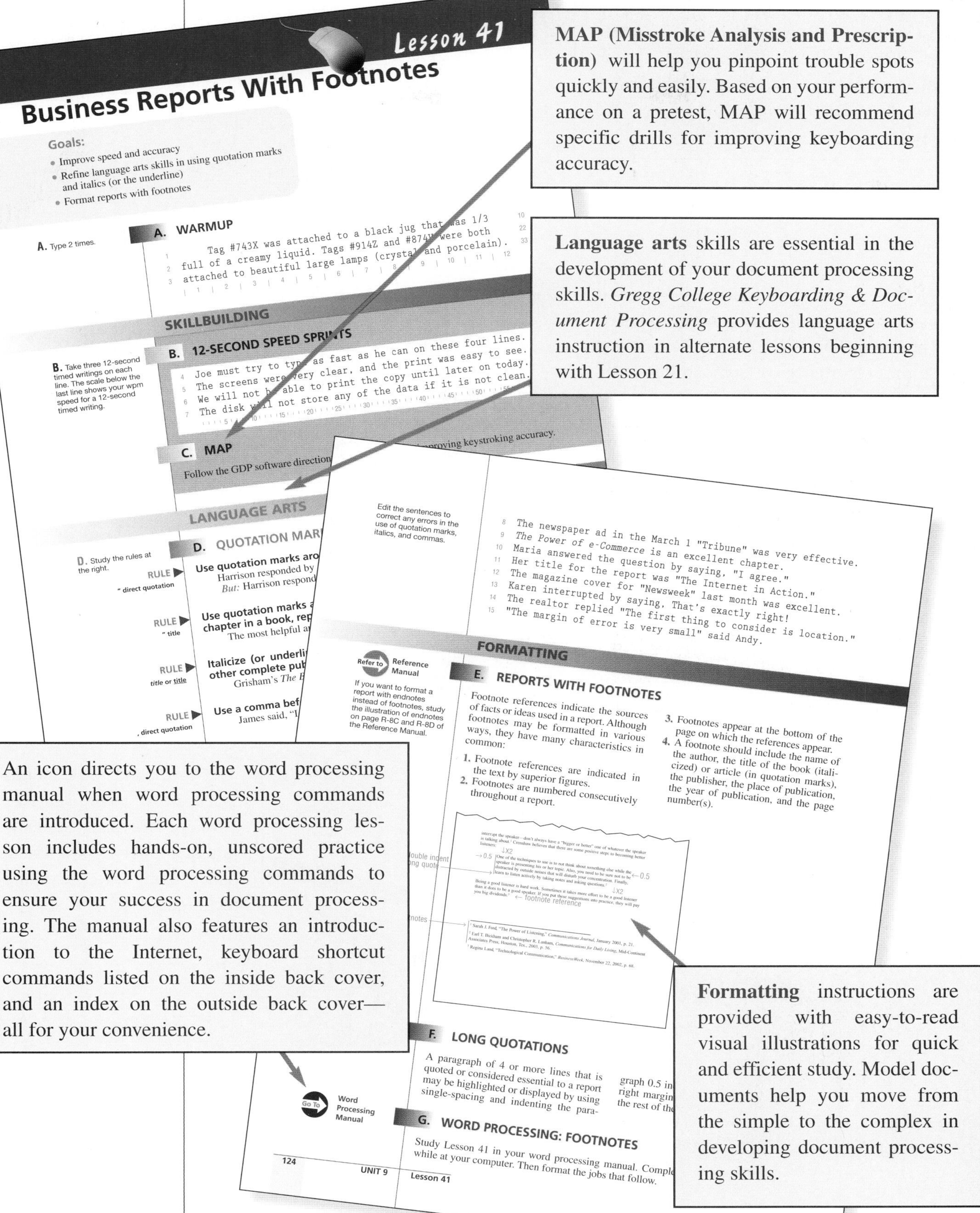

MAP (Misstroke Analysis and Prescription) will help you pinpoint trouble spots quickly and easily. Based on your performance on a pretest, MAP will recommend specific drills for improving keyboarding accuracy.

Language arts skills are essential in the development of your document processing skills. *Gregg College Keyboarding & Document Processing* provides language arts instruction in alternate lessons beginning with Lesson 21.

An icon directs you to the word processing manual when word processing commands are introduced. Each word processing lesson includes hands-on, unscored practice using the word processing commands to ensure your success in document processing. The manual also features an introduction to the Internet, keyboard shortcut commands listed on the inside back cover, and an index on the outside back cover—all for your convenience.

Formatting instructions are provided with easy-to-read visual illustrations for quick and efficient study. Model documents help you move from the simple to the complex in developing document processing skills.

The last document processing exercise in most units is designated as a Progress Check/Proofreading Check. Make it your goal is to have zero typographical errors when the GDP software first scores the document.

Special features are designed to enhance your study of keyboarding. The *Keyboarding Connection* features illustrate the importance of keyboarding skills outside of the classroom. The *Strategies for Career Success* features offer an employment-related narrative, including useful hints for succeeding in any career.

The Appendix contains instructions for the Ten-Key Numeric Keypad. Students practice entering numerical data using touch-typing techniques.

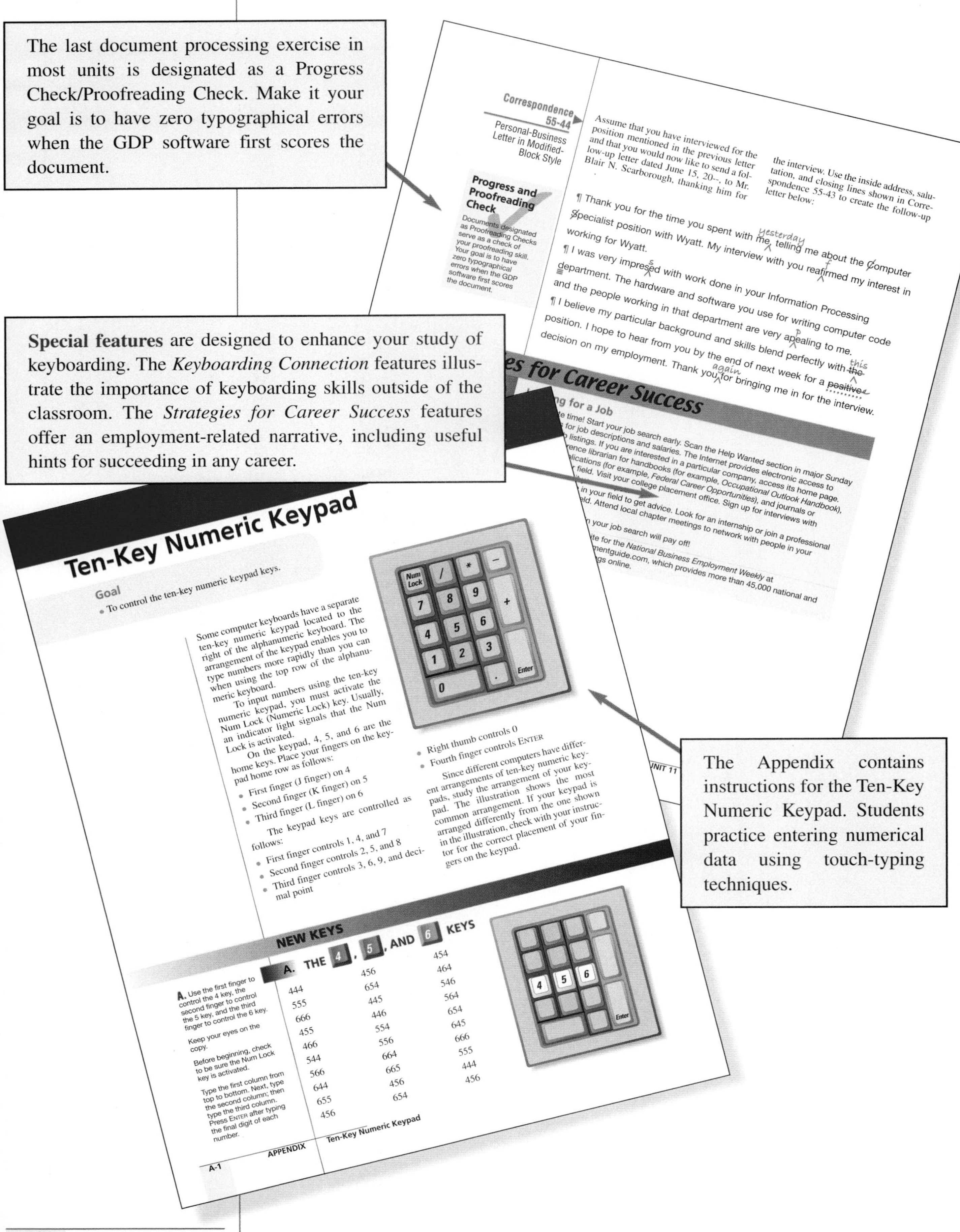

Correspondence 55-44

Personal-Business Letter in Modified-Block Style

Assume that you have interviewed for the position mentioned in the previous letter and that you would now like to send a follow-up letter dated June 15, 20--, to Mr. Blair N. Scarborough, thanking him for the interview. Use the inside address, salutation, and closing lines shown in Correspondence 55-43 to create the follow-up letter below:

Progress and Proofreading Check

Documents designated as Proofreading Checks serve as a check of your proofreading skill. Your goal is to have zero typographical errors when the GDP software first scores the document.

¶ Thank you for the time you spent with me, telling me about the Computer Specialist position with Wyatt. My interview with you reafirmed my interest in working for Wyatt.

¶ I was very impresed with work done in your Information Processing department. The hardware and software you use for writing computer code and the people working in that department are very apealing to me.

¶ I believe my particular background and skills blend perfectly with the position. I hope to hear from you by the end of next week for a positive decision on my employment. Thank you for bringing me in for the interview.

Ten-Key Numeric Keypad

Goal

- To control the ten-key numeric keypad keys.

Some computer keyboards have a separate ten-key numeric keypad located to the right of the alphanumeric keyboard. The arrangement of the keypad enables you to type numbers more rapidly than you can when using the top row of the alphanumeric keyboard.

To input numbers using the ten-key numeric keypad, you must activate the Num Lock (Numeric Lock) key. Usually, an indicator light signals that the Num Lock is activated.

On the keypad, 4, 5, and 6 are the home keys. Place your fingers on the keypad home row as follows:

- First finger (J finger) on 4
- Second finger (K finger) on 5
- Third finger (L finger) on 6

The keypad keys are controlled as follows:

- First finger controls 1, 4, and 7
- Second finger controls 2, 5, and 8
- Third finger controls 3, 6, 9, and decimal point
- Right thumb controls 0
- Fourth finger controls ENTER

Since different computers have different arrangements of ten-key numeric keypads, study the arrangement of your keypad. The illustration shows the most common arrangement. If your keypad is arranged differently from the one shown in the illustration, check with your instructor for the correct placement of your fingers on the keypad.

NEW KEYS

A. THE 4, 5, AND 6 KEYS

A. Use the first finger to control the 4 key, the second finger to control the 5 key, and the third finger to control the 6 key.

Keep your eyes on the copy.

Before beginning, check to be sure the Num Lock key is activated.

Type the first column from top to bottom. Next, type the second column; then type the third column. Press ENTER after typing the final digit of each number.

444 555 666 455 466 544 566 644 655 456

456 654 445 446 554 556 664 665 456 654

454 464 546 564 654 645 666 555 444 456

A-1 APPENDIX Ten-Key Numeric Keypad

The back-of-the book skillbuilding routines are designed with YOU in mind. The Paced Practice skillbuilding paragraphs use an upbeat, motivational storyline with guidance in career choices. The Supplementary Timed Writings relate critical thinking skills to careers.

SKILLBUILDING

70wpm Indexing is the ability of a word processor to accumulate a list of words that appear in a document, including page numbers, and then print a revised list in alphabetic order.

72wpm When a program needs information from you, a dialog box will appear on the desktop. Once the dialog box appears, you must identify the option you desire and then choose that option.

74wpm A facsimile is an exact copy of a document, and it is also a process by which images, such as typed letters, graphs, and signatures, are scanned, transmitted, and then printed on paper.

76wpm Compatibility refers to the ability of a computer to share information with another computer or to communicate with some other apparatus. It can be accomplished by using hardware or software.

78wpm Some operators like to personalize their desktops when they use Windows by making various changes. For example, they can change their screen colors and the pointer so that they will have more fun.

80wpm Wraparound is the ability of a word processor to move words from one line to another line and from one page to the next page as a result of inserting and deleting text or changing the size of margins.

82wpm It is possible when using Windows to evaluate the contents of different directories o... screen at the very same time. You can then choose to ... particular file from one directory to anoth...

84wpm List processing is a ... lists of data that c... numeric order. A li... is stored in one's ...

86wpm A computer is a wo... input and then pr... computer performs... programs, which ...

88wpm The configurati... processing sys... used for enter... one disk driv...

SB-9 SKILLBUILDING Progressive Pr...

Supplementary Timed Writing 3

SKILLBUILDING

Office employees perform a variety of tasks during 10
their workday. These tasks vary from handling telephone 21
calls to forwarding personal messages, from sending short 33
e-mail messages to compiling complex office reports, and 44
from writing simple letters to assembling detailed letters 56
with tables, graphics, and imported data. Office workers 67
are a fundamental part of a company's structure. 77

The office worker uses critical thinking in order to 88
accomplish a wide array of daily tasks. Some of the tasks 100
are more urgent than other tasks and should be completed 111
first. Some tasks take only a short time, while others take 123
a lot more time. Some tasks demand a quick response, while 135
others may be taken up as time permits or even postponed 147
until the future. Some of the tasks require input from 158
coworkers or managers. Whether a job is simple or complex, 170
big or small, the office worker must decide what is to be 182
tackled first by determining the priority of each task. 193

When setting priorities, critical thinking skills are 204
essential. The office worker evaluates each aspect of the 216
task. It is a good idea to identify the size of the task, 228
determine its complexity, estimate its effort, judge its 239
importance, and set its deadline. Once the office worker 250
assesses each task that is to be finished within a certain 262
period of time, then the priority for completing all tasks 274
can be set. Critical thinking skills, if applied well, 285
can save the employer money or, if executed poorly, can 296
cost the employer. 300

| 1 | 2 | 3 | 4 | 5 | 6 | 7 | 8 | 9 | 10 | 11 | 12

SKILLBUILDING Supplementary Timed Writings SB-30

Reference Manual

A. MAJOR PARTS OF A MICROCOMPUTER SYSTEM

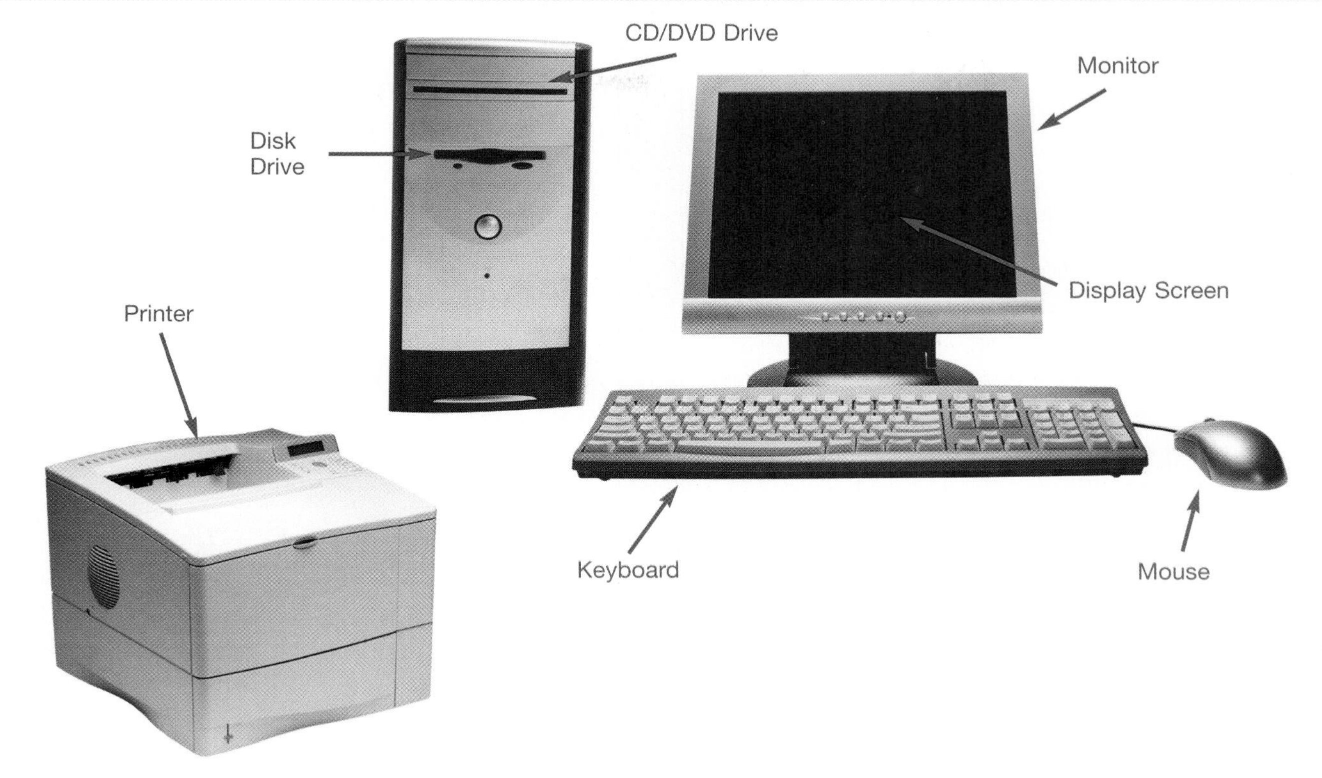

B. THE COMPUTER KEYBOARD

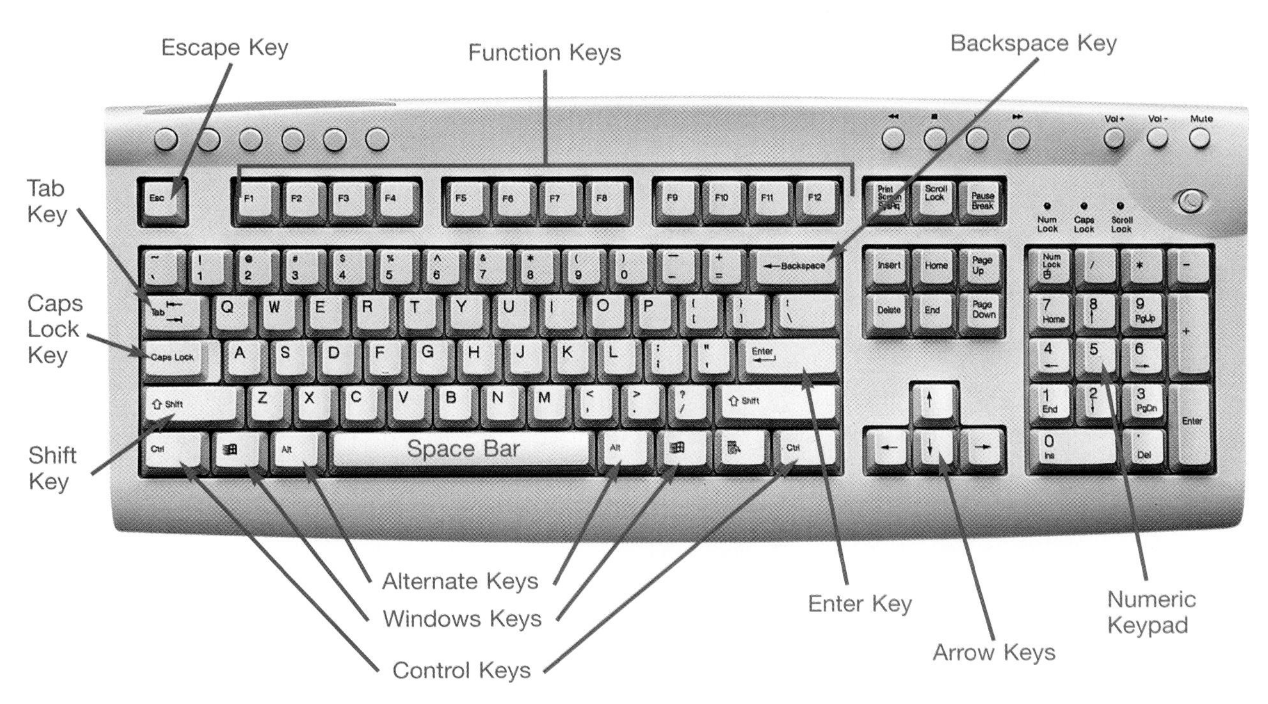

Reference Manual

A. BUSINESS LETTER IN BLOCK STYLE

(with standard punctuation)

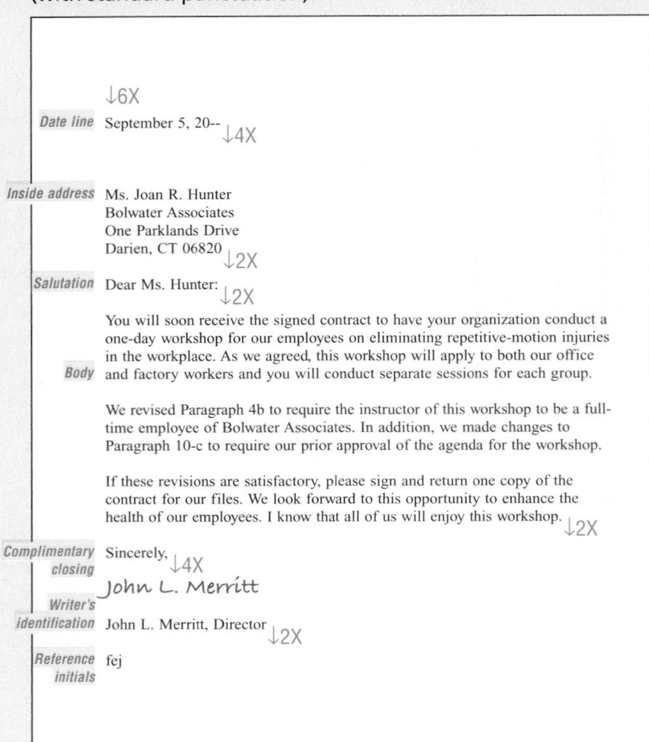

↓6X

Date line — September 5, 20-- ↓4X

Inside address — Ms. Joan R. Hunter
Bolwater Associates
One Parklands Drive
Darien, CT 06820 ↓2X

Salutation — Dear Ms. Hunter: ↓2X

Body — You will soon receive the signed contract to have your organization conduct a one-day workshop for our employees on eliminating repetitive-motion injuries in the workplace. As we agreed, this workshop will apply to both our office and factory workers and you will conduct separate sessions for each group.

We revised Paragraph 4b to require the instructor of this workshop to be a full-time employee of Bolwater Associates. In addition, we made changes to Paragraph 10-c to require our prior approval of the agenda for the workshop.

If these revisions are satisfactory, please sign and return one copy of the contract for our files. We look forward to this opportunity to enhance the health of our employees. I know that all of us will enjoy this workshop. ↓2X

Complimentary closing — Sincerely, ↓4X

John L. Merritt

Writer's identification — John L. Merritt, Director ↓2X

Reference initials — fej

B. BUSINESS LETTER IN MODIFIED-BLOCK STYLE

(with open punctuation, multiline list, and enclosure notation)

Left tab: 3"

↓6X

→tab to centerpoint — May 15, 20-- ↓4X

Mr. Ichiro Xie
Bolwater Associates
One Parklands Drive
Darien, CT 06820 ↓2X

Dear Mr. Xie ↓2X

I am returning a signed contract to have your organization conduct a one-day workshop for our employees on eliminating repetitive-motion injuries in the workplace. We have made the following changes to the contract:

Multiline list

1. We revised Paragraph 4b to require the instructor of this workshop to be a full-time employee of Bolwater Associates.

2. We made changes to Paragraph 10-c to require our prior approval of the agenda for the workshop.

If these revisions are satisfactory, please sign and return one copy of the contract for our files. We look forward to this opportunity to enhance the health of our employees. I know that all of us will enjoy this workshop. ↓2X

→tab to centerpoint — Sincerely ↓4X

Reinalda Guerrero

Reinalda Guerrero, Director ↓2X

pec

Enclosure notation — Enclosure

C. BUSINESS LETTER IN SIMPLIFIED STYLE

(with single-line list, enclosure notation, and copy notation)

↓6X

October 5, 20-- ↓4X

Mr. Dale P. Griffin
Bolwater Associates
One Parklands Drive
Darien, CT 06820 ↓3X

Subject line — WORKSHOP CONTRACT ↓3X

I am returning the signed contract, Ms. Hunter, to have your organization conduct a one-day workshop for our employees on eliminating repetitive-motion injuries in the workplace. We have amended the following sections of the contract:

Single-line list

- Paragraph 4b
- Table 3
- Attachment 2

If these revisions are satisfactory, please sign and return one copy of the contract for our files. We look forward to this opportunity to enhance the health of our employees. I know that all of us will enjoy this workshop. ↓4X

Kachina Haddad

KACHINA HADDAD, DIRECTOR ↓2X

iww
Enclosure

Copy notation — c: Legal Department

D. PERSONAL-BUSINESS LETTER IN MODIFIED-BLOCK STYLE

(with international address and standard punctuation)

Left tab: 3"

↓6X

→tab to centerpoint — July 15, 20-- ↓4X

International Address — Mr. Luis Fernandez, President
Arvon Industries, Inc.
21 St. Claire Avenue East
Toronto, ON M4T IL9
CANADA ↓2X

Dear Mr. Fernandez: ↓2X

As a former employee and present stockholder of Arvon Industries, I wish to protest the planned sale of the Consumer Products Division.

According to published reports, consumer products accounted for 19 percent of last year's corporate profits, and they are expected to account for even more this year. In addition, Dun & Bradstreet predicts that consumer products nationwide will outpace the general economy for the next five years.

I am concerned about the effect that this planned sale will have on overall corporate profits, on cash dividends for investors, and on the economy of Melbourne, where the two consumer-products plants are located. Please ask your board of directors to reconsider this matter. ↓2X

→tab to centerpoint — Sincerely, ↓4X

Roger J. Michaelson

Return address — Roger J. Michaelson
901 East Benson, Apt. 3
Fort Lauderdale, FL 33301

A. BUSINESS LETTER ON EXECUTIVE STATIONERY

(7.25" x 10.5"; 1" side margins; with delivery notation and standard punctuation.)

↓6X

July 18, 20-- ↓4X

Mr. Rodney Eastwood
BBL Resources
52A Northern Ridge
Fayetteville, PA 17222 ↓2X

Dear Rodney: ↓2X

I see no reason why we should continue to consider the locality around Geraldton for our new plant. Even though the desirability of this site from an economic view is undeniable, there is insufficient housing readily available for our workers.

In trying to control urban growth, the city has been turning down the building permits for new housing or placing so many restrictions on foreign investment as to make it too expensive.

Please continue to seek out other areas of exploration where we might form a joint partnership. ↓2X

Sincerely, ↓4X

Dalit Chande

Dalit Chande
Vice President for Operations ↓2X

mme
Delivery notation — By Fax

B. BUSINESS LETTER ON HALF-PAGE STATIONERY

(5.5" x 8.5"; 0.75" side margins and standard punctuation)

↓4X

July 18, 20-- ↓4X

Mr. Aristeo Olivas
BBL Resources
52A Northern Ridge
Fayetteville, PA 17222 ↓2X

Dear Aristeo: ↓2X

We should continue considering Geraldton for our new plant. Even though the desirability of this site from an economic view is undeniable, there is insufficient housing readily available.

Please continue to search out other areas of new exploration where we might someday form a joint partnership. ↓2X

Sincerely, ↓4X

Mieko Nakamura

Mieko Nakamura
Vice President for Operations ↓2X

adk

C. BUSINESS LETTER FORMATTED FOR A WINDOW ENVELOPE

(with standard punctuation)

↓6X

July 18, 20-- ↓3X

Ms. Reinalda Guerrero
BBL Resources
52A Northern Ridge
Fayetteville, PA 17222 ↓3X

Dear Ms. Guerrero: ↓2X

I see no reason why we should continue to consider the locality around Geraldton for our new plant. Even though the desirability of this site from an economic view is undeniable, there is insufficient housing readily available for our workers.

In trying to control urban growth, the city has been turning down the building permits for new housing or placing so many restrictions on foreign investment as to make it too expensive.

Please continue to seek out other areas of exploration where we might form a joint partnership. ↓2X

Sincerely, ↓4X

Arlyn J. Bunch

Arlyn J. Bunch
Vice President for Operations ↓2X

woc

D. MEMO

(with table and attachment notation)

↓6X →tab

MEMO TO: Nancy Price, Executive Vice President ↓2X

FROM: Arlyn J. Bunch, Operations *ajb* ↓2X

DATE: July 18, 20-- ↓2X

SUBJECT: New Plant Site ↓2X

As you can see from the attached letter, I've informed BBL Resources that I see no reason why we should continue to consider the locality around Geraldton for our new plant. Even though the desirability of this site from an economic standpoint is undeniable, there is insufficient housing available. In fact, as of June 25, the number of appropriate single-family houses listed for sale within a 25-mile radius of Geraldton was as follows: ↓2X

Agent	Units
Belle Real Estate	123
Castleton Homes	11
Red Carpet	9
Geraldton Homes	5

↓1X

In addition, in trying to control urban growth, Geraldton has been either turning down building permits for new housing or placing excessive restrictions on them.

Because of this deficiency of housing for our employees, we have no choice but to look elsewhere. ↓2X

woc
Attachment notation — Attachment

A. MULTIPAGE BUSINESS LETTER

(page 1; with on-arrival notation, international address, subject line, table, and standard punctuation)

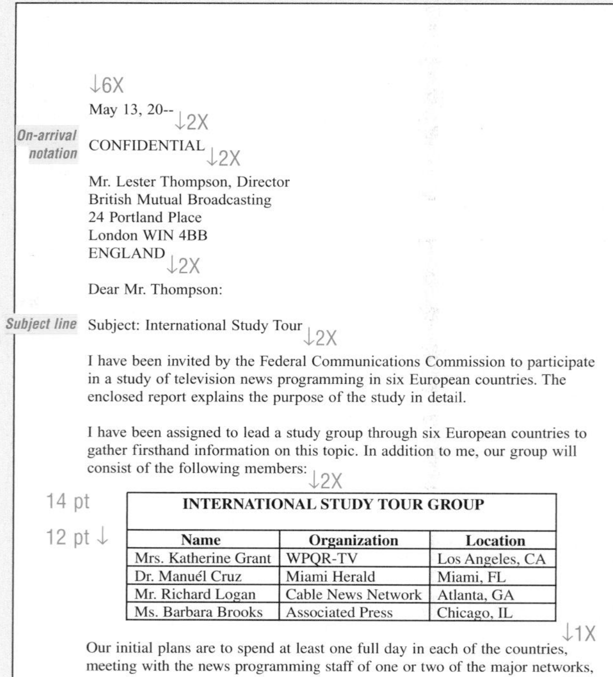

↓6X

May 13, 20-- ↓2X

On-arrival notation CONFIDENTIAL ↓2X

Mr. Lester Thompson, Director
British Mutual Broadcasting
24 Portland Place
London WIN 4BB
ENGLAND ↓2X

Dear Mr. Thompson:

Subject line Subject: International Study Tour ↓2X

I have been invited by the Federal Communications Commission to participate in a study of television news programming in six European countries. The enclosed report explains the purpose of the study in detail.

I have been assigned to lead a study group through six European countries to gather firsthand information on this topic. In addition to me, our group will consist of the following members: ↓2X

14 pt

12 pt ↓

INTERNATIONAL STUDY TOUR GROUP		
Name	**Organization**	**Location**
Mrs. Katherine Grant	WPQR-TV	Los Angeles, CA
Dr. Manuél Cruz	Miami Herald	Miami, FL
Mr. Richard Logan	Cable News Network	Atlanta, GA
Ms. Barbara Brooks	Associated Press	Chicago, IL

↓1X

Our initial plans are to spend at least one full day in each of the countries, meeting with the news programming staff of one or two of the major networks,

B. MULTIPAGE BUSINESS LETTER

(page 2; with company name; multiline list; enclosure, delivery, copy, postscript, blind copy notations; and standard punctuation)

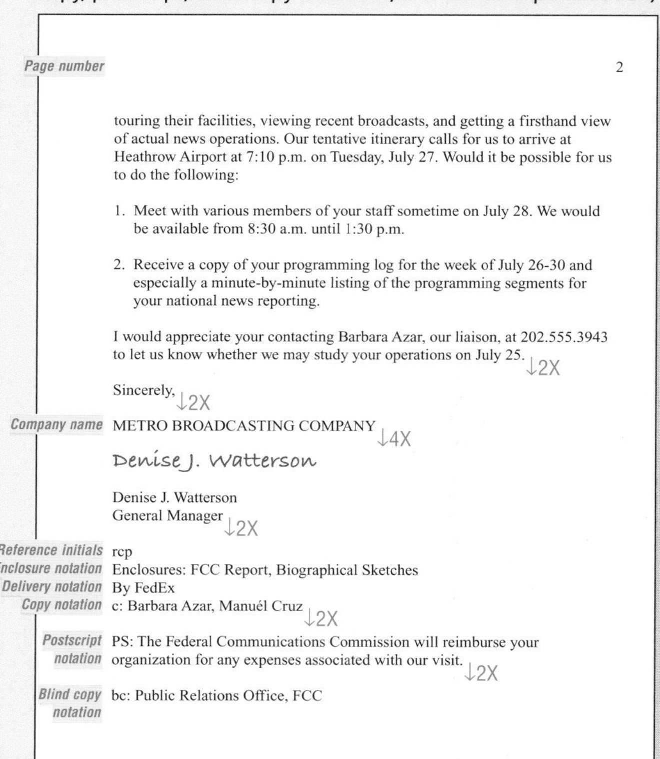

Page number 2

touring their facilities, viewing recent broadcasts, and getting a firsthand view of actual news operations. Our tentative itinerary calls for us to arrive at Heathrow Airport at 7:10 p.m. on Tuesday, July 27. Would it be possible for us to do the following:

1. Meet with various members of your staff sometime on July 28. We would be available from 8:30 a.m. until 1:30 p.m.

2. Receive a copy of your programming log for the week of July 26-30 and especially a minute-by-minute listing of the programming segments for your national news reporting.

I would appreciate your contacting Barbara Azar, our liaison, at 202.555.3943 to let us know whether we may study your operations on July 25. ↓2X

Sincerely, ↓2X

Company name METRO BROADCASTING COMPANY ↓4X

Denise J. Watterson

Denise J. Watterson
General Manager ↓2X

Reference initials rcp
Enclosure notation Enclosures: FCC Report, Biographical Sketches
Delivery notation By FedEx
Copy notation c: Barbara Azar, Manuél Cruz ↓2X

Postscript notation PS: The Federal Communications Commission will reimburse your organization for any expenses associated with our visit. ↓2X

Blind copy notation bc: Public Relations Office, FCC

C. E-MAIL MESSAGE IN MICROSOFT OUTLOOK/ INTERNET EXPLORER

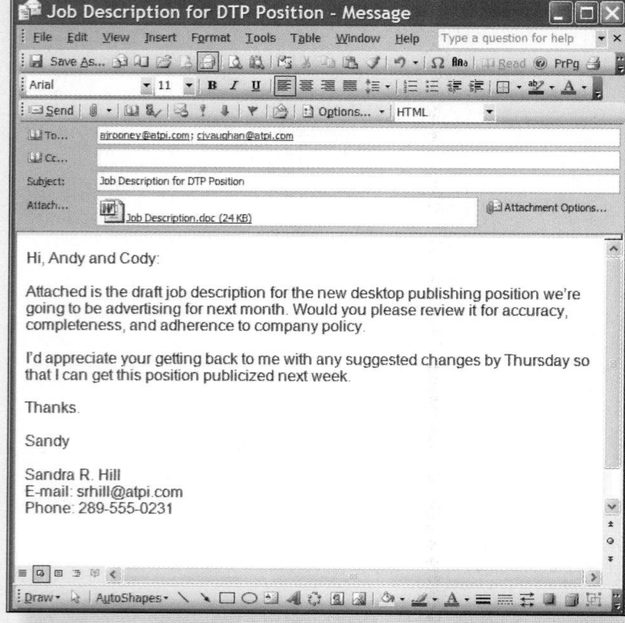

Job Description for DTP Position - Message

To... ajrooney@atpi.com; cjvaughan@atpi.com
Cc...
Subject: Job Description for DTP Position
Attach... Job Description.doc (24 KB)

Hi, Andy and Cody:

Attached is the draft job description for the new desktop publishing position we're going to be advertising for next month. Would you please review it for accuracy, completeness, and adherence to company policy.

I'd appreciate your getting back to me with any suggested changes by Thursday so that I can get this position publicized next week.

Thanks.

Sandy

Sandra R. Hill
E-mail: srhill@atpi.com
Phone: 289-555-0231

D. E-MAIL MESSAGE IN YAHOO!

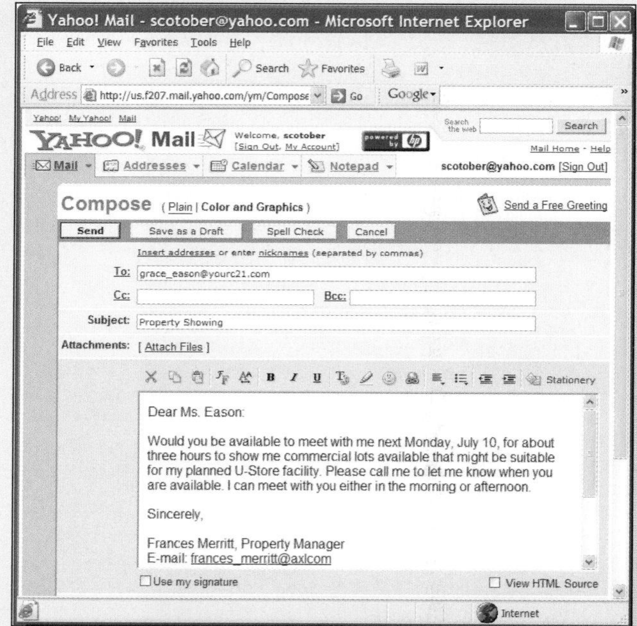

Yahoo! Mail - scotober@yahoo.com - Microsoft Internet Explorer

Compose

To: grace_eason@yourc21.com
Cc:
Bcc:
Subject: Property Showing
Attachments: [Attach Files]

Dear Ms. Eason:

Would you be available to meet with me next Monday, July 10, for about three hours to show me commercial lots available that might be suitable for my planned U-Store facility. Please call me to let me know when you are available. I can meet with you either in the morning or afternoon.

Sincerely,

Frances Merritt, Property Manager
E-mail: frances_merritt@axl.com

A. FORMATTING ENVELOPES

A standard large (No. 10) envelope is 9.5 by 4.125 inches. A standard small (No. 6¼) envelope is 6.5 by 3.625 inches. Although either address format shown below is acceptable, the format shown for the large envelope (all caps and no punctuation) is recommended by the U.S. Postal Service for mail that will be sorted by an electronic scanning device.

Window envelopes are often used in a word processing environment because of the difficulty of aligning envelopes correctly in some printers. A window envelope requires no formatting, since the letter is formatted and folded so that the inside address is visible through the window.

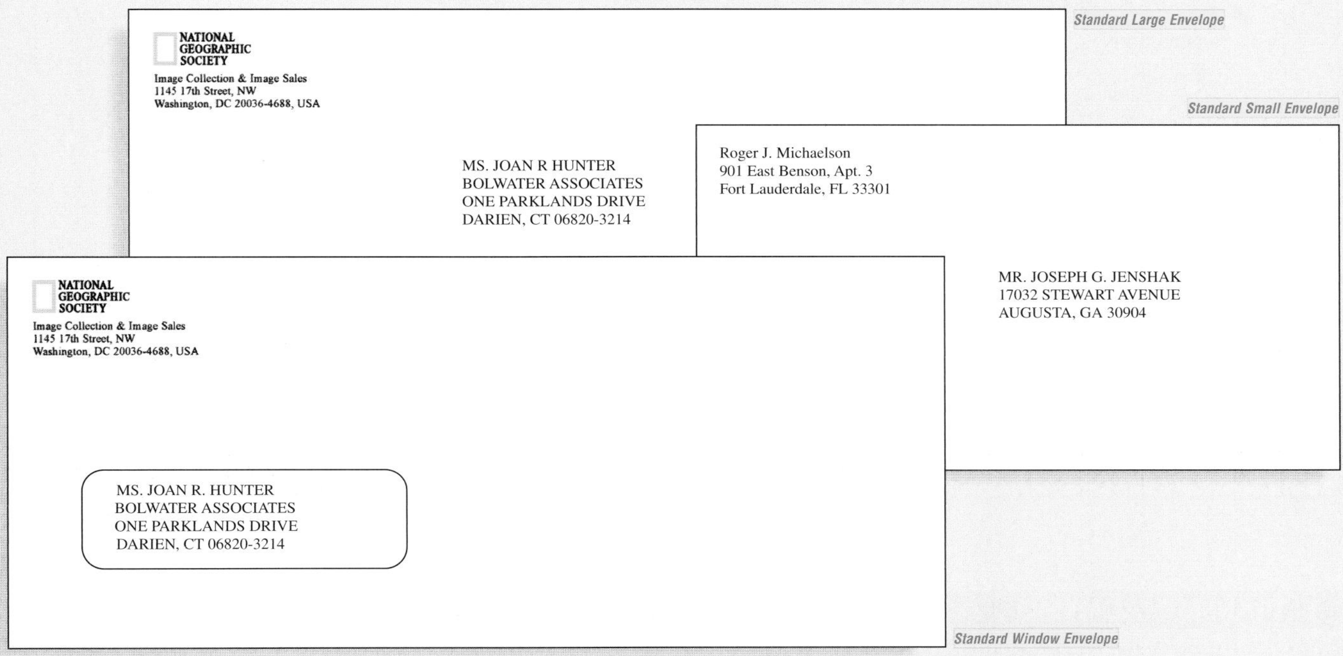

B. FOLDING LETTERS

To fold a letter for a large envelope:

1. Place the letter *face up* and fold up the bottom third.
2. Fold the top third down to 0.5 inch from the bottom edge.
3. Insert the last crease into the envelope first, with the flap facing up.

To fold a letter for a small envelope:

1. Place the letter *face up* and fold up the bottom half to 0.5 inch from the top.
2. Fold the right third over to the left.
3. Fold the left third over to 0.5 inch from the right edge.
4. Insert the last crease into the envelope first, with the flap facing up.

To fold a letter for a window envelope:

1. Place the letter *face down* with the letterhead at the top and fold the bottom third of the letter up.
2. Fold the top third down so that the address shows.
3. Insert the letter into the envelope so that the address shows through the window.

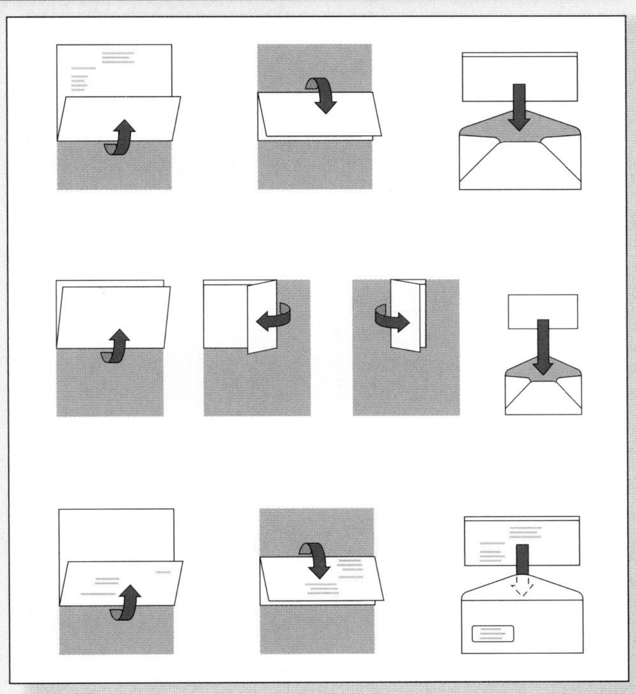

A. OUTLINE

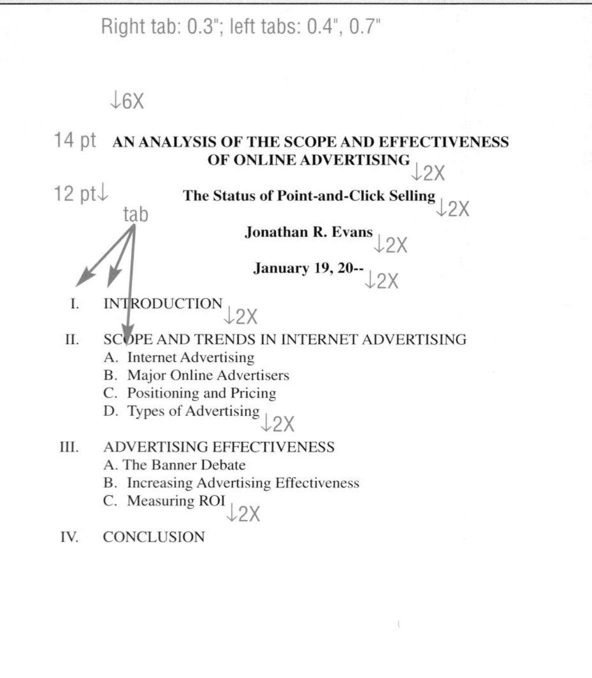

Right tab: 0.3"; left tabs: 0.4", 0.7"

↓6X

14 pt **AN ANALYSIS OF THE SCOPE AND EFFECTIVENESS OF ONLINE ADVERTISING** ↓2X

12 pt↓ **The Status of Point-and-Click Selling** ↓2X

tab

Jonathan R. Evans ↓2X

January 19, 20-- ↓2X

I. INTRODUCTION ↓2X

II. SCOPE AND TRENDS IN INTERNET ADVERTISING
   A. Internet Advertising
   B. Major Online Advertisers
   C. Positioning and Pricing
   D. Types of Advertising ↓2X

III. ADVERTISING EFFECTIVENESS
   A. The Banner Debate
   B. Increasing Advertising Effectiveness
   C. Measuring ROI ↓2X

IV. CONCLUSION

B. TITLE PAGE

center page↓

14 pt **AN ANALYSIS OF THE SCOPE AND EFFECTIVENESS OF ONLINE ADVERTISING** ↓2X

12 pt↓ **The Status of Point-and-Click Selling** ↓12X

Submitted to ↓2X

Luis Torres
General Manager
ViaWorld, International ↓12X

Prepared by ↓2X

Jonathan R. Evans
Assistant Marketing Manager
ViaWorld, International ↓2X

January 19, 20--

C. TRANSMITTAL MEMO

(with 2-line subject line and attachment notation)

↓6X

→ tab

MEMO TO: Luis Torres, General Manager ↓2X

FROM: Jonathan R. Evans, Assistant Marketing Manager *jre* ↓2X

DATE: January 19, 20-- ↓2X

SUBJECT: An Analysis of the Scope and Effectiveness of Online Advertising ↓2X

Here is the report analyzing the scope and effectiveness of Internet advertising that you requested on January 5, 20--.

The report predicts that the total value of the business-to-business e-commerce market will reach $1.3 trillion by 2003, up from $190 billion in 1999. New technologies aimed at increasing Internet ad interactivity and the adoption of standards for advertising response measurement and tracking will contribute to this increase. Unfortunately, as discussed in this report, the use of "rich media" and interactivity in Web advertising will create its own set of problems.

I enjoyed working on this assignment, Luis, and learned quite a bit from my analysis of the situation. Please let me know if you have any questions about the report. ↓2X

plw
Attachment

D. TABLE OF CONTENTS

Left tab: 0.5"; right dot-leader tab: 6".

↓6X

14 pt **CONTENTS** ↓2X

12 pt↓ INTRODUCTION .... 1 ↓2X

SCOPE AND TRENDS IN ONLINE ADVERTISING .... 3 ↓2X

→tab Internet Advertising Spending 4
Major Online Advertisers 5
Positioning and Pricing 7
Types of Advertising .... 8 ↓2X

ADVERTISING EFFECTIVENESS .... 9 ↓2X

The Banner Debate 9
Increasing Advertising Effectiveness 11
Measuring ROI .... 12 ↓2X

CONCLUSION .... 13 ↓2X

APPENDIX ↓2X

Sample Internet Advertising 15
Proposed WEFA Standards .... 18 ↓2X

BIBLIOGRAPHY 19

A. BUSINESS REPORT

(page 1; with footnotes and multiline list)

↓6X

Title 14 pt **AN ANALYSIS OF THE SCOPE AND EFFECTIVENESS OF ONLINE ADVERTISING** ↓2X

Subtitle 12 pt↓ **The Status of Point-and-Click Selling** ↓2X

Byline **Jonathan R. Evans** ↓2X

Date **January 19, 20--** ↓2X

Over the past three years, the number of American households online has tripled, from an estimated 15 million in 1996 to 45 million in 1999. Jupiter Communications, predicts that by the year 2003, 70 million households, representing about 62 percent of all U.S. households, will be online. ↓2X

Side head **GROWTH FACTORS** ↓2X

Online business has grown in tandem with the expanding number of Internet users. Forrester Research Inc. predicts that the total value of business-to-business e-commerce will reach $109 billion in 1999 and is likely to reach $1.3 trillion by 2003.[1] ↓2X

Paragraph head **Uncertainty**. The uncertainties surrounding advertising on the Internet remain one of the major impediments to the expansion. The Internet advertising industry is today in a state of flux. ↓2X

Reasons for Not Advertising Online. A recent Association of National Advertisers survey found two main reasons cited for not advertising online:[2] ↓2X

1. The difficulty of determining return on investment, especially in terms of repeat business
2. The lack of reliable tracking and measurement data

Footnotes

[1] George Anders, "Buying Frenzy," *The Wall Street Journal*, July 12, 1999, p. R6.
[2] "eStats: Advertising Revenues and Trends," *eMarketer*, August 11, 1999, <http:www.emarketer.com/estats/ad>, accessed on January 7, 2000.

B. BUSINESS REPORT

(page 3; with long quotation and table)

3

who argue that banners have a strong potential for advertising effectiveness point out that it is not the banner format itself which presents a problem to advertising effectiveness, but rather the quality of the banner and the attention to its placement. According to Mike Windsor, president of Ogilvy Interactive: ↓2X

indent 0.5″→ ←indent 0.5″

Long quotation

> It's more a case of bad banner ads, just like there are bad TV ads. The space itself has huge potential. As important as using the space within the banner creatively is to aim it effectively. Unlike broadcast media, the Web offers advertisers the opportunity to reach a specific audience based on data gathered about who is surfing at a site and what their interests are[1]

Thus, while some analysts continue to argue that the banner advertisement is passé, there is little evidence of its abandonment. Instead, ad agencies are focusing on increasing the banner's effectiveness. ↓2X

SCOPE AND TRENDS IN ONLINE ADVERTISING ↓2X

Starting from zero in 1994, analysts agree that the volume of Internet advertising spending has risen rapidly. However, as indicated in Table 3, analysts provide a wide range of the exact amount of such advertising. ↓2X

14 pt 12 pt ↓

TABLE 3. INTERNET ADVERTISING
1998 Estimates

Source	Estimate
Internet Advertising Board	$1.92 billion
Forester	1.30 billion
IDC	1.20 billion
Burst! Media	560 million

Table source: Source: "Advertising Age Teams with eMarketer for Research Report," *Advertising Age*, May 3, 1999, p. 24. ↓1X

The differences in estimates of total Web advertising spending is generally attributed to the different methodologies used by the research agencies to

[1] Lisa Napoli, "Banner Ads Are Under the Gun—And On the Move," *The New York Times*, June 17, 1999, p. D1.

C. ACADEMIC REPORT

(page 1; with endnotes and multiline list)

↓3DS

14 pt **AN ANALYSIS OF THE SCOPE AND EFFECTIVENESS** ↓1DS
OF ONLINE ADVERTISING ↓1DS

12 pt↓ **The Status of Point-and-Click Selling** ↓1DS

Jonathan R. Evans ↓1DS

January 19, 20-- ↓1DS

Over the past three years, the number of American households online has tripled, from an estimated 15 million in 1996 to 45 million in 1999. Jupiter Communications, predicts that by the year 2003, 70 million households, representing about 62 percent of all U.S. households, will be online. ↓1DS

GROWTH FACTORS ↓1DS

Online business has grown in tandem with the expanding number of Internet users. Forrester Research Inc. predicts that the total value of business-to-business e-commerce will reach $109 billion in 1999.[i]

Reasons for Not Advertising Online. A recent Association of National Advertisers survey found two main reasons cited for not advertising online:[ii]

1. The difficulty of determining return on investment, especially in terms of repeat business.
2. The lack of reliable tracking and measurement data.

Some analysts argue that advertising on the Internet can and should follow the same principles as advertising on television.[iii] Other visual media

D. ACADEMIC REPORT

(last page; with long quotation and endnotes)

14

advertising effectiveness, but rather the quality of the banner and the attention to its placement. According to Mike Windsor, president of Ogilvy Interactive: ↓1DS

indent 0.5″→ ←indent 0.5″

Long quotation

> It's more a case of bad banner ads, just like there are bad TV ads. The space itself has huge potential. As important as using the space within the banner creatively is to aim it effectively. Unlike broadcast media, the Web offers advertisers the opportunity to reach a specific audience based on data gathered about who is surfing at a site and what their interests are.[vii] ↓1SS

From the advertiser's perspective, the most effective Internet ads do more than just deliver information to the consumer and grab the consumer's attention—they also gather information about consumers (e.g., through "cookies" and other methodologies). From the consumer's perspective, this type of interactivity may represent an intrusion and an invasion of privacy. There appears to be a shift away from the ad-supported model and toward the transaction model, wherein users pay for the content they want and the specific transactions they perform.

Endnotes

i George Anders, "Buying Frenzy," *The Wall Street Journal*, July 12, 1999, p. R6.
ii "eStats: Advertising Revenues and Trends," *eMarketer*, August 11, 1999, <http:www.emarketer.com/estats/ad>, accessed on August 11, 1999.
iii Bradley Johnson, "Nielsen/NetRatings Index Shows 4% Rise in Web Ads," *Advertising Age*, July 19, 2003, p. 18.
iv Tom Hyland, "Web Advertising: A Year of Growth," *Internet Advertising Board*, November 13, 1999, <http:www.iab.net/advertise>, accessed on January 8, 2000.
v Adrian Mand, "Click Here: Free Ride Doles Out Freebies to Ad Surfers," *Brandweek*, March 8, 1999, p. 30.
vi Andrea Petersen, "High Price of Internet Banner Ads Slips Amid Increase in Web Sites," *The Wall Street Journal*, March 2, 1999, p. B20.
vii Lisa Napoli, "Banner Ads Are Under the Gun—And On the Move," *The New York Times*, June 17, 1999, p. D1.

A. LEFT-BOUND BUSINESS REPORT

(page 1; with endnotes and single-line list)

Left margin: 1.75″ Right margin: *default* (1.25″)

↓6X

14 pt **AN ANALYSIS OF THE SCOPE AND EFFECTIVENESS OF ONLINE ADVERTISING** ↓2X

12 pt↓ **The Status of Point-and-Click Selling** ↓2X

Jonathan R. Evans ↓2X

January 19, 20-- ↓2X

Over the past three years, the number of American households online has tripled, from an estimated 15 million in 1996 to 45 million in 1999. Jupiter Communications predicts that by the year 2003, 70 million households will be online. ↓2X

GROWTH FACTORS ↓2X

Online business has grown in tandem with the expanding number of Internet users. Forrester Research Inc. predicts that the total value of business-to-business e-commerce will reach $109 billion in 1999 and is likely to reach $1.3 trillion by 2003.[i] ↓2X

Uncertainty. The uncertainties surrounding advertising on the Internet remain one of the major impediments to the expansion. Dating from just 1994, when the first banner ads appeared on the Hotwired home page, the Internet advertising industry is today in a state of flux. ↓2X

Some analysts argue that advertising on the Internet can and should follow the same principles as advertising on television and other visual media. Others contend that advertising on the Internet should reflect the unique characteristics of this new medium. ↓2X

Reasons for Not Advertising Online. A recent Association of National Advertisers survey found two main reasons cited for not advertising online:[ii] ↓2X

1. The difficulty of determining return on investment
2. The lack of reliable tracking and measurement data

B. BIBLIOGRAPHY

(for business or academic style using either endnotes or footnotes)

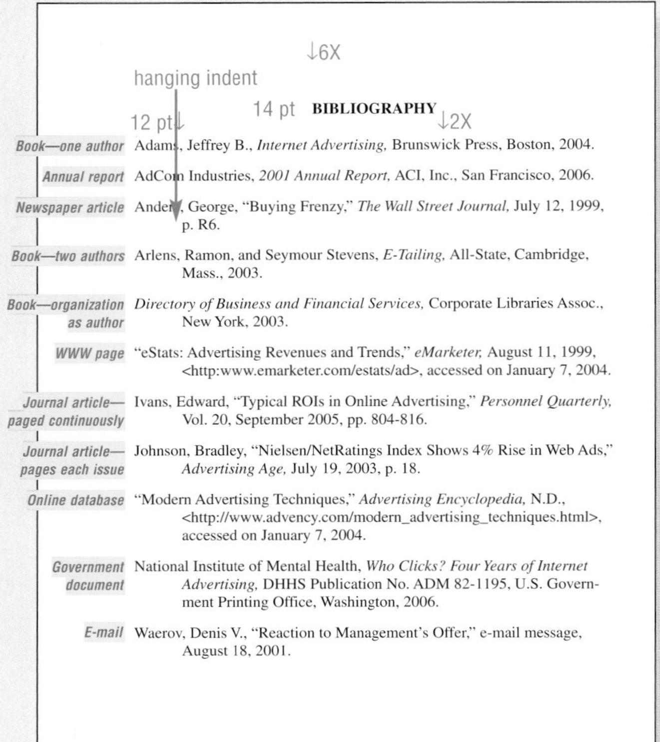

↓6X

hanging indent

12 pt↓ 14 pt **BIBLIOGRAPHY** ↓2X

Book—one author	Adams, Jeffrey B., *Internet Advertising,* Brunswick Press, Boston, 2004.
Annual report	AdCom Industries, *2001 Annual Report,* ACI, Inc., San Francisco, 2006.
Newspaper article	Anders, George, "Buying Frenzy," *The Wall Street Journal,* July 12, 1999, p. R6.
Book—two authors	Arlens, Ramon, and Seymour Stevens, *E-Tailing,* All-State, Cambridge, Mass., 2003.
Book—organization as author	*Directory of Business and Financial Services,* Corporate Libraries Assoc., New York, 2003.
WWW page	"eStats: Advertising Revenues and Trends," *eMarketer,* August 11, 1999, <http:www.emarketer.com/estats/ad>, accessed on January 7, 2004.
Journal article—paged continuously	Ivans, Edward, "Typical ROIs in Online Advertising," *Personnel Quarterly,* Vol. 20, September 2005, pp. 804-816.
Journal article—pages each issue	Johnson, Bradley, "Nielsen/NetRatings Index Shows 4% Rise in Web Ads," *Advertising Age,* July 19, 2003, p. 18.
Online database	"Modern Advertising Techniques," *Advertising Encyclopedia,* N.D., <http://www.advency.com/modern_advertising_techniques.html>, accessed on January 7, 2004.
Government document	National Institute of Mental Health, *Who Clicks? Four Years of Internet Advertising,* DHHS Publication No. ADM 82-1195, U.S. Government Printing Office, Washington, 2006.
E-mail	Waerov, Denis V., "Reaction to Management's Offer," e-mail message, August 18, 2001.

C. MEMO REPORT

(page 1, with single-line list)

↓6X

→tab

MEMO TO: Luis Torres, General Manager ↓2X

FROM: Jonathan R. Evans, Assistant Marketing Manager *jre* ↓2X

DATE: January 19, 20-- ↓2X

SUBJECT: An Analysis of the Scope and Effectiveness of Online Advertising ↓2X

According to a July 12, 1999, Wall Street Journal article, over the past three years, the number of American households online has tripled, from an estimated 15 million in 1996 to 45 million in 1999. Jupiter Communications, predicts that by the year 2003, 70 million households, representing 62 percent of all U.S. households, will be online. Online business has grown in tandem with the expanding number of Internet users. Forrester Research Inc. predicts that the total value of business-to-business e-commerce will reach $109 billion in 1999 and is likely to reach $1.3 trillion by 2003. ↓2X

UNCERTAINTY ↓2X

The uncertainties surrounding advertising on the Internet remain one of the major impediments to the expansion. Dating from just 1994, when the first banner ads appeared on the Hotwired home page, the Internet advertising industry is today in a state of flux.

Some analysts argue that advertising on the Internet can and should follow the same principles as advertising on television and other visual media. Others contend that all of the advertising on the Internet should reflect the unique characteristics of this new medium.

A recent Association of National Advertisers survey found two main reasons cited for not advertising online:

1. The difficulty of determining return on investment
2. The lack of reliable tracking and measurement data

D. REPORTS: SPECIAL FEATURES

Margins and Spacing. Use a 2-inch top margin for the first page of each section of a report (for example, the table of contents, first page of the body, and bibliography page) and a 1-inch top margin for other pages. Use default side margins (1.25 inches) and bottom margins (1 inch) for all pages. If the report is going to be bound on the left, add 0.5 inch to the left margin. Single-space business reports and double-space academic reports.

Headings. Center the report title in 14-point font (press ENTER to space down before switching to 12-point font). Single-space multiline report titles in a single-spaced report and double-space multiline titles in a double-spaced report. Insert 1 blank line before and after all parts of a heading block (consisting of the title, subtitle, author, and/or date) and format all lines in bold.

Insert 1 blank line before and after side headings and format in bold, beginning at the left margin. Format paragraph headings in bold; begin at the left margin for single-spaced reports and indent for double-spaced reports. The text follows on the same line, preceded by a period and 1 space.

Citations. For business and academic reports, format citations using your word processor's footnote (or endnote) feature. For reports formatted in APA or MLA style, use the format shown on page R-10.

A. REPORT IN APA STYLE

(page 1; with author/year citations)

Top, bottom, and side margins: 1″

Online Advertising 3 *header*

An Analysis of the Scope and Effectiveness

of Online Advertising

Jonathan R. Evans

Over the past three years, the number of American households online has tripled, from an estimated 15 million in 1996 to 45 million in 1999. Jupiter Communications predicts that by the year 2003, 70 million households, which represent 62 percent of all U.S. households, will be online (Napoli, 2003).

main head Growth Factors

Online business has grown in tandem with the expanding number of Internet users. Forrester Research Inc. predicts that the total value of business-to-business e-commerce will reach $109 billion in 2003 (Arlens & Stevens, 2003).

subhead *Uncertainty*

The uncertainties surrounding advertising on the Internet remain one of the major impediments to the expansion. Dating from just 1994. when the first banner ads appeared on the Hotwired home page, the Internet advertising industry is today in a state of flux.

Some analysts argue that advertising on the Internet can and should follow the same principles as advertising on television and other visual media ("eStats," 2004). Others contend that advertising on the Internet should reflect

B. REFERENCES IN APA STYLE

Top, bottom, and side margins: 1″

Double-space throughout.

Online Advertising 14 *header*

hanging indent

References

Book—one author Adams, J. B. (2004). *Internet advertising.* Boston: Brunswick Press.

Annual report AdCom Industries. (2006). 2005 *annual report.* San Francisco: ACI, Inc.

Newspaper article Anders, G. (2003, July 12). Buying frenzy. *The Wall Street Journal,* p. R6.

Book—two authors Arlens, R., & Stevens, S. (2003). *E-tailing.* Cambridge, MA: All-State.

Book—organization as author *Directory of business and financial services.* (2003). New York: Corporate Libraries Association.

WWW page eStats: Advertising revenues and trends. (n.d.). New York: eMarketer. Retrieved August 11, 2004, from the World Wide Web: http://www.emarketer.com/estats/ad

Journal article—paged continuously Ivans, E. (2005). Typical ROIs in online advertising. *Personnel Quarterly,* 20, 804-816.

Journal article—paged each issue Johnson, B. (2003, July 19). Nielsen/NetRatings Index shows 4% rise in Web ads. Advertising Age, 39, 18.

Online database *Modern advertising techniques.* (1998, January). *Advertising Encyclopedia.* Retrieved January 7, 2004, from http://www.advency.com/ads.html

Government document National Institute of Mental Health *Who clicks? Four years of Internet advertising* (DHHS Publication No. ADM 82-1195). Washington, DC. (2006).

C. REPORT IN MLA STYLE

(page 1; with author/page citations)

Top, bottom, and side margins: 1″

Double-space throughout.

Evans 1 *header*

Jonathan R. Evans

Professor Inman

Management 302

19 January 20--

An Analysis of the Scope and Effectiveness

of Online Advertising

Over the past three years, the number of American households online has tripled, from an estimated 15 million in 1996 to 45 million in 1999. Jupiter Communications predicts that by the year 2003, 70 million households, representing about 62% of all U.S. households, will be online (Napoli D1). Online business has grown in tandem with the expanding number of Internet users. Forrester Research Inc. predicts that the total value of business-to-business e-commerce will reach $109 billion in 1999 and is likely to reach $1.3 trillion by 2003 (Arlens & Stevens 376-379).

The uncertainties surrounding advertising on the Internet remain one of the major impediments to the expansion. Dating from just 1994, when the first banner ads appeared on the Hotwired home page, the Internet advertising industry is today in a state of flux.

Some analysts argue that advertising on the Internet can and should follow the same principles as advertising on television and other visual media ("eStats"). Others contend that advertising on the Internet should reflect the

D. WORKS CITED IN MLA STYLE

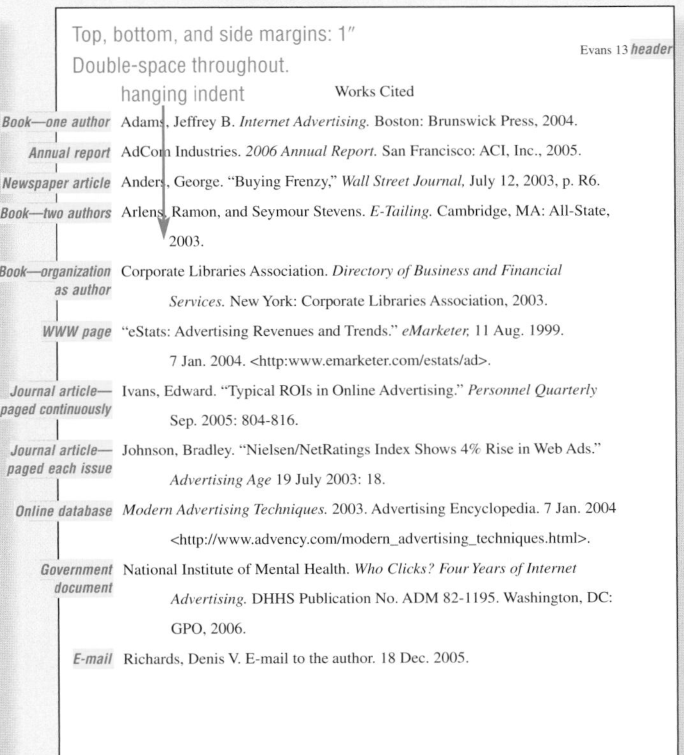

Top, bottom, and side margins: 1″

Double-space throughout.

Evans 13 *header*

hanging indent

Works Cited

Book—one author Adams, Jeffrey B. *Internet Advertising.* Boston: Brunswick Press, 2004.

Annual report AdCom Industries. *2006 Annual Report.* San Francisco: ACI, Inc., 2005.

Newspaper article Anders, George. "Buying Frenzy," *Wall Street Journal,* July 12, 2003, p. R6.

Book—two authors Arlens, Ramon, and Seymour Stevens. *E-Tailing.* Cambridge, MA: All-State, 2003.

Book—organization as author Corporate Libraries Association. *Directory of Business and Financial Services.* New York: Corporate Libraries Association, 2003.

WWW page "eStats: Advertising Revenues and Trends." *eMarketer,* 11 Aug. 1999. 7 Jan. 2004. <http:www.emarketer.com/estats/ad>.

Journal article—paged continuously Ivans, Edward. "Typical ROIs in Online Advertising." *Personnel Quarterly* Sep. 2005: 804-816.

Journal article—paged each issue Johnson, Bradley. "Nielsen/NetRatings Index Shows 4% Rise in Web Ads." *Advertising Age* 19 July 2003: 18.

Online database *Modern Advertising Techniques.* 2003. Advertising Encyclopedia. 7 Jan. 2004 <http://www.advency.com/modern_advertising_techniques.html>.

Government document National Institute of Mental Health. *Who Clicks? Four Years of Internet Advertising.* DHHS Publication No. ADM 82-1195. Washington, DC: GPO, 2006.

E-mail Richards, Denis V. E-mail to the author. 18 Dec. 2005.

A. MEETING AGENDA

↓6X

14 pt **MILES HARDWARE EXECUTIVE COMMITTEE** ↓2X

12 pt↓ **Meeting Agenda** ↓2X

June 7, 20--, 3 p.m. ↓2X

1. Call to order ↓2X
2. Approval of minutes of May 5 meeting
3. Progress report on building addition and parking lot restrictions (Norman Hodges and Anthony Pascarelli)
4. May 15 draft of Five-Year Plan
5. Review of National Hardware Association annual convention
6. Employee grievance filed by Ellen Burrows (John Landstrom)
7. New expense-report forms (Anne Richards)
8. Announcements
9. Adjournment

B. MINUTES OF A MEETING

↓6X

14 pt **RESOURCE COMMITTEE** ↓2X 12 pt↓ **Minutes of the Meeting** ↓2X **March 13, 20--** ↓1X	
ATTENDANCE	The Resource Committee met on March 13, 20--, at the Airport Sheraton in Portland, Oregon, with all members present. Michael Davis, chairperson, called the meeting to order at 2:30 p.m. ↓1X
APPROVAL OF MINUTES	The minutes of the January 27 meeting were read and approved. ↓1X
OLD BUSINESS	The members of the committee reviewed the sales brochure on electronic copyboards and agreed to purchase one for the conference room. Cynthia Giovanni will secure quotations from at least two suppliers. ↓1X
NEW BUSINESS	The committee reviewed a request from the Purchasing Department for three new computers. After extensive discussion regarding the appropriate use of the computers and software to be purchased, the committee approved the request. ↓1X
ADJOURNMENT	The meeting was adjourned at 4:45 p.m. ↓2X Respectfully submitted, ↓4X *D. S. Madsen* D. S. Madsen, Secretary

(Note: Table shown with "Show Gridlines" active.)

C. ITINERARY

↓6X

14 pt **ITINERARY** ↓2X 12 pt↓ **For Arlene Gilsdorf** ↓2X **March 12-15, 20--** ↓1X	
THURSDAY, MARCH 12	↓1X
5:10 p.m.-7:06 p.m.	Flight from Detroit to Portland; Northwest 83 (Phone: 800-555-1212); e-ticket; Seat 8D; nonstop; dinner ↓2X Jack Weatherford (Home: 503-555-8029; Office: 503-555-7631) will meet your flight on Thursday, provide transportation during your visit, and return you to the airport on Saturday morning. ↓2X Airport Sheraton (503-555-4032) King-sized bed, nonsmoking room; late arrival guaranteed (Reservation No. 30ZM6-02) ↓1X
FRIDAY, MARCH 13	
9 a.m.-5:30 p.m.	Portland Sales Meeting 1931 Executive Way, Suite 10 Portland (503-555-7631)
Evening	On your own
SATURDAY, MARCH 14	
7:30 a.m.-2:47 p.m.	Flight from Portland to Detroit; Northwest 360; e-ticket; Seat 9a; nonstop; breakfast

(Note: Table shown with "Show Gridlines" active.)

D. LEGAL DOCUMENT

Left tabs: 1″, 3″

↓6X

12 pt↓ POWER OF ATTORNEY ↓2X

KNOW ALL MEN BY THESE PRESENTS that I, ATTORNEY LEE FERNANDEZ, of the City of Tulia, County of Swisher, State of Texas, do hereby appoint my son, Robert Fernandez, of this City, County, and State as my attorney-in-fact to act in my name, place, and stead as my agent in the management of my business operating transactions.

I give and grant unto my said attorney full power and authority to do and perform every act and thing requisite and necessary to be done in the said management as fully, to all intents and purposes, as I might or could do if personally present, with full power of revocation, hereby ratifying all that my said attorney shall lawfully do.

IN WITNESS WHEREOF, I have hereunto set my hand and seal this _____ day of ____________________, 20--. ↓2X

5 underscores ↑ 20 underscores ↑

→tab to centerpoint ______________________________ ↓2X

SIGNED and affirmed in the presence of: ↓4X

______________________________ ↓4X

____

A. RESUME

↓6X

14 pt **TERRY M. MARTINA** ↓2X

12 pt ↓ **250 Maxwell Avenue, Boulder, CO 80305**
Phone: 303-555-9311; e-mail: tmartina@ecc.edu ↓1X

↓1X

OBJECTIVE	Position in resort management anywhere in Colorado or the Southwest. ↓1X
EDUCATION	A.A. in hotel management to be awarded May 2005 Edgewood Community College, Boulder, Colorado. ↓1X
EXPERIENCE	*Assistant Manager, Burger King Restaurant* Boulder, Colorado: 2003-Present • Achieved grade point average of 3.1 (on 4.0 scale). • Received Board of Regents tuition scholarship. • Financed all college expenses. ↓2X *Student Intern, Ski Valley Haven* Aspen, Colorado: September-December 2004 • Worked as an assistant to the night manager. • Gained experience in operating First-Guest software. • Was in charge of producing daily occupancy reports. • Received Employee-of-the-Month award. ↓1X
PERSONAL	• Speak and write fluent Spanish. • Competent in Microsoft Office 2003. • Secretary of ECC Hospitality Services Association. • Special Olympics volunteer: Summer 2004. ↓1X
REFERENCES	Available upon request

(Note: Table shown with "Show Gridlines" active.)

B. APPLICATION LETTER IN BLOCK STYLE

(with standard punctuation)

↓6X

March 1, 20-- ↓4X

Mr. Lou Mansfield, Director
Human Resources Department
Rocky Resorts International
P.O. Box 1412
Denver, CO 80214 ↓2X

Dear Mr. Mansfield: ↓2X

Please consider me an applicant for the position of concierge for Suite Retreat, as advertised in last Sunday's *Denver Times*.

I will receive my A.A. degree in hotel administration from Edgewood Community College in May and will be available for full-time employment immediately. In addition to my extensive coursework in hospitality services and business, I've had experience in working for a ski lodge similar to Suite Retreats in Aspen. As a lifelong resident of Colorado and an avid skier, I would be able to provide your guests with any information they request.

After you've reviewed my enclosed resume, I would appreciate having an opportunity to discuss with you why I believe I have the right qualifications and personality to serve as your concierge. I can be reached at 303-555-9311. ↓2X

Sincerely, ↓4X

Terry M. Martina

Terry M. Martina
250 Maxwell Avenue, Apt. 8
Boulder, CO 80305 ↓2X

Enclosure

C. FORMATTING LISTS

Numbers or bullets may be used in letters, memos, and reports to call attention to items in a list. If the sequence of the items is important, use numbers rather than bullets.

- ❑ Begin the number or bullet at the paragraph point, that is, at the left margin for blocked paragraphs and indented 0.5 inch for indented paragraphs.
- ❑ Insert 1 blank line before and after the list.
- ❑ Within the list, use the same spacing (single or double) as is used in the rest of the document.
- ❑ For single-spaced documents, if all items require no more than 1 line, single-space the items in the list. If any item requires more than 1 line, single-space each item and insert 1 blank line between each item.

To format a list:

1. Type the list unformatted.
2. Select the items in the list.
3. Apply the number or bullet feature.
4. If necessary, use the Decrease Indent or Increase Indent button in Microsoft Word to adjust the position of the list.

The three bulleted and numbered lists shown at the right are all formatted correctly.

D. EXAMPLES OF DIFFERENT TYPES OF LISTS

According to PricewaterhouseCoopers and the Internet Advertising Bureau, the following are the most common types of advertising on the Internet:

- Banner ads that feature some type of animation to attract the viewer's attention.

- Sponsorship, in which an advertiser sponsors a content-based Web site.

- Interstitials, ads that flash up while a page downloads.

There is now considerable controversy about the effectiveness of banner ads. As previously noted, a central goal of banner advertisements is to increase the

***

According to PricewaterhouseCoopers, the following are the most common types of advertising on the Internet, shown in order of popularity:

1. Banner ads
2. Sponsorship
3. Interstitials

There is now considerable controversy about the effectiveness of banner ads. As previously noted, a central goal of banner advertisements is to increase the

***

According to PricewaterhouseCoopers, the following are the most common types of advertising on the Internet:

- Banner ads that feature some type of animation to attract the viewer's attention.
- Sponsorship, in which an advertiser sponsors a Web site.
- Interstitials, ads that flash up while a page downloads.

There is now considerable controversy about the effectiveness of banner advertising. As previously noted, a central goal of banner advertisements is to

A. BOXED TABLE (DEFAULT STYLE)

(with subtitle, braced headings, total line, and table note.)

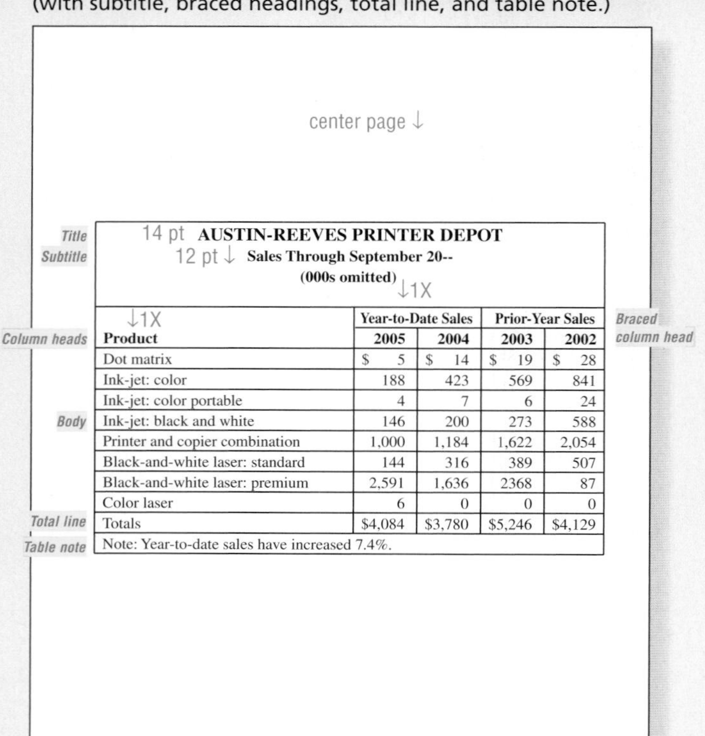

center page ↓

14 pt **AUSTIN-REEVES PRINTER DEPOT**

12 pt ↓ **Sales Through September 20--**

(000s omitted) ↓1X

↓1X Product	Year-to-Date Sales		Prior-Year Sales	
	2005	**2004**	**2003**	**2002**
Dot matrix	$ 5	$ 14	$ 19	$ 28
Ink-jet: color	188	423	569	841
Ink-jet: color portable	4	7	6	24
Ink-jet: black and white	146	200	273	588
Printer and copier combination	1,000	1,184	1,622	2,054
Black-and-white laser: standard	144	316	389	507
Black-and-white laser: premium	2,591	1,636	2368	87
Color laser	6	0	0	0
Totals	$4,084	$3,780	$5,246	$4,129

Note: Year-to-date sales have increased 7.4%.

B. OPEN TABLE

(with subtitle, blocked column headings, and 2-line heading)

center page ↓

14 pt **SUITE RETREAT**

12 pt ↓ **New Lodging Rates** ↓1X

↓1X **Location**	**Rack Rate**	**Discount Rate**	↓1X **Saving**
Bozeman, Montana	$ 95.75	$ 91.50	4.4%
Chicago, Illinois	159.00	139.50	12.3%
Dallas, Texas	249.50	219.00	12.2%
Las Vegas, Nevada	98.50	89.95	8.7%
Los Angeles, California	179.00	139.00	22.3%
Minneapolis, Minnesota	115.00	95.00	17.4%
New York, New York	227.50	175.00	23.1%
Orlando, Florida	105.75	98.50	6.3%
Portland, Maine	93.50	93.50	0.0%
Seattle, Washington	143.75	125.75	12.5%

C. RULED TABLE

(with table number and centered column headings)

2

an effort to reduce errors and provide increased customer support, we have recently added numerous additional telephone support services, some of which are available 24 hours a day and others available during the workday. These are shown in Table 2. ↓2X

14 pt **Table 2. COMPUTER SUPPLIES SUPPORT SERVICES** ↓1X

12 pt↓

Support Service	Telephone	Hours
Product literature	800-555-3867	6 a.m. to 5 p.m.
Replacement parts	303-555-3388	24 hours a day
Technical documentation	408-555-3309	24 hours a day
Troubleshooting	800-555-8277	10 a.m. to 5 p.m.
Printer drivers	800-555-2377	6 a.m. to 5 p.m.
Software notes	800-555-3496	24 hours a day
Technical support	800-555-1205	24 hours a day
Hardware information	303-555-4289	6 a.m. to 5 p.m.

↓1X

We hope you will take advantage of these additional services to ensure that the computer hardware and software you purchase from Computer Supplies continues to provide you the quality and service you have come to expect from our company.

Sincerely,

Douglas Pullis

Douglas Pullis
General Manager

cds

D. TABLES: SPECIAL FEATURES

Vertical Placement. Vertically center a table that appears on a page by itself. Insert 1 blank line before and after a table appearing with other text.

Heading Block. Center and bold all lines of the heading, typing the title in all caps and 14-point font and the subtitle in upper- and lowercase and in 12-point font. If a table has a number, type the word *Table* in upper- and lowercase. Follow the table number with a period and 1 space.

Column Headings. If *all* columns in the table consist of text (such as words, phone numbers, or years), center all column headings and left-align all column entries. In all other situations, left-align all text column headings and text column entries and right-align all quantity column headings and quantity column entries. Regardless of the type of column, center braced headings. Use bold upper- and lowercase.

Column Capitalization. Capitalize only the first word and proper nouns in column entries.

Percentages and Dollars. Repeat the % sign for each number in a column (unless the heading identifies the data as percentages). Insert the $ sign only before the first amount and before a total amount. Align the $ sign with the longest amount in the column, inserting spaces after the $ sign as needed (leaving 2 spaces for each digit and 1 space for each comma).

Total Line. Add a border above a total line. Use the word *Total* or *Totals* as appropriate.

Reference Manual

A. FORMATTING BUSINESS FORMS

Many business forms can be created and filled in by using templates that are provided within commercial word processing software. Template forms can be used "as is" or they can be edited. Templates can also be used to create customized forms for any business.

When a template is opened, the form is displayed on screen. The user can then fill in the necessary information, including personalized company information. Data are entered into cells or fields, and you can move quickly from field to field with a single keystroke—usually by pressing TAB or ENTER.

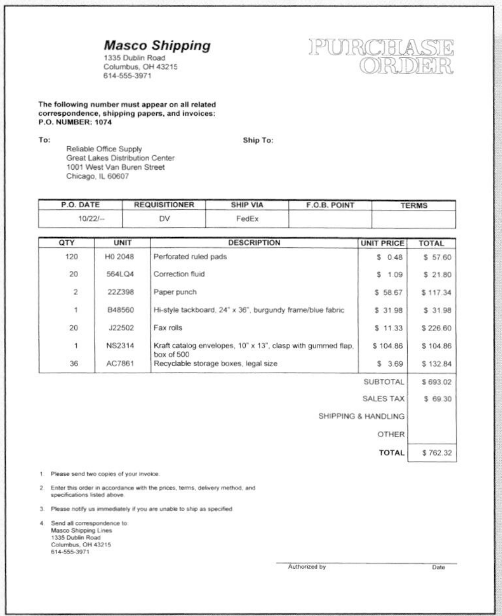

Masco Shipping
1335 Dublin Road
Columbus, OH 43215
614-555-3971

PURCHASE ORDER

The following number must appear on all related correspondence, shipping papers, and invoices:
P.O. NUMBER: 1074

To:
Reliable Office Supply
Great Lakes Distribution Center
1001 West Van Buren Street
Chicago, IL 60607

Ship To:

P.O. DATE	REQUISITIONER	SHIP VIA	F.O.B. POINT	TERMS
10/22/--	DV	FedEx		

QTY	UNIT	DESCRIPTION	UNIT PRICE	TOTAL
120	H0 2048	Perforated ruled pads	$ 0.48	$ 57.60
20	564LQ4	Correction fluid	$ 1.09	$ 21.80
2	22Z398	Paper punch	$ 58.67	$ 117.34
1	B48560	Hi-style tackboard, 24" x 36", burgundy frame/blue fabric	$ 31.98	$ 31.98
20	J22502	Fax rolls	$ 11.33	$ 226.60
1	NS2314	Kraft catalog envelopes, 10" x 13", clasp with gummed flap, box of 500	$ 104.86	$ 104.86
36	AC7861	Recyclable storage boxes, legal size	$ 3.69	$ 132.84
			SUBTOTAL	$ 693.02
			SALES TAX	$ 69.30
			SHIPPING & HANDLING	
			OTHER	
			TOTAL	$ 762.32

1. Please send two copies of your invoice.
2. Enter this order in accordance with the prices, terms, delivery method, and specifications listed above.
3. Please notify us immediately if you are unable to ship as specified.
4. Send all correspondence to:
   Masco Shipping Lines
   1335 Dublin Road
   Columbus, OH 43215
   614-555-3971

Authorized by　　　　Date

B. U.S. POSTAL SERVICE ABBREVIATIONS

(for States, Territories, and Canadian Provinces)

States and Territories

Alabama	AL
Alaska	AK
Arizona	AZ
Arkansas	AR
California	CA
Colorado	CO
Connecticut	CT
Delaware	DE
District of Columbia	DC
Florida	FL
Georgia	GA
Guam	GU
Hawaii	HI
Idaho	ID
Illinois	IL
Indiana	IN
Iowa	IA
Kansas	KS
Kentucky	KY
Louisiana	LA
Maine	ME
Maryland	MD
Massachusetts	MA
Michigan	MI
Minnesota	MN
Mississippi	MS
Missouri	MO
Montana	MT
Nebraska	NE
Nevada	NV
New Hampshire	NH
New Jersey	NJ
New Mexico	NM
New York	NY
North Carolina	NC
North Dakota	ND
Ohio	OH
Oklahoma	OK
Oregon	OR
Pennsylvania	PA
Puerto Rico	PR
Rhode Island	RI
South Carolina	SC
South Dakota	SD
Tennessee	TN
Texas	TX
Utah	UT
Vermont	VT
Virgin Islands	VI
Virginia	VA
Washington	WA
West Virginia	WV
Wisconsin	WI
Wyoming	WY

Canadian Provinces

Alberta	AB
British Columbia	BC
Labrador	LB
Manitoba	MB
New Brunswick	NB
Newfoundland	NF
Northwest Territories	NT
Nova Scotia	NS
Ontario	ON
Prince Edward Island	PE
Quebec	PQ
Saskatchewan	SK
Yukon Territory	YT

C. PROOFREADERS' MARKS

Proofreaders' Marks	Draft	Final Copy
Omit space	data base	database
V or ∧ Insert	if he's going (not)	if he's not going,
≡ Capitalize	Maple street	Maple Street
Delete	a final draft	a draft
# Insert space	allready to	all ready to
when Change word	and if you	and when you
/ Use lowercase letter	our President	our president
¶ Paragraph	… to use it.¶We can	… to use it. We can
••• Don't delete	a true story	a true story
○ Spell out	the only (1)	the only one
∽ Transpose	they all see	they see all
ss Single-space	ss [first line second line	first line second line
ds Double-space	ds [first line second line	first line second line
Move right	Please send	Please send
Move left	May I	May I
Bold	Column Heading	**Column Heading**
ital Italic	ital Time magazine	*Time* magazine
u/l Underline	u/l Time magazine	Time magazine
Move as shown	readers will see	will see readers

Language Arts for Business

(50 "must-know" rules)

PUNCTUATION

COMMAS

RULE 1 , direct address (L. 21)

Use commas before and after a name used in direct address.

Thank you, John, for responding to my e-mail so quickly.

Ladies and gentlemen, the program has been canceled.

RULE 2 , independent clause (L. 27)

Use a comma between independent clauses joined by a coordinate conjunction (unless both clauses are short).

Ellen left her job with IBM, and she and her sister went to Paris.

But: Ellen left her job with IBM and went to Paris with her sister.

But: John drove and I navigated.

Note: An independent clause is one that can stand alone as a complete sentence. The most common coordinate conjunctions are *and, but, or,* and *nor.*

RULE 3 , introductory expression (L. 27)

Use a comma after an introductory expression (unless it is a short prepositional phrase).

Before we can make a decision, we must have all the facts.

But: In 2004 our nation elected a new president.

Note: An introductory expression is a group of words that come before the subject and verb of the independent clause. Common prepositions are *to, in, on, of, at, by, for,* and *with.*

RULE 4 , direct quotation (L. 41)

Use a comma before and after a direct quotation.

James said, "I shall return," and then left.

RULE 5 , date (L. 57)

Use a comma before and after the year in a complete date.

We will arrive on June 2, 2006, for the conference.

But: We will arrive on June 2 for the conference.

RULE 6 , place (L. 57)

Use a comma before and after a state or country that follows a city (but not before a ZIP Code).

Joan moved to Vancouver, British Columbia, in May.

Send the package to Douglasville, GA 30135, by Express Mail.

But: Send the package to Georgia by Express Mail.

RULE 7 ▶
, series
(L. 61)

Use a comma between each item in a series of three or more.

We need to order paper, toner, and font cartridges_ for the printer.

They saved their work, exited their program, and turned off their computers_ when they finished.

Note: Do not use a comma after the last item in a series.

RULE 8 ▶
, transitional expression
(L. 61)

Use a comma before and after a transitional expression or independent comment.

It is critical, therefore, that we finish the project on time.

Our present projections, you must admit, are inadequate.

But: You must admit_ our present projections are inadequate.

Note: Examples of transitional expressions and independent comments are *in addition to, therefore, however, on the other hand, as a matter of fact,* and *unfortunately.*

RULE 9 ▶
, nonessential expression
(L. 71)

Use a comma before and after a nonessential expression.

Andre, who was there, can verify the statement.

But: Anyone_ who was there_ can verify the statement.

Van's first book, *Crisis of Management,* was not discussed.

Van's book_ *Crisis of Management*_ was not discussed.

Note: A nonessential expression is a group of words that may be omitted without changing the basic meaning of the sentence. Always examine the noun or pronoun that comes before the expression to determine whether the noun needs the expression to complete its meaning. If it does, the expression is *essential* and does *not* take a comma.

RULE 10 ▶
, adjacent adjectives
(L. 71)

Use a comma between two adjacent adjectives that modify the same noun.

We need an intelligent, enthusiastic_ individual for this job.

But: Please order a new_ bulletin board for our main_ conference room.

Note: Do not use a comma after the second adjective. Also, do not use a comma if the first adjective modifies the combined idea of the second adjective and the noun (for example, *bulletin board* and *conference room* in the second example above).

SEMICOLONS

RULE 11 ▶
; no conjunction
(L. 97)

Use a semicolon to separate two closely related independent clauses that are *not* joined by a conjunction (such as *and, but, or,* or *nor*).

Management favored the vote; stockholders did not.

But: Management favored the vote, but stockholders did not.

RULE 12 ▶
; series
(L. 97)

Use a semicolon to separate three or more items in a series if any of the items already contain commas.

Staff meetings were held on Thursday, May 7; Monday, June 7; and Friday, June 12.

Note: Be sure to insert the semicolon *between* (not within) the items in a series.

HYPHENS

RULE 13 ▶
- number
(L. 57)

Hyphenate compound numbers between twenty-one and ninety-nine and fractions that are expressed as words.

Twenty-nine recommendations were approved by at least three-fourths of the members.

RULE 14 ▶
- compound adjective
(L. 67)

Hyphenate compound adjectives that come before a noun (unless the first word is an adverb ending in *-ly*).

We reviewed an up-to-date report on Wednesday.

But: The report was up_to_date.

But: We reviewed the highly_rated report.

Note: A compound adjective is two or more words that function as a unit to describe a noun.

APOSTROPHES

RULE 15 ▶
' singular noun
(L. 37)

Use *'s* to form the possessive of singular nouns.

The hurricane's force caused major damage to North Carolina's coastline.

RULE 16 ▶
' plural noun
(L. 37)

Use only an apostrophe to form the possessive of plural nouns that end in *s.*

The investors' goals were outlined in the stockholders' report.

But: The investors_outlined their goals in the report to the stockholders_.

But: The women's and children's clothing was on sale.

RULE 17 ▶
' pronoun
(L. 37)

Use *'s* to form the possessive of indefinite pronouns (such as *someone's* or *anybody's*); do not use an apostrophe with personal pronouns (such as *hers, his, its, ours, theirs,* and *yours*).

She could select anybody's paper for a sample.

It's time to put the file back into its_cabinet.

COLONS

RULE 18 ▶ : explanatory material (L. 91)

Use a colon to introduce explanatory material that follows an independent clause.

The computer satisfies three criteria: speed, cost, and power.

But: The computer satisfies the three criteria of speed, cost, and power.

Remember this: only one coupon is allowed per customer.

Note: An independent clause can stand alone as a complete sentence. Do not capitalize the word following the colon.

PERIODS

RULE 19 ▶ . polite request (L. 91)

Use a period to end a sentence that is a polite request.

Will you please call me if I can be of further assistance.

Note: Consider a sentence a polite request if you expect the reader to respond by doing as you ask rather than by giving a yes-or-no answer.

QUOTATION MARKS

RULE 20 ▶ " quotation (L. 41)

Use quotation marks around a direct quotation.

Harrison responded by saying, "Their decision does not affect us."

But: Harrison responded by saying that their decision does not affect us.

RULE 21 ▶ " title (L. 41)

Use quotation marks around the title of a newspaper or magazine article, chapter in a book, report, and similar terms.

The most helpful article I found was "Multimedia for All."

ITALICS (OR UNDERLINE)

RULE 22 ▶ *title* (L. 41)

Italicize (or underline) the titles of books, magazines, newspapers, and other complete published works.

Grisham's *The Brethren* was reviewed in a recent *USA Today* article.

GRAMMAR

SENTENCES

RULE 23 ▶ fragment (L. 21)

Avoid sentence fragments.

Not: She had always wanted to be a financial manager. But had not had the needed education.

But: She had always wanted to be a financial manager but had not had the needed education.

Note: A fragment is a part of a sentence that is incorrectly punctuated as a complete sentence. In the first example above, "but had not had the needed education" is not a complete sentence because it does not contain a subject.

RULE 24 ▶ run-on (L. 21)

Avoid run-on sentences.

Not: Mohamed is a competent worker he has even passed the MOS exam.

Not: Mohamed is a competent worker, he has even passed the MOS exam.

But: Mohamed is a competent worker; he has even passed the MOS exam.

Or: Mohamed is a competent worker. He has even passed the MOS exam.

Note: A run-on sentence is two independent clauses that run together without any punctuation between them or with only a comma between them.

AGREEMENT

RULE 25 ▶ agreement singular agreement plural (L. 67)

Use singular verbs and pronouns with singular subjects; use plural verbs and pronouns with plural subjects.

I was happy with my performance.

Janet and Phoenix were happy with their performance.

Among the items discussed were our raises and benefits.

RULE 26 ▶ agreement pronoun (L. 81)

Some pronouns *(anybody, each, either, everybody, everyone, much, neither, no one, nobody,* and *one)* are always singular and take a singular verb. Other pronouns *(all, any, more, most, none,* and *some)* may be singular or plural, depending on the noun to which they refer.

Each of the employees has finished his or her task.

Much remains to be done.

Most of the pie was eaten, but most of the cookies were left.

RULE 27 ▶ agreement intervening words (L. 81)

Disregard any intervening words that come between the subject and verb when establishing agreement.

The box containing the books and pencils has not been found.

Alex, accompanied by Tricia, is attending the conference and taking his computer.

RULE 28 ▶ agreement nearer noun (L. 101)

If two subjects are joined by *or, either/or, neither/nor,* or *not only/but also,* make the verb agree with the subject nearer to the verb.

Neither the coach nor the players are at home.

Not only the coach but also the referee is at home.

But: Both the coach and the referee are at home.

PRONOUNS

RULE 29 ▶ nominative pronoun (L. 107)

Use nominative pronouns (such as *I, he, she, we, they,* and *who)* as subjects of a sentence or clause.

The programmer and he are reviewing the code.

Barb is a person who can do the job.

RULE 30 ▶ objective pronoun (L. 107)

Use objective pronouns (such as *me, him, her, us, them,* and *whom)* as objects of a verb, preposition, or infinitive.

The code was reviewed by the programmer and him.

Barb is the type of person whom we can trust.

ADJECTIVES AND ADVERBS

RULE 31 ▶ adjective/adverb (L. 101)

Use comparative adjectives and adverbs (*-er, more,* and *less)* when referring to two nouns or pronouns; use superlative adjectives and adverbs *(-est, most,* and *least)* when referring to more than two.

The shorter of the two training sessions is the more helpful one.

The longest of the three training sessions is the least helpful one.

WORD USAGE

RULE 32 ▶ accept/except (L. 117)

***Accept* means "to agree to"; *except* means "to leave out."**

All employees except the maintenance staff should accept the agreement.

RULE 33 ▶ affect/effect (L. 117)

***Affect* is most often used as a verb meaning "to influence"; *effect* is most often used as a noun meaning "result."**

The ruling will affect our domestic operations but will have no effect on our Asian operations.

RULE 34 ▶ farther/further (L. 117)

***Farther* refers to distance; *further* refers to extent or degree.**

The farther we drove, the further agitated he became.

RULE 35 ▶ personal/personnel (L. 117)

***Personal* means "private"; *personnel* means "employees."**

All personnel agreed not to use e-mail for personal business.

RULE 36 ▶ principal/principle (L. 117)

***Principal* means "primary"; *principle* means "rule."**

The principle of fairness is our principal means of dealing with customers.

MECHANICS

CAPITALIZATION

RULE 37 ▶ **Capitalize the first word of a sentence.**
≡ sentence
(L. 31)

Please prepare a summary of your activities.

RULE 38 ▶ **Capitalize proper nouns and adjectives derived from proper nouns.**
≡ proper noun
(L. 31)

Judy Hendrix drove to Albuquerque in her new Pontiac convertible.

Note: A proper noun is the official name of a particular person, place, or thing.

RULE 39 ▶ **Capitalize the names of the days of the week, months, holidays, and religious days (but do not capitalize the names of the seasons).**
≡ time
(L. 31)

On Thursday, November 25, we will celebrate Thanksgiving, the most popular holiday in the fall.

RULE 40 ▶ **Capitalize nouns followed by a number or letter (except for the nouns *line, note, page, paragraph,* and *size*).**
≡ noun #
(L. 77)

Please read Chapter 5, which begins on page 94.

RULE 41 ▶ **Capitalize compass points (such as *north, south,* or *northeast*) only when they designate definite regions.**
≡ compass point
(L. 77)

From Montana we drove south to reach the Southwest.

RULE 42 ▶ **Capitalize common organizational terms (such as *advertising department* and *finance committee*) only when they are the actual names of the units in the writer's own organization and when they are preceded by the word *the*.**
≡ organization
(L. 111)

The report from the Advertising Department is due today.

But: Our advertising department will submit its report today.

RULE 43 ▶ **Capitalize the names of specific course titles but not the names of subjects or areas of study.**
≡ course
(L. 111)

I have enrolled in Accounting 201 and will also take a marketing course.

NUMBER EXPRESSION

RULE 44 ▶ **In general, spell out numbers zero through ten, and use figures for numbers above ten.**
general
(L. 41)

We rented two movies for tonight.

The decision was reached after 27 precincts sent in their results.

RULE 45 ▶
figure
(L. 41)

Use figures for

❑ **Dates. (Use *st, d,* or *th* only if the day comes before the month.)**
The tax report is due on April 15 (*not* April 15th)
We will drive to the camp on the 23d (or *23rd* or *23rd*) of May.

❑ **All numbers if two or more *related* numbers both above and below ten are used in the same sentence.**
Mr. Carter sent in 7 receipts, and Ms. Cantrell sent in 22.
But: The 13 accountants owned three computers each.

❑ **Measurements (time, money, distance, weight, and percent).**
The $500 statue we delivered at 7 a.m. weighed 6 pounds.

❑ **Mixed numbers.**
Our sales are up 9½ (or *9 1/2*) percent over last year.

RULE 46 ▶
word
(L. 57)

Spell out

❑ **A number used as the first word of a sentence.**
Seventy-five people attended the conference in San Diego.

❑ **The shorter of two adjacent numbers.**
We have ordered 3 two-pound cakes and one 5-pound cake for the reception.

❑ **The words *million* and *billion* in even amounts (do not use decimals with even amounts).**
Not: A $5.00 ticket can win $28,000,000 in this month's lottery.
But: A $5 ticket can win $28 million in this month's lottery.

❑ **Fractions.**
Almost one-half of the audience responded to the question.

Note: When fractions and the numbers twenty-one through ninety-nine are spelled out, they should be hyphenated.

ABBREVIATIONS

RULE 47 ▶
abbreviate none
(L. 67)

In general business writing, do not abbreviate common words (such as *dept.* or *pkg.*), compass points, units of measure, or the names of months, days of the week, cities, or states (except in addresses).

Almost one-half of the audience indicated they were at least 5 feet_8 inches tall.

Note: Do not insert a comma between the parts of a single measurement.

RULE 48 ▶
abbreviate measure
(L. 87)

In technical writing, on forms, and in tables, abbreviate units of measure when they occur frequently. Do not use periods.

14 oz   5 ft 10 in   50 mph   2 yrs 10 mo

RULE 49 ▶
abbreviate lowercase
(L. 87)

In most lowercase abbreviations made up of single initials, use a period after each initial but no internal spaces.

a.m.   p.m.   i.e.   e.g.   e.o.m.
Exceptions: mph   mpg   wpm

RULE 50 ▶
abbreviate ≡
(L. 87)

In most all-capital abbreviations made up of single initials, do not use periods or internal spaces.

OSHA   PBS   NBEA   WWW   VCR   MBA
Exceptions: U.S.A.   A.A.   B.S.   Ph.D.   P.O.   B.C.   A.D.

Part 1

The Alphabet, Number, and Symbol Keys

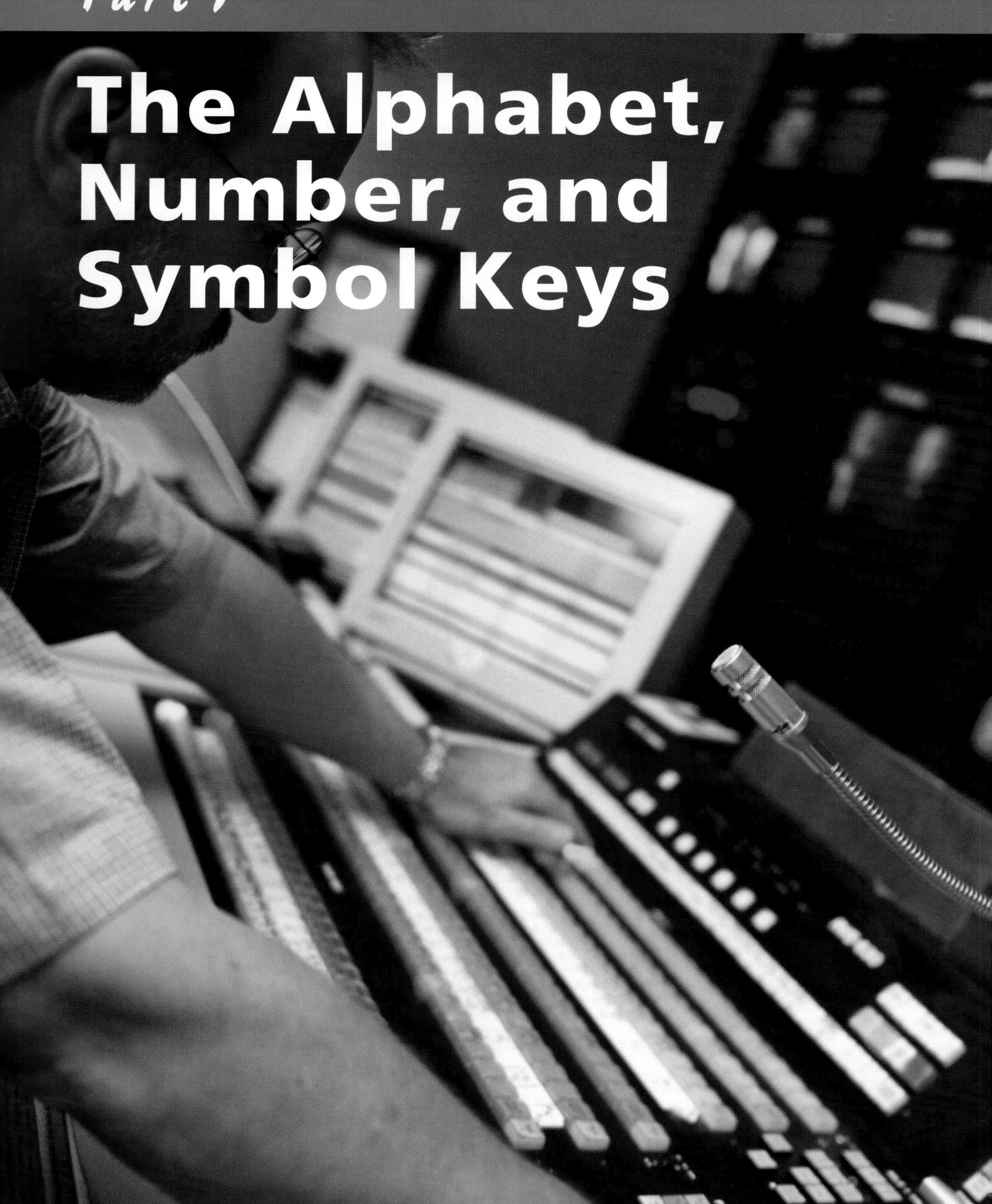

Keyboarding in Arts, Audio, Video Technology, and Communications Services

Occupations in this cluster deal with organizing and communicating information to the public in various forms and media. This cluster includes jobs in radio and television broadcasting, journalism, motion pictures, the recording industry, the performing arts, multimedia publishing, and the entertainment services. Book editors, computer artists, technical writers, radio announcers, news correspondents, and camera operators are just a few jobs within this cluster.

Qualifications and Skills

Strong oral and written communication skills and technical skills are necessary for anyone in communications and media. Without a doubt, competent keyboarding skill is extremely advantageous.

Working in the media requires creativity, talent, and accurate use of language. In journalism, being observant, thinking clearly, and seeing the significance of events are all of utmost importance. Announcers must have exceptional voices, excellent speaking skills, and a unique style. The ability to work under pressure is important in all areas of media.

Objectives

KEYBOARDING

- Operate by touch the letter, number, and symbol keys.
- Demonstrate proper typing technique.
- Use the correct spacing with punctuation.
- Type at least 28 words per minute on a 2-minute timed writing with no more than 5 errors.

TECHNICAL

- Answer correctly at least 90 percent of the questions on an objective test.

Keyboarding: The Alphabet

LESSON 1
A S D F J K L ;
ENTER SPACE BAR

LESSON 2
H E O R

LESSON 3
M T P C

LESSON 4
RIGHT SHIFT V . W

LESSON 5
Review

Home Keys

Goals

- Touch-type the home keys (A S D F J K L ;)
- Touch-type the SPACE BAR
- Touch-type the ENTER key
- Type at least 10wpm/1′/3e

LEFT HAND
First Finger F
Second Finger D
Third Finger S
Fourth Finger A

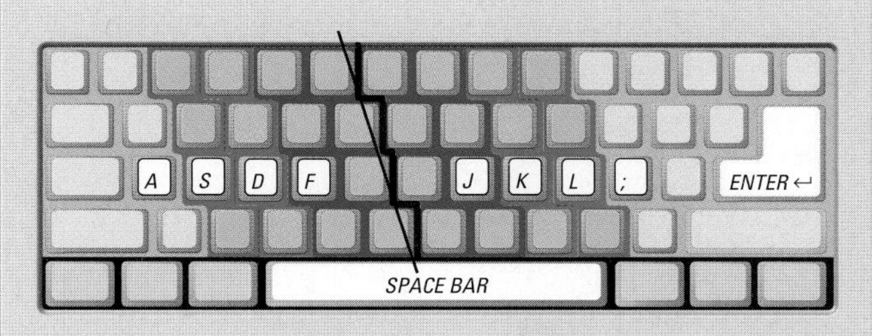

RIGHT HAND
J First Finger
K Second Finger
L Third Finger
; Fourth Finger
SPACE BAR Thumb

NEW KEYS

A. Follow the directions to become familiar with the home keys.

The semicolon (;) is commonly called the sem key.

A. THE HOME KEYS

The **A S D F J K L ;** keys are known as the home keys.

1. Place the fingers of your left hand on the home keys as follows: first finger on **F**; second finger on **D**; third finger on **S**; fourth finger on **A**.
2. Place the fingers of your right hand on the home keys as follows: first finger on **J**; second finger on **K**; third finger on **L**; and fourth finger on **;**.
3. Curve your fingers.
4. Using the correct fingers, type each character as you say it to yourself: `a s d f j k l ;`.
5. Remove your fingers from the keyboard and replace them on the home keys.
6. Press each home key again as you say each character: `a s d f j k l ;`.

B. THE SPACE BAR

The SPACE BAR, located beneath the letter keys, is used to space between words and after marks of punctuation.

1. With fingers held motionless on the home keys, poise your right thumb about a half inch above the SPACE BAR.
2. Type the characters and then press the SPACE BAR 1 time. Bounce your thumb off.

C. Type each line 1 time, pressing the SPACE BAR where you see a space and pressing the ENTER key at the end of a line.

C. THE ENTER↵ KEY

The ENTER key moves the insertion point to the beginning of a new line. Reach to the ENTER key with the fourth finger of your right hand. Keep your J finger at home. Lightly press the ENTER key. Practice using the ENTER key until you can do so with confidence and without looking at your hands.

```
asdf jkl; asdf jkl; ↵
asdf jkl; asdf jkl; ↵
```

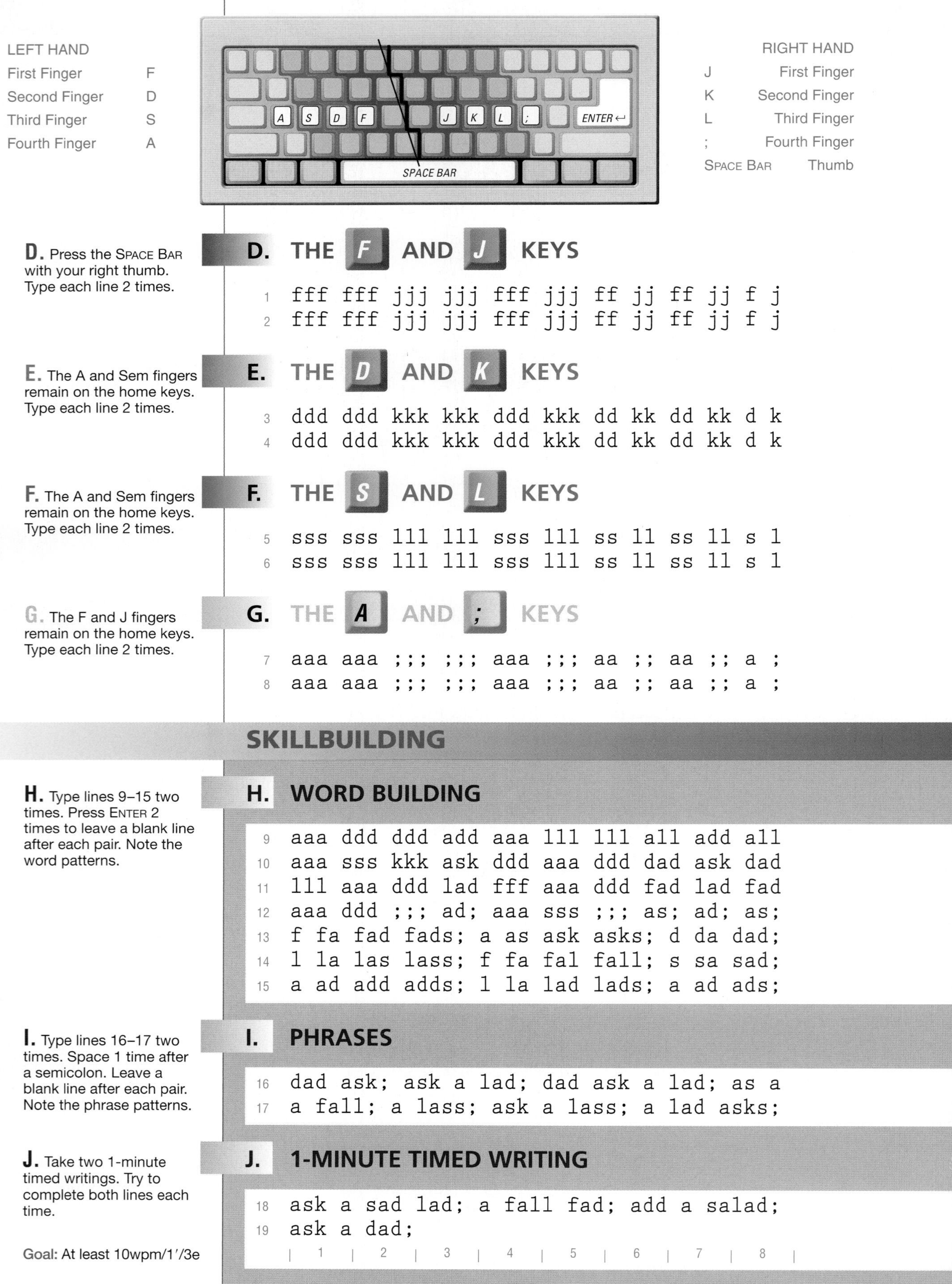

LEFT HAND	
First Finger	F
Second Finger	D
Third Finger	S
Fourth Finger	A

	RIGHT HAND
J	First Finger
K	Second Finger
L	Third Finger
;	Fourth Finger
SPACE BAR	Thumb

D. Press the SPACE BAR with your right thumb. Type each line 2 times.

D. THE F AND J KEYS

```
1  fff fff jjj jjj fff jjj ff jj ff jj f j
2  fff fff jjj jjj fff jjj ff jj ff jj f j
```

E. The A and Sem fingers remain on the home keys. Type each line 2 times.

E. THE D AND K KEYS

```
3  ddd ddd kkk kkk ddd kkk dd kk dd kk d k
4  ddd ddd kkk kkk ddd kkk dd kk dd kk d k
```

F. The A and Sem fingers remain on the home keys. Type each line 2 times.

F. THE S AND L KEYS

```
5  sss sss lll lll sss lll ss ll ss ll s l
6  sss sss lll lll sss lll ss ll ss ll s l
```

G. The F and J fingers remain on the home keys. Type each line 2 times.

G. THE A AND ; KEYS

```
7  aaa aaa ;;; ;;; aaa ;;; aa ;; aa ;; a ;
8  aaa aaa ;;; ;;; aaa ;;; aa ;; aa ;; a ;
```

SKILLBUILDING

H. Type lines 9–15 two times. Press ENTER 2 times to leave a blank line after each pair. Note the word patterns.

H. WORD BUILDING

```
9   aaa ddd ddd add aaa lll lll all add all
10  aaa sss kkk ask ddd aaa ddd dad ask dad
11  lll aaa ddd lad fff aaa ddd fad lad fad
12  aaa ddd ;;; ad; aaa sss ;;; as; ad; as;
13  f fa fad fads; a as ask asks; d da dad;
14  l la las lass; f fa fal fall; s sa sad;
15  a ad add adds; l la lad lads; a ad ads;
```

I. Type lines 16–17 two times. Space 1 time after a semicolon. Leave a blank line after each pair. Note the phrase patterns.

I. PHRASES

```
16  dad ask; ask a lad; dad ask a lad; as a
17  a fall; a lass; ask a lass; a lad asks;
```

J. Take two 1-minute timed writings. Try to complete both lines each time.

Goal: At least 10wpm/1′/3e

J. 1-MINUTE TIMED WRITING

```
18  ask a sad lad; a fall fad; add a salad;
19  ask a dad;
    | 1 | 2 | 3 | 4 | 5 | 6 | 7 | 8 |
```

New Keys

Goals

- Touch-type the H, E, O, and R keys
- Type at least 11wpm/1′/3e

Fingers are named for home keys. (Example: The middle finger of the left hand is the D finger.)

A. Type 2 times.

A. WARMUP

```
fff jjj ddd kkk sss lll aaa ;;; fff jjj
a salad; a lad; alas a fad; ask a lass;
```

NEW KEYS

B. Type each line 2 times. Space 1 time after a semicolon.

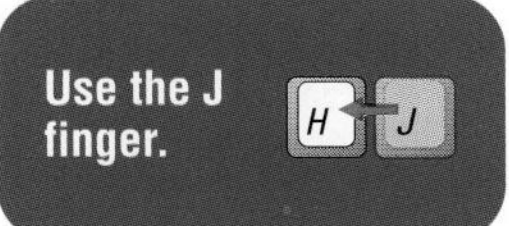

Use the J finger.
H
J

B. THE H KEY

```
jjj jhj jhj hjh jjj jhj jhj hjh jjj jhj
has has hah hah had had aha aha ash ash
hash half sash lash dash hall shad shah
as dad had; a lass has half; add a dash
```

C. Type each line 2 times. Keep your eyes on the copy as you type.

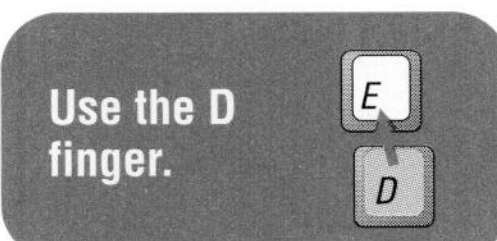

Use the D finger.
E
D

C. THE E KEY

```
ddd ded ded ede ddd ded ded ede ddd ded
lea led he; he see; eke fed sea lee fee
feed keel ease heal held seal lead fake
he fed a seal; she held a lease; a keel
```

D. Type each line 2 times. Keep fingers curved.

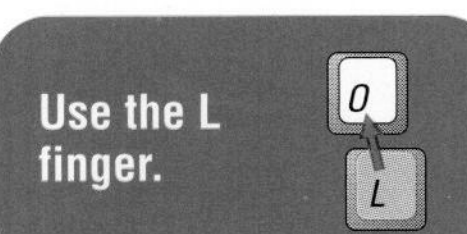

Use the L finger.
O
L

D. THE O KEY

```
lll lol lol olo lll lol lol olo lll lol
doe off foe hod oh; oak odd ode old sod
shoe look kook joke odes does solo oleo
he held a hook; a lass solos; old foes;
```

E. Type each line 2 times. Keep the A finger at home.

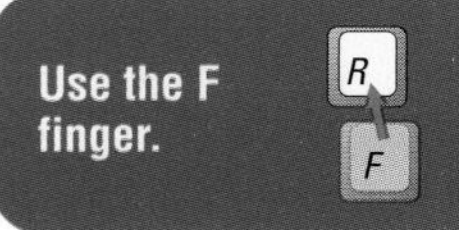

E. THE R KEY

15 fff frf frf rfr fff frf frf rfr fff frf
16 red ark ore err rah era rod oar her are
17 oars soar dear fare read role rare door
18 a dark red door; he read a rare reader;

SKILLBUILDING

F. Type each line 2 times. Do not type the red vertical lines.

F. WORD PATTERNS

19 dale kale sale hale | fold sold hold old;
20 feed deed heed seed | dash sash lash ash;
21 lake rake sake fake | dear sear rear ear;

G. Take two 1-minute timed writings. Try to complete both lines each time. Press ENTER only at the end of line 23.

Goal: At least 11wpm/1′/3e

G. 1-MINUTE TIMED WRITING

22 she asked for a rare old deed; he held
23 a red door ajar;
| 1 | 2 | 3 | 4 | 5 | 6 | 7 | 8 |

Keyboarding Connection

What Is the Internet?

What is the easiest way to go to the library? Try using your fingertips! The Internet creates a "virtual library"—a library with no walls. Nothing can match the Internet as a research device. It is not just one computer but an immense connection of computers talking to one another and organizing and exchanging information.

The Internet is synonymous with cyberspace, a word describing the power and control of information. The Internet has been called "a network of networks" linked together to deliver information to users. The Internet connects more than 200 million people to over 3 million computer networks.

The Internet is considered a wide area network (WAN) because the computers on it span the entire world. Each day the Net increases at about 1000 new users every hour.

YOUR TURN List some ways the Internet, as a virtual library, enhances your research activities.

New Keys

Goals

- Touch-type the M, T, P, and C keys
- Type at least 12wpm/1′/3e

A. Type 2 times.

A. WARMUP

1 aa ;; ss ll dd kk ff jj hh ee oo rr aa;
2 he held a sale for her as she had asked

NEW KEYS

B. Type each line 2 times.

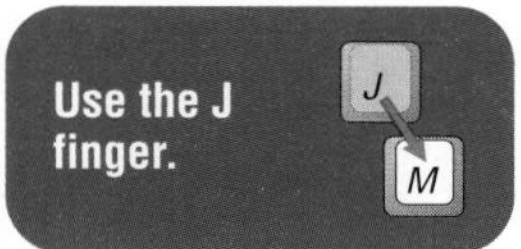

B. THE M KEY

3 jjj jmj jmj mjm jjj jmj jmj mjm jjj jmj
4 mad mom me; am jam; ram dam ham mar ma;
5 arms loam lame roam make fame room same
6 she made more room for some of her ham;

C. Type each line 2 times.

C. THE T KEY

7 fff ftf ftf tft fff ftf ftf tft fff ftf
8 tar tam mat hot jot rat eat lot art sat
9 told take date late mart mate tool fate
10 he told her to set a later date to eat;

D. Type each line 2 times.

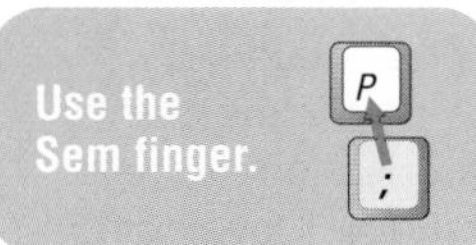

D. THE P KEY

11 ;;; ;p; ;p; p;p ;;; ;p; ;p; p;p ;;; ;p;
12 pat pal sap rap pet par spa lap pad mop
13 pale palm stop drop pelt plea slap trap
14 please park the red jeep past the pool;

E. Type each line 2 times.

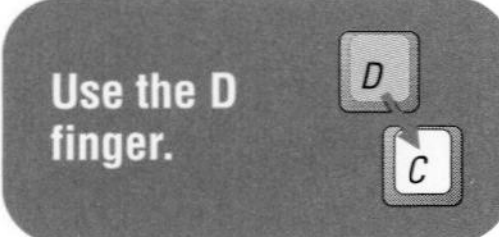

E. THE C KEY

15 ddd dcd dcd cdc ddd dcd dcd cdc ddd dcd
16 cot cod sac act car coo arc ace cop cat
17 pack tack chat coat face aces deck cost
18 call her to race cool cars at the track

SKILLBUILDING

F. Sit in the correct position as you type these drills. Refer to the illustration in the Introduction. Type each line 2 times. Do not type the red vertical lines.

F. SHORT PHRASES

19 as so | she had | has met | let her | fast pace
20 to do | ask her | for the | had pop | look past
21 do as | lap top | her pad | let pat | halt them
22 as he | had for | red cap | she let | fast plot

G. Take two 1-minute timed writings. Try to complete both lines each time. Use word wrap. Press ENTER only at the end of line 24.

Goal: At least 12wpm/1′/3e

G. 1-MINUTE TIMED WRITING

23 the old store at home had lots of cheap
24 stools for the sale;

| 1 | 2 | 3 | 4 | 5 | 6 | 7 | 8 |

Strategies for Career Success

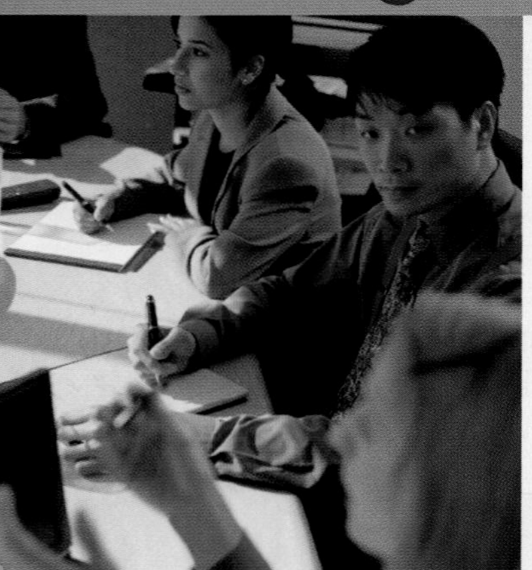

Being a Good Listener

Silence is golden! Listening is essential for learning, getting along, and forming relationships.

Do you tend to forget people's names after being introduced? Do you look away from the speaker instead of making eye contact? Do you interrupt the speaker before he or she finishes talking? Do you misunderstand people? Answering yes can indicate poor listening skills.

To improve your listening skills, follow these steps. *Hear the speaker clearly.* Do not interrupt; let the speaker develop his or her ideas before you speak. *Focus on the message.* At the end of a conversation, identify major items discussed. Mentally ask questions to help you assess the points the speaker is making. *Keep an open mind.* Do not judge. Developing your listening skills benefits everyone.

YOUR TURN Assess your listening behavior. What techniques can you use to improve your listening skills? Practice them the next time you have a conversation with someone.

New Keys

Goals

- Touch-type the RIGHT SHIFT, V, period, and W keys
- Count errors
- Type at least 13wpm/1′/3e

A. Type 2 times.

A. WARMUP

```
1 the farmer asked her to feed the mares;
2 the late callers came to mop the floor;
```

NEW KEYS

B. Type each line 2 times.

B. THE RIGHT  KEY

To capitalize letters on the left half of the keyboard:

1. With the J finger at home, press and hold down the RIGHT SHIFT key with the Sem finger.
2. Press the letter key.
3. Release the RIGHT SHIFT key and return fingers to home position.

```
3 ;;; ;A; ;A; ;;; ;S; ;S; ;;; ;D; ;D; ;;;
4 Art Alf Ada Sal Sam Dee Dot Flo Ted Tom
5 Amos Carl Chet Elsa Fred Sara Todd Elda
6 Carl Amos took Sara Carter to the races
```

C. Type each line 2 times.

C. THE V KEY

```
7 fff fvf fvf vfv fff fvf fvf vfv fff fvf
8 Val eve Eva vet Ava vat Eve ova Vel vee
9 have vase Vera ever vast Reva dove vest
10 Dave voted for Vassar; Val voted for me
```

D. Type each line 2 times. Space 1 time after a period following an abbreviation; do not space after a period within an abbreviation; space 1 time after a period ending a sentence.

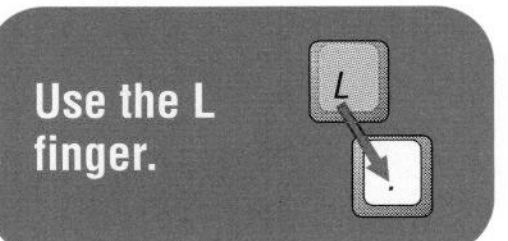

D. THE . KEY

```
11 lll l.l l.l .l. lll l.l l.l .l. lll l.l
12 dr. dr. ea. ea. sr. sr. Dr. Dr. Sr. Sr.
13 a.m. acct. A.D. p.m. Corp. amt. Dr. Co.
14 Selma left. Dave left. Sarah came home.
```

E. Type each line 2 times.

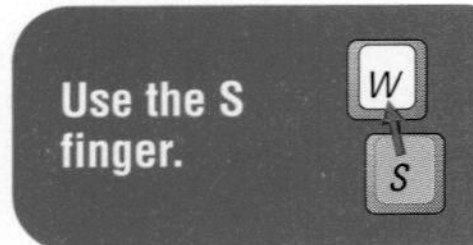

E. THE W KEY

```
15 sss sws sws wsw sss sws sws wsw sss sws
16 wow sow war owe was mow woe few wee row
17 wake ward wart wave wham whom walk what
18 Wade watched Walt Shaw walk for a week.
```

SKILLBUILDING

F. Type each line 2 times.

F. BUILD SKILL ON SENTENCES

```
19 Amos Ford saw Emma Dale feed the mares.
20 Dr. Drake called Sam; he asked for Ted.
21 Vera told a tale to her old classmates.
22 Todd asked Cale to move some old rakes.
```

G. Type each line 1 time. After typing all the lines, count your errors. Refer to the Introduction if you need help.

G. COUNTING ERRORS IN SENTENCES

```
23 Ada lost her letter; Dee lost her card.
24 Dave sold some of the food to a market.
25 Alva asked Walt for three more matches.
26 Dale asked Seth to watch the last show.
```

H. Take two 1-minute timed writings. Try to complete both lines each time.

Goal: At least 13wpm/1′/3e

H. 1-MINUTE TIMED WRITING

```
27 Val asked them to tell the major to see
28 Carla at that local farm.
   |  1  |  2  |  3  |  4  |  5  |  6  |  7  |  8  |
```

Review

Goals

- Reinforce new-key reaches
- Type at least 14wpm/1′/3e

A. Type 2 times.

A. WARMUP

```
Dave called Drew to ask for a road map.
Elsa took three old jars to her mother.
```

SKILLBUILDING

B. Type each line 2 times. Do not type the red vertical lines.

B. WORD PATTERNS

```
feed seed deed heed|fold cold mold told
fame tame lame same|mate late date fate
lace face mace race|vast last cast fast
park dark hark mark|rare dare fare ware
```

C. Type each line 2 times.

C. PHRASES

```
at the|he has|her hat|for the|come home
or the|he had|her top|ask the|late date
to the|he met|her mop|ask her|made more
of the|he was|her pop|ask too|fast pace
```

D. Type each line 2 times.

D. BUILD SKILL ON SENTENCES

```
She asked Dale to share the jar of jam.
Cal took the tools from store to store.
Darel held a sale to sell some clothes.
Seth watched the old cat chase the car.
```

E. Take a 1-minute timed writing on each line. Review your speed and errors.

E. SENTENCES

```
Carl loved to talk to the tall teacher.
She dashed to take the jet to her home.
Walt asked her to deed the farm to Ted.
| 1 | 2 | 3 | 4 | 5 | 6 | 7 | 8 | = Number of 5-stroke words
```

F. Take two 1-minute timed writings on the paragraph. Press ENTER only at the end of the paragraph. Review your speed and errors.

F. PARAGRAPH

CUMULATIVE WORDS

```
Rachael asked Sal to take her to school        8
for two weeks. She had to meet Freda or       16
Walt at the school to work on the maps.       24
| 1 | 2 | 3 | 4 | 5 | 6 | 7 | 8 |
```

G. Take two 1-minute timed writings. Review your speed and errors.

Goal: At least 14wpm/1′/3e

G. 1-MINUTE TIMED WRITINGS

```
Dot Crews asked Al Roper to meet her at        8
the tree to look for a jacket.                14
| 1 | 2 | 3 | 4 | 5 | 6 | 7 | 8 |
```

Keyboarding Connection

Using Search Engines

How can you most efficiently find information on the Web? Use a search engine! A search engine guides you to the Web's resources. It analyzes the information you request, navigates the Web's many networks, and retrieves a list of relevant documents. Popular search engines include Google, Excite, Alta Vista, and Yahoo.

A search engine examines electronic databases, wire services, journals, article summaries, articles, home pages, and user group lists. It can access material found in millions of Web sites. When you request a specific keyword search, a search engine scans its large database and searches the introductory lines of text, as well as the title, headings, and subheadings of a Web page. The search engine displays the information that most closely matches your request.

YOUR TURN Try different search engines and see which ones you like best. Choose three of your favorite search engines. Then conduct a search using the keywords "touch typing." (Don't forget the quotation marks.) Compare the results for each search engine.

Unit 2

Keyboarding: The Alphabet

LESSON 6
I Left Shift - G

LESSON 7
U B : X

LESSON 8
Y , Q /

LESSON 9
N Z ? Tab

LESSON 10
Review

New Keys

Goals

- Touch-type the I, LEFT SHIFT, hyphen, and G keys
- Type at least 15wpm/1′/3e

A. Type 2 times.

A. WARMUP

1 The major sold three wool hats at cost.
2 Dale took her cats to the vet at three.

NEW KEYS

B. Type each line 2 times.

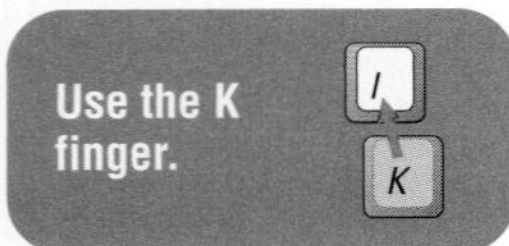

B. THE I KEY

3 kkk kik kik iki kkk kik kik iki kkk kik
4 aid did fir him kid lid mid pit sip tip
5 chip dice itch film hide iris kite milk
6 This time he left his tie at the store.

C. Type each line 2 times.

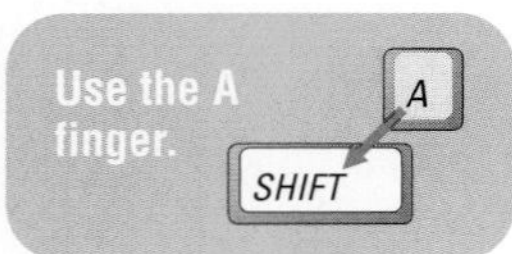

C. THE LEFT SHIFT KEY

To capitalize letters on the right half of the keyboard:

1. With the F finger at home, press and hold down the LEFT SHIFT key with the A finger.
2. Press the letter key.
3. Release the LEFT SHIFT key and return fingers to the home position.

7 aaa Jaa Jaa aaa Kaa Kaa aaa Laa Laa aaa
8 Joe Kip Lee Hal Mat Pat Jim Kim Les Pam
9 Jake Karl Lake Hope Mark Jack Kate Hale
10 Les Lee rode with Pat Mace to the park.

D. Type each line 2 times. Do not space before or after a hyphen; keep the J finger in home position.

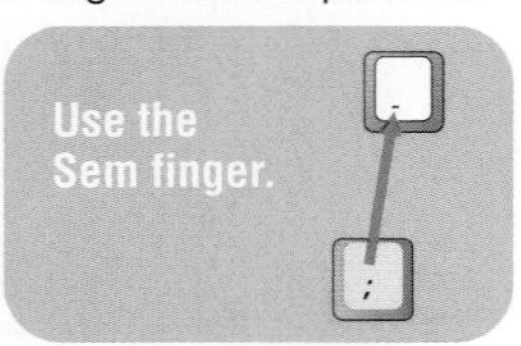

D. THE - KEY

11 ;;; ;p; ;-; ;-; -;- ;;; ;-; -;- ;;; ;-;
12 two-thirds two-fifths trade-off tip-off
13 look-alike jack-of-all-trades free-fall
14 I heard that Ms. Lee-Som is well-to-do.

E. Type each line 2 times. Keep wrists low but not resting on the keyboard.

E. THE G KEY

```
fff fgf fgf gfg fff fgf fgf gfg fff fgf
age cog dig fig hog jog lag peg rag sag
gold rage sage grow page cage gate wage
Gail G. Grove greeted the great golfer.
```

SKILLBUILDING

F. Type each line 2 times.

F. TECHNIQUE PRACTICE: SPACE BAR

```
Vic will meet. Ed is here. Ava is here.
See them. Do it. Make these. Hold this.
See Lester. See Kate. See Dad. See Mom.
Take this car. Make the cakes. Hide it.
```

G. Type each line 2 times.

G. TECHNIQUE PRACTICE: HYPHEN KEY

```
Two-thirds were well-to-do look-alikes.
Jo Hames-Smith is a jack-of-all-trades.
Phil saw the trade-offs at the tip-off.
Two-fifths are packed for Jo Mill-Ross.
```

H. Take two 1-minute timed writings. Review your speed and errors.

Goal: At least 15wpm/1′/3e

H. 1-MINUTE TIMED WRITING

	WORDS
Al Hall left the firm two weeks ago. I	8
will see him at the office at three.	15
| 1 | 2 | 3 | 4 | 5 | 6 | 7 | 8 |	

New Keys

Goals

- Touch-type the U, B, colon, and X keys
- Type at least 16wpm/1′/3e

A. Type 2 times.

A. WARMUP

1 Evette jogged eight miles with Christi.
2 Philip gave Shari the award for spirit.

NEW KEYS

B. Type each line 2 times. Keep your other fingers at home as you reach to U.

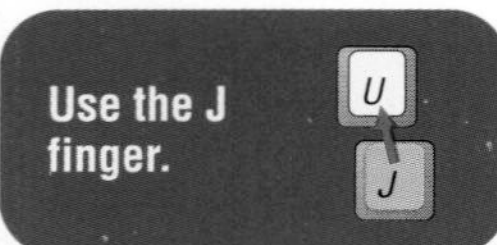

B. THE U KEY

3 jjj juj juj uju jjj juj juj uju jjj juj
4 cue due hue put rut cut dug hut pup rum
5 cult duet fuel hulk just lump mule pull
6 Hugh urged us to put out the hot fires.

C. Type each line 2 times.

C. THE B KEY

7 fff fbf fbf bfb fff fbf fbf bfb fff fbf
8 bag cab bad lab bat rib bar tab beg web
9 bake back bead beef bath bail beam both
10 Bart backed Bill for a big blue bumper.

D. The colon is the shift of the semicolon key. Type each line 2 times. Space 1 time after a period following an abbreviation and 1 time after a colon.

Use the Sem finger.

D. THE : KEY

11 ;:; ;:; ;:; :;: ;:; ;:; ;:; :;: ;:; ;:;
12 Dr. Poole: Ms. Shu: Mr. Rose: Mrs. Tam:
13 Dear Ed: Dear Flo: Dear James: Dear Di:
14 Date: To: From: Subject: for the dates:

E. Type each line 2 times.

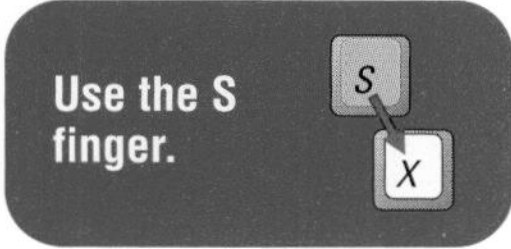

E. THE X KEY

sss sxs sxs xsx sss sxs sxs xsx sss sxs
box fox hex lax lux mix six tax vex wax
apex axle exam flax flex flux taxi text
Max asked six pals to fix a sixth taxi.

SKILLBUILDING

F. Type each line 2 times.

F. TECHNIQUE PRACTICE: COLON KEY

as follows: these people: this example:
Dear Sirs: Dear Madam: Dear Mrs. Smith:
Dear Di: Dear Bo: Dear Peter: Dear Mom:
for this part: as listed: the projects:

G. Type each line 2 times.

G. WORD PRACTICE

Top row

We were told to take our truck to Hugo.
There were two tired people at the hut.
Please write to their home to tell Tom.

Home row

Jake asked his dad for small red flags.
Sara added a dash of salt to the salad.
Dale said she had a fall sale at Drake.

Bottom row

He came to the mall at five to meet me.
Victoria came to vote with ample vigor.
Mable Baxter visited via the Marta bus.

H. Take two 1-minute timed writings. Review your speed and errors.

Goal: At least 16wpm/1′/3e

H. 1-MINUTE TIMED WRITING

WORDS

Dear Jack: Fred would like to take Jill 8
Wells to the home game at five tomorrow. 16

| 1 | 2 | 3 | 4 | 5 | 6 | 7 | 8 |

New Keys

Goals

- Touch-type the Y, comma, Q, and slash keys
- Type at least 17wpm/1′/3e

A. Type 2 times.

A. WARMUP

1 Jack asked Philip if Charlie came home.
2 Kim had a short meal with Victor Baker.

NEW KEYS

B. Type each line 2 times.

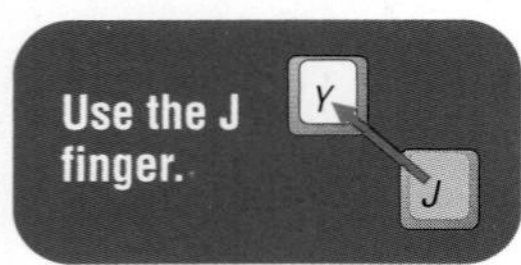

Use the J finger.
Y
J

B. THE Y KEY

3 jjj jyj jyj yjy jjj jyj jyj yjy jjj jyj
4 boy cry day eye fly guy hay joy key may
5 yard year yelp yoke yolk your yule play
6 Peggy told me that she may try to stay.

C. Type each line 2 times.

Use the K finger.
K
,

C. THE , KEY

7 kkk k,k k,k ,k, kkk k,k k,k ,k, kkk k,k
8 as, at, do, if, is, it, of, oh, or, so,
9 if so, if it is, what if, what of, too,
10 Dale, Barbra, Sadie, or Edith left too.

D. Type each line 2 times.

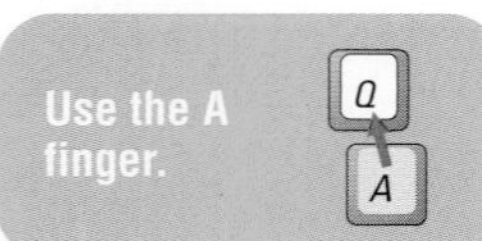

Use the A finger.
Q
A

D. THE Q KEY

11 aaa aqa aqa qaq aaa aqa aqa qaq aaa aqa
12 quip quit quack quail quake quart quash
13 quest quick quilts quotes quaver queasy
14 Four quiet squires quilted aqua quilts.

E. Type each line 2 times. Do not space before or after a slash.

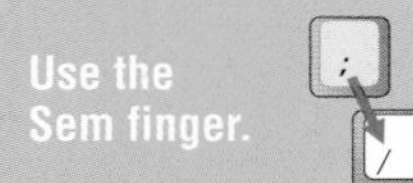

E. THE / KEY

15 ;;; ;/; ;/; /;/ ;;; ;/; ;/; /;/ ;;; ;/;
16 his/her him/her he/she either/or ad/add
17 do/due/dew hale/hail fir/fur heard/herd
18 Ask him/her if he/she chose true/false.

SKILLBUILDING

F. Type each line 2 times.

F. PHRASES

19 if it is|she will do|will he come|he is
20 he said so|who left them|will she drive
21 after all|he voted|just wait|to ask her
22 some said it|for that firm|did she seem

G. Type each line 2 times.

G. TECHNIQUE PRACTICE: SHIFT KEY

23 Ada, Idaho; Kodiak, Alaska; Lima, Ohio;
24 Lula, Georgia; Sully, Iowa; Alta, Utah;
25 Mr. Ray Tims; Mr. Ed Chu; Mr. Cal York;
26 Ms. Vi Close; Ms. Di Ray; Ms. Sue Ames;

H. Take two 1-minute timed writings. Review your speed and errors.

Goal: At least 17wpm/1′/3e

H. 1-MINUTE TIMED WRITING

27 George predicted that Lu will have five 8
28 boxed quilts. David Quayle was to pack 16
29 a mug. 17

| 1 | 2 | 3 | 4 | 5 | 6 | 7 | 8 |

New Keys

Goals

- Touch-type the N, Z, question mark, and TAB keys
- Type at least 18wpm/1′/3e

A. Type 2 times.

A. WARMUP

1 I quit the sales job at Huber, Georgia.
2 Alice packed two boxes of silver disks.

NEW KEYS

B. Type each line 2 times.

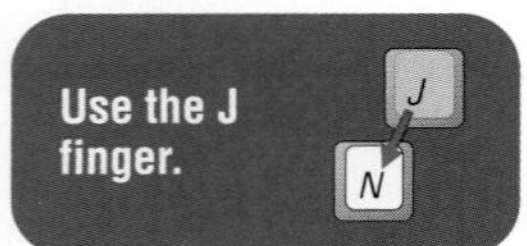

B. THE N KEY

3 jjj jnj jnj njn jjj jnj jnj njn jjj jnj
4 and ban can den end fan nag one pan ran
5 aunt band chin dent find gain hang lawn
6 Al and Dan can enter the main entrance.

C. Type each line 2 times. Keep the F finger at home as you reach to the Z.

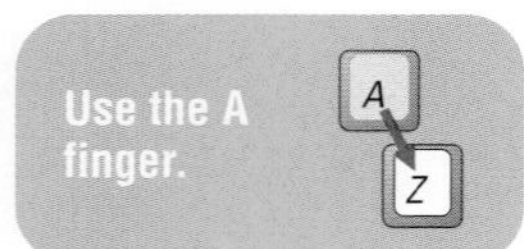

C. THE Z KEY

7 aaa aza aza zaz aaa aza aza zaz aaa aza
8 zap zig buzz gaze haze jazz mazes oozes
9 zip zoo zinc zing zone zoom blaze craze
10 The size of the prized pizza amazed us.

D. The question mark is the shift of the slash. Space 1 time after a question mark at the end of a sentence. Type each line 2 times.

D. THE ? KEY

11 ;;; ;?; ;?; ?;? ;;; ;?; ;?; ?;? ;;; ;?;
12 Can John go? If not Jane, who? Can Ken?
13 Who will see? Can this be? Is that you?
14 Why not quilt? Can they go? Did he ask?

E. The word counts in this book credit you with 1 stroke for each paragraph indention in a timed writing. Press the Tab key after the timing starts.

E. THE TAB KEY

The Tab key is used to indent paragraphs. Reach to the Tab key with the A finger. Keep your other fingers on the home keys as you quickly press the Tab key. Pressing the Tab key moves the insertion point 0.5 inch (the default setting) to the right.

F. Type each paragraph 2 times. Press Enter only at the end of the paragraph.

F. PRACTICE THE TAB KEY

```
15  Each  Tab→  day   Tab→  set   Tab→  your   Tab→  goal
16  to          type        with        more         speed.

17  You         will        soon        reach        your
18  goal        if          you         work         hard.
```

SKILLBUILDING

G. Type each line 2 times.

G. TECHNIQUE PRACTICE: QUESTION MARK

```
19  Who? Why? How? When? What? True? False?
20  Is it Mo? Why not? What for? Which one?
21  Did Mary go? Is Clinton ready? Why not?
22  Who competed with me? Dana? James? Kay?
```

H. Type each line 2 times.

H. PHRASES

```
23  and the|for the|she is able|can they go
24  for him|ask him|they still|did they fly
25  of them|with us|can he send|ought to be
26  has been able|they need it|he will call
```

I. Type each paragraph 2 times.

I. TECHNIQUE PRACTICE: HYPHEN

Hyphens are used:

- To show that a word is divided (lines 27 and 31).
- To make a dash using two hyphens with no space before or after (lines 28 and 31).
- To join words in a compound word (lines 29, 30, and 32).

27 Can Larry go to the next tennis tourna-
28 ment? I am positive he--like Lane--will find
29 the event to be a first-class sports event.
30 If he can go, I will get first-rate seats.
31 Larry--like Ella--enjoys going to tourna-
32 ments that are always first-rate, first-class
33 sporting events.

J. Space 1 time after a semicolon, colon, and comma and 1 time after a period and question mark at the end of a sentence. Type each line 2 times.

J. PUNCTUATION PRACTICE

34 Kate writes; John sings. Are they good?
35 Send these items: pens, pencils, clips.
36 Hal left; she stayed. Will they attend?
37 Wes made these stops: Rome, Bern, Kiev.

K. Take two 1-minute timed writings. Review your speed and errors.

Goal: At least 18wpm/1′/3e

K. 1-MINUTE TIMED WRITING

38 Zelda judged six typing contests 7
39 that a local firm held in Piqua. Vick 14
40 Bass was a winner. 18

| 1 | 2 | 3 | 4 | 5 | 6 | 7 | 8 |

Strategies for Career Success

Preparing a Job Interview Portfolio

Don't go empty-handed to that job interview! Take a portfolio of items with you. Definitely include copies of your resume and your list of references, with at least three professional references. Your academic transcript is useful, especially if you are asked to complete a company application form. Appropriate work samples and copies of certificates and licenses are also helpful portfolio items.

The interview process provides you the opportunity to interview the organization. Include a list of questions you want to ask during the interview.

A comprehensive portfolio of materials will benefit you by giving you a measure of control during the interview process.

YOUR TURN Start today to compile items for your interview portfolio. Include copies of your resume, your reference list, and copies of certificates and licenses. Begin developing a list of interview questions. Think about appropriate work samples to include in your portfolio.

Review

Goals

- Reinforce new key reaches
- Type at least 19wpm/1′/3e

A. Type 2 times.

A. WARMUP

She expects to work hard at her job.
Keith had a very quiet, lazy afternoon.

SKILLBUILDING

B. Take a 1-minute timed writing on each paragraph. Review your speed and errors.

B. SHORT PARAGRAPHS

You can utilize your office skills 7
to complete tasks. Some types of jobs 15
require more skills. 19

You will be amazed at how easily 7
and quickly you complete your task when 15
you can concentrate. 19

| 1 | 2 | 3 | 4 | 5 | 6 | 7 | 8 |

C. Type each line 2 times.

C. WORD PATTERNS

banister minister adapter filter master
disable disband discern discord discuss
embargo emerge embody empty employ emit
enforce endure energy engage engine end
precept precise predict preside premier
subtract subject subsist sublime subdue
teamster tearful teaches teak team tear
theater theirs theory thefts therm them
treason crimson season prison bison son
tribune tribute tripod trial tribe trim

D. Type each line 2 times. Keep fingers curved and wrists low but not resting on the keyboard as you practice these lines.

D. ALPHABET REVIEW

Alda asked Alma Adams to fly to Alaska.
Both Barbara and Bill liked basketball.
Carl can accept a classic car in Cairo.
David dined in a dark diner in Detroit.
Elmo said Eddie edited the entire text.
Five friars focused on the four fables.
Guy gave a bag of green grapes to Gina.
Haughty Hugh hoped Hal had helped Seth.
Irene liked to pickle pickles in brine.
Jon Jones joined a junior jogging team.
Kenny kept a kayak for a trek to Akron.
Lowell played a well-planned ball game.
Monica made more money on many markups.
Ned knew ten men in a main dining room.
Opal Orem opened four boxes of oranges.
Pat paid to park the plane at the pump.
Quincy quickly quit his quarterly quiz.
Robin read rare books in their library.
Sam signed, sealed, and sent the lease.
Todd caught trout in the little stream.
Uncle Rubin urged Julie to go to Utica.
Viva Vista vetoed the five voice votes.
Walt waited while Wilma went to Weston.
Xu mixed extra extract exactly as told.
Yes, your young sister played a cymbal.
Zesty zebras zigzagged in the Ohio zoo.

E. Take two 1-minute timed writings. Review your speed and errors.

Goal: At least 19wpm/1′/3e

E. 1-MINUTE TIMED WRITING

Zoe expected a quiet morning to do 7
all of her work. Jean Day was to bring 15
five of the tablets. 19

| 1 | 2 | 3 | 4 | 5 | 6 | 7 | 8 |

Unit 3

Keyboarding: The Numbers

LESSON 11
5 7 3 9

LESSON 12
Review

LESSON 13
8 2 0

LESSON 14
4 6 1

LESSON 15
Review

Number Keys

Goals

- Touch-type the 5, 7, 3, and 9 keys
- Type at least 19wpm/2′/5e

A. Type 2 times.

A. WARMUP

```
1      The law firm of Quayle, Buster, Given, and      9
2  Rizzo processed all the cases last June and July;  19
3  however, we will seek a new law firm next summer.  29
   |  1  |  2  |  3  |  4  |  5  |  6  |  7  |  8  |  9  |  10  |
```

NEW KEYS

B. Type each line 2 times.

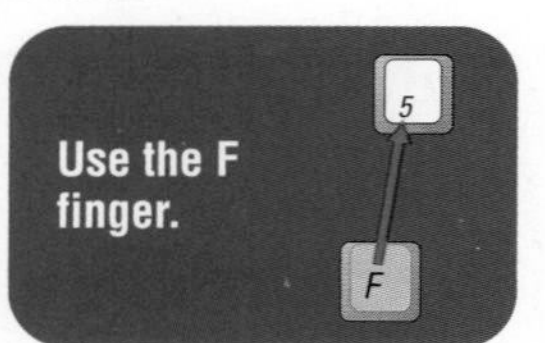

B. THE 5 KEY

```
4  fr5f fr5f f55f f55f f5f5 f5f5 5 55 555 5,555 5:55
5  55 fibs 55 foes 55 fibs 55 fads 55 furs 55 favors
6  The 55 students read the 555 pages in 55 minutes.
7  He found Item 55 that weighed 55 pounds 5 ounces.
```

C. Type each line 2 times.

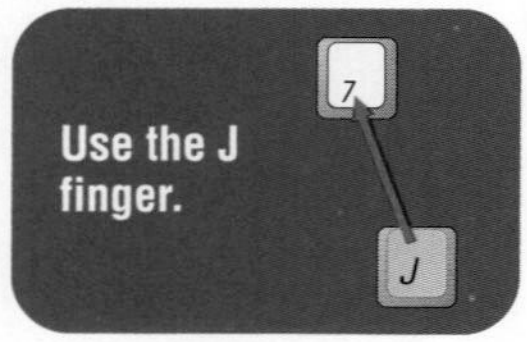

C. THE 7 KEY

```
8   ju7j ju7j j77j j77j j7j7 j7j7 7 77 777 7,777 7:77
9   77 jigs 77 jobs 77 jugs 77 jets 77 jars 77 jewels
10  The 77 men bought Items 77 and 777 for their job.
11  Joe had 57 books and 77 tablets for a 7:57 class.
```

D. Type each line 2 times.

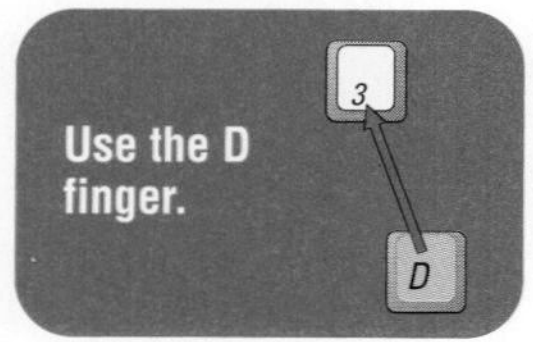

D. THE 3 KEY

```
12  de3d de3d d33d d33d d3d3 d3d3 3 33 333 3,333 3:33
13  33 dots 33 dies 33 dips 33 days 33 dogs 33 drains
14  The 33 vans moved 73 cases in less than 33 hours.
15  Add 55 to 753; subtract 73 to get a total of 735.
```

E. Type each line 2 times.

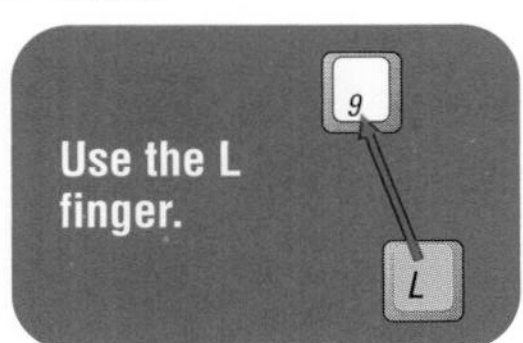

E. THE 9 KEY

```
1o91 1o91 1991 1991 1919 1919 9 99 999 9,999 9:99
99 lads 99 lights 99 labs 99 legs 99 lips 99 logs
Their 99 cans of No. 99 were sold to 99 managers.
He had 39 pens, 59 pads, 97 pencils, and 9 clips.
```

SKILLBUILDING

F. Type each line 2 times.

F. NUMBER PRACTICE: 5, 7, 3, AND 9

```
The 57 tickets were for the April 3 show at 9:59.
Mary was to read pages 33, 57, 95, and 97 to him.
Kate planted 53 tulips, 39 mums, and 97 petunias.
Only 397 of the 573 coeds could register at 5:39.
```

G. Type each line 2 times. Keep other fingers at home as you reach to the SHIFT keys.

G. TECHNIQUE PRACTICE: SHIFT KEY

```
Vera Rosa Tao Fay Jae Tab Pat Yuk Sue Ann Sal Joe
Andre Fidel Pedro Chong Alice Mike Juan Fern Dick
Carlos Caesar Karen Ojars Julie Marta Scott Maria
Marge Jerry Joan Mary Bill Ken Bob Ray Ted Mel Al
```

H. PROGRESSIVE PRACTICE: ALPHABET

If you are not using the GDP software, turn to page SB-7 and follow the directions for this activity.

I. Take two 2-minute timed writings. Review your speed and errors.

Goal: At least 19wpm/2'/5e

I. 2-MINUTE TIMED WRITING

```
     Zach paid for six seats and quit because he      9
could not get the views he wanted near the middle    19
of the field. In August he is thinking of going      29
to the ticket office early to purchase tickets.      38
|  1  |  2  |  3  |  4  |  5  |  6  |  7  |  8  |  9  |  10
```

Review

Goal

- Type at least 20wpm/2′/5e

A. Type 2 times.

A. WARMUP

     Rex played a very quiet game of bridge with 9
Zeke. In March they played in competition with 18
39 players; in January they played with 57 more. 28
| 1 | 2 | 3 | 4 | 5 | 6 | 7 | 8 | 9 | 10

SKILLBUILDING

B. Take three 12-second timed writings on each line. The scale below the last line shows your wpm speed for a 12-second timed writing.

B. 12-SECOND SPEED SPRINTS

A good neighbor paid for these ancient ornaments.
Today I sit by the big lake and count huge rocks.
The four chapels sit by the end of the old field.
The signal means help is on its way to the child.
5 10 15 20 25 30 35 40 45 50

C. Take a 1-minute timed writing on the first paragraph to establish your base speed. Then take four 1-minute timed writings on the remaining paragraphs. As soon as you equal or exceed your base speed on one paragraph, advance to the next, more difficult paragraph.

C. SUSTAINED PRACTICE: SYLLABIC INTENSITY

     People continue to rent autos for personal 9
use and for their work, and car rental businesses 19
just keep growing. You may want to try one soon. 29

     It is likely that a great deal of insurance 9
protection is part of the standard rental cost to 19
you. You may, however, make many other choices. 28

     Perhaps this is not necessary, as you might 9
already have the kind of protection you want in a 19
policy that you currently have on the automobile. 29

     Paying separate mileage charges could evolve 9
into a very large bill. This will undoubtedly be 19
true if your trip involves distant destinations. 29

D. Type each line 2 times.

D. ALPHABET PRACTICE

Packing jam for the dozen boxes was quite lively.
Fay quickly jumped over the two dozen huge boxes.
We vexed Jack by quietly helping a dozen farmers.
The quick lynx from the zoo just waved a big paw.
Lazy brown dogs do not jump over the quick foxes.

E. Type each line 2 times.

E. NUMBER PRACTICE

Mary was to read pages 37, 59, 75, and 93 to Zoe.
He invited 53 boys and 59 girls to the 7:35 show.
The 9:37 bus did not come to our stop until 9:55.
Purchase Order 53 listed Items 35, 77, 93, and 9.
Flight 375 will be departing Gate 37 at 9:59 p.m.

F. Type each sentence on a separate line. Type 2 times.

F. TECHNIQUE PRACTICE: ENTER KEY

Can he go? If so, what? We are lost. Jose is ill.
Did she type the memos? Tina is going. Jane lost.
Max will drive. Xenia is in Ohio. She is tallest.
Nate is fine. Ty is not. Who won? Where is Nancy?
No, she cannot go. Was he here? Where is Roberta?

G. Type each line 2 times. Space without pausing.

G. TECHNIQUE PRACTICE: SPACE BAR

a b c d e f g h i j k l m n o p q r s t u v w x y
an as be by go in is it me no of or to we but for
Do you go to Ada or Ida for work every day or so?
I am sure he can go with you if he has some time.
He is to be at the car by the time you get there.

H. Take two 2-minute timed writings. Review your speed and errors.

Goal: At least 20wpm/2′/5e

H. 2-MINUTE TIMED WRITING

Jack and Alex ordered six pizzas at a price 9
that was quite a bit lower than was the one they 19
ordered yesterday. They will order from the same 29
place tomorrow for the parties they are planning 38
to have. 40

| 1 | 2 | 3 | 4 | 5 | 6 | 7 | 8 | 9 | 10

Number Keys

Goals

- Touch-type the 8, 2, and 0 keys
- Type at least 21wpm/2′/5e

A. Type 2 times.

A. WARMUP

     Mary, Jenny, and Quinn packed 79 prizes in 9
53 large boxes for the party. They will take all 19
of the boxes to 3579 North Capitol Avenue today. 29

| 1 | 2 | 3 | 4 | 5 | 6 | 7 | 8 | 9 | 10

NEW KEYS

B. Type each line 2 times.

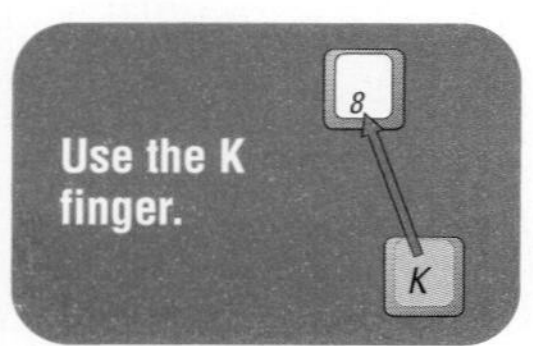

B. THE 8 KEY

ki8k ki8k k88k k88k k8k8 k8k8 8 88 888 8,888 8:88
88 inks 88 inns 88 keys 88 kits 88 kids 88 knives
Bus 38 left at 3:38 and arrived here at 8:37 p.m.
Kenny called Joe at 8:38 at 883-7878 or 585-3878.

C. Type each line 2 times.

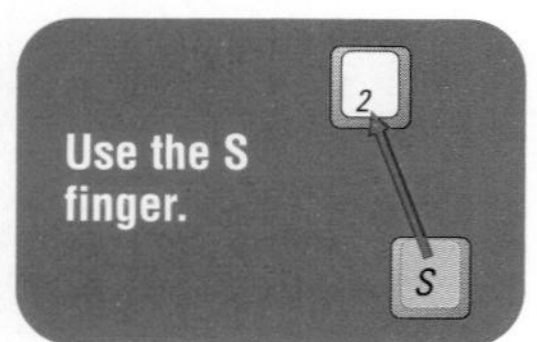

C. THE 2 KEY

sw2s sw2s s22s s22s s2s2 s2s2 2 22 222 2,222 2:22
22 seas 22 sets 22 sons 22 subs 22 suns 22 sports
The 22 seats sold at 2:22 to 22 coeds in Room 22.
He added Items 22, 23, 25, 27, and 28 on Order 2.

D. Type each line 2 times.

D. THE 0 KEY

;p0; ;p0; ;00; ;00; ;0;0 ;0;0 0 00 000 0,000 0:00
20 pads 30 pegs 50 pens 70 pins 80 pits 900 parks
You will get 230 when you add 30, 50, 70, and 80.
The 80 men met at 3:05 with 20 agents in Room 90.

E. Type each line 2 times.

E. NUMBER PRACTICE

```
Jill bought 55 tickets for the 5:50 or 7:50 show.
Maxine called from 777-7370 or 777-7570 for Mary.
Sally had 23 cats, 23 dogs, and 22 birds at home.
Items 35, 37, 38, and 39 were sent on October 30.
Did Flight 2992 leave from Gate 39 at 9:39 today?
Sue went from 852 28th Street to 858 28th Street.
He sold 20 tires, 30 air filters, and 200 wipers.
```

F. Type each sentence on a separate line. For each sentence, press TAB, type the sentence, and then press ENTER. After you have typed all 11 sentences, insert a blank line and type them all a second time.

F. TECHNIQUE PRACTICE: TAB KEY

```
     Casey left to go home. Where is John? Did
Susan go home with them?

     Isaiah drove my car to work. Sandy parked
the car in the lot. They rode together.

     Pat sold new cars for a new dealer. Dana
sold vans for the same dealer.

     Nick bought the nails to finish the job.
Chris has the bolts. Dave has the wood.
```

G. PACED PRACTICE

If you are not using the GDP software, turn to page SB-14 and follow the directions for this activity.

H. PROGRESSIVE PRACTICE: ALPHABET

If you are not using the GDP software, turn to page SB-7 and follow the directions for this activity.

I. Take two 2-minute timed writings. Review your speed and errors.

Goal: At least 21wpm/2′/5e

I. 2-MINUTE TIMED WRITING

```
     Jim told Bev that they must keep the liquid      9
oxygen frozen so that it could be used by the new    19
plant managers tomorrow. The oxygen will then be     29
moved quickly to its new location by transport or    39
rail on Tuesday.                                     42
|  1  |  2  |  3  |  4  |  5  |  6  |  7  |  8  |  9  |  10
```

Number Keys

Goals

- Touch-type the 4, 6, and 1 keys
- Type at least 22wpm/2′/5e

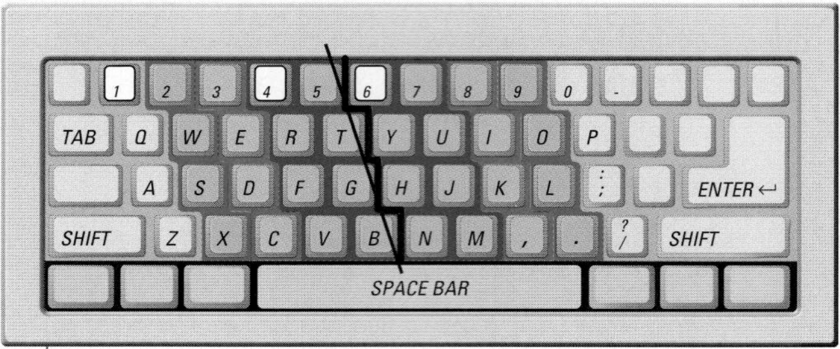

A. Type 2 times.

A. WARMUP

1 We quickly made 30 jars of jam and won a big 9
2 prize for our efforts on March 29. Six of the jam 19
3 jars were taken to 578 Culver Drive on April 28. 29

| 1 | 2 | 3 | 4 | 5 | 6 | 7 | 8 | 9 | 10

NEW KEYS

B. Type each line 2 times.

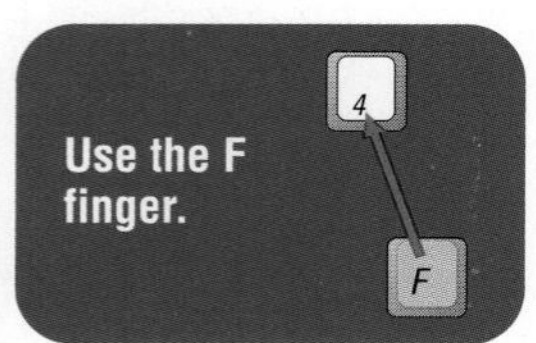

B. THE 4 KEY

4 fr4f fr4f f44f f44f f4f4 f4f4 4 44 444 4,444 4:44
5 44 fans 44 feet 44 figs 44 fins 44 fish 44 flakes
6 The 44 boys had 44 tickets for the games at 4:44.
7 Matthew read 4 books, 54 articles, and 434 lines.

C. Type each line 2 times.

C. THE 6 KEY

8 jy6j jy6j j66j j66j j6j6 j6j6 6 66 666 6,666 6:66
9 66 jabs 66 jams 66 jobs 66 jars 66 jots 66 jewels
10 Tom Lux left at 6:26 on Train 66 to go 600 miles.
11 There were 56,640 people in Bath; 26,269 in Hale.

D. Type each line 2 times.

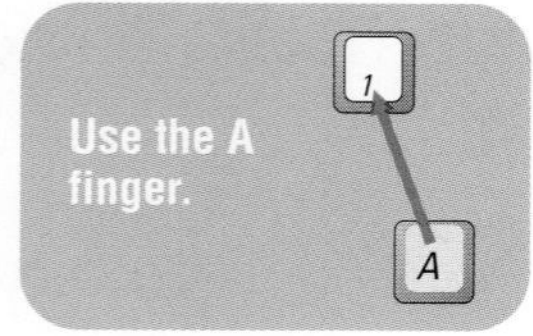

D. THE 1 KEY

12 aq1a aq1a a11a a11a a1a1 a1a1 1 11 111 1,111 1:11
13 11 aces 11 arms 11 aims 11 arts 11 axes 11 arenas
14 Sam left here at 1:11, Sue at 6:11, Don at 11:11.
15 Eric moved from 1661 Main Street to 1116 in 1995.

SKILLBUILDING

E. Type each line 2 times. Focus on accuracy rather than speed as you practice the number drills.

E. NUMBER PRACTICE

```
Adding 10 and 20 and 30 and 40 and 70 totals 170.
Al selected Nos. 15, 16, 17, 18, and 19 to study.
The test took Sam 10 hours, 8 minutes, 3 seconds.
Did the 39 men drive 567 miles on Route 23 or 27?
The 18 shows were sold out by 8:37 on October 18.
On April 29-30 we will be open from 7:45 to 9:30.
```

F. PROGRESSIVE PRACTICE: NUMBERS

If you are not using the GDP software, turn to page SB-11 and follow the directions for this activity.

G. Take two 1-minute timed writings. Review your speed and errors.

G. HANDWRITTEN PARAGRAPH

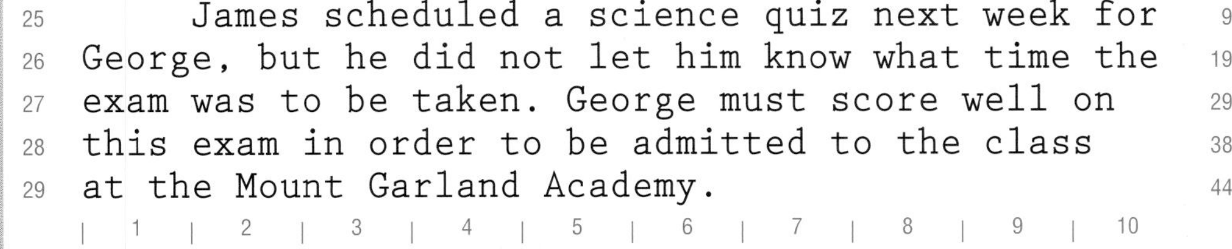
Good writing skills are critical for success 9
in business. Numerous studies have shown 18
that these skills are essential for job advancement. 27

| 1 | 2 | 3 | 4 | 5 | 6 | 7 | 8 | 9 | 10

H. PACED PRACTICE

If you are not using the GDP software, turn to page SB-14 and follow the directions for this activity.

I. Take two 2-minute timed writings. Review your speed and errors.

Goal: At least 22wpm/2′/5e

I. 2-MINUTE TIMED WRITING

```
     James scheduled a science quiz next week for    9
George, but he did not let him know what time the   19
exam was to be taken. George must score well on     29
this exam in order to be admitted to the class      38
at the Mount Garland Academy.                       44
| 1 | 2 | 3 | 4 | 5 | 6 | 7 | 8 | 9 | 10
```

Review

Goal

- Type at least 23wpm/2′/5e

A. Type 2 times.

A. WARMUP

    Jeffrey Mendoza quickly plowed six fields so 9
that he could plant 19 rows of beets, 28 rows of 19
corn, 37 rows of grapes, and 45 rows of olives. 28

| 1 | 2 | 3 | 4 | 5 | 6 | 7 | 8 | 9 | 10

SKILLBUILDING

B. Take three 12-second timed writings on each line. The scale below the last line shows your wpm speed for a 12-second timed writing.

B. 12-SECOND SPEED SPRINTS

The lane to the lake might make the auto go away.
They go to the lake by bus when they work for me.
He just won and lost, won and lost, won and lost.
The man and the girl rush down the paths to town.

5 10 15 20 25 30 35 40 45 50

C. Press Tab 1 time between columns. Type 2 times.

C. TECHNIQUE PRACTICE: TAB KEY

aisle	Tab→ break	Tab→ crank	Tab→ draft	Tab→ earth
Frank	Guinn	Henry	Ivan	Jacob
knack	learn	mason	night	ocean
print	quest	rinse	slide	title
Umberto	Victor	Wally	Xavier	Zenger

D. Type each line 2 times. Try not to slow down for the capital letters.

D. TECHNIQUE PRACTICE: SHIFT KEY

Sue, Pat, Ann, and Gail left for Rome on June 10.
The St. Louis Cardinals and New York Mets played.
Dave Herr took Flight 481 for Memphis and Toledo.
An address for Karen Cook is 5 Bar Street, Provo.
Harry Truman was born in Missouri on May 8, 1884.

E. Type each line 2 times.

E. PUNCTUATION PRACTICE: HYPHEN

```
Jan Brooks-Smith was a go-between for the author.
The off-the-record comment led to a free-for-all.
Louis was a jack-of-all-trades as a clerk-typist.
Ask Barbara--who is in Central Data--to find out.
Joanne is too old-fashioned to be that outspoken.
```

PPP PRETEST → PRACTICE → POSTTEST

PRETEST
Take a 1-minute timed writing. Review your speed and errors.

F. PRETEST: Vertical Reaches

```
     A few of our business managers attribute the    9
success of the bank to a judicious and scientific   19
reserve program. The bank cannot drop its guard.    29
| 1 | 2 | 3 | 4 | 5 | 6 | 7 | 8 | 9 | 10
```

PRACTICE
Speed Emphasis: If you made 2 or fewer errors on the Pretest, type each *individual line* 2 times.
Accuracy Emphasis: If you made 3 or more errors, type each *group* of lines (as though it were a paragraph) 2 times.

G. PRACTICE: Up Reaches

```
at atlas plate water later batch fatal match late
dr draft drift drums drawn drain drama dress drab
ju jumpy juror junky jumbo julep judge juice just
```

H. PRACTICE: Down Reaches

```
ca cable cabin cadet camel cameo candy carve cash
nk trunk drink prank rinks brink drank crank sink
ba batch badge bagel baked banjo barge basis bank
```

POSTTEST
Repeat the Pretest timed writing and compare performance.

I. POSTTEST: Vertical Reaches

J. PROGRESSIVE PRACTICE: ALPHABET

If you are not using the GDP software, turn to page SB-7 and follow the directions for this activity.

K. Take two 2-minute timed writings. Review your speed and errors.

Goal: At least 23wpm/2′/5e

K. 2-MINUTE TIMED WRITING

```
     Jeff Malvey was quite busy fixing all of the    9
frozen pipes so that his water supply would not     19
be stopped. Last winter Jeff kept the pipes from    29
freezing by wrapping them with an insulated tape    38
that protected them from snow and ice.              46
| 1 | 2 | 3 | 4 | 5 | 6 | 7 | 8 | 9 | 10
```

Unit 4

Keyboarding: The Symbols

LESSON 16
$ ( ) !

LESSON 17
Review

LESSON 18
*** # '**

LESSON 19
& % " @

LESSON 20
Review

Symbol Keys

Goals

- Touch-type the $ ( ) and ! keys
- Type at least 24wpm/2′/5e

A. Type 2 times.

A. WARMUP

```
     Gill was quite vexed by that musician who       9
played 5 jazz songs and 13 country songs at the     18
fair. He wanted 8 rock songs and 4 blues songs.     28
|  1  |  2  |  3  |  4  |  5  |  6  |  7  |  8  |  9  |  10
```

NEW KEYS

B. DOLLAR is the shift of 4. Do not space between the dollar sign and the number. Type each line 2 times.

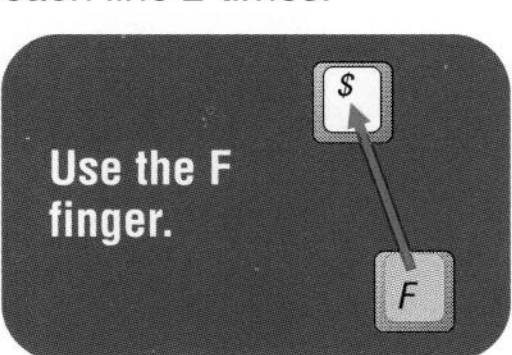

B. THE $ KEY

```
frf fr4f f4f f4$f f$$f f$$f $44 $444 $4,444 $4.44
I quoted $48, $64, and $94 for the set of chairs.
Her insurance paid $150; our insurance paid $175.
Season concert seats were $25, $30, $55, and $75.
```

C. PARENTHESES are the shifts of 9 and 0. Do not space between the parentheses and the text within them. Type each line 2 times.

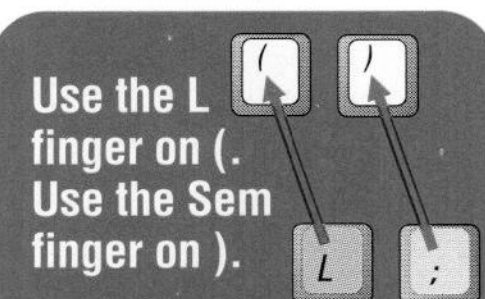

Use the L finger on (.
Use the Sem finger on).
( )
L ;

C. THE (AND) KEYS

```
lo91 lo91 lo(1 lo(1 1((1 ;p0; ;p0; ;p); ;p); ;));
Please ask (1) Al, (2) Pat, (3) Ted, and (4) Dee.
Sue has some (1) skis, (2) sleds, and (3) skates.
Mary is (1) prompt, (2) speedy, and (3) accurate.

Our workers (Lewis, Jerry, and Ty) were rewarded.
The owner (Ms. Parks) went on Friday (August 18).
The Roxie (a cafe) had fish (salmon) on the menu.
The clerk (Ms. Fay Green) will vote yes (not no).
```

D. Exclamation is the shift of 1. Space 1 time after an exclamation point at the end of a sentence. Type each line 2 times.

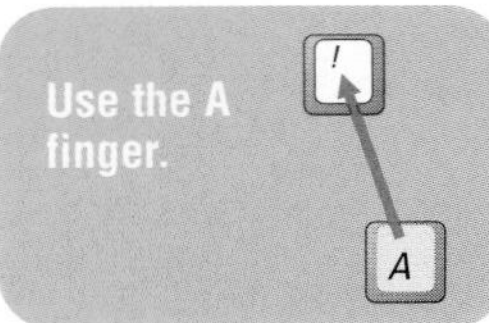

D. THE ! KEY

aqa aq!a aq!a a!!a a!!a Where! Whose! What! When!
Put those down! Do not move them! Leave it there!
He did say that! Jake cannot take a vacation now!
You cannot leave at this time! Janie will go now!

SKILLBUILDING

E. Type the paragraph 2 times.

E. TECHNIQUE PRACTICE: SPACE BAR

We will all go to the race if I win the one I am going to run today. Do you think I will be able to run at the front of the pack and win it?

F. Take three 12-second timed writings on each line. The scale below the last line shows your wpm speed for a 12-second timed writing.

F. 12-SECOND SPEED SPRINTS

Walking can perk you up if you are feeling tired.
Your heart and lungs can work harder as you walk.
It may be that a walk is often better than a nap.
If you walk each day, you may have better health.
5 | 10 | 15 | 20 | 25 | 30 | 35 | 40 | 45 | 50

G. PACED PRACTICE

If you are not using the GDP software, turn to page SB-14 and follow the directions for this activity.

H. Take two 2-minute timed writings. Review your speed and errors.

Goal: At least 24wpm/2′/5e

H. 2-MINUTE TIMED WRITING

Katie quit her zoo job seven days after she 9
learned that she was expected to travel to four 19
different zoos in the first month of employment. 28
After quitting that job, she found an excellent 38
position which did not require her to travel much. 48
| 1 | 2 | 3 | 4 | 5 | 6 | 7 | 8 | 9 | 10

Review

Goal

- Type at least 25wpm/2′/5e

A. Type 2 times.

A. WARMUP

```
     Yes! We object to the dumping of 25 toxic          9
barrels at 4098 Nix Street. A larger number (36)       19
were dumped on the 7th, costing us over $10,000.       28
|  1  |  2  |  3  |  4  |  5  |  6  |  7  |  8  |  9  |  10
```

SKILLBUILDING

B. Type each line 2 times.

B. NUMBER PRACTICE

```
we 23 pi 08 you 697 row 492 tire 5843 power 09234
or 94 re 43 eye 363 top 590 quit 1785 witty 28556
up 70 ye 63 pit 085 per 034 root 4995 wrote 24953
it 85 ro 49 rip 480 two 529 tour 5974 quite 17853
yi 68 to 59 toy 596 rot 495 tier 5834 queue 17373
op 90 qo 19 wet 235 pet 035 rope 4903 quote 17953
```

C. Type each line 2 times.

C. WORD BEGINNINGS

```
tri trinkets tribune trifle trick trial trip trim
mil million mileage mildew mills milky miles mild
spo sponsor sponge sports spore spoon spool spoke
for forgiving forbear forward forbid forced force

div dividend division divine divide diving divers
vic vicinity vicious victory victims victor vices
aff affliction affiliates affirms affords affairs
tab tablecloth tabulates tableau tabloids tablets
```

D. Type each line 2 times.

D. WORD ENDINGS

```
ive repulsive explosive alive drive active strive
est nearest invest attest wisest nicest jest test
ply supply simply deeply damply apply imply reply
ver whenever forever whoever quiver waiver driver
```

```
tor inventor detector debtor orator doctor factor
lly industrially logically legally ideally really
ert convert dessert expert invert diverts asserts
ink shrink drink think blink clink pink sink rink
```

E. PROGRESSIVE PRACTICE: ALPHABET

If you are not using the GDP software, turn to page SB-7 and follow the directions for this activity.

F. Take two 1-minute timed writings. Review your speed and errors.

F. HANDWRITTEN PARAGRAPH

In this book you have learned the reaches 9
for all alphabetic and number keys. You have 18
also learned a few of the symbol keys. In the 27
remaining lessons you will learn the other 36
symbol keys. You will also build your speed 45
and accuracy when typing. 50

| 1 | 2 | 3 | 4 | 5 | 6 | 7 | 8 | 9 | 10

G. DIAGNOSTIC PRACTICE: NUMBERS

If you are not using the GDP software, turn to page SB-5 and follow the directions for this activity.

H. Take two 2-minute timed writings. Review your speed and errors.

Goal: At least 25wpm/2′/5e

H. 2-MINUTE TIMED WRITING

```
     From the tower John saw that those six big      9
planes could crash as they zoomed quickly over      18
treetops on their way to the demonstration that     28
was scheduled to begin very soon. We hope there     37
is no accident and that the pilots reach their      47
airports safely.                                    50
| 1 | 2 | 3 | 4 | 5 | 6 | 7 | 8 | 9 | 10
```

Strategies for Career Success

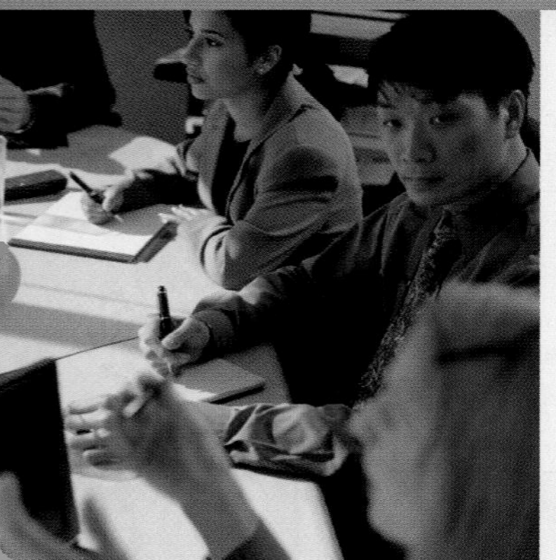

Goodwill Messages

Would you like to strengthen your relationship with a customer, coworker, or boss? Send an unexpected goodwill message! Your expression of goodwill has a positive effect on business relationships.

Messages of congratulations or appreciation provide special opportunities to express goodwill. These messages can be quite brief. If your handwriting is good, send a handwritten note on a professional note card. Otherwise, send a letter or e-mail.

A note of congratulations might be "I just heard the news about your (award, promotion, etc.). My very best wishes." An appreciation note could be "Thank you for referring me to. . . . Your confidence and trust are sincerely appreciated."

YOUR TURN Send a goodwill message to someone to express congratulations or appreciation.

Symbol Keys

Goals

- Touch-type * # and ' keys
- Type at least 26wpm/2′/5e

A. Type 2 times.

A. WARMUP

```
     Bill Waxmann quickly moved all 35 packs of      9
gear for the Amazon trip (worth $987) 26 miles      18
into the jungle. The move took 14 days in all.      27
|  1  |  2  |  3  |  4  |  5  |  6  |  7  |  8  |  9  |  10
```

NEW KEYS

B. Asterisk is the shift of 8. Type each line 2 times.

B. THE * KEY

```
kik ki8k k8*k k8*k k**k k**k This book* is great.
Use an * to show that a table source is included.
Asterisks keyed in a row (*******) make a border.
The article quoted Hanson,* Pyle,* and Peterson.*
```

C. Number (if before a figure) or Pounds (if after a figure) is the shift of 3. Type each line 2 times.

C. THE # KEY

```
de3d de3#d d3#d d3#d d##d d##d #3 #33 #333 #3,333
Al wants 33# of #200 and 38# of #400 by Saturday.
My favorite seats are #2, #34, #56, #65, and #66.
Please order 45# of #245 and 13# of #24 tomorrow.
```

D. Apostrophe is to the right of the semicolon. Type each line 2 times.

D. THE ' KEY

```
;'; ';' ;'; ';' Can't we go in Sue's or Al's car?
It's Bob's job to cover Ted's work when he's out.
What's in Joann's lunch box for Sandra's dessert?
He's gone to Ty's banquet, which is held at Al's.
```

SKILLBUILDING

E. PACED PRACTICE

If you are not using the GDP software, turn to page SB-14 and follow the directions for this activity.

F. PROGRESSIVE PRACTICE: NUMBERS

If you are not using the GDP software, turn to page SB-11 and follow the directions for this activity.

G. Take two 1-minute timed writings. Review your speed and errors.

G. HANDWRITTEN PARAGRAPH

You have completed the first segment of 8
your class. You have learned to type all of 17
the alphabetic keys, the number keys, and some 26
of the symbol keys. Next you will learn the 35
remaining symbol keys on the top row. 42

| 1 | 2 | 3 | 4 | 5 | 6 | 7 | 8 | 9 | 10

H. Take two 2-minute timed writings. Review your speed and errors.

Goal: At least 26wpm/2′/5e

H. 2-MINUTE TIMED WRITING

```
     Max had to make one quick adjustment to his          9
television set before the football game began.          18
The picture during the last game was fuzzy and           28
hard to see. If he cannot fix the picture, he may        38
have to purchase a new television set; and that          47
may be difficult to do.                                  52
```

| 1 | 2 | 3 | 4 | 5 | 6 | 7 | 8 | 9 | 10

Symbol Keys

Goals

- Touch-type & % " and @ keys
- Type at least 27wpm/2'/5e

A. Type 2 times.

A. WARMUP

```
     The teacher (James Quayle) gave us some work    9
to do for homework for 11-28-05. Chapters 3 and 4   19
from our text* are to be read for a hard quiz.      28
|  1  |  2  |  3  |  4  |  5  |  6  |  7  |  8  |  9  |  10
```

NEW KEYS

B. Ampersand (sign for *and*) is the shift of 7. Space before and after the ampersand. Type each line 2 times.

B. THE & KEY

```
juj ju7j j7j j7&j j&&j j&&j Max & Dee & Sue & Ken
Brown & Sons shipped goods to Crum & Lee Company.
Johnson & Loo brought a case against May & Green.
Ball & Trump vs. Vens & See is being decided now.
```

C. Percent is the shift of 5. Do not space between the number and the percent sign. Type each line 2 times.

C. THE % KEY

```
ft5f ft5%f f5%f f5%f f%%f f%%f 5% 55% 555% 5,555%
Robert quoted rates of 8%, 9%, 10%, 11%, and 12%.
Pat scored 82%, Jan 89%, and Ken 90% on the test.
Only 55% of the students passed 75% of the exams.
```

D. QUOTATION is the shift of the apostrophe. Do not space between quotation marks and the text they enclose. Type each line 2 times.

D. THE " KEY

```
12  ;'; ";" ;"; ";" "That's a super job," said Mabel.
13  The theme of the meeting is "Improving Your Job."
14  John said, "Those were good." Sharon said, "Yes."
15  Allison said, "I'll take Janice and Ed to Flint."
```

E. AT is the shift of 2. Space before and after @ except when used in an e-mail address. Type each line 2 times.

E. THE @ KEY

```
16  sws sw2s s2@s s2@s s@@s s@@s Buy 15 @ $5 in June.
17  He can e-mail us at this address: projec@edu.com.
18  Order 12 items @ $14 and another 185 items @ $16.
19  Lee said, "I'll buy 8 shares @ $6 and 5 @ $7.55."
```

FORMATTING

F. Read these rules about the placement of quotation marks. Then type lines 20-23 two times.

F. PLACEMENT OF QUOTATION MARKS

1. The closing quotation mark is always typed *after* a period or comma but *before* a colon or semicolon.
2. The closing quotation mark is typed *after* a question mark or exclamation point if the quoted material itself is a question or an exclamation; otherwise, the quotation mark is typed *before* the question mark or exclamation point.

```
20  "Hello," I said. "My name is Hal; I am new here."
21  Zack read the article "Can She Succeed Tomorrow?"
22  James said, "I'll mail the check"; but he didn't.
23  Did Amy say, "We lost"? She said, "I don't know."
```

G. ALPHABET AND SYMBOL PRACTICE

G. Type each line 2 times.

Gaze at views of my jonquil or red phlox in back.
Jan quickly moved the six dozen big pink flowers.
Joe quietly picked six razors from the woven bag.
Packing jam for the dozen boxes was quite lively.

Mail these "Rush": #38, #45, and #67 (software).
No! Joe's note did not carry a rate of under 9%.
Lee read "The Computer Today." It's here Monday.
The book* cost us $48.10, 12% higher than yours.

H. SUSTAINED PRACTICE: NUMBERS AND SYMBOLS

H. Take a 1-minute timed writing on the first paragraph to establish your base speed. Then take four 1-minute timed writings on the remaining paragraphs. As soon as you equal or exceed your base speed on one paragraph, advance to the next, more difficult paragraph.

We purchased several pieces of new computer 9
equipment for our new store in Boston. We were 19
amazed at all the extra work we could get done. 28

For our department, we received 5 printers, 9
12 computers, and 3 fax machines. We heard that 19
the equipment cost us several thousand dollars. 28

Next week 6 computers (Model ZS86), 4 old 9
copiers (drums are broken), and 9 shredders will 18
need to be replaced. Total cost will be high. 28

Last year $150,890 was spent on equipment 9
for Iowa's offices. Breaman & Sims predicted a 18
17% to 20% increase (*over '99); that's amazing. 28

| 1 | 2 | 3 | 4 | 5 | 6 | 7 | 8 | 9 | 10

I. 2-MINUTE TIMED WRITING

I. Take two 2-minute timed writings. Review your speed and errors.

Goal: At least 27wpm/2'/5e

Topaz and onyx rings were for sale at a very 9
reasonable price last week. When Jeanette saw the 19
rings with these stones, she quickly bought them 29
both for her sons. These jewels were difficult to 39
find, and Jeanette was pleased she could purchase 49
those rings when she did. 54

| 1 | 2 | 3 | 4 | 5 | 6 | 7 | 8 | 9 | 10

Review

Goal

- Type at least 28wpm/2′/5e

A. Type 2 times.

A. WARMUP

     Vin went to see Exhibits #794 and #860. He 9
had quickly judged these zany projects that cost 19
$321 (parts & labor)--a 5% markup from last year. 29
| 1 | 2 | 3 | 4 | 5 | 6 | 7 | 8 | 9 | 10

SKILLBUILDING

B. Type each line 2 times.

B. PUNCTUATION PRACTICE

period: Go to Reno. Drive to Yuma. Call Mary. Get Samuel.
comma: We saw Nice, Paris, Bern, Rome, Munich, and Bonn.
semicolon: Type the memo; read reports. Get pens; get paper.
colon, hyphen: Read the following pages: 1-10, 12-22, and 34-58.
exclamation point: No! Stop! Don't look! Watch out! Move over! Jump!

question mark: Can you wait? Why not? Can he drive? Where is it?
colon, apostrophe: I have these reports: Susan's, Bill's, and Lou's.
dash: It's the best--and cheapest! Don't lose it--ever.
quotation marks: "I can," she said, "right now." Val said, "Wait!"
parentheses: Quint called Rome (GA), Rome (NY), and Rome (WI).

PRETEST
Take a 1-minute timed writing. Review your speed and errors.

C. PRETEST: Alternate- and One-Hand Words

     The chairman should handle the tax problem 9
downtown. If they are reversed, pressure tactics 19
might have changed the case as it was discussed. 28
| 1 | 2 | 3 | 4 | 5 | 6 | 7 | 8 | 9 | 10

PRACTICE
Speed Emphasis: If you made 2 or fewer errors on the Pretest, type each *individual* line 2 times.
Accuracy Emphasis: If you made 3 or fewer errors, type each *group* of lines (as though it were a paragraph) 2 times.

D. PRACTICE: Alternate-Hand Words

the with girl right blame handle antique chairman
for wish town their panel formal problem downtown
pan busy they flair signs thrown signals problems

E. PRACTICE: One-Hand Words

lip fact yolk poplin yummy affect reverse pumpkin
you cast kill uphill jumpy grease wagered opinion
tea cage lump limply hilly served bravest minimum

POSTTEST
Repeat the Pretest timed writing and compare performance.

F. POSTTEST: Alternate- and One-Hand Words

G. Take three 12-second timed writings on each line. The scale below the last line shows your wpm speed for a 12-second timed writing.

G. 12-SECOND SPEED SPRINTS

Paul likes to work for the bank while in college.
They will make a nice profit if the work is done.
The group of friends went to a movie at the mall.
The man sent the forms after she called for them.
| | | | 5 | | | | 10 | | | | 15 | | | | 20 | | | | 25 | | | | 30 | | | | 35 | | | | 40 | | | | 45 | | | | 50

H. Take two 1-minute timed writings. Review your speed and errors.

H. HANDWRITTEN PARAGRAPH

In your career, you will use the 7
skills you are learning in this course. 15
However, you will soon discover that you 23
must also possess human relations skills. 31

I. MAP

Follow the GDP software directions for this exercise in improving keystroking accuracy.

J. DIAGNOSTIC PRACTICE: NUMBERS

If you are not using the GDP software, turn to page SB-5 and follow the directions for this activity.

K. Take two 2-minute timed writings. Review your speed and errors.

Goal: At least 28wpm/2′/5e

K. 2-MINUTE TIMED WRITING

Jake or Peggy Zale must quickly fix the fax 9
machine so that we can have access to regional 18
reports that we think might be sent within the 28
next few days. Without the fax, we will not be 37
able to complete all our monthly reports by the 47
deadlines. Please let me know of any problems. 56
| 1 | 2 | 3 | 4 | 5 | 6 | 7 | 8 | 9 | 10

Part 2

Basic Business Documents

Keyboarding in Business and Administrative Services

Opportunities in Business and Administrative Careers

Occupations in the business and administrative services cluster focus on providing management and support services for various companies. The many positions found in this cluster include receptionist, bookkeeper, administrative professional or assistant, claim examiner, accountant, word processor, office manager, and chief executive officer.

Managers and administrators are in charge of planning, organizing, and controlling businesses. Management support workers gather and analyze data to help company executives make decisions. Administrative support workers perform a variety of tasks, such as recordkeeping, operating office equipment, managing their own projects and assignments, and developing high-level integrated software skills as well as Internet research skills. Ideally, everyone in business should be patient, detail-oriented, and cooperative. Excellent written and oral communication skills are definitely an asset as well.

Many companies have been revolutionized by advances in computer technology. As a result, keyboarding skill provides a definite advantage for those who work in business and administrative services. Now, more than ever, success in the business world is dependent upon adaptability and education.

Objectives

KEYBOARDING

- Operate the keyboard by touch.
- Type at least 36 words per minute on a 3-minute timed writing with no more than 4 errors.

LANGUAGE ARTS

- Develop proofreading skills and correctly use proofreaders' marks.
- Use capitals, commas, and apostrophes correctly.
- Develop composing and spelling skills.

WORD PROCESSING

- Use the word processing commands necessary to complete the document processing activities.

DOCUMENT PROCESSING

- Format e-mail, business and academic reports, business letters in block style, envelopes, memos, and tables.

TECHNICAL

- Answer at least 90 percent of the questions correctly on an objective test.

Unit 5

E-Mail and Word Processing

LESSON 21
Orientation to Word Processing: A

LESSON 22
Orientation to Word Processing: B

LESSON 23
Orientation to Word Processing: C

LESSON 24
Orientation to Word Processing: D

LESSON 25
E-Mail Basics

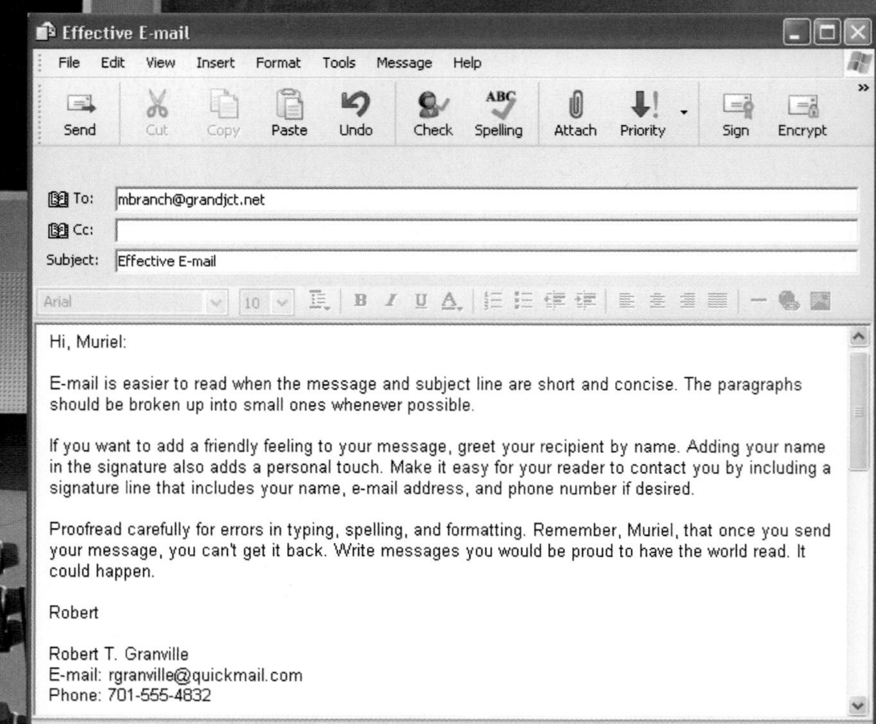
Effective E-mail
File Edit View Insert Format Tools Message Help
Send Cut Copy Paste Undo Check Spelling Attach Priority Sign Encrypt
To: mbranch@grandjct.net
Cc:
Subject: Effective E-mail
Arial 10
Hi, Muriel:
E-mail is easier to read when the message and subject line are short and concise. The paragraphs should be broken up into small ones whenever possible.
If you want to add a friendly feeling to your message, greet your recipient by name. Adding your name in the signature also adds a personal touch. Make it easy for your reader to contact you by including a signature line that includes your name, e-mail address, and phone number if desired.
Proofread carefully for errors in typing, spelling, and formatting. Remember, Muriel, that once you send your message, you can't get it back. Write messages you would be proud to have the world read. It could happen.
Robert
Robert T. Granville
E-mail: rgranville@quickmail.com
Phone: 701-555-4832

Orientation to Word Processing: A

Goals

- Improve speed and accuracy
- Refine language arts skills in punctuation and grammar
- Practice basic word processing commands

A. Type 2 times.

A. WARMUP

```
     Juan Valdez will lead 10 managers during this sales      10
period; his expert input has always been valuable. Will       22
Quentin earn 8% commission ($534) after order #K76 arrives?   34
|  1  |  2  |  3  |  4  |  5  |  6  |  7  |  8  |  9  |  10  |  11  |  12
```

SKILLBUILDING

B. PROGRESSIVE PRACTICE: NUMBERS

If you are not using the GDP software, turn to page SB-11 and follow the directions for this activity.

C. PACED PRACTICE

If you are not using the GDP software, turn to page SB-14 and follow the directions for this activity.

LANGUAGE ARTS

D. Study the rules at the right.

D. COMMAS AND SENTENCES

Note: The callout signals in the left margin indicate which language arts rule from this lesson has been applied.

RULE ▶ , direct address

Use commas before and after a name used in direct address.

Thank you, John, for responding to my e-mail so quickly.

Ladies and gentlemen, the program has been canceled.

RULE ▶ fragment

Avoid sentence fragments.

Not: She had always wanted to be a financial manager. But had not had the needed education.

But: She had always wanted to be a financial manager but had not had the needed education.

Note: A fragment is a part of a sentence that is incorrectly punctuated as a complete sentence. In the first sentence above, "but had not had the needed education" is not a complete sentence because it does not contain a subject.

RULE ▶ run-on

Avoid run-on sentences.

Not: Mohamed is a competent worker he has even passed the MCSE exam.

Not: Mohamed is a competent worker, he has even passed the MCSE exam.

But: Mohamed is a competent worker; he has even passed the MCSE exam.

Or: Mohamed is a competent worker. He has even passed the MCSE exam.

Note: A run-on sentence is two independent clauses that run together without any punctuation between them or with only a comma between them.

Edit the paragraph to insert any needed punctuation and to correct any errors in grammar.

```
     You must be certain, Sean that every e-mail message is concise. And also complete. In addition, Sean, use a clear subject line the subject line describes briefly the principal content of the e-mail message. You should use a direct style of writing, use short lines and paragraphs. The recipient of your e-mail message will be more likely to read and respond to a short message. Than a long one. Your reader will be grateful for any writing techniques. That save time. Another thing you should do Sean is to include an appropriate closing, your reader should know immediately who wrote the message.
```

FORMATTING

Word Processing Manual

E. WORD PROCESSING

Study Lesson 21 in your word processing manual. Complete all of the shaded steps while at your computer.

Keyboarding Connection

Defining the E-Mail Address

With most e-mail software, a header at the top of each e-mail message contains the sender's address. What is the meaning of the strange configuration of an e-mail address?

An e-mail address contains three parts: anyname@server.com. First is the e-mail user's name (before the @ symbol). Next is the name of the host computer the person uses (before the period). The third part is the zone, or domain, for the type of organization or institution to which the host belongs (e.g., *edu* = education; *gov* = government; *com* = company).

Be careful to include each part of an e-mail address and punctuate the address completely and correctly. Even a small error will prevent your message from reaching the recipient.

YOUR TURN Have you ever sent an e-mail that did not reach its recipient because of an address error? What type of error did you make?

Orientation to Word Processing: B

Goals

- Practice hyphenation
- Type at least 28wpm/3′/5e
- Practice basic word processing commands

A. Type 2 times.

A. WARMUP

```
1      Zenobia bought 987 reams of 16# bond paper from V & J   11
2 Co. @ $5/ream. Part of this week's order is usable. About    23
3 24 percent is excellent quality; the rest cannot be used.    34
  | 1 | 2 | 3 | 4 | 5 | 6 | 7 | 8 | 9 | 10 | 11 | 12
```

SKILLBUILDING

B. Type each line 2 times.

B. HYPHEN PRACTICE

Hyphens are used:

1. To show that a word is divided (lines 4 and 8).
2. To make a dash by typing two hyphens with no space before or after (lines 5 and 8).
3. To join words in a compound (lines 6, 7, and 9).

```
4 Can Larry possibly go with us next week to the golf tourna-
5 ment? I am positive that he--like you--would enjoy the game
6 and realize that it is a first-class sporting event. If you
7 think he can go, I will get first-class reservations on the
8 next plane. Larry--just like Tom and me--always likes every-
9 thing to be first-class and first-rate. Money is no object.
```

Note: In your word processing program, when you type text followed by two hyphens (--) followed by more text and then a space, an em dash (—) will automatically be inserted.

C. PROGRESSIVE PRACTICE: ALPHABET

If you are not using the GDP software, turn to page SB-7 and follow the directions for this activity.

D. Take two 3-minute timed writings. Review your speed and errors.

Goal: At least 28wpm/3′/5e

D. 3-MINUTE TIMED WRITING

```
     Once you learn to use a variety of software programs,    11
you will feel confident and comfortable as you are using a    23
computer. All you have to do is take that first step and      34
decide to strive for excellence.                              41
     Initially, you might have several questions as you       52
gaze up at a screen that is filled with icons. If you try     62
to learn to use just one or two commands each day, you may    75
soon find that using software is very exciting.               84
| 1 | 2 | 3 | 4 | 5 | 6 | 7 | 8 | 9 | 10 | 11 | 12
```

FORMATTING

Word Processing Manual

E. WORD PROCESSING

Study Lesson 22 in your word processing manual. Complete all of the shaded steps while at your computer.

Strategies for Career Success

Preparing to Conduct a Meeting

Do you want to conduct a successful meeting? Meetings tend to fail because they last too long and attendees do not stay focused. First, determine the meeting's purpose (e.g., to make a decision or obtain/provide information).

Decide who needs to attend the meeting. Include those who can significantly contribute, as well as decision makers. Prepare an agenda, that is, a list of items to be discussed. Distribute it to attendees a few days before the meeting.

Choose where you will conduct the meeting and schedule the room. Determine if you will be teleconferencing, videoconferencing, or needing audiovisual equipment. If appropriate, arrange for refreshments. Check the room temperature, acoustics, and lighting. Attention to these details will increase your chances for a successful outcome.

YOUR TURN Think about a meeting you attended that was a failure. What could the meeting leader have done to better prepare for the meeting?

Orientation to Word Processing: C

Goals

- Improve speed and accuracy
- Refine language arts skills in composing
- Practice basic word processing commands

A. Type 2 times.

A. WARMUP

```
1      We expect the following sizes to be mailed promptly     11
2  on January 8: 5, 7, and 9. Send your payment quickly so     22
3  that the items will be sure to arrive before 2:35* (*p.m.)! 33
   | 1 | 2 | 3 | 4 | 5 | 6 | 7 | 8 | 9 | 10 | 11 | 12
```

SKILLBUILDING

B. Take a 1-minute timed writing on the first paragraph to establish your base speed. Then take four 1-minute timed writings on the remaining paragraphs. As soon as you equal or exceed your base speed on one paragraph, advance to the next, more difficult paragraph.

B. SUSTAINED PRACTICE: CAPITALS

```
4      The insurance industry will see some changes because     11
5  of the many natural disasters the United States has seen in 23
6  the last few years in places like California and Florida.   34

7      The major earthquakes in San Francisco, Northridge,      11
8  and Loma Prieta cost thousands of dollars. Faults like      22
9  the San Andreas are being watched carefully for activity.   33

10     Some tropical storms are spawned in the West Indies      11
11 and move from the Caribbean Sea into the Atlantic Ocean.    22
12 They could affect Georgia, Florida, Alabama, and Texas.     33

13     Some U.S. cities have VHF-FM radio weather stations.     11
14 NASA and NOAA are agencies that launch weather satellites   23
15 to predict the locations, times, and severity of storms.    34
```

C. DIAGNOSTIC PRACTICE: SYMBOLS AND PUNCTUATION

If you are not using the GDP software, turn to page SB-2 and follow the directions for this activity.

LANGUAGE ARTS

D. Answer each question with a complete sentence.

D. COMPOSING SENTENCES

16 Do you prefer Word as a word processing software, or do you prefer something else?
17 What search engine do you prefer when you search for information on the Web?
18 Do you like Internet Explorer, or do you prefer Netscape Navigator as a Web browser?
19 What class are you now taking that is best preparing you for the workplace?
20 If you could work in any foreign country, which one would you choose?
21 What documents do you type most frequently as a student: letters, reports, or tables?

FORMATTING

Word Processing Manual

E. WORD PROCESSING

Study Lesson 23 in your word processing manual. Complete all of the shaded steps while at your computer.

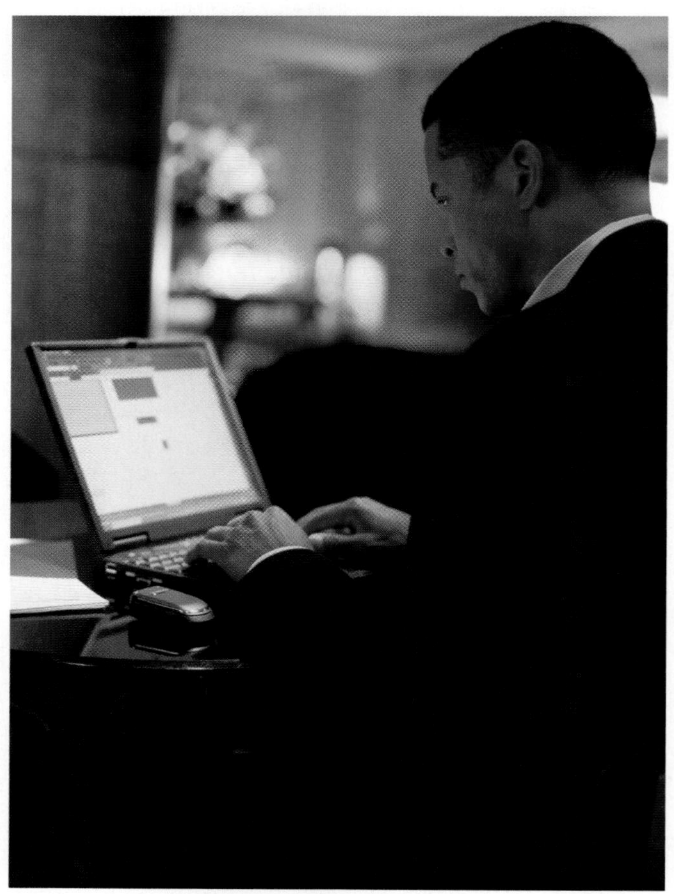

Orientation to Word Processing: D

Goals

- Type at least 29wpm/3′/5e
- Practice basic word processing commands

A. Type 2 times.

A. WARMUP

The experts quickly realized that repairs could cost 11
"$985 million" and might exceed 60% of their budget. Will 22
Valdez & Co. begin work before 12 or just wait until 4:30? 34
| 1 | 2 | 3 | 4 | 5 | 6 | 7 | 8 | 9 | 10 | 11 | 12

SKILLBUILDING

B. Take three 12-second timed writings on each line. The scale below the last line shows your wpm speed for a 12-second timed writing.

B. 12-SECOND SPEED SPRINTS

Mary will be able to go home when she can run fast and far.
Sam can come to the store if he is able to stop for a soda.
Suzy knows that she must send the mail out by noon or else.
Only a few good desks will be made by the end of this week.
5 10 15 20 25 30 35 40 45 50 55 60

PPP PRETEST → PRACTICE → POSTTEST

PRETEST
Take a 1-minute timed writing. Review your speed and errors.

C. PRETEST: Common Letter Combinations

He tried to explain the delay in a logical way. The 11
man finally agreed to insure the package and demanded to 22
know why the postal worker did not record the total amount. 34
| 1 | 2 | 3 | 4 | 5 | 6 | 7 | 8 | 9 | 10 | 11 | 12

PRACTICE
Speed Emphasis:
If you made 2 or fewer errors on the Pretest, type each *individual* line 2 times.
Accuracy Emphasis:
If you made 3 or more errors, type each *group* of lines (as though it were a paragraph) 2 times.

D. PRACTICE: Word Beginnings

re reuse react relay reply return reason record results red
in inset inept incur index indeed intend inning insured ink
de dents dealt death delay detest devote derive depicts den

E. PRACTICE: Word Endings

ly lowly dimly apply daily barely unruly deeply finally sly
ed cured tamed tried moved amused tasted billed creamed fed
al canal total equal local postal plural rental logical pal

POSTTEST
Repeat the Pretest timed writing and compare performance.

F. POSTTEST: Common Letter Combinations

G. Take two 3-minute timed writings. Review your speed and errors.

Goal: At least 29wpm/3′/5e

G. 3-MINUTE TIMED WRITING

```
     If you ever feel tired as you are typing, you should    11
take a rest. Question what you are doing that is causing     22
your muscles to be fatigued. You will realize that you       33
can change the fundamental source of your anxiety.           43
     Take a deep breath and enjoy the relaxing feeling as    54
you exhale slowly. Check your posture to be sure that        65
you are sitting up straight with your back against the       76
chair. Stretch your neck and back for total relaxation.      87
| 1 | 2 | 3 | 4 | 5 | 6 | 7 | 8 | 9 | 10 | 11 | 12
```

FORMATTING

Word Processing Manual

H. WORD PROCESSING

Study Lesson 24 in your word processing manual. Complete all of the shaded steps while at your computer.

Keyboarding Connection

Business E-Mail Style Guide

Watch those e-mail p's and q's! Even though e-mail is relatively informal, you need to be succinct and clear. Greet your reader with a formal "Dear . . . ," or an informal "Hi . . . ," etc. Put the most important part of your message first. Watch the length of your paragraphs; four to five lines per paragraph won't put off your reader.

Use asterisks, caps, dashes, etc., for emphasis. Avoid unfamiliar abbreviations, slang, or jargon. Not everyone who receives your business e-mail may know a particular catchword or phrase. Proofread your e-mail. Be concerned about grammar, punctuation, and word choice. Use your e-mail's spell checker.

End your business e-mail politely. Expressions of appreciation (e.g., "Thanks") or goodwill (e.g., "Best wishes") let your reader know you are finishing your message.

YOUR TURN In Lesson 25 you will learn how to format and compose e-mail messages. Create an e-mail message to send to a coworker, colleague, or friend. Review the e-mail for adherence to the guidelines listed above.

E-Mail Basics

Goals

- Improve speed and accuracy
- Refine language arts skills in proofreading
- Format and compose a basic e-mail message

A. Type 2 times.

A. WARMUP

```
1       Exactly 610 employees have quit smoking! About half      11
2   of them just quit recently. They realized why they can't     22
3   continue to smoke inside the buildings and decided to stop.  34
    | 1 | 2 | 3 | 4 | 5 | 6 | 7 | 8 | 9 | 10 | 11 | 12
```

SKILLBUILDING

B. Tab 1 time between columns. Type 2 times.

B. TECHNIQUE PRACTICE: TAB KEY

4	A. Uyeki	B. Vorton	C. Wetzel	D. Xenios	E. Young
5	F. Zeller	G. Ambrose	H. Brown	I. Carter	J. Denney
6	K. Elmer	L. Fraser	M. Greene	N. Hawkins	O. Irvin
7	P. Jarvis	Q. Krueger	R. Larkin	S. Majors	T. Norris
8	U. Vassar	V. Hagelin	W. Wesley	X. Bernet	Y. Robins

C. MAP

Follow the GDP software directions for this exercise in improving keystroking accuracy.

LANGUAGE ARTS

D. Study the proofreading techniques at the right.

D. PROOFREADING YOUR DOCUMENTS

Proofreading and correcting errors are essential parts of document processing. To become an expert proofreader:

1. Use the spelling feature of your word processing software to check for spelling errors; then read the copy aloud to see if it makes sense.
2. Proofread for all kinds of errors, especially repeated, missing, or transposed words; grammar and punctuation; and numbers and names.
3. Check for formatting errors such as line spacing, tabs, margins, and use of bold.

E. Compare these lines with lines 4–7 in the 12-second speed sprints on page 57. Edit the lines to correct any errors.

E. PROOFREADING

```
9   Mary will be able to go when she can run fast and far.
10  Sam can come to the store if she is able to stop for soda.
11  Suzy know that she must send the mail out by noon or else.
12  Only a few good disks will be made by the end of this week.
```

F. BASIC PARTS OF AN E-MAIL MESSAGE

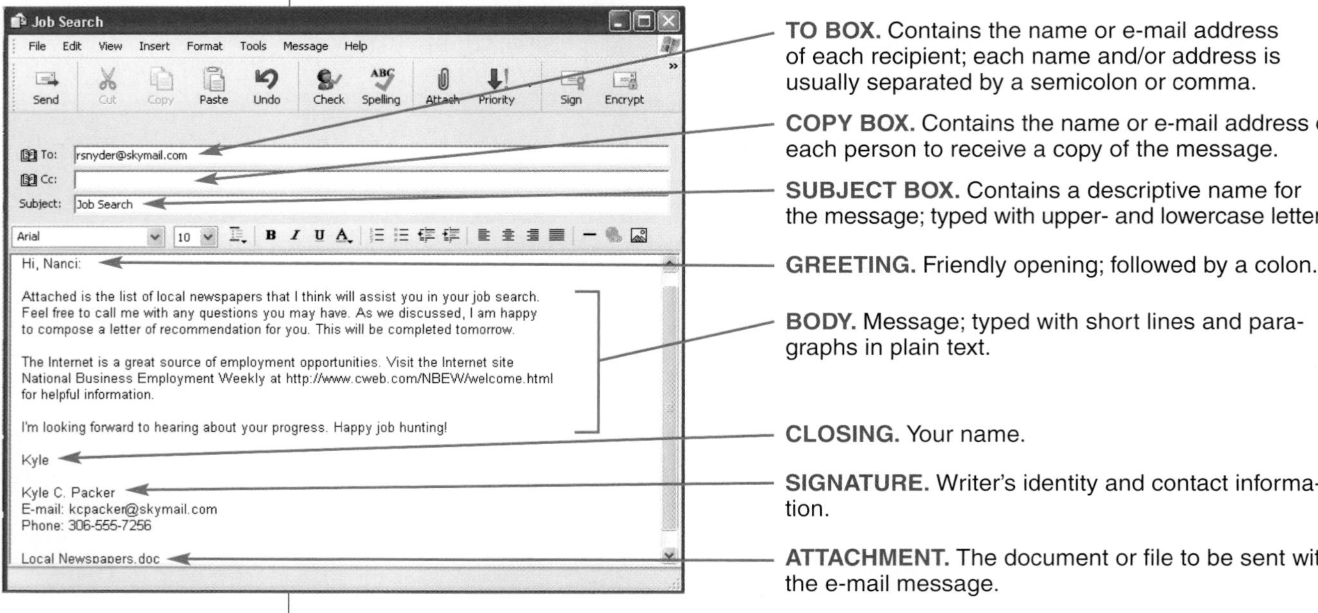
Job Search
File Edit View Insert Format Tools Message Help
Send Cut Copy Paste Undo Check Spelling Attach Priority Sign Encrypt
To: rsnyder@skymail.com
Cc:
Subject: Job Search
Arial 10
Hi, Nanci:
Attached is the list of local newspapers that I think will assist you in your job search. Feel free to call me with any questions you may have. As we discussed, I am happy to compose a letter of recommendation for you. This will be completed tomorrow.
The Internet is a great source of employment opportunities. Visit the Internet site National Business Employment Weekly at http://www.cweb.com/NBEW/welcome.html for helpful information.
I'm looking forward to hearing about your progress. Happy job hunting!
Kyle
Kyle C. Packer
E-mail: kcpacker@skymail.com
Phone: 306-555-7256
Local Newspapers.doc
TO BOX. Contains the name or e-mail address of each recipient; each name and/or address is usually separated by a semicolon or comma.
COPY BOX. Contains the name or e-mail address of each person to receive a copy of the message.
SUBJECT BOX. Contains a descriptive name for the message; typed with upper- and lowercase letters.
GREETING. Friendly opening; followed by a colon.
BODY. Message; typed with short lines and paragraphs in plain text.
CLOSING. Your name.
SIGNATURE. Writer's identity and contact information.
ATTACHMENT. The document or file to be sent with the e-mail message.

G. FORMATTING AND COMPOSING AN E-MAIL MESSAGE

E-mail formats will vary, depending on your e-mail provider. Most e-mail message screens will allow space for the *To*, *Cc*, and *Subject* entries as well as a separate area for the e-mail message. The attachment feature is often displayed on the toolbar as a paper clip icon.

1. Use the address book feature or type the e-mail address of each recipient in the *To, Cc,* or *Bcc* boxes. A semicolon or comma is usually automatically inserted to separate several names.
2. If you use the reply feature, include the original message if it helps the reader remember the topic(s) more easily.
3. Use a descriptive, concise subject line with upper- and lowercase letters.

   Example: Items for Meeting Agenda
4. Use the attachment feature if you need to attach a file or document.
5. Use a friendly greeting. Follow the greeting with a colon. Use the recipient's first name or a courtesy title and last name for a more businesslike greeting.

   Example: Hi, Jim: or Dear Jim:

   Example: Jim: or Mr. Andrews:
6. Use short lines (about 60 characters) with plain text, or let the lines word wrap if your e-mail program supports word wrap.
7. Keep paragraphs short and type them with normal capitalization and punctuation in plain text. Typing in all-caps is considered shouting.
8. Type paragraphs single-spaced and blocked at the left with 1 blank line between them.
9. A closing is optional. Type your name in the closing, and leave 1 blank line above and below the closing.

   Example: Sandy Hill or Sandy
10. Use a signature line so the recipient clearly knows your identity and contact information.

    Example:
    Sandra R. Hill
    E-mail: srhill@server.com
    Phone: 661-555-1223
11. Revise and proofread your message carefully before sending it. You can't get it back!

H. WORD PROCESSING: E-MAIL A DOCUMENT

Study Lesson 25 in your word processing manual. Complete all of the shaded steps while at your computer. Then format the jobs that follow.

DOCUMENT PROCESSING

Correspondence 25-1

E-Mail Message

1. Type the greeting and body for the e-mail message below.
2. Type the sender's name 1 blank line below the final line of the e-mail message.
3. Type the sender's signature line, including the e-mail address, 1 blank line below the sender's name
4. Type the phone number below the signature line.
5. Proofread your e-mail message for typing, spelling, and formatting errors.

Hi, Muriel: ↓2X

E-mail is easier to read when the message and subject line are short and concise. The paragraphs should be broken up into small ones whenever possible. ↓2X

If you want to add a friendly feeling to your message, greet your recipient by name. Adding your name in the signature also adds a personal touch. Make it easy for your reader to contact you by including a signature line that includes your name, e-mail address, and phone number if desired. ↓2X

Proofread carefully for errors in typing, spelling, and formatting. Remember, Muriel, that once you send your message, you can't get it back. Write messages you would be proud to have the world read. It could happen. ↓2X

Robert ↓2X

Robert T. Granville
E-mail: rgranville@quickmail.com
Phone: 701-555-4832

Correspondence 25-2

E-Mail Message

1. Type an e-mail message to `Ernesto Sanchez`.
2. Type the greeting as: `Hi, Ernesto:`
3. Type the following message: `I now have e-mail access using my new cable modem. You can now send me the photos you took at our annual meeting, because I will be able to access them at a much faster rate.`

   `Thank you, Ernesto, for bringing your digital camera to the meeting so that we could all enjoy the photos you took.`
4. Type the closing as `Karen` and the signature line as `Karen Drake`.
5. Type Karen Drake's e-mail address as `kdrake@brightway.net` and her phone number as `404-555-6823`.
6. Proofread your e-mail message for typing, spelling, and formatting errors.

Unit 6

Reports

LESSON 26
One-Page Business Reports

LESSON 27
Multipage Rough-Draft Business Reports

LESSON 28
Business Reports With Lists

LESSON 29
Academic Reports

LESSON 30
Academic Reports With Displays

AN ANALYSIS OF CORPORATE SICK-LEAVE POLICIES

Recent Trends in the Business World

Linda C. Motonaga

April 5, 20--

Corporate sick-leave policies must be studied carefully in order to maximize employee productivity and minimize excessive absenteeism. The reasons for absences and the responsiveness of employers to the needs of the employees must be examined in order to determine some practical alternatives to current policies.

REASONS FOR ABSENCE

There are many reasons employees are absent from work. Illness and personal emergency are common reasons for absenteeism. However, recent surveys have shown that about 28% of reported sick time isn't due to illness. This percentage is on the rise. Recent studies have also shown that absences due to personal needs and stress are increasing. Also, many workers believe that they are "entitled" to a day off now and then. Perhaps it is time for employers to revamp their sick-leave policies and make these policies more responsive to the needs of the employees.

RESPONSIVENESS OF EMPLOYERS

If employees are finding it necessary to take sick days when they are not ill, it makes sense to conclude that possibly employers are either not aware of why absenteeism exists or have chosen not to respond to their employees' needs. One thing is certain—ignoring the problem will not make it go away.

POSSIBLE SOLUTIONS

Flexible scheduling is one creative way in which employers can respond to the needs of employees. If workers are given the opportunity for a flexible working schedule, stress levels should go down, and personal needs can be handled during the time they are off. Another solution might be to give employees a fixed number of days off each year for reasons other than illness. This gives workers a legitimate reason for a planned absence and gives employers some advance notice so that absences do not hurt productivity.

ENDING PROCRASTINATION

Judy Baca

Everyone at one time or another has put off some task, goal, or important plan at work for any number of reasons. Perhaps you think time is too short or the task isn't really that important. Either way, procrastination can lead to a stalled life and career.

EVALUATE YOUR SITUATION

Joyce Winfrey of Time Management Incorporated has some very good advice that will help you begin to move forward. She says that you should ask yourself two very basic questions about why you are procrastinating:

1. Am I procrastinating because the task at hand is not really what I want?
2. Is there a valid reason for my procrastination?

After you have asked yourself these questions, Ms. Winfrey suggests that you do the following:

> Look deep within yourself. If you are looking for excuses, then the process of asking these questions will be a waste of your time. However, if you answer these questions honestly, you might find answers that surprise you and that will help clarify your situation.

She also recommends several techniques that can help you get back on task and put an end to procrastination.

PRACTICE NEW TECHNIQUES

Identifying and understanding the techniques that follow is the first step. Once you know what to do, you can begin to practice these steps daily.

2

Take Baby Steps. Don't make any task bigger than it really is by looking at the whole thing at once. Break it down into baby steps that are manageable.

Don't Strive for Perfectionism. If you are waiting for the perfect solution or the perfect opportunity, you will be immobilized. Accept the fact that no one and nothing is perfect. Then accept your mistakes and move on.

Enjoy the Task. Enjoy the task at hand and find something in it that is positive and rewarding. Confront your fears with a plan of action.

Remind yourself of all these techniques daily. Post them by your telephone, by your desk, or in your car. You will find that your personal life and career will gain momentum, and success will soon be yours.

One-Page Business Reports

Goals

- Type at least 30wpm/3′/5e
- Format one-page business reports

A. Type 2 times.

A. WARMUP

```
     Mr. G. Yoneji ordered scanners* (*800 dots per inch)    11
in vibrant 24-bit color! He quickly realized that exactly    22
31% of the work could be scanned in order to save money.     34
| 1 | 2 | 3 | 4 | 5 | 6 | 7 | 8 | 9 | 10 | 11 | 12
```

SKILLBUILDING

B. Take three 12-second timed writings on each line. The scale below the last line shows your wpm speed for a 12-second timed writing.

B. 12-SECOND SPEED SPRINTS

```
She went to the same store to find some good books to read.
Frank will coach eight games for his team when he has time.
Laura sent all the mail out today when she left to go home.
These pages can be very hard to read when the light is dim.
5 10 15 20 25 30 35 40 45 50 55 60
```

C. DIAGNOSTIC PRACTICE: SYMBOLS AND PUNCTUATION

If you are not using the GDP software, turn to page SB-2 and follow the directions for this activity.

D. Take two 3-minute timed writings. Review your speed and errors.

Goal: At least 30wpm/3′/5e

D. 3-MINUTE TIMED WRITING

```
     Holding a good business meeting may require a great     11
deal of thought and planning. The meeting must be well       22
organized, and an agenda must be prepared. It may be hard    33
to judge how long a meeting will take or how many people     45
will discuss important issues.                               51
     A good leader is required to execute the agenda. He or  62
she must know when to move on to the next topic or when to   73
continue debate on a topic. After a productive meeting, a    85
leader should be pleased.                                    90
| 1 | 2 | 3 | 4 | 5 | 6 | 7 | 8 | 9 | 10 | 11 | 12
```

Refer to page R-8C of the Reference Manual for an illustration of a report in academic style.

E. BASIC PARTS OF A REPORT

There are two basic styles of reports: business and academic. The illustration that follows is for a business report.

↓6X

14 pt **AN ANALYSIS OF CORPORATE SICK-LEAVE POLICIES** ↓2X

12 pt↓ **Recent Trends in the Business World**

Linda C. Motonaga ↓2X

April 5, 2003 ↓2X

Corporate sick-leave policies must be studied carefully in order to maximize employee productivity and minimize excessive absenteeism. The reasons for absences and the responsiveness of employers to the needs of the employees must be examined in order to determine some practical alternatives to current policies. ↓2X

REASONS FOR ABSENCE ↓2X

There are many reasons employees are absent from work. Illness and personal emergency are common reasons for absenteeism. ↓2X

Illness. Illness is often caused by all the stress in the workplace. Employees may have to care for parents and children. ↓2X

Personal Needs. Recent studies have also shown that absences due to personal needs are increasing. Two important questions must be addressed: ↓2X

1. Should employers rethink their sick-leave policies? ↓2X

2. How can a newly instituted sick-leave policy be more responsive to the needs of the employee? ↓2X

POSSIBLE SOLUTIONS ↓2X

Flexible scheduling is one creative way in which employers can respond to the needs of employees. If workers are given the opportunity for a flexible working schedule, stress levels should go down and personal needs can be handled during the time they are off. Another solution might be to give employees a fixed number of days off each year for reasons other than illness. This gives workers a legitimate reason for a planned absence and gives employers some advance notice so that absences do not hurt productivity.

TITLE. Subject of the report; centered; typed about 2 inches from the top of the page in bold and all-caps, with a 14-point font size; 2-line titles are single-spaced.

SUBTITLE. Secondary or explanatory title; centered; typed 1 blank line below the title, in bold, with upper- and lowercase letters.

BYLINE. Name of the writer; centered; typed 1 blank line below the previous line, in bold.

DATE. Date of the report; centered; typed 1 blank line below the previous line, in bold.

BODY. Text of the report; typed 1 blank line below the previous line, single-spaced and positioned at the left margin, with 1 blank line between paragraphs.

SIDE HEADING. Major subdivision of the report; typed 1 blank line below the previous line and beginning at the left margin, in bold and all-caps.

PARAGRAPH HEADING. Minor subdivision of the report; typed 1 blank line below the previous line at the left margin, in bold, with upper- and lowercase letters; followed by a period (also in bold).

LIST. Numbered or bulleted items in a report; typed at the left margin, single-spaced, with 1 blank line above and below the list. If the list includes multiline items, insert 1 blank line between the individual items.

F. BUSINESS REPORTS

To format a business report:

- Single-space business reports.
- Press ENTER 6 times to begin the first line of the report approximately 2 inches from the top of the page.
- Change the font size to 14 point, and type the title in all-caps, centered, in bold. Single-space a 2-line title.
- Press ENTER 2 times and change the font size to 12 point.
- If the report includes a subtitle, byline, or date, type each item centered and in bold upper- and lowercase letters.
- Press ENTER 2 times after each line in the heading block.
- Insert 1 blank line after all paragraphs.
- Do not number the first page of a report.

G. REPORTS WITH SIDE HEADINGS

To format side headings:

- Insert 1 blank line before and after side headings.
- Type side headings at the left margin, in bold, and in all-caps.

Word Processing Manual

H. WORD PROCESSING: ALIGNMENT AND FONT SIZE

Study Lesson 26 in your word processing manual. Complete all of the shaded steps while at your computer. Then format the jobs that follow.

DOCUMENT PROCESSING

Report 26-1

Business Report

Type this report in standard format for a business report with side headings.

Type the actual current year in place of 20--.

↓6X

14 pt. **AN ANALYSIS OF CORPORATE SICK-LEAVE POLICIES** ↓1X ↓2X

14 pt.↓ **Recent Trends in the Business World** ↓2X

Linda C. Motonaga ↓2X

April 5, 20-- ↓2X

Corporate sick-leave policies must be studied carefully in order to maximize employee productivity and minimize excessive absenteeism. The reasons for absences and the responsiveness of employers to the needs of the employees must be examined in order to determine some practical alternatives to current policies. ↓2X

REASONS FOR ABSENCE ↓2X

There are many reasons employees are absent from work. Illness and personal emergency are common reasons for absenteeism. However, recent surveys have shown that about 28 percent of reported sick time isn't due to illness. This percentage is on the rise. Recent studies have also shown that absences due to personal needs and stress are increasing. Also, many workers believe that they are "entitled" to a day off now and then. Perhaps it is time for employers to revamp their sick-leave policies and make these policies more responsive to the needs of the employees. ↓2X

In your word processor, when you type text followed by two hyphens (--), followed by more text and then a space, an em dash (—) will automatically be inserted.

RESPONSIVENESS OF EMPLOYERS ↓2X

If employees are finding it necessary to take sick days when they are not ill, it makes sense to conclude that possibly employers either are not aware of why absenteeism exists or have chosen not to respond to their employees' needs. One thing is certain—ignoring the problem will not make it go away. ↓2X

(Continued on next page)

POSSIBLE SOLUTIONS ↓2X

Flexible scheduling is one creative way in which employers can respond to the needs of employees. If workers are given the opportunity for a flexible working schedule, stress levels should go down and personal needs can be handled during the time they are off. Another solution might be to give employees a fixed number of days off each year for reasons other than illness. This gives workers a legitimate reason for a planned absence and gives employers some advance notice so that absences do not hurt productivity.

Report 26-2

Business Report

Open the file for Report 26-1 and make the following changes:

1. Delete the subtitle, and change the byline to `Amy Ho`.
2. Change the date to `October 23`.
3. Change the second side heading to `EMPLOYER RESPONSIVENESS`.
4. Delete the last two sentences in the last paragraph at the end of the report. Add the following sentences to the end of the last paragraph:

```
Employees will not feel the
need to invent elaborate
reasons for their absences.
They will feel as if they are
in control of their schedule
outside of work so that they
can determine the best way to
schedule their time off. When
they return to work, they will
feel relaxed and ready to work.
```

Multipage Rough-Draft Business Reports

Goals

- Improve speed and accuracy
- Refine language arts skills in punctuation
- Identify and apply basic proofreaders' marks
- Format multipage rough-draft business reports

A. Type 2 times.

A. WARMUP

1 On 7/23 the office will convert to a new phone system. 11
2 A freeze on all toll calls is requested for July. Account 23
3 #GK95 has a balance of $68 and isn't expected to "pay up." 35
| 1 | 2 | 3 | 4 | 5 | 6 | 7 | 8 | 9 | 10 | 11 | 12

SKILLBUILDING

B. Take a 1-minute timed writing on the first paragraph to establish your base speed. Then take four 1-minute timed writings on the remaining paragraphs. As soon as you equal or exceed your base speed on one paragraph, advance to the next, more difficult paragraph.

B. SUSTAINED PRACTICE: PUNCTUATION

4 Anyone who is successful in business realizes that the 11
5 needs of the customer must always come first. A satisfied 23
6 consumer is one who will come back to buy again and again. 34

7 Consumers must learn to lodge a complaint in a manner 11
8 that is fair, effective, and efficient. Don't waste time 22
9 talking to the wrong person. Go to the person in charge. 34

10 State your case clearly; be prepared with facts and 11
11 figures to back up any claim--warranties, receipts, bills, 22
12 and checks are all very effective. Don't be intimidated. 34

13 If the company agrees to work with you, you're on the 11
14 right track. Be specific: "I'll expect a check Tuesday," 22
15 or "I'll expect a replacement in the mail by Saturday." 33

C. PROGRESSIVE PRACTICE: ALPHABET

If you are not using the GDP software, turn to page SB-7 and follow the directions for this activity.

LANGUAGE ARTS

D. Study the rules at the right.

D. COMMAS AND SENTENCES

Note: The callout signals in the left margin indicate which language arts rule from this lesson has been applied.

RULE ▶ **, independent**

Use a comma between independent clauses joined by a coordinate conjunction (unless both clauses are short).

Ellen left her job with IBM, and she and her sister went to Paris.

But: Ellen left her job with IBM and went to Paris with her sister.

But: John drove and I navigated.

The underline calls attention to a point in the sentence where a comma might mistakenly be inserted.

Note: An independent clause is one that can stand alone as a complete sentence. The most common coordinate conjunctions are *and, but, or,* and *nor*.

RULE ▶ **, introductory**

Use a comma after an introductory expression (unless it is a short prepositional phrase).

Before we can make a decision, we must have all the facts.

But: In 2000 our nation elected a new president.

Note: An introductory expression is a group of words that come before the subject and verb of the independent clause. Common prepositions are *to, in, on, of, at, by, for,* and *with*.

Edit the paragraph to insert any needed punctuation and to correct any errors in grammar.

```
     Business reports should be single-spaced and all lines in
the heading block should be typed in bold. If the report title
has two lines it should be single-spaced and in all caps.
Include a subtitle below the title. You should type the
subtitle 1 blank line below the title and it should be typed
in both upper- and lowercase letters. Most reports include a
byline and a date. After the date begin typing the report
body. If there is a side heading type it in all caps and bold.
```

FORMATTING

E. BASIC PROOFREADERS' MARKS

Proofreaders' marks are used to indicate changes or corrections to be made in a document (called a *rough draft*) that is being revised for final copy. Study the chart to learn what each proofreaders' mark means.

Proofreaders' Marks		Draft	Final copy
⁀	Omit space	data base	database
∨ or ∧	Insert	if hes going, (’ not inserted)	if he's not going,
≡	Capitalize	Maple street	Maple Street
↗	Delete	a ~~final~~ draft	a draft
# ∧	Insert space	allready to	all ready to

(Continued on next page)

> Note that a new paragraph may be formatted either by inserting a blank line before it in a single-spaced document or by indenting the first line 0.5 inch (⇥) in a double-spaced document.

Proofreaders' Marks		Draft	Final Copy
~~if~~ ^when	Change word	and ~~if~~ ^when you	and when you
/	Use lowercase letter	our /President	our president
∽	Transpose	they all see (transposed)	they see all
ss	Single-space	ss [first line second line	first line second line
¶	New paragraph	. . . to use it. ¶ We can	. . . to use it. We can

F. MULTIPAGE BUSINESS REPORTS

To format a multipage report:

- Use the same side margins for all pages of the report.
- Leave an approximate 2-inch top margin on page 1.
- Leave an approximate 1-inch bottom margin on all pages.

Note: When you reach the end of a page, your word processing software will automatically insert a soft page break. If a soft page break separates a side heading from the paragraph that follows it, insert a hard page break just above the side heading to keep them together.

- Leave a 1-inch top margin on continuing pages.
- Do not number the first page. However, number all continuing pages at the top right margin.

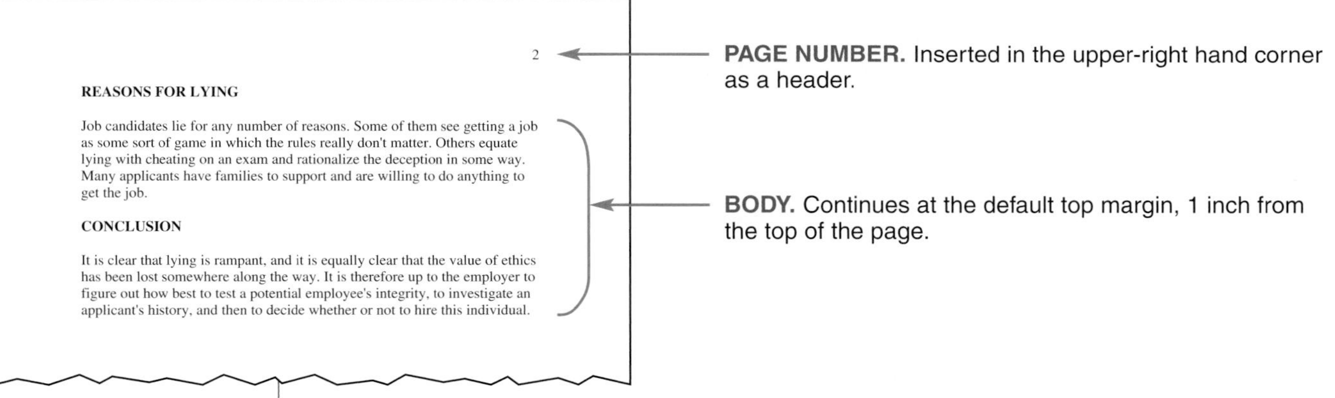

2

REASONS FOR LYING

Job candidates lie for any number of reasons. Some of them see getting a job as some sort of game in which the rules really don't matter. Others equate lying with cheating on an exam and rationalize the deception in some way. Many applicants have families to support and are willing to do anything to get the job.

CONCLUSION

It is clear that lying is rampant, and it is equally clear that the value of ethics has been lost somewhere along the way. It is therefore up to the employer to figure out how best to test a potential employee's integrity, to investigate an applicant's history, and then to decide whether or not to hire this individual.

PAGE NUMBER. Inserted in the upper-right hand corner as a header.
BODY. Continues at the default top margin, 1 inch from the top of the page.

G. BUSINESS REPORTS WITH PARAGRAPH HEADINGS

To format paragraph headings:

- Type paragraph headings at the left margin in bold and in upper- and lowercase letters.
- Follow the paragraph heading by a bold period and 1 space.

Go To

Word Processing Manual

H. WORD PROCESSING: PAGE NUMBERING AND PAGE BREAK

Study Lesson 27 in your word processing manual. Complete all of the shaded steps while at your computer. Then format the jobs that follow.

Report 27-3

Business Report

Note: The report lines are shown with extra spacing to accommodate the proofreaders' marks. Use standard business report spacing when you type the report.

1. Type the report using standard business report format.
2. Type side headings at the left margin in bold and all-caps.
3. Type any paragraph headings at the left margin in bold and in upper- and lowercase letters, followed by a bold period and 1 space.
4. Insert a page number at the top right, and suppress the page number on the first page.
5. Spell-check, preview, and proofread your document for spelling and formatting errors before printing it.

The ¶ symbol indicates the start of a new paragraph. In a business report, paragraphs are blocked (not indented).

THE INTEGRITY AND ~~MORALS~~ ETHICS

OFJOB APPLICANTS

~~By~~ Elizabeth Reddix

April 5, 20--

INTRODUCTION

¶ Some studies have found that about ~~9 out of 10~~ 90 percent of job applicants have lied in someway in order to land a job. The lies range from small exaggerations to blatant and completely fraudulent information such as lying about a degree or perhaps about ones history of earnings. After tallying the results of a survey of a large group of College students, one psychologist found that ~~approximately~~ about 90 out of 100 of them were willing to lie ~~in order~~ to land a job that they really wanted.

, introductory

¶ One way to help screen out the deceptions from the truth is to identify the most common deceptions. A nother way is to try to understand why applicants feel the need to lie. After these factors are identified and understood it will be easier tomake some judgment calls on the ethical integrity of an applicant.

, introductory

COMMON DECEPTIONS

¶ There are ~~a great~~ many areas in which job applicants are willing to make false statements in order to get a job. These could include verbal statements or written ones.

School activities. Many ~~job~~ applicants are willing to exaggerate or totally falsify ~~totally~~ their participation in school activities. In order to prove leader ship ability, an applicant might be willing to say that he or she was president of a nonexistent club or perhaps organized some type of fund-raising fictional activity.

, introductory

(Continued on next page)

, introductory

, introductory

, independent

Former Job titles. Another area rampant with deception is the list of previous Job Titles. In order to make a ~~previous~~ former job sound more impressive, a job contender might add a word or two to the title or perhaps rename the title al together.

Computer Experience. Since we live in an age of computer technology, most employers are looking for people with computer experience. Usually the more computer experience a ~~person~~ candidate has, the better off he or she willbe in terms of competing with others for the same position.

REASONS FOR LYING

¶ Job Candidates lie for any number of reasons. Some of them see getting a job as some sort of game in which the rules don't really matter. Others equate lying with cheating on an exam and rationalize the deception in some way. Many applicants have families to support and are willing to do any thing to get the job.

Conclusion

¶ It is clear that lying is ~~quite~~ rampant, and it is equally clear that the value of ethics has been lost some where along the way. It is therefore up to the employer to figure out how best to test a potential employee's integrity, to investigate an applicant's history, and then to decide whether or not to hire this individual.

Report 27-4

Business Report

Open the file for Report 27-3 and make the following changes:

1. Change the byline to `Diane Jackson`.
2. Change the date to `July 7`.
3. Change the third side heading to `COMMON REASONS FOR LYING`.
4. Add this sentence to the end of the last paragraph:

   `The importance of ethics in a future employee should never be underestimated.`

Business Reports With Lists

Goals

- Type at least 31wpm/3′/5e
- Format business reports with bulleted and numbered lists

A. Type 2 times.

A. WARMUP

    At 8:30, Horowitz & Co. will fax Order #V546 to us for 11
immediate processing! Just how many additional orders they 23
will request isn't known. About 7% of the orders are here. 35
| 1 | 2 | 3 | 4 | 5 | 6 | 7 | 8 | 9 | 10 | 11 | 12

SKILLBUILDING

B. Take three 12-second timed writings on each line. The scale below the last line shows your wpm speed for a 12-second timed writing.

B. 12-SECOND SPEED SPRINTS

Mary will not be able to meet them at the game later today.
The class is not going to be able to meet if they are gone.
They could not open that old door when the chair fell over.
This very nice piece of paper may be used to print the job.
5 10 15 20 25 30 35 40 45 50 55 60

PRETEST → PRACTICE → POSTTEST

PRETEST
Take a 1-minute timed writing. Review your speed and errors.

C. PRETEST: Close Reaches

    The growth in the volume of company assets is due to 11
the astute group of twenty older employees. Their answers 23
were undoubtedly the reason for the increase in net worth. 35
| 1 | 2 | 3 | 4 | 5 | 6 | 7 | 8 | 9 | 10 | 11 | 12

PRACTICE
Speed Emphasis:
If you made 2 or fewer errors on the Pretest, type each *individual* line 2 times.
Accuracy Emphasis:
If you made 3 or more errors, type each *group* of lines (as though it were a paragraph) 2 times.

D. PRACTICE: Adjacent Keys

as ashes cases class asset astute passes chased creased ask
we weave tweed towed weigh wealth twenty fewest answers wet
rt worth alert party smart artist sorted charts turtles art

E. PRACTICE: Consecutive Fingers

un undue bunch stung begun united punish outrun untie funny
gr grand agree angry grade growth egress hungry group graph
ol older solid tools spool volume evolve uphold olive scold

POSTTEST
Repeat the Pretest timed writing and compare performance.

F. POSTTEST: Close Reaches

G. Take two 3-minute timed writings. Review your speed and errors.

Goal: At least 31wpm/3′/5e

G. 3-MINUTE TIMED WRITING

Credit cards can make shopping very convenient, and 11
they frequently help you record and track your spending. 22
However, many card companies charge high fees for using 33
their credit cards. 37
You must realize that it may be better to pay in cash 48
and not use a credit card. Look at all your options. Some 60
card companies do not charge yearly fees. Some may give 71
you extended warranties on goods you buy with their credit 83
cards. Judge all the details; you may be surprised. 93

| 1 | 2 | 3 | 4 | 5 | 6 | 7 | 8 | 9 | 10 | 11 | 12

FORMATTING

H. BULLETED AND NUMBERED LISTS

- Numbers or bullets call attention to items in a list. If the sequence of the items is important, use numbers rather than bullets.
- Numbers and bullets either appear at the left margin or are indented to the same point as the paragraphs in the document.
- The numbers and bullets themselves are followed by an indent, and carry-over lines are indented automatically to align with the text in the previous line, not the bullet or number.

I. BUSINESS REPORTS WITH LISTS

To format a list in a business report:

- Press Enter 2 times to insert 1 blank line above the list.
- Type the list *unformatted* (without the bullets or numbers) at the left margin.
- If all the items in the list are 1 line long, single-space the entire list.
- If any items in the list are multiline, single-space each item in the list but insert a blank line between the items for readability.
- Press Enter 2 times to insert 1 blank line below the list.
- Select all lines of the list and apply the number or bullet feature to the selected lines of the list only.

Word Processing Manual

J. WORD PROCESSING: BULLETS AND NUMBERING

Study Lesson 28 in your word processing manual. Complete all of the shaded steps while at your computer. Then format the jobs that follow.

Report 28-5

Business Report

1. Type the report using standard business report format.
2. Use the bullet and numbering feature to add bullets or numbers to the list after typing the list unformatted.

INCREASING YOUR ENERGY
Shannon Wahlberg
August 21, 20--

When your energy level is running high, you are more creative, happier, and more relaxed. Some people believe that we are born with a personality that is innately energetic, lethargic, or somewhere in between. However, we are all capable of generating more energy in our lives at home or at work.

CREATING MORE ENERGY

There are many ways in which you can generate more energy before you leave for work. These two methods are simple and can be practiced without a great deal of planning:

1. Wake up to natural light by opening your curtains before you go to bed. The light coming in signals your body to stop releasing melatonin, a hormone that tells your body to continue sleeping.
2. Play music that is lively and upbeat. This will set the tone for the day.

MAINTAINING MORE ENERGY

Once you have raised your energy level at home, you can also learn to maintain your energy level at work.

- Remain positive throughout the day.
- Avoid people who are negative and have low energy. Instead, seek out those who are cheerful and positive. They will boost your energy level.
- Avoid high-fat foods, sweets, and heavy meals during the working day.
- Accept your periods of low energy as natural rhythms, knowing that they will pass. This will help you relax.

If you practice these methods to create and maintain your energy levels, you will find that these techniques will become a natural part of your daily life. Enjoy the change and experiment with your own techniques!

Report 28-6

Business Report

Open the file for Report 28-5 and make the following changes:

1. Change the first side heading to `HOW TO CREATE MORE ENERGY.`
2. Change the second side heading to `HOW TO MAINTAIN MORE ENERGY.`
3. Change the third bulleted item to this: `Avoid foods with caffeine, such as sodas and coffee.`
4. Change the fourth bulleted item to this: `Monitor your sleep. Sleeping too long can make you just as tired as sleeping too little.`

Academic Reports

Goals

- Improve speed and accuracy
- Refine language arts skills in proofreading
- Format academic reports

A. Type 2 times.

A. WARMUP

```
     Will the package arrive at 9:45 or 11:29? The exact        11
answer to this question could mean the difference between      23
losing or saving their account; Joyce also realizes this.      34
|  1  |  2  |  3  |  4  |  5  |  6  |  7  |  8  |  9  |  10  |  11  |  12
```

SKILLBUILDING

B. Type each paragraph 1 time. Change every masculine pronoun to a ferminine pronoun. Change every feminine pronoun to a masculine pronoun.

B. TECHNIQUE PRACTICE: CONCENTRATION

```
     She will finish composing the report as soon as he has
given her all the research. Her final draft will be turned in
to her boss; he will submit it to the company president.
     His new job with her company was fascinating. When the
chance to join her firm came up, he jumped at it immediately.
I wonder if she will give him a promotion anytime soon.
```

C. PACED PRACTICE

If you are not using the GDP software, turn to page SB-14 and follow the directions for this activity.

Strategies for Career Success

Turning Negative Messages Positive

Accentuate the positive. When communicating bad news (e.g., layoffs, product recalls, price increases, personnel problems), find the positive.

People respond better to positive rather than negative language, and they are more likely to cooperate if treated fairly and with respect. Avoid insults, accusations, criticism, or words with negative connotations (e.g., *failed*, *delinquent*, *bad*). Focus on what the reader can do rather than on what you won't or can't let the reader do. Instead of "You will not qualify unless . . . ," state "You will qualify if you are . . . ."

Assuage your audience's response by providing an explanation to support your decision and examples of how they might benefit. Analyze your audience and decide whether to give the negative news in the beginning, middle, or end of your message. Regardless of your approach, always maintain goodwill.

YOUR TURN Review some of your written documents and observe if they have a positive tone.

LANGUAGE ARTS

D. Type these frequently misspelled words, paying special attention to any spelling problems in each word.

D. SPELLING

```
10 personnel information its procedures their committee system
11 receive employees which education services opportunity area
12 financial appropriate interest received production contract
13 important through necessary customer employee further there
14 property account approximately general control division our
```

Edit the sentences to correct any misspellings.

```
15 All company personel will receive important information.
16 Are division has some control over there financial account.
17 There comittee has received approximately three contracts.
18 The employe and the customer have an oportunity to attend.
19 We have no farther interest in the property or it's owner.
20 When it is necessary, apropriate proceedures are followed.
```

FORMATTING

E. MORE PROOFREADERS' MARKS

1. Review the most frequently used proofreaders' marks introduced in Lesson 27.
2. Study the additional proofreaders' marks presented here.

Proofreaders' Marks	Draft	Final Copy
ds Double-space	ds first line second line	first line second line
...... Don't delete	a true story	a true story
◯ Spell out	the only 1	the only one
Move right	Please send	Please send
Move left	May 1	May 1
Bold	Column Heading	**Column Heading**
ital Italic	ital Time magazine	*Time* magazine
u/l Underline	u/l Time magazine	Time magazine
Move as shown	readers will see	readers will see

Note that a new paragraph may be formatted either by inserting a blank line before it in a single-spaced document or by indenting the first line 0.5 inch ( ) in a double-spaced document.

F. ACADEMIC REPORTS

To format an academic report:

1. Double-space academic reports.
2. After you have set the line spacing to double, press ENTER 3 times to begin the first line of the academic report about 2 inches from the top of the page.
3. Type the title in all-caps, centered, in bold, and change the font size to 14 point. Double-space a 2-line title.
4. Press ENTER 1 time and change the font size to 12 point.
5. If the report includes a subtitle, byline, or date, type each item centered, in bold and upper- and lowercase letters; press ENTER 1 time after each line in the heading block.
6. Type side headings at the left margin, in bold and all-caps.
7. Press TAB 1 time at the start of paragraphs and paragraph headings to indent them 0.5 inch.
8. Type paragraph headings in bold and in upper- and lowercase letters, and follow the paragraph heading with a bold period and 1 space.
9. Insert an approximate 1-inch bottom margin on all pages, and insert a 1-inch top margin on continuation pages.
10. Do not number the first page. However, number all continuation pages at the top right margin.

Word Processing Manual

G. WORD PROCESSING: LINE SPACING

Study Lesson 29 in your word processing manual. Complete all of the shaded steps while at your computer. Then format the jobs that follow.

DOCUMENT PROCESSING

Report 29-7

Academic Report

1. Type this report in standard format for an academic report.
2. Type the 2-line title double-spaced, and use standard format for the rest of the heading block.
3. Insert a page number at the top right, and suppress the page number on the first page.
4. Spell-check, preview, and proofread your document for spelling and formatting errors before printing it.

Reference Manual

See page R-8C and R-8D of the Reference Manual for an illustration of a multipage report in academic style.

Indent paragraphs in an academic report.

Highlighted words are spelling words from the language arts activities.

ELECTRONIC SAFEGUARDS IN
THE DIGITAL WORLD

Trends in Technology

Kevin Nguyen

July 13, 20--

More and more people are using computers and the Internet for a wide variety of reasons, both personal and professional. Most of the technology requires the use of passwords, user names, pin numbers, and miscellaneous other important codes for users to access their accounts. Unfortunately, at times it seems as if the number of codes that are necessary is increasing in geometric proportions. The problem is how to maintain accurate records of these various security codes and still preserve a secure environment, technologically speaking.

(Continued on next page)

SECURITY CODE OVERLOAD

People need 1 or sometimes 2 security codes just to log on to their computers. Several more are needed to access web sites, trade stocks, and shop and bank online, just to name a few activities. In addition most people need to remember codes for their home phones, work phones, cell phones, and voice mail. Banks require codes to withdraw money and use credit cards and ATMs. With so many security codes proliferating on a daily basis, its no wonder that we are often frustrated and frazzled as we move through our daily lives going about our personal and professional business. To add insult to injury we are often being asked to change our passwords and codes on a regular basis.

MANAGING SECURITY CODES

Several things can be done to help manage this ever-growing list of security codes. Try to choose passwords that are in some way meaningful to you but that cannot be guessed at by an intruder. Use a combination of letters and numbers. An article in the magazine Technology Bytes suggests using using street addresses or names of pets that can be easily remembered but that have no logical association with anything else.

If you decide to keep a list of security codes, make sure to protect the file in an appropriate way. If you must write down your passwords, physically lock them up. You must control and manage these important and necessary security codes to protect your personal and financial information.

Report 29-8

Academic Report

Open the file for Report 29-7 and make the following changes:

1. Change the byline to Nancy Dodson.
2. Add this paragraph below the last paragraph at the end of the report:

   A number of Web sites are available to help you remember your passwords and user names. However, these sites can help you do much more than simply manage your security codes. Some sites can provide instant registration at new sites with just one click. They also offer price comparisons while you shop anywhere on the Web, and they bring together the best search engines all in one place for easier searching. They can also filter e-mail to help you eliminate cluttered e-mail boxes full of junk.

Lesson 30

Academic Reports With Displays

Goals

- Type at least 32wpm/3′/5e
- Format rough-draft academic reports with indented lists and displays

A. Type 2 times.

A. WARMUP

```
     Did Zagorsky & Sons charge $876 for the renovation?    11
An invoice wasn't quite right; the exact amount charged in  22
July can be found in an e-mail message to zagsons@post.com. 34
|  1  |  2  |  3  |  4  |  5  |  6  |  7  |  8  |  9  |  10  |  11  |  12
```

SKILLBUILDING

B. MAP

Follow the GDP software directions for this exercise in improving keystroking accuracy.

C. DIAGNOSTIC PRACTICE: NUMBERS

If you are not using the GDP software, turn to page SB-5 and follow the directions for this activity.

D. Take two 3-minute timed writings. Review your speed and errors.

Goal: At least 32wpm/3′/5e

D. 3-MINUTE TIMED WRITING

```
     If you want to work in information processing, you      10
may realize that there are steps that you must take to      21
plan for such an exciting career. First, you must decide    33
whether or not you have the right personality traits.       44
     Then you must be trained in the technical skills you   54
need in such an important field. The technology is changing 66
each day. You must stay focused on keeping up with these    78
changes. Also, you must never quit wanting to learn new     89
skills each day you are on the job.                         96
|  1  |  2  |  3  |  4  |  5  |  6  |  7  |  8  |  9  |  10  |  11  |  12
```

FORMATTING

E. ACADEMIC REPORTS WITH LISTS

To format a list in an academic report:

- Press ENTER 1 time to begin the list.
- Type the list *unformatted* at the left margin, double-spaced.
- Press ENTER 1 time after the last line in the list.
- Select all lines of the list and apply the number or bullet feature to the selected lines of the list only. Do not include the blank lines above and below the list in your selection.
- Increase or decrease the indent of the list as needed so that the list begins at the same point of indention as the paragraphs in the report.

F. ACADEMIC REPORTS WITH INDENTED DISPLAYS

A paragraph having 4 lines or more that are quoted or having lines that need special emphasis should be formatted so that the paragraph stands out from the rest of the report. To format academic reports with indented displays:

- Type the paragraph single-spaced and indented 0.5 inch from both the left and the right margins (instead of enclosing it in quotation marks).
- Use the indent command in your word processing software to format a displayed paragraph.

Word Processing Manual

G. WORD PROCESSING: INCREASE INDENT AND CUT, COPY, AND PASTE

Study Lesson 30 in your word processing manual. Complete all of the shaded steps while at your computer. Then format the jobs that follow.

DOCUMENT PROCESSING

Report 30-9

Academic Report

1. Type the report using standard academic report format.
2. Type the list using standard format for lists in an academic report. Use the number feature to add numbers to the list after you have typed the list unformatted. Use the cut-and-paste feature to move the second numbered item.
3. Type the display using standard format for indented displays in an academic report.
4. Type paragraph headings indented 0.5 inch, in bold, and in upper- and lowercase letters, and follow the paragraph heading with a bold period and 1 space.
5. Insert a page number at the top right margin, and suppress the page number on the first page.

Reference Manual

See page R-8D of the Reference Manual for an illustration of a multipage report in academic style with a displayed paragraph.

ENDING PROCRASTINATION

Judy Baca

Every one at one time or another has put of f some task, goal or important plan at work for any number of reasons. perhaps you think time is too short or the task isn't really that important. Either way, procrastination can lead to a stalled life and career.

(Continued on next page)

EVALUATE YOUR SITUATION

Joyce Winfrey of Time Management Incorporated has some very good advice that will help you to begin to move forward. She says that you should ask yourself 2 very basic questions about why you are procrastinating:

1. Is there a valid reason for my procrastination?
2. Am I procrastinating because the task at hand is not really what I want?

After you have asked yourself these questions, ms. Winfrey suggests that you do the following:

Look deep within yourself. If you are looking for excuses, then the process of asking these questions will be a waste of your time. However, if you answer these questions honestly, you might find answers that surprise you and that will help clarify your situation.

She also recommends several techniques can help your get back on task and put an end to procrastination.

PRACTICE NEW TECHNIQUES

Identifying and understanding the techniques which follow is the first step. Once you know what to do you can begin to practice these steps daily.

Take Baby Steps. Don't make any task bigger than it really is by looking at the whole thing at once. Break it down into babysteps that are manageable.

Dont Strive for Perfectionism. If you are waiting for the perfect solution or the perfect opportunity, you will immobilized. Accept the fact that no one and nothing is perfect. Then accept your mistakes and move on.

Enjoy the Task. Enjoy the task at hand and find something in it that is positive and rewarding. Confront your fears with a plan of action.

Remind yourself of all these techniques daily. Post them by your telephone, your desk, or your car. You will find that your personal life and career will gain momentum, and success will soon be yours.

Report 30-10

Academic Report

Progress and Proofreading Check

Documents designated as Proofreading Checks serve as a check of your proofreading skill. Your goal is to have zero typographical errors when the GDP software first scores the document.

1. Type the report using standard academic report format for a multipage academic report with a list.

2. Make all changes as indicated by the proofreaders' marks.

TIPS FOR HELPING YOU
PREPARE FOR YOUR EXAM

Betty Goldberg
June 8, 20--

in school you have taken ~~some~~ many exams. Whether you are an excellent exam taker or a novice at the task, you probably have experienced a degree of stress related to your performance on an exam. There are some steps you can take to reduce the stress of taking an exam, and these suggestions will likely help you throughout your life.

PREPARING FOR THE EXAM

Of course, it's always easier to take an exam from an Instructor whom you have had in previous classes, because you know what to expect. From past experience, you know whether the Instructor likes to use objective questions or subjective questions, whether the Instructor focuses on the textbook or on class notes, and the difficulty of the questions the Instructor asks.

If you don't know what to expect, however, you need to prepare for all possibilities. Be sure that you review all pertinent materials for the exam—whether they come from classnotes, the textbook, field trips, or class room presentations.

SURVIVING THE DAY BEFORE THE EXAM

Be sure you know where and at what time the exam will be administered. Organize the materials you need to bring with you to the exam. You may need pencils, pens, calculators, disks, or paper. Try to get a good night's sleep the night before the exam, and don't upset your usual routine.

Taking The Exam

Now that the day of the exam has arrived, there are several actions you should take to ensure that you perform well:

1. Arrive at the test ~~sight~~ site early so that you are ready to take the exam when the instructor announces the beginning time. That means that before you have to be sure to get up early enough to have a light breakfast leaving for the exam.
2. Read very carefully the instructions provided on the exam to be sure you answer the questions correctly.
3. Keep track of time so that you don't get stuck and spend too much of your time on any one part of the exam.
4. Try to keep a positive attitude.
5. Relax as best you can—a relaxed performance is much more productive than a stressed performance.

Unit 7

Correspondence

LESSON 31
Business Letters

LESSON 32
Business Letters With Enclosure Notations

LESSON 33
Envelopes and Labels

LESSON 34
Memos

LESSON 35
Correspondence Review

April 3, 20--

Ms. Linda Lopez
Account Manager
The Internet Connection
7625 Maple Avenue
Pomona, CA 91765

Dear Ms. Lopez:

Our company is interested in hosting an educational seminar this spring that will focus on meeting the growing need for information industry professionals to keep abreast of emerging new technologies and trends. We are specifically interested in information on high-speed Internet connections.

I understand that The Internet Connection specializes in these seminars and will also help businesses analyze their needs and choose an appropriate solution. I am in the process of contacting several companies similar to yours who might be interested in conducting these seminars. Please contact me by Thursday or Friday at the latest so that we can discuss this matter further.

I appreciate the fine service we have always received from you in the past, Ms. Lopez, and I look forward to hearing from you.

Sincerely,

Ruzanna Petroska
Technology Specialist

urs

MEMO TO: All Salaried Employees

FROM: Amy Vigil, Human Resources

DATE: November 2, 20--

SUBJECT: Health Care Benefit Plan

Effective January 1, Allied Aerospace Industries will contract with MedNet to begin a new health benefits program for all eligible salaried personnel. A brochure outlining important program information will be mailed to you soon.

An open enrollment period will be in effect during the entire month of January. If you and your family are interested in one of the MedNet health plan options, you may transfer yourself and your dependents into any appropriate plan. All applications must be received no later than midnight, January 31. You may also access your plan over the Internet at www.mednet.com if it is more convenient.

If you have any questions or need any help understanding your options, please call me at Ext. 134. I will be happy to help you select the plan that is best for you.

urs

Trend Electronics
2206 31st Street
Minneapolis, MN 55407-1911

Mr. Charles Goldstein
Software Solutions
2981 Canwood Street
Roselle, IL 60172

Business Letters

Goals

- Improve speed and accuracy
- Refine language arts skills in capitalization
- Format a business letter in block style

A. Type 2 times.

A. WARMUP

```
     You can save $1,698 when you buy the 20-part video      10
series! Just ask for Series #MX5265 in the next 7 days;      22
ordering early qualifies you for a sizable discount of 5%.   33
| 1 | 2 | 3 | 4 | 5 | 6 | 7 | 8 | 9 | 10 | 11 | 12
```

SKILLBUILDING

B. Take three 12-second timed writings on each line. The scale below the last line shows your wpm speed for a 12-second timed writing.

B. 12-SECOND SPEED SPRINTS

```
Mary will be able to go home when she can run fast and far.
Sam can come to the store if he is able to stop for a soda.
Suzy knows that she must send the mail out by noon or else.
Only a few good desks will be made by the end of this week.
5 10 15 20 25 30 35 40 45 50 55 60
```

C. PROGRESSIVE PRACTICE: ALPHABET

If you are not using the GDP software, turn to page SB-7 and follow the directions for this activity.

D. PROGRESSIVE PRACTICE: NUMBERS

If you are not using the GDP software, turn to page SB-11 and follow the directions for this activity.

LANGUAGE ARTS

E. Study the rules at the right.

E. CAPITALIZATION

Note: The callout signals in the left margin indicate which language arts rule from this lesson has been applied.

RULE ▶ ≡ sentence

Capitalize the first word of a sentence.
Please prepare a summary of your activities.

RULE ▶ ≡ proper

Capitalize proper nouns and adjectives derived from proper nouns.
Judy Hendrix drove to Albuquerque in her new Pontiac convertible.

Note: A proper noun is the official name of a particular person, place, or thing.

(Continued on next page)

RULE ▶ ≡ time

Capitalize the names of the days of the week, months, holidays, and religious days (but do not capitalize the names of the seasons).

On Thursday, November 25, we will celebrate Thanksgiving, the most popular holiday in the fall.

Edit the paragraph to insert or delete capitalization.

```
The american flag can be seen flying over the White House in Washington. Our Country's flag is often seen flying over Government buildings on holidays like July 4, independence day. Memorial Day signals the end of spring and the start of Summer. Most Americans consider Labor day the beginning of the fall season. In december many people observe christmas and Hanukkah. most government holidays are scheduled to fall on either a Monday or a friday. Sometimes the birthdays of Historical figures are also celebrated.
```

FORMATTING

F. BASIC PARTS OF A BUSINESS LETTER

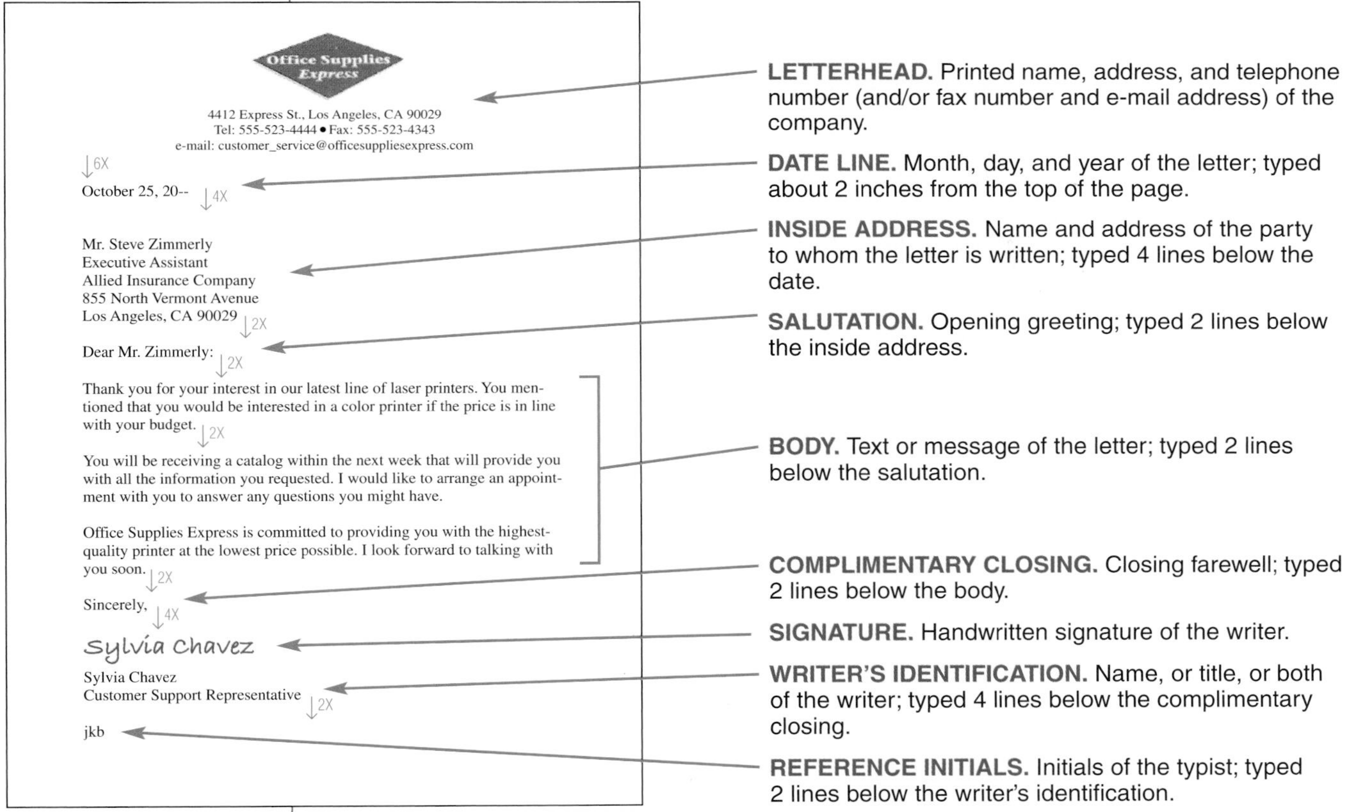

Office Supplies Express

4412 Express St., Los Angeles, CA 90029
Tel: 555-523-4444 • Fax: 555-523-4343
e-mail: customer_service@officesuppliesexpress.com

↓6X

October 25, 20-- ↓4X

Mr. Steve Zimmerly
Executive Assistant
Allied Insurance Company
855 North Vermont Avenue
Los Angeles, CA 90029 ↓2X

Dear Mr. Zimmerly: ↓2X

Thank you for your interest in our latest line of laser printers. You mentioned that you would be interested in a color printer if the price is in line with your budget. ↓2X

You will be receiving a catalog within the next week that will provide you with all the information you requested. I would like to arrange an appointment with you to answer any questions you might have.

Office Supplies Express is committed to providing you with the highest-quality printer at the lowest price possible. I look forward to talking with you soon. ↓2X

Sincerely, ↓4X

Sylvia Chavez

Sylvia Chavez
Customer Support Representative ↓2X

jkb

LETTERHEAD. Printed name, address, and telephone number (and/or fax number and e-mail address) of the company.
DATE LINE. Month, day, and year of the letter; typed about 2 inches from the top of the page.
INSIDE ADDRESS. Name and address of the party to whom the letter is written; typed 4 lines below the date.
SALUTATION. Opening greeting; typed 2 lines below the inside address.
BODY. Text or message of the letter; typed 2 lines below the salutation.
COMPLIMENTARY CLOSING. Closing farewell; typed 2 lines below the body.
SIGNATURE. Handwritten signature of the writer.
WRITER'S IDENTIFICATION. Name, or title, or both of the writer; typed 4 lines below the complimentary closing.
REFERENCE INITIALS. Initials of the typist; typed 2 lines below the writer's identification.

G. BUSINESS LETTERS IN BLOCK STYLE

1. Type all lines beginning at the left margin.
2. Press ENTER 6 times to begin the first line of the letter about 2 inches from the top of the page, and then type the date.
3. After the date, press ENTER 4 times and type the inside address. Leave 1 space between the state and the ZIP Code.

(Continued on next page)

4. After the inside address, press ENTER 2 times and type the salutation. For standard punctuation, type a colon after the salutation. Press ENTER 2 times after the salutation.
5. Single-space the body of the letter, but press ENTER 2 times between paragraphs. Do not indent paragraphs.
6. Press ENTER 2 times after the last paragraph and type the complimentary closing. For standard punctuation, type a comma after the complimentary closing.
7. Press ENTER 4 times after the complimentary closing and type the writer's identification.
8. Press ENTER 2 times after the writer's identification and type your reference initials in lowercase letters with no periods or spaces.

Word Processing Manual

H. WORD PROCESSING: INSERT DATE

Study Lesson 31 in your word processing manual. Complete all of the shaded steps while at your computer. Then format the jobs that follow.

DOCUMENT PROCESSING

Correspondence 31-3

Business Letter in Block Style

1. Type the letter using standard block style.
2. Use standard punctuation: a colon after the salutation and a comma after the complimentary closing.
3. Use word wrap for the paragraphs. Press ENTER only at the end of each paragraph. Your lines may end differently from those shown in the illustration.
4. Type your initials for the reference initials.
5. Spell-check, preview, and proofread your letter for typing, spelling, and formatting errors.

↓6X
March 27, 20-- ↓4X

≡ proper

Ms. Linda Lopez
Account Manager
The Internet Connection
7625 Maple Avenue
Pomona, CA 91765 ↓2X

≡ proper

Dear Ms. Lopez: ↓2X

≡ sentence, ≡ time

≡ proper

Our company is interested in hosting an educational seminar this spring that will focus on meeting the growing need for information industry professionals to keep abreast of emerging new technologies and trends. We are specifically interested in information on high-speed Internet connections. ↓2X

≡ sentence

≡ time

I understand that The Internet Connection specializes in these seminars and will also help businesses analyze their needs and choose an appropriate solution. I am in the process of contacting several companies similar to yours who might be interested in conducting these seminars. Please contact me by Thursday or Friday at the latest so that we can discuss this further. ↓2X

(Continued on next page)

≡ sentence

≡ proper

I appreciate the fine service we have always received from you in the past, Ms. Lopez, and look forward to hearing from you. ↓2X

Sincerely,↓4X

≡ proper

≡ proper

Ruzanna Petroska
Technology Specialist ↓2X

urs

Remember to type your initials in place of urs.

Correspondence 31-4

Business Letter in Block Style

Open the file for Correspondence 31-3 and make the following changes:

1. Change the date to `May 8`.
2. Change the writer's identification to: `Gail Madison` and her job title to `Technology Engineer`.

Correspondence 31-5

Business Letter in Block Style

Note: The | symbol indicates the end of a line. The ¶ symbol indicates the start of a new paragraph.

1. Type the letter using standard block style.
2. Spell-check, preview, and proofread your letter for typing, spelling, and formatting errors.

≡ time

≡ proper

≡ proper

≡ proper

The ¶ symbol indicates the start of a new paragraph. In a business letter, paragraphs are blocked (not indented).

≡ time

May 25, 20-- | Ms. Linda Lopez | Account Manager | The Internet Connection | 7625 Maple Avenue | Pomona, CA 91765 | Dear Ms. Lopez:

¶ Thank you so much for hosting the educational seminar last Tuesday that focused on the topic of high-speed Internet connections. Our company and our employees are now well prepared to make a decision about the best type of Internet connection for their particular needs.

¶ Because this seminar was so successful, I have been authorized to contract with The Internet Connection for a continuing series of seminars on any topics related to emerging new technologies and trends as they apply to the needs of our company and our employees. I will call you on Monday so that we can arrange for a meeting to finalize some contractual issues.

¶ Once again, thank you for a very successful and productive seminar!

Sincerely, | Ruzanna Petroska | Technology Specialist |

urs

Business Letters With Enclosure Notations

Goals

- Type at least 33wpm/3′/5e
- Format a business letter with an enclosure notation

A. Type 2 times.

A. WARMUP

```
     Sales by two travel agencies (Quill, Virgil, & Johnson  11
and Keef & Zane) exceeded all prior amounts. Total sales     23
for that year were as follows: $1,540,830 and $976,233.      34
| 1 | 2 | 3 | 4 | 5 | 6 | 7 | 8 | 9 | 10 | 11 | 12
```

SKILLBUILDING

B. Type each line 2 times.

Technique Tip: Press the BACKSPACE key with the Sem finger without looking at your keyboard.

B. TECHNIQUE PRACTICE: BACKSPACE KEY

1. Type each letter (or group of letters) as shown.
2. When you reach the backspace sign (←), backspace 1 time to delete the last keystroke.
3. Type the next group of letters. The result will be a new word. For example, if you see "hi← at," you would type "hi," backspace 1 time, and then type "at," resulting in the new word "hat" instead of the original word "hit."

```
p←cat c←tab b←peg p←but p←tie t←pop m←pat f←sit m←but t←cub
t←mop b←fib r←fat w←fin p←tin c←top p←ban f←can y←get m←let
di←ye be←ag ge←um ri←ob mu←ad la←id fi←an bi←ad to←ip ro←id
pa←it ti←on fi←un ra←un pi←an ge←ot ba←it fa←it ma←it sa←it
bin←t any←t new←t was←r sea←t tap←n fan←t lap←d for←x fin←x
pin←t ham←d sod←n rid←p rap←n tap←n dip←n sin←p lip←d put←n
```

PRETEST → PRACTICE → POSTTEST

PRETEST
Take a 1-minute timed writing. Review your speed and errors.

PRACTICE
Speed Emphasis: If you made 2 or fewer errors on the Pretest, type each *individual* line 2 times.
Accuracy Emphasis: If you made 3 or more errors, type each *group* of lines (as though it were a paragraph) 2 times.

C. PRETEST: Discrimination Practice

```
     Steven saw the younger, unruly boy take flight as he    11
threw the coin at the jury. The brave judge stopped the      22
fight. He called out to the youth, who recoiled in fear.     33
| 1 | 2 | 3 | 4 | 5 | 6 | 7 | 8 | 9 | 10 | 11 | 12
```

D. PRACTICE: Left Hand

```
vbv verb bevy vibes bevel brave above verbal bovine behaves
wew west weep threw wedge weave fewer weight sewing dewdrop
fgf gulf gift fight fudge fugue flags flight golfer feigned
```

E. PRACTICE: Right Hand

```
uyu buys your usury unity youth buoys unruly untidy younger
oio coin lion oiled foils foist prior recoil iodine rejoice
jhj jury huge enjoy three judge habit adjust slight jasmine
```

POSTTEST
Repeat the Pretest timed writing and compare performance.

F. POSTTEST: Discrimination Practice

G. Take two 3-minute timed writings. Review your speed and errors.

Goal: At least 33wpm/3′/5e

G. 3-MINUTE TIMED WRITING

```
     Be zealous in your efforts when you write business     10
letters. Your business writing must convey clearly what     22
it is you want people to read. All of your letters should   33
be formatted neatly in proper business letter format.       44
     Before sending your letters, read them quickly just to 55
make sure that they explain clearly what you want to say.   67
Proofread the letters you write for correct grammar and     78
spelling. Use all of your writing skills to display the     89
best image. Your readers will welcome the effort.           99
| 1 | 2 | 3 | 4 | 5 | 6 | 7 | 8 | 9 | 10 | 11 | 12
```

FORMATTING

H. ENCLOSURE NOTATION

- To indicate that an item is enclosed with a letter, type the word *Enclosure* on the line below the reference initials.

Example: urs
Enclosure

- If more than one item is being enclosed, type the word *Enclosures*.

DOCUMENT PROCESSING

Correspondence 32-6

Business Letter in Block Style

Reference Manual

See page R-3B and R-3C of the Reference Manual for an illustration of a business letter with an enclosure notation.

The | symbol indicates the end of a line.

1. Type the letter using standard business letter format.
2. Spell-check, preview, and proofread your document for spelling and formatting errors.

October 10, 20-- | Ms. Denise Bradford | Worldwide Travel, Inc. | 1180 Alvarado, SE | Albuquerque, NM 87108 | Dear Ms. Bradford:

¶ Our company has decided to hold its regional sales meeting in Scottsdale, Arizona, during the second week of January. I need information on a suitable conference site.

(Continued on next page)

The ¶ symbol indicates the start of a new paragraph.

¶ We will need a meeting room with the following items: 30 computer workstations with an Internet connection, copy stands, mouse pads, and adjustable chairs; an LCD projector with a large screen; and a microphone and podium. The hotel should have a fax machine and on-site secretarial services. We might also need a messenger service.
¶ A final decision on the conference site must be made within the next two weeks. Please send me any information you have available for a suitable location in Scottsdale immediately. I have enclosed a list of conference attendees and their room preferences. Thank you for your help.
Sincerely yours, | Bill McKay | Marketing Manager | urs | Enclosure

Correspondence 32-7

Business Letter in Block Style

1. Open the file for Correspondence 32-6.
2. Change the inside address to `1032 San Pedro, SE.`
3. Change the first sentence as follows:
   `Our company has decided to hold its annual national sales meeting during the first week of February in Scottsdale, Arizona.`
4. In the first sentence of the second paragraph, change the information after the colon as follows:
   `30 computer workstations, an LCD projector with a large screen, and a microphone and podium.`

Correspondence 32-8

Business Letter in Block Style

October 20, 20-- | Mr. Bill McKay | Marketing Manager | Viatech Communications | 9835 Osuna Road, NE | Albuquerque, NM 87111 | Dear Mr. McKay:
¶ Thank you for your inquiry, regarding a conference site in Scottsdale, Arizona, for 35 people during the second week of January.
¶ I have enclosed the following brochures with detailed information on some properties in Scottsdale that provide exclusive service to businesses like yours: Camelback Resorts, Shadow Pines Suites, and Desert Inn Resorts and Golf Club. All these properties have meeting rooms that will accommodate your needs and also offer additional services you might be interested in using.

(Continued on next page)

¶ Please call me when you have reached a decision. I will be happy to make the final arrangements as well as issue any airline tickets you may need. Yours truly, | Ms. Denise Bradford | Travel Agent | urs | Enclosures

Envelopes and Labels

Goals

- Improve speed and accuracy
- Refine language arts skills in composing sentences
- Format envelopes and labels and fold letters

A. Type 2 times.

A. WARMUP

```
     Does Quentin know if half of the January order will be  11
ready on 1/7/05? At 4:20 only 36% of the orders had been     23
mailed! Mr. Gray expects a very sizable loss this month.     34
| 1 | 2 | 3 | 4 | 5 | 6 | 7 | 8 | 9 | 10 | 11 | 12
```

SKILLBUILDING

B. Take three 12-second timed writings on each line. The scale below the last line shows your wpm speed for a 12-second timed writing.

B. 12-SECOND SPEED SPRINTS

```
Today we want to find out if our work will be done on time.
Doug will be able to drive to the store if the car is here.
Jan will sign this paper when she has done all of the work.
This time she will be sure to spend two days with her sons.
5 | 10 | 15 | 20 | 25 | 30 | 35 | 40 | 45 | 50 | 55 | 60
```

C. PACED PRACTICE

If you are not using the GDP software, turn to page SB-14 and follow the directions for this activity.

LANGUAGE ARTS

D. Answer each question with a complete sentence.

D. COMPOSING: SENTENCES

What are your best traits that you will bring to your job when you graduate?
What are the best traits that you will want to see in your new boss?
Would you rather work for a large or a small company?
How much money do you expect to earn on your first job?
Would you like your first job to be in a small town or a large city?
What do you see yourself doing in ten years?
What types of benefits do you think you would like to have?

E. ENVELOPES

The envelope feature of your word processor simplifies your task of addressing a No. 10 envelope. The standard size for business envelopes is 9½ by 4⅛ inches. A business envelope should include the following:

- **Return Address**. If necessary, type the sender's name and address in upper- and lowercase style in the upper left corner. Business stationery usually has a printed return address. Use the default placement and the default font of your word processor for the return address.
- **Mailing Address**. Type the recipient's name and address in upper- and lowercase style (or in all-capital letters without any punctuation) toward the center of the envelope. Use the default placement and the default font of your word processor for the mailing address.

Note: Postal scanners read addresses more efficiently if they are typed in all-capital letters without any punctuation.

Trend Electronics
2206 31st Street
Minneapolis, MN 55407-1911

Mr. Charles R. Harrison
Reliable Software, Inc.
5613 Brunswick Avenue
Minneapolis, MN 55406

Standard large envelope, No. 10, is 9½ 3 4⅛ inches.

F. FOLDING LETTERS

To fold a letter for a No. 10 envelope:

1. Place the letter face up, and fold up the bottom third of the page.
2. Fold the top third of the page down to about 0.5 inch from the bottom edge of the page.
3. Insert the last crease into the envelope first with the flap facing up.

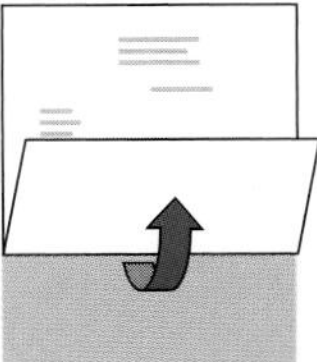

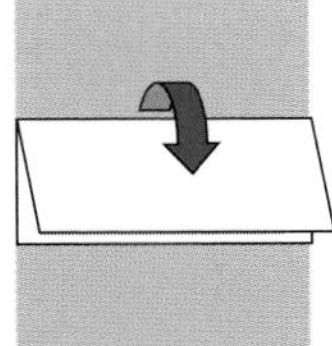

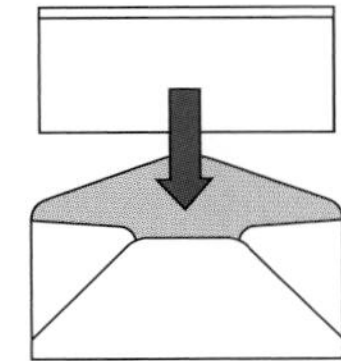

G. LABELS

The label feature of your word processor simplifies the task of preparing various labels. You can use different label settings to print a full sheet of labels or to print a single label. You may want to use a mailing label as an alternative to printing an envelope.

When preparing labels, test the label settings by printing your labels on a blank page before you print them on the actual label form.

H. WORD PROCESSING: ENVELOPES AND LABELS

Study Lesson 33 in your word processing manual. Complete all of the shaded steps while at your computer. Then format the jobs that follow.

DOCUMENT PROCESSING

Correspondence 33-9
Envelope

1. Prepare an envelope with the following mailing address:

   Mr. Charles Goldstein | Software Solutions | 2981 Canwood Street | Roselle, IL 60172

2. Insert the following return address.

   Shannon Stone | Data Systems, Inc. | 2201 South Street | Racine, WI 53404

3. Add the envelope to a blank document.

Correspondence 33-10
Envelope

1. Open the file for Correspondence 32-8 and prepare an envelope for the letter.
2. Do not insert a return address.
3. Add the envelope to the letter.

Correspondence 33-11
Mailing Labels

1. Select an address label product about 1 inch deep, large enough to fit a 4-line address. Label choices will vary; however, Avery standard, 5160, Address is a good choice for laser and ink jet printers.
2. Prepare address labels for the names and addresses that follow.
3. Type the addresses in order from left to right as you see them displayed below in the first group.
4. Move to the second group of labels and type them again from left to right.

Purchasing Dept.
Abbott Laboratories
Abbott Park
Chicago, IL 60064

Frank Zimmerly
Cartridges, Etc.
1220 Charleston Road
Oso Park, CA 90621

John Sanchez
Adobe Systems
1585 Charleston Road
Los Angeles, CA 90029

Mike Rashid
Internet Services
901 Thompson Place
Sunnyvale, CA 94088

Jennifer Reagan
Aetna Life
151 Farmington Avenue
Hartford, CT 06156

Bob Patterson
Affiliated Publishing
135 Morrisey Boulevard
Boston, MA 02107

Correspondence 33-12

Mailing Labels

1. Select an address label product about 1 inch deep, large enough to fit a 4-line address. Label choices will vary; however, Avery standard, 5160, Address is a good choice for laser and ink jet printers.
2. Prepare a full page of the same label with the following address:

    Shipping and Receiving|E-Office Outlet|1122 North Highland Street|Arlington, VA 22201

Correspondence 33-13

Envelope

1. Open the file for Correspondence 32-6 and prepare an envelope for the letter.
2. Insert the following return address:

    Bill McKay|Viatech Communications|9835 Osana Road, NE|Albuquerque, NM 87111

3. Add the envelope to the letter.

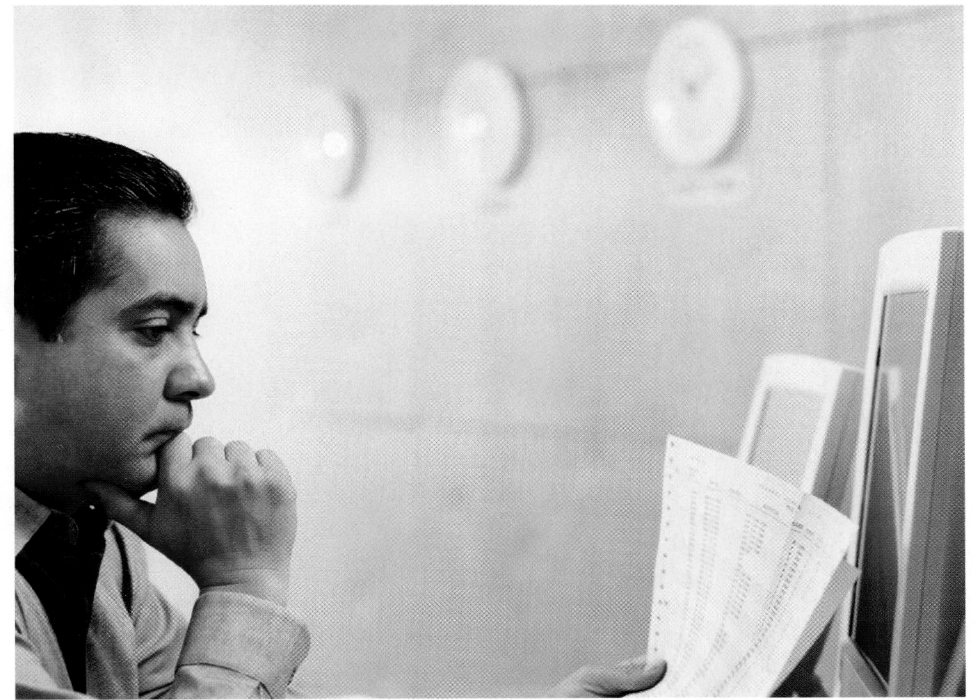

Memos

Goals

- Type at least 34wpm/3′/5e
- Format interoffice memos

A. Type 2 times.

A. WARMUP

```
     The series* (*6 films, 28 minutes) by J. Zeller goes      11
beyond the "basics" of computers. Viewers keep requesting      22
an extension on the following due dates: 3/2, 5/5, and 8/9.    34
|  1  |  2  |  3  |  4  |  5  |  6  |  7  |  8  |  9  |  10  |  11  |  12
```

SKILLBUILDING

B. DIAGNOSTIC PRACTICE: SYMBOLS AND PUNCTUATION

If you are not using the GDP software, turn to page SB-2 and follow the directions for this activity.

C. PROGRESSIVE PRACTICE: ALPHABET

If you are not using the GDP software, turn to page SB-7 and follow the directions for this activity.

D. Take two 3-minute timed writings. Review your speed and errors.

Goal: At least 34wpm/3′/5e

D. 3-MINUTE TIMED WRITING

```
     Companies that place their ads on the Internet use a      11
process called data mining. They look for patterns in the      22
quantities of data they get from those who visit Web sites.    34
     Data mining tracks buying habits of customers and then    46
decides to send ads to them based on their current and past    58
buying patterns. Data mining can also be used to explain       69
buyer behavior and to look at trends. First, a survey is       80
filled out, and then the results are gathered and stored in    92
a file to be analyzed in detail at a later time.              102
|  1  |  2  |  3  |  4  |  5  |  6  |  7  |  8  |  9  |  10  |  11  |  12
```

FORMATTING

E. MEMOS

A memo is usually sent from one person to another in the same organization. To format a memo on plain paper or on letterhead stationery:

1. Press ENTER 6 times for a top margin of about 2 inches.
2. Type the headings (including the colons) in all-caps and bold: `MEMO TO:`, `FROM:`, `DATE:`, and `SUBJECT:`.
3. Press TAB 1 time after typing the colon to reach the point where the heading entries begin.
4. Insert 1 blank line between the heading lines and between the heading lines and the memo body.
5. Insert 1 blank line between paragraphs. Most memos are typed with blocked paragraphs (no indentions).
6. Insert 1 blank line between the body and the reference initials.

DOCUMENT PROCESSING

Correspondence 34-14

Memo

Refer to page R-7C of the Reference Manual for an illustration of a memo.

1. Type the memo using standard memo format.
2. Spell-check, preview, and proofread your document for spelling and formatting errors before printing it.

↓6X

MEMO TO: All Salaried Employees ↓2X

FROM: Amy Vigil, Human Resources ↓2X

DATE: November 2, 20-- ↓2X

SUBJECT: Health Care Benefit Plan ↓2X

Effective January 1, Allied Aerospace Industries will contract with MedNet to begin a new health benefits program for all eligible salaried personnel. A brochure outlining important program information will be mailed to you soon. ↓2X

An open enrollment period will be in effect during the entire month of January. If you and your family are interested in one of the MedNet health plan options, you may transfer yourself and your dependents into any appropriate plan. All applications must be received no later than midnight, January 31. You may also access your plan over the Internet at www.mednet.com if it is more convenient. ↓2X

If you have any questions or need any help understanding your options, please call me at Ext. 134. I will be happy to help you select the plan that is best for you. ↓2X

urs

Correspondence 34-15

Memo

> The ¶ symbol indicates the start of a new paragraph. In a memo, paragraphs are blocked (not indented).

MEMO TO: Amy Vigil, Human Resources | **FROM:** Dan Westphal | **DATE:** November 23, 20-- | **SUBJECT:** MedNet Benefit Plan

¶ Thank you for the brochure detailing the various options for employees under the MedNet plan. I would like clarification on some of the services included in the plan.

¶ Because both my wife and I are employees of Allied Aerospace Industries, do we have the choice of enrolling separately under different options? In our present plan, I know that this is possible.

¶ We have two dependents. Is it possible to enroll both dependents under different options of the plan, or do they both fall under either one option or the other? I know that in the past you have asked for evidence of dependent status and dates of birth.

¶ If you need any further information, please let me know. Thank you very much for your help.

urs

Correspondence 34-16

Memo

Open the file for Correspondence 34-14 and make the following changes:

1. Send the memo to `All Allied Aerospace Industries Employees.`
2. Change the date to `December 2.`
3. Change the subject line to `Health Care Open Enrollment Period.`

Keyboarding Connection

Searching the Web

Research projects on the World Wide Web! Access up-to-date information from all over the world.

To conduct a search, specify keywords and certain relationships among them. Many search engines use arithmetic operators to symbolize Boolean relationships. A plus sign (+) is used instead of AND, a minus sign (−) instead of NOT, and no sign instead of OR.

Simple document searches match a single keyword (e.g., *cherry*). Advanced searches might match any of the words (e.g., *cherry pie*); all words (e.g., *+cherry +pie*); a phrase (e.g., "*cherry pie*"); or some words and not others (e.g., *+cherry +pie −tree*). There is no space between the plus or minus sign and its word.

YOUR TURN From your Web browser, open a Web search engine site. Type various searches in the entry box of the search engine and start the search. Compare the results.

Correspondence Review

Goals

- Improve speed and accuracy
- Refine language arts skills in proofreading
- Format various types of correspondence with an attachment notation
- Practice italicizing and underlining

A. Type 2 times.

A. WARMUP

Item #876 won't be ordered until 9/10. Did you gather 11
all requests and input them exactly as they appeared? Zack 23
will never be satisfied until he contacts jack@orders.com. 34

| 1 | 2 | 3 | 4 | 5 | 6 | 7 | 8 | 9 | 10 | 11 | 12

SKILLBUILDING

B. MAP

Follow the GDP software directions for this exercise in improving keystroking accuracy.

C. Take a 1-minute timed writing on the first paragraph to establish your base speed. Then take four 1-minute timed writings on the remaining paragraphs. As soon as you equal or exceed your base speed on one paragraph, advance to the next, more difficult paragraph.

C. SUSTAINED PRACTICE: ALTERNATE-HAND WORDS

When eight of them began a formal discussion on some 11
of the major issues, the need for a chair was very evident. 23
A chair would be sure to handle the usual work with ease. 35

The eight people in that group decided that the work 11
would be done only if they selected one person to be chair 23
of their group. They began to debate all the major issues. 35

One issue that needed to be settled right up front was 11
the question of how to handle proxy votes. It seemed for a 23
short time that a fight over this very issue would result. 35

The group worked diligently in attempting to solve the 11
issues that were being discussed. All of the concerns that 23
were brought to the group were reviewed in depth by them. 34

| 1 | 2 | 3 | 4 | 5 | 6 | 7 | 8 | 9 | 10 | 11 | 12

LANGUAGE ARTS

D. Edit this paragraph to correct any typing or formatting errors.

D. PROOFREADING

```
     It doesnt matter how fast you can  type or how well
you now a software program if you produce documents taht
are filled with errors. You must learn to watch for errors
in spelling punctuation, and formatting. Look carefully
between words and sentences.Make sure that after a period
at the end of a sentence, you see one space. Sometime it
helps to look at the characters in the sentence justabove
the one you are proofreading to ensure accuracy.
```

FORMATTING

E. ATTACHMENT NOTATION

The word *Attachment* (rather than *Enclosure*) is typed below the reference initials when material is physically attached (stapled or clipped) to a memo.

Example: urs
Attachment

Word Processing Manual

F. WORD PROCESSING: ITALIC AND UNDERLINE

Study Lesson 35 in your word processing manual. Complete all of the shaded steps while at your computer. Then format the jobs that follow.

DOCUMENT PROCESSING

Correspondence 35-17

Memo

MEMO TO: All Executive Assistants | **FROM:** Barbara Azar, Staff Development Coordinator | **DATE:** March 25, 20-- | **SUBJECT:** Standardizing Document Formats

¶ Last month we received our final shipment of new laser printers. The installation of these printers in your offices marked the final phase-out of all ink-jet printers.

¶ Because all of us can now use a variety of standardized fonts in our correspondence, please note the following change: <u>From now on, all book and journal titles should be set in Arial Narrow.</u> This new formatting change will help us to standardize our correspondence.

¶ The latest edition of the book *Quick Reference for the Automated Office* has two pages of helpful information on laser printers, which I have attached. Please read these pages carefully, and we will discuss them at our next meeting.

urs | Attachment

Correspondence 35-18

Memo

MEMO TO: Barbara Azar, Staff Development Coordinator | **FROM:** Sharon Hearshen, Executive Assistant | **DATE:** April 3, 20-- | **SUBJECT:** Laser Printer Workshop

¶ The new laser printers we received are fabulous! I know that you worked very hard to get these printers for us, and all of us in the Sales and Marketing Department certainly appreciate your effort.

¶ Several of us would be very interested in seeing the printers demonstrated. Would it be possible to have a workshop with some hands-on training? We are particularly interested in learning about font selection, paper selection, and envelopes and labels.

¶ I have attached an article on laser printers from the latest issue of *Office Technology*. It is very informative, and you might like to include it as a part of the workshop. Please let me know if I can help you in any way.

urs | Attachment

Correspondence 35-19

Business Letter in Block Style

Progress and Proofreading Check

Documents designated as Proofreading Checks serve as a check of your proofreading skill. Your goal is to have zero typographical errors when the GDP software first scores the document.

1. Type the following business letter, and then prepare an envelope for the document.
2. Do not include a return address.
3. Add the envelope to the letter.

October 1, 20-- | Mrs. Elizabeth McGraw | 844 Lincoln Boulevard | Santa Monica, CA 90403 | Dear Mrs. McGraw:

¶ The League of Women Voters is looking for volunteers to work at the various polling places during the upcoming elections. If you think you will be able to volunteer your time, please fill out and mail the following enclosed items: registration form, schedule of availability, and insurance waiver form.

¶ After I receive these items, I will contact you to confirm a location, time, and date.

¶ Your efforts are greatly appreciated, Mrs. McGraw. Concerned citizens like you make it possible for the public to have a convenient place to vote. Thank you for your interest in this very worthy cause!

Sincerely yours, | Ashley Abbott | Public Relations Volunteer | urs | Enclosures

Unit 8

Tables

LESSON 36
Boxed Tables

LESSON 37
Open Tables With Titles

LESSON 38
Open Tables With Column Headings

LESSON 39
Ruled Tables With Number Columns

LESSON 40
Formatting Review

PERSONAL ASSET ACCOUNTS
Wanda Nelson

Account	Amount	Interest Rate
Interest Checking	$ 972.55	3.10%
Money Market	4,500.35	4.90%
	3,250.76	5.07%
sit	550.00	7.41%

GENERAL EQUITY MUTUAL FUNDS

Fund	Current
Duncan Insurance	16.3%
Strident Nova	9.3%
First Value	10.7%
Safeguard Policy	11.1%
Vanguard Life	8.5%

CABLE SERVICES AVAILABILITY

Type of Service	Currently Available
Basic	Phoenix
Lifeline	Scottsdale
Expanded	Glendale
Expanded (per channel)	Camelback City

Boxed Tables

Goals

- Type at least 35wpm/3′/4e
- Format boxed tables

A. Type 2 times.

A. WARMUP

```
     A plain paper reader/printer must be ordered; it must      11
accept jackets and have a footprint of 15 x 27* (*inches).      23
Please ask Gary to request Model Z-340 whenever he arrives.     35
|  1  |  2  |  3  |  4  |  5  |  6  |  7  |  8  |  9  |  10  |  11  |  12
```

SKILLBUILDING

B. Take three 12-second timed writings on each line. The scale below the last line shows your wpm speed for a 12-second timed writing.

B. 12-SECOND SPEED SPRINTS

```
The book that is on top of the big desk will be given away.
Bill must pay for the tape or he will have to give it back.
They left the meeting after all of the group had gone away.
The third person to finish all of the work today may leave.
    5    10    15    20    25    30    35    40    45    50    55    60
```

C. DIAGNOSTIC PRACTICE: SYMBOLS AND PUNCTUATION

If you are not using the GDP software, turn to page SB-2 and follow the directions for this activity.

D. Take two 3-minute timed writings. Review your speed and errors.

Goal: At least 35wpm/3′/4e

D. 3-MINUTE TIMED WRITING

```
     Technology that tracks eye movements is used by Web          11
designers to judge how people interact with Web pages. It         22
must find out which zone of the page is viewed first, which       34
feature is viewed most often, and how quickly a page comes        46
to the screen.                                                    49
     Eye movements are tracked by use of hardware and data        60
analysis software. A camera is employed to find out the eye       72
movements of people who watch a screen. Pupil dilations and       84
scanning patterns of the eyes are measured to document the        96
amount of mental strain that has been exerted.                   105
|  1  |  2  |  3  |  4  |  5  |  6  |  7  |  8  |  9  |  10  |  11  |  12
```

FORMATTING

E. BASIC PARTS OF A TABLE

- Tables have vertical columns (identified by a letter in the illustration) and horizontal rows (identified by a number in the illustration).
- A cell, or "box," is created where a column and a row intersect.
- Tables formatted with borders all around (as shown in the illustration) are called boxed tables.
- Tables formatted with no borders are called open tables.
- Center a table vertically when it appears alone on the page.
- Center a table horizontally if the cell widths have been adjusted automatically to fit the contents.

Note: You will learn to center tables vertically and horizontally in Lesson 38.

↓ center page

14 pt **ALASKAN VACATIONS** 12 pt↓ **Sailing Dates and Prices** ↓1X				Row 1
↓1X **Northern Departures**	**Interior Stateroom**	**Ocean View Stateroom**	↓1X **Guest**	Row 2
January 12	$599	$699	$ 99	Row 3
February 14	599	699	99	Row 4
March 11	699	799	199	Row 5
April 2	699	799	199	Row 6
May 11	699	799	299	Row 7
June 6	799	899	399	Row 8
July 1	799	899	399	Row 9
August 21	799	899	399	Row 10
Column A	Column B	Column C	Column D	

TITLE. Center and type in all-caps and bold, with a 14-point font. If there is no subtitle, insert 1 blank line after the title.

SUBTITLE. Center on the line below the title, and type in upper- and lowercase letters and bold. Press Enter 1 time to insert a blank line below the subtitle.

HEADING BLOCK. Title and subtitle.

COLUMN HEADINGS. Center or left-align (for text) or right-align (for numbers). Press ENTER to split a 2-line column heading or to move a 1-line column heading down 1 line.

COLUMN ENTRIES. Align text entries at the left; align number entries at the right. Capitalize only the first word and proper nouns. Add spaces after the dollar sign to align with the widest column entry below (add 2 spaces for each digit and 1 space for each comma).

Word Processing Manual

F. WORD PROCESSING: TABLE—INSERT AND AUTOFIT TO CONTENTS

Study Lesson 36 in your word processing manual. Complete all of the shaded steps while at your computer. Then format the jobs that follow.

DOCUMENT PROCESSING

Table 36-1

Boxed Table

Simple tables often do not have titles, subtitles, or column headings.

1. Insert a boxed table with 3 columns and 3 rows.
2. Left-align all column entries.
3. Automatically adjust the column widths for all columns.

Mary Spangler	President	Administration
Joyce Moore	Dean	Jefferson Hall
Thelma Day	Chairperson	Da Vinci Hall

Table 36-2
Boxed Table

1. Insert a boxed table with 2 columns and 4 rows.
2. Left-align all column entries.
3. Automatically adjust the column widths for all columns.

Marie Covey, Executive Editor	Santa Clarita, California
Albert Russell, Associate Editor	Newport, Rhode Island
Bob Harris, Contributing Writer	St. Louis, Missouri
Sylvestra Zimmerly, Art Director	Albuquerque, New Mexico

Table 36-3
Boxed Table

1. Open the file for Table 36-2.
2. Change the name and title in Row 4, Column A, to `Theodore Easton, Film Editor.`
3. Change the city in Row 4, Column B, to `Socorro.`

Table 36-4
Boxed Table

Barbara Azar	Professor	Computer Technologies
Ken Kennedy	Professor	Foreign Languages
Bonnie Marquette	Instructor	Computer Technologies
Kevin Nguyen	Assistant	Social Sciences

Strategies for Career Success

Nonverbal Communication

"It's not what he said, but how he said it." More than 90 percent of your spoken message contains nonverbal communication that expresses your feelings and desires. People respond to this nonverbal language.

Posture can convey your mood. For example, leaning toward a speaker indicates interest. Leaning backward suggests dislike or indifference. Your handshake, an important nonverbal communicator, should be firm but not overpowering.

Your head position provides many nonverbal signals. A lowered head usually expresses shyness or withdrawal. An upright head conveys confidence and interest. A tilted head signifies curiosity or suspicion. Nodding your head shows positive feeling, while left-right head shakes signify negative feeling. Your face strongly expresses your emotions. Narrow, squinting eyes signify caution, reflection, or uncertainty. Wide-open eyes convey interest and attention.

YOUR TURN Turn off the sound on a television program. How much of the plot can you understand just from the nonverbal communication signals?

Lesson 37

Open Tables With Titles

Goals

- Improve speed and accuracy
- Refine language arts skills in punctuation
- Format open tables with titles

A. Type 2 times.

A. WARMUP

```
     The check for $432.65 wasn't mailed on time! Late    10
charges of up to 10% can be expected. To avoid a sizable  22
penalty, just send an e-mail message to quickpay@epay.com. 33
| 1 | 2 | 3 | 4 | 5 | 6 | 7 | 8 | 9 | 10 | 11 | 12
```

SKILLBUILDING

B. Take a 1-minute timed writing on the first paragraph to establish your base speed. Then take four 1-minute timed writings on the remaining paragraphs. As soon as you equal or exceed your base speed on one paragraph, advance to the next, more difficult paragraph.

B. SUSTAINED PRACTICE: ROUGH DRAFT

```
     Various human responses are asymmetrical. This means    11
that we ask more from one side of the body than the other    23
each time we wave, wink, clap our hands, or cross our legs.  35

     Each one of these actions demands a clear desision,     11
usually unconscious and instantaneous, to start the course   23
of moving parts of the body in different directions.        34

All children go though remarkably involved steps as they     12
develop their preferried. As children grows she or he may   23
favor the right hand, the left, or both the same at times.   35

When most kids are eihgt or seven, stability ocurrs,         11
and one hand is permanently dominent over the other. Fore   22
some unnown reason, choose the right hand.                  34
| 1 | 2 | 3 | 4 | 5 | 6 | 7 | 8 | 9 | 10 | 11 | 12
```

C. PACED PRACTICE

If you are not using the GDP software, turn to page SB-14 and follow the directions for this activity.

LANGUAGE ARTS

D. Study the rules at the right.

D. APOSTROPHE

Note: The callout signals in the left margin indicate which language arts rule from this lesson has been applied.

RULE ▶ ' singular

Use *'s* to form the possessive of singular nouns.

The hurricane's force caused major damage to North Carolina's coastline.

RULE ▶ ' plural

Use only an apostrophe to form the possessive of plural nouns that end in *s*.

The investors' goals were outlined in the stockholders' report.

But: The investors outlined their goals in the report to the stockholders.

But: The women's and children's clothing was on sale.

RULE ▶ ' pronoun

Use *'s* to form the possessive of indefinite pronouns (such as *someone's* or *anybody's*); do not use an apostrophe with personal pronouns (such as *hers, his, its, ours, their,* and *yours*).

She could select anybody's paper for a sample.

It's time to put the file back into its cabinet.

Edit the sentences to insert any needed punctuation.

16 The womans purse was stolen as she held her childs hand.
17 If the book is yours, please return it to the library now.
18 The girls decided to send both parents donations to school.
19 The childs toy was forgotten by his mothers good friend.
20 The universities presidents submitted the joint statement.
21 The four secretaries salaries were raised just like yours.
22 One boys presents were forgotten when he left the party.
23 If these blue notebooks are not ours, they must be theirs.
24 The plant was designed to recycle its own waste products.

FORMATTING

E. TABLE HEADING BLOCK

Note: The title and subtitle (if any) make up the table heading block.

To format a table heading block:

- Type the title centered in all-caps and bold, with a 14-point font in Row 1 of the table. If the table does not have a subtitle, insert 1 blank line after the title.
- Type the subtitle (if any) with a 12-point font centered on the line below the title in upper- and lowercase letters in bold.
- Insert 1 blank line after the subtitle.

Word Processing Manual

F. WORD PROCESSING: TABLE—MERGE CELLS AND BORDERS

Study Lesson 37 in your word processing manual. Complete all of the shaded steps while at your computer. Then format the jobs that follow.

Table 37-5

Open Table

1. Insert a table with 2 columns and 5 rows.
2. Merge the cells in Row 1; then center and type the title in bold and all-caps, with a 14-point font.
3. Press ENTER once to insert 1 blank line after the title.
4. Left-align all column entries.
5. Automatically adjust the column widths for all columns.
6. Remove the table borders.

' singular

PC CONNECTION'S LOCATIONS

Valencia Mall	Santa Clarita, California
Town Center Square	Stevenson Ranch, California
Northridge Mall	Northridge, California
Granary Square	Valencia, California

Table 37-6

Open Table

1. Insert a table with 3 columns and 5 rows.
2. Merge the cells in Row 1; then center and type the title in bold and all-caps, with a 14-point font.
3. Press ENTER 1 time, change to a 12-point font, and type the subtitle centered in bold.
4. Press ENTER 1 time to insert 1 blank line after the subtitle.
5. Left-align all column entries.
6. Automatically adjust the column widths for all columns.
7. Remove the table borders.

' singular

' plural

NEWHALL DISTRICT'S REGISTRATION
Seniors' Schedule

Meadows	Monday, February 14	11 a.m.
Stevenson Ranch	Monday, February 21	10 a.m.
Old Orchard	Monday, February 28	11 a.m.
Wiley Canyon	Monday, March 7	10 a.m.

Table 37-7

Open Table

' singular

1. Insert a table with 2 columns and 6 rows.
2. Use standard table format for an open table with a title and subtitle.

MAR VISTA REALTY'S TOP SELLERS
First Quarter

James Kinkaid	Santa Clarita
Deborah Springer	Northbridge
Patricia Morelli	Woodland Hills
Jan McKay	Malibu
Daniel Aboud	San Luis Obispo

Open Tables With Column Headings

Goals

- Type at least 35wpm/3′/4e
- Format open tables with column headings

A. Type 2 times.

A. WARMUP

Jerry wrote a great article entitled "Interviewing 10
Techniques" on pp. 23 and 78! A&B@bookstore.com expected a 22
sizable number of requests; thus far, 65% have been sold. 33

| 1 | 2 | 3 | 4 | 5 | 6 | 7 | 8 | 9 | 10 | 11 | 12

SKILLBUILDING

B. Take three 12-second timed writings on each line. The scale below the last line shows your wpm speed for a 12-second timed writing.

B. 12-SECOND SPEED SPRINTS

Blake was paid to fix the handle on the bowls that he made.
Alan led the panel of four men until the work was all done.
Jan will sign this paper when she has done all of the work.
They will focus on their main theme for the last six weeks.

5 | 10 | 15 | 20 | 25 | 30 | 35 | 40 | 45 | 50 | 55 | 60

C. PROGRESSIVE PRACTICE: ALPHABET

If you are not using the GDP software, turn to page SB-7 and follow the directions for this activity.

D. Take two 3-minute timed writings. Review your speed and errors.

Goal: At least 35wpm/3′/4e

D. 3-MINUTE TIMED WRITING

Telecommuting is a word you may have heard before but 11
do not quite understand. Very simply, it means working at 23
home instead of driving in to work. Many people like the 34
convenience of working at home. They realize they can save 46
money on expenses like gas, food, and child care. 56
Most home office workers use a computer in their job. 67
When their work is done, they can just fax or e-mail it to 79
the office. If they must communicate with other workers, 90
they can use the phone, fax, or computer and never have to 102
leave your home. 105

| 1 | 2 | 3 | 4 | 5 | 6 | 7 | 8 | 9 | 10 | 11 | 12

FORMATTING

Reference Manual

E. COLUMN HEADINGS

Column headings describe the information contained in the column entries. Refer to page R-13A in the Reference Manual for an illustration of column headings.

To format column headings:

- Type the column headings in upper- and lowercase letters and bold.
- If a table has a combination of 1- and 2-line column headings, press ENTER 1 time before typing the 1-line column heading to push the heading down so that it aligns vertically at the bottom of the cell.
- Center column headings in tables with all-text columns.
- Left-align column headings in a column with all text.
- Right-align column headings in a column with all numbers.

Word Processing Manual

F. WORD PROCESSING: TABLE—CENTER HORIZONTALLY AND CENTER PAGE

Study Lesson 38 in your word processing manual. Complete all of the shaded steps while at your computer. Then format the jobs that follow.

DOCUMENT PROCESSING

Table 38-8

Open Table

Note: Center all tables horizontally and vertically from now on.

1. Insert a table with 2 columns and 6 rows.
2. Type the title block in standard table title block format.
3. Type the column headings centered in upper- and lowercase letters and bold.
4. Left-align the column entries.
5. Automatically adjust the column widths for all columns.
6. Remove all table borders.

↓center page

VENDOR LIST
July 1, 20-- ↓1X

Product	**Vendor**
Laser printers	Office Supplies Unlimited
Workstations	PC Junction, Inc.
Cell phones	Satellite Communications
Scanners	Atlantic-Pacific Digital

Table 38-9

Open Table

1. Insert a table with 2 columns and 6 rows.
2. Type the title block in standard table title block format.
3. Type the column headings centered in upper- and lowercase letters and bold.
4. In Column A, press ENTER 1 time to split the column heading into two lines as shown.
5. In Column B, press ENTER 1 time before typing the 1-line column heading to push the heading down so that it aligns vertically at the bottom of the cell.
6. Left-align the column entries.
7. Automatically adjust the column widths for all columns.
8. Remove all table borders.

Press ENTER to create a column heading of 2 lines or to move a single-line heading down 1 line.

COMMITTEE ASSIGNMENTS

Academic Committee Assignments	**Professor**
Institutional Integrity	Anne McCarthy
Educational Programs	Bill Zimmerman
Student Services	John Yeh
Financial Resources	Steve Williams

Table 38-10

Open Table

1. Open the file for Table 38-8.
2. Change the date to `September 30.`
3. Change the 4 products in Column A as follows:

```
Copiers
Processors
Controller cards
Modems
```

Table 38-11

Open Table

CABLE SERVICES AVAILABILITY ↓1X

Type of Service	**Currently Available**
Basic	Phoenix
Lifeline	Scottsdale
Expanded	Glendale
Expanded (per channel)	Camelback City

Ruled Tables With Number Columns

Goals

- Improve speed and accuracy
- Refine language arts skills in spelling
- Format ruled tables with number columns

A. Type 2 times.

A. WARMUP

Does Xavier know that around 8:04 a.m. his July sales 11
quota was realized? Invoice #671 indicates a 9% increase! 23
Several of the employees weren't able to regain their lead. 34
| 1 | 2 | 3 | 4 | 5 | 6 | 7 | 8 | 9 | 10 | 11 | 12

SKILLBUILDING

B. Type the paragraph 2 times. Use the CAPS LOCK key to type a word or series of words in all-caps. Tap the CAPS LOCK key with the A finger.

B. TECHNIQUE PRACTICE: SHIFT KEY AND CAPS LOCK

The new computer has CD-ROM, PCI IDE HDD controller,
and an SVGA card. Mr. J. L. Jones will order one from PC
EXPRESS out of Orem, Utah. IT ARRIVES NO LATER THAN JULY.

PPP PRETEST → PRACTICE → POSTTEST

PRETEST
Take a 1-minute timed writing. Review your speed and errors.

C. PRETEST: Horizontal Reaches

The chief thinks the alarm was a decoy for the armed 11
agent who coyly dashed away. She was dazed as she dodged 22
a blue sedan. He lured her to the edge of the high bluff. 33
| 1 | 2 | 3 | 4 | 5 | 6 | 7 | 8 | 9 | 10 | 11 | 12

PRACTICE
Speed Emphasis:
If you made 2 or fewer errors on the Pretest, type each *individual* line 2 times.
Accuracy Emphasis:
If you made 3 or more errors, type each *group* of lines (as though it were a paragraph) 2 times.

D. PRACTICE: In Reaches

oy foyer loyal buoys enjoy decoy coyly royal cloy ploy toys
ar argue armed cared alarm cedar sugar radar area earn hear
lu lucid lunch lured bluff value blunt fluid luck lush blue

E. PRACTICE: Out Reaches

ge geese genes germs agent edges dodge hinge gear ages page
da daily dazed dance adapt sedan adage panda dash date soda
hi hints hiked hired chief think ethic aphid high ship chip

POSTTEST
Repeat the Pretest timed writing and compare performance.

F. POSTTEST: Horizontal Reaches

LANGUAGE ARTS

G. Type these frequently misspelled words, paying special attention to any spelling problems in each word.

G. SPELLING

```
16 prior activities additional than faculty whether first with
17 subject material equipment receiving completed during basis
18 available please required decision established policy audit
19 section schedule installation insurance possible appreciate
20 benefits requirements business scheduled office immediately
```

Edit the sentences to correct any misspellings.

```
21 We requierd the office to schedule all prior activities.
22 The business scheduled the instalation of the equipment.
23 The decision established the basis of the insurance policy.
24 Please audit any additionl material available to faculty.
25 If possible, they would appreciate recieving them soon.
26 Section requirements to receive benefits were completed.
```

FORMATTING

H. RULED TABLES WITH NUMBER COLUMNS

Review the use of borders in Lesson 37 or in your word processing manual as needed.

To format a ruled table with number columns:

1. Remove all table borders.
2. Apply borders to the top and bottom of Row 2 and to the bottom of the last row.
3. Right-align column headings and column entries with numbers.
4. If the column entry includes a dollar sign, add spaces after the dollar sign to align the dollar sign just to the left of the widest column entry below it as follows: add 2 spaces for each number and 1 space for each comma. In the example below, 3 spaces were added after the dollar sign.

Example:

$ 375
2,150
49

Word Processing Manual

I. WORD PROCESSING: TABLE—ALIGN TEXT IN A COLUMN

Study Lesson 39 in your word processing manual. Complete all of the shaded steps while at your computer. Then format the jobs that follow.

Table 39-12

Ruled Table

1. Insert a ruled table with 3 columns and 5 rows.
2. Type the heading block and table in standard table format.
3. Add spaces after the dollar sign as needed to align the dollar sign just to the left of the widest column entry below it.
4. Remove all table borders and apply borders to the top and bottom of Row 2 and to the bottom of the last row.

Highlighted words are spelling words from the language arts activity.

↓center page

NORTHERN BELL PHONES
Inside Wire Repair Service ↓1X

Per-Month Plan	Today's Rates	1995 Rates
Residence	$ .60	$1.00
Business	1.30	1.30
Private Line	3.50	4.50

Table 39-13

Ruled Table

1. Insert a ruled table with 4 columns and 7 rows.
2. Type the heading block and table in standard table format.
3. Add spaces after the dollar sign to align the dollar sign just to the left of the widest column entry below it.
4. Remove all table borders; then apply borders to the top and bottom of Row 2 and to the bottom of the last row.

To align the dollar sign correctly, add 2 spaces for each digit.

↓center page

HOLIDAY RESORT SUITES
Available Rates ↓1X

Hotel	Rack Rate	Club Rate	3-Night Savings
Porter Ranch Inn	$ 92.00	$36.00	$ 68.00
Jamaican Inn	119.00	59.50	178.50
Casitas Suites	120.00	60.00	180.00
The Desert Inn Resort	135.00	75.50	178.50
Sannibel Courtyard	150.00	75.00	225.00

Table 39-14

Ruled Table

GENERAL EQUITY MUTUAL FUNDS

Fund	Current Year	Previous Year
Duncan Insurance	16.3%	2.0%
Strident Nova	9.3%	3.5%
First Value	10.7%	12.1%
Safeguard Policy	11.1%	9.7%
Vanguard Life	8.5%	10.1%

Formatting Review

Goals

- Type at least 36wpm/3′/4e
- Format tables with a variety of features
- Format documents with a variety of features

A. Type 2 times.

A. WARMUP

```
     On July 15, a check for exactly $329.86 was mailed to   11
Zak & Quinn, Inc.; they never received Check #104. Does      22
Gary know if the check cleared the company's bank account?   34
|  1  |  2  |  3  |  4  |  5  |  6  |  7  |  8  |  9  |  10  |  11  |  12
```

SKILLBUILDING

B. MAP

Follow the GDP software directions for this exercise in improving keystroking accuracy.

C. DIAGNOSTIC PRACTICE: NUMBERS

If you are not using the GDP software, turn to page SB-5 and follow the directions for this activity.

D. Take two 3-minute timed writings. Review your speed and errors.

Goal: At least 36wpm/3′/4e

D. 3-MINUTE TIMED WRITING

```
     Employee complaints are often viewed as a negative       10
force in a workplace. In fact, these complaints should be     22
viewed as a chance to communicate with the employee and to    34
improve morale. To ignore the complaint does not make it go   46
away. If you just listen to complaints, you may help to       57
solve small problems before they turn into bigger ones.       68
     Often workers expect a chance to be heard by a person    79
who is willing to listen to them quite openly. That person    90
should recognize that the employee has concerns that need    102
to be addressed at this time.                                108
|  1  |  2  |  3  |  4  |  5  |  6  |  7  |  8  |  9  |  10  |  11  |  12
```

Report 40-11

Academic Report

RELATIONSHIPS AT WORK

Jensen Zhao

¶ Do you believe that as long as you get your work done at the end of the day, you have had a successful day on the job? If so, you are badly mistaken. Doing the work is only half the job. The other half is relating to and working with the people around you.

TAKE A TEAM APPROACH

¶ Everything you do and every action you take affects those around you in a close working relationship. Operating as a team means thinking about others and taking actions that will help them reach their goals and achieve the goals of the company.

MAINTAIN A SPIRIT OF COOPERATION

¶ When you work in a spirit of cooperation, those around you will reflect that spirit. Your job will be easier because you will minimize resistance. It takes much more energy to resist one another than it does to cooperate and work together.

VALIDATE THE OPINIONS OF OTHERS

¶ You will find that this simple act of validation will go a long way in helping the spirit of your coworkers. Here are two simple ways to validate the opinions of others:

1. Take time to listen to the issues and accomplishments of those around you.
2. Reflect their opinions in your own words in a spirit of genuine interest.

There is a saying that states, "Your success is my success." Adopt this as your motto, and you will find a great deal of satisfaction at the end of each day.

Correspondence 40-20

Business Letter in Block Style

Note: Omit the return address on the envelope.

December 1, 20--| Mrs. Yvonne Spillotro | 105 North Field Avenue | Edison NJ 08837 | Dear mrs. Spillotro:

Thank you for choosing Insurance Alliance Of America. Open enrollment for your insurance medical plan is scheduled to begin the first day of January. I hope it was possible for you to review the materials you received last week. Selecting the right benefit plan for you and your family can be an over whelming task. To make this decision a little easier, I have enclosed a brochure with this letter summarizing the key features of each policy.

(Continued on next page)

Please call me if I can help in any way.

You might want to browse through our website at www.IAA.com for further details.

Sincerely, | Denise Broers | Customer Support | urs | enclosure

Table 40-15

Three-Column Boxed Table

Progress and Proofreading Check

Documents designated as Proofreading Checks serve as a check of your proofreading skill. Your goal is to have zero typographical errors when the GDP software first scores the document.

PERSONAL ASSET ACCOUNTS Wanda Nelson		
Account	**Amount**	**Interest Rate**
Interest Checking	$ 972.55	3.10%
Money Market	4,500.35	4.90%
Smart Saver	3,250.76	5.07%
Certificate of Deposit	550.00	7.41%

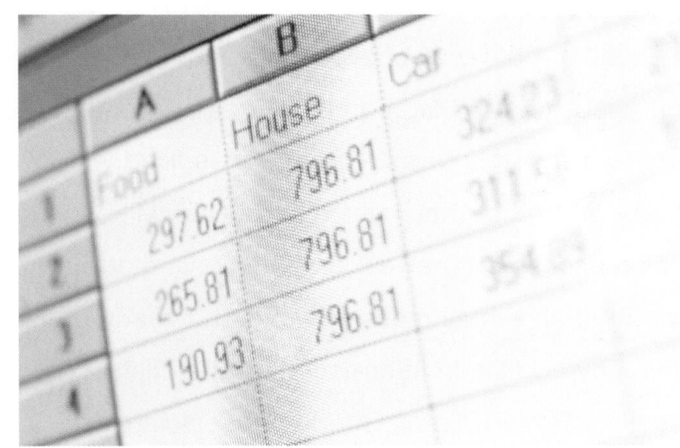

Skills Assessment on Part 2

3-Minute Timed Writing

From the first day of class, you have continuously 10
worked to improve your typing skill. You have worked hard 22
to increase your typing speed and accuracy. You have also 34
learned to format letters, memos, reports, and tables. All 46
of this work is quite an amazing accomplishment. 56
In your lessons, you have worked on learning a wide 66
range of word processing skills. You can expect to make 78
even more progress if you practice your skills regularly. 90
Learn as much as you can each day. Ask questions, and then 102
move toward a new goal each day. 108

| 1 | 2 | 3 | 4 | 5 | 6 | 7 | 8 | 9 | 10 | 11 | 12

Correspondence Test 2-21

Business Letter in Block Style

Note: Omit the return address on the envelope.

March 17 , 20-- | Ms. ~~Arlene~~ Dorothy Turner | Global Moving and Storage | 6830 Via Del Monte | San Jose, CA 95119 | Dear Ms. Turner:

¶ Thank you ~~you~~ for registering your pc Graphics software so promptly. As a registered user, you are entitled to free technical support 24 hours a day. The brochure enclosed will explain in detail how you can reach us ~~either~~ by fax, e-mail or phone whenever you need help. Also, help is always available on our website at www.pcgraphics.com. All our PC Graphics users will receive our monthly newsletter, which is filled with tips on using your new software and other material we know you will be interested in ~~seeing~~ reading. You can also access our newest graphics online at our Web site. Please call me or send me an e-mail message if you have any questions or would like to receive any additional information. Your satisfaction is our number 1 priority. Sincerely | Roy Phillips | Support Technician | urs | enclosure

Report Test 2-12

Academic Report

TELECOMMUTERS
Visibility at Work
Roy Phillips

¶ Have you ever wondered how to remain "visible" at work when you aren't there for most of the work week? This is a problem many telecommuters are struggling to overcome as

(Continued on next page)

more and more people do their work from home. We all know the advantages of working at home, but it may come with a heavy price unless you work smart. Here are some ways for telecommuters to increase visibility at work.

ATTEND KEY MEETINGS

¶ Make sure that you are notified by e-mail of all key meetings so that you can be sure to be there and make your opinions and your presence known. If meeting agendas or schedules normally are distributed through office mail, make sure there is a procedure in place that distributes these important documents electronically.

COMMUNICATE WITH YOUR SUPERVISOR

¶ Don't think that there is any virtue in keeping quiet about your accomplishments. Make your accomplishments known in an assertive, regular manner. This can be done easily in several different ways.

¶ E-Mail. Use e-mail messages or attachments to e-mail messages to summarize your accomplishments on a project. It would also be a good idea to send your list of work objectives for the week to your supervisor. When a project is finished, send the final documents related to the project. If a picture could help, invest in a digital camera or a scanner and attach a picture.

¶ Answering Machines and Pagers. Make it easy for your boss to contact you. Check your pager and answering machine frequently and return calls promptly. All of these techniques will help ensure your visibility when you aren't there.

Table Test 2-16

Boxed Table

SIENNA VILLA CONDOMINIUMS Association Fees		
Category	**Average Monthly Bill**	**Proposed Increase**
Insurance	$150	$25
Earthquake rider	75	32
Water	65	20
Landscaping	30	5

Part 3

Reports, Correspondence, and Employment Documents

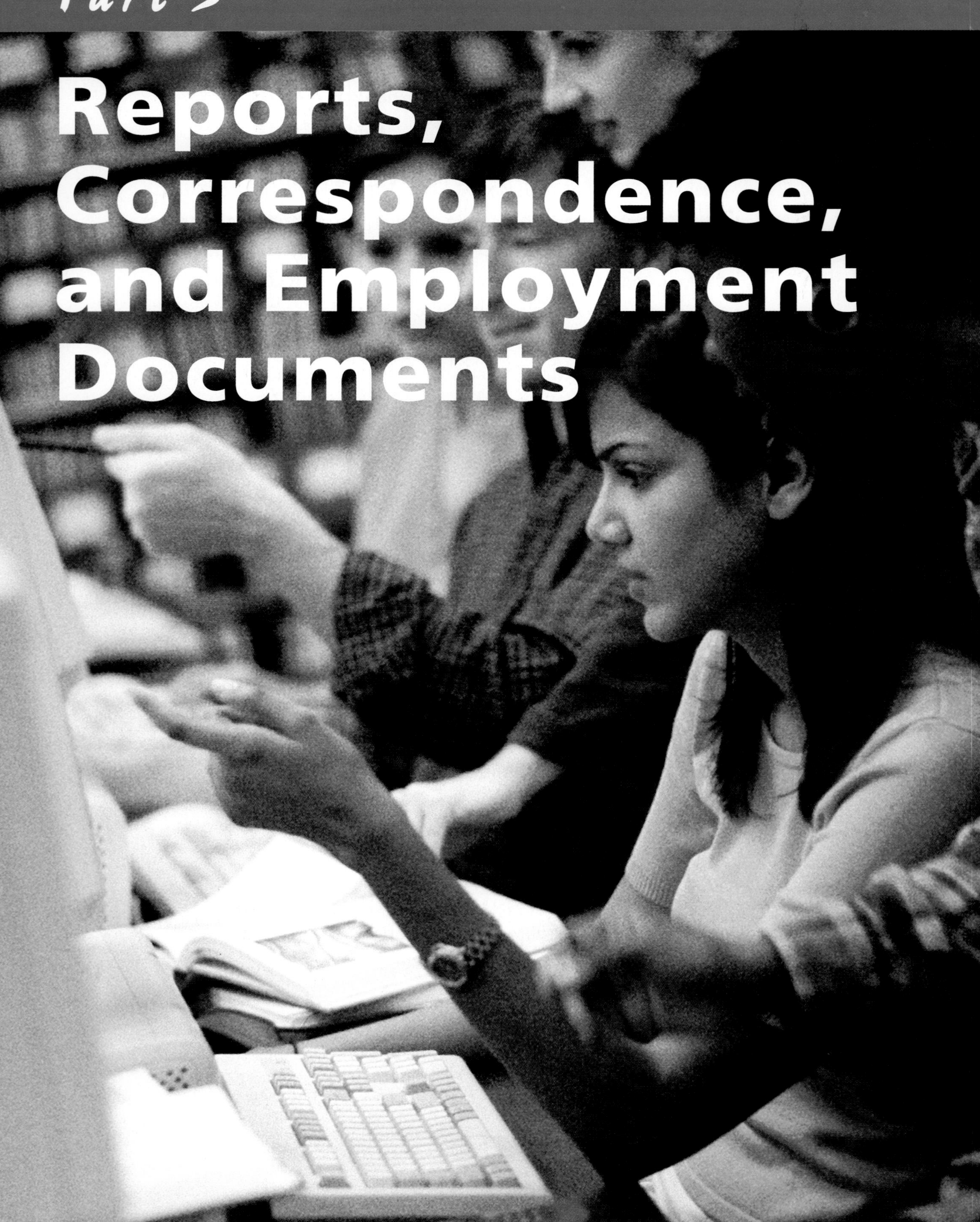

Keyboarding in Education Careers

The education field has many career opportunities, including positions such as teacher, counselor, teacher assistant, administrator, and curriculum designer. Although two of three workers in educational services have professional and related occupations, the education field employs many administrative support, managerial, and service workers.

Teacher assistants provide support for classroom teachers in many ways, allowing instructors more time for lesson planning and actual teaching. Teacher assistants also grade assignments and tests, check homework, keep attendance records, and perform typing, data entry, and filing. Office administration staff perform similar functions for the heads of departments in colleges and universities and for the principals and education boards of elementary and secondary schools.

The use of computer technology in the educational setting is constantly growing. Being proficient with a computer, including keyboarding and formatting skills, is essential for success in the field. The use of the Internet in classrooms has expanded greatly, helping instructors and students to communicate with each other, as well as to perform research for class assignments. Distance learning is growing, too. Increasing numbers of higher education institutions use Internet-based technology to post lessons and coursework electronically. *The Gregg College Keyboarding & Document Processing* text and software are good examples of this development.

Objectives

KEYBOARDING

- Type at least 40 words per minute on a 5-minute timed writing with no more than 5 errors.

LANGUAGE ARTS

- Refine proofreading skills and correctly use proofreaders' marks.
- Use punctuation and grammar correctly.
- Improve composing and spelling skills.

WORD PROCESSING

- Use the word processing commands necessary to complete the document processing activities.

DOCUMENT PROCESSING

- Format business and academic reports, personal-business letters, memos, business letters in modified-block style, and resumes.

TECHNICAL

- Answer at least 90 percent of the questions correctly on an objective test.

Unit 9

Reports

LESSON 41
Business Reports With Footnotes

LESSON 42
Reports in APA Style

LESSON 43
Reports in MLA Style

LESSON 44
Report Citations

LESSON 45
Preliminary Report Pages

Computer Generations 4

Fourth-Generation Computers

This generation is placed in the 1971 to 1999 time category. Again, computers became smaller and faster, and the Intel chip was responsible for most of the changes taking place in this 29-year period.

Enhancements in Speed

Because of the rapid miniaturization that took place with the chip, the CPU, memory, and input/output controls could now be placed on a single chip. Computers were becoming faster and faster, and they were being used in everyday items such as microwave ovens, televisions, and automobiles.

Commercial Applications

Word processing and spreadsheet applications made their debut in this generation, as did home and video game systems. Names such as Pac Man and Atari were very popular with computer users.

Fifth-Generation Computers

According to Allen, the turn of the century marks this generation, and it will be ... en word instructions, and superconductor technology, ... e or no resistance (2005, p. 130).

SHOPPING FOR A HOME

Luisa Rodriguez

Buying a home is a process that many of us will go thr... many other prospective buyers, we will experience this... in our working years. A home is typically the largest p... therefore deserves our careful attention.

"Most people think that the most important criterion i... The site should be on land that is well drained and fre... city zoning plan to determine if you have chosen a site... high water levels. You should also check to see if the g... considerably can cause cracks in foundations and walls...

Moreau suggests that a house survey be undertaken in...

> Key problems are encroachments such as trees, ... the house that overlap the property line or may ... The solution can be as simple as moving or rem...

The buying of a house is a major undertaking with a l... investigated. To ensure that the building is structurally... use the services of a building inspector.

The walls, ceiling, and floors (if you have a basement)... insulation. "Both the depth and 'R' factor need to be c... addition, cross braces should have been used between...

Check the roof carefully. Walk around the entire house... all roof lines and angles. Are there any shingles missin...

[1] James Nelson, "A New Home for the Millennium," *Home Plan...*

[2] Eva Bartlett, "Settlement Issues When Buying a New Home," ...

[3] "Home Construction in the 21st Century," *Family Living,* Octo...

[4] Karen Ostrowski, "A Short Course in Buying a Home," *Home...* Company, Boston, 2004, p. 37.

Computer Generations 3

A Brief History of Computer Generations

Joshua T. Reynolds

The invention of the computer did not occur in the past two centuries; in fact, the first computer was probably the abacus, which was used about 5,000 years ago in Asia Minor. As we know them today, computers were first used just after the Second World War, around 1945. Since then, several computer advancements have occurred that make it possible to classify computer power by one of the significant advancements that can be associated with particular time periods or generations. The .following paragraphs summarize the major developments that occurred in each of these generations.

First-Generation Computers

The first generation of computers generally runs from 1945 to 1956. During this time, the first vacuum tube computer, the ENIAC, was invented. The first commercial computer was called the UNIVAC, and it was used by the U.S. Census Bureau. It was also used to predict President Eisenhower's victory in the 1952 presidential election (Baker, 2003).

Second-Generation Computers

During this period, 1956 to 1963, computers were run by transistors. These computers were known for their ability to accept instructions for a specific function that could be stored in the computer's memory. This is also the period when COBOL and FORTRAN were used for computer operations. The entire software industry began in this generation.

Third-Generation Computers

This computer generation ran from 1964 to 1971, and it is characterized by the use of integrated circuits to replace the transistors of the previous generation. As a result of this invention, computers became smaller, faster, and more powerful (Diaz & Moore, 2004).

Business Reports With Footnotes

Goals:

- Improve speed and accuracy
- Refine language arts skills in using quotation marks and italics (or the underline)
- Format reports with footnotes

A. Type 2 times.

A. WARMUP

```
     Tag #743X was attached to a black jug that was 1/3     10
full of a creamy liquid. Tags #914Z and #874V were both     22
attached to beautiful large lamps (crystal and porcelain).  33
| 1 | 2 | 3 | 4 | 5 | 6 | 7 | 8 | 9 | 10 | 11 | 12
```

SKILLBUILDING

B. Take three 12-second timed writings on each line. The scale below the last line shows your wpm speed for a 12-second timed writing.

B. 12-SECOND SPEED SPRINTS

```
Joe must try to type as fast as he can on these four lines.
The screens were very clear, and the print was easy to see.
We will not be able to print the copy until later on today.
The disk will not store any of the data if it is not clean.
5 10 15 20 25 30 35 40 45 50 55 60
```

C. MAP

Follow the GDP software directions for this exercise in improving keystroking accuracy.

LANGUAGE ARTS

D. Study the rules at the right.

D. QUOTATION MARKS AND ITALICS (OR UNDERLINE)

RULE ▶ " direct quotation

Use quotation marks around a direct quotation.

Harrison responded by saying, "Their decision does not affect us."

But: Harrison responded by saying that their decision does not affect us.

RULE ▶ " title

Use quotation marks around the title of a newspaper or magazine article, chapter in a book, report, and similar terms.

The most helpful article I found was "Multimedia for All."

RULE ▶ *title* or title

Italicize (or underline) the titles of books, magazines, newspapers, and other complete published works.

Grisham's *The Brethren* was reviewed in a recent *USA Today* article.

RULE ▶ , direct quotation

Use a comma before and after a direct quotation.

James said, "I shall return," and then left.

(Continued on next page)

Edit the sentences to correct any errors in the use of quotation marks, italics, and commas.

8 The newspaper ad in the March 1 "Tribune" was very effective.
9 *The Power of e-Commerce* is an excellent chapter.
10 Maria answered the question by saying, "I agree."
11 Her title for the report was "The Internet in Action."
12 The magazine cover for "Newsweek" last month was excellent.
13 Karen interrupted by saying, That's exactly right!
14 The realtor replied "The first thing to consider is location."
15 "The margin of error is very small" said Andy.

FORMATTING

Reference Manual

If you want to format a report with endnotes instead of footnotes, study the illustration of endnotes on page R-8C and R-8D of the Reference Manual.

E. REPORTS WITH FOOTNOTES

Footnote references indicate the sources of facts or ideas used in a report. Although footnotes may be formatted in various ways, they have many characteristics in common:

1. Footnote references are indicated in the text by superior figures.
2. Footnotes are numbered consecutively throughout a report.
3. Footnotes appear at the bottom of the page on which the references appear.
4. A footnote should include the name of the author, the title of the book (italicized) or article (in quotation marks), the publisher, the place of publication, the year of publication, and the page number(s).

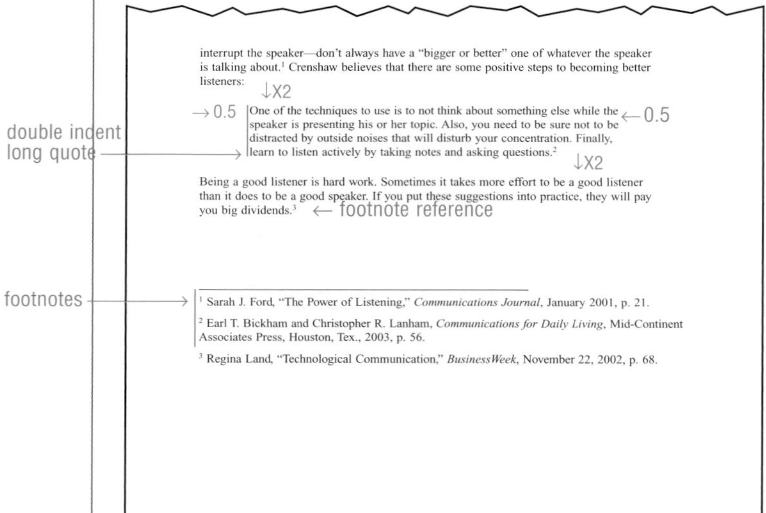

interrupt the speaker—don't always have a "bigger or better" one of whatever the speaker is talking about.[1] Crenshaw believes that there are some positive steps to becoming better listeners:

> One of the techniques to use is to not think about something else while the speaker is presenting his or her topic. Also, you need to be sure not to be distracted by outside noises that will disturb your concentration. Finally, learn to listen actively by taking notes and asking questions.[2]

Being a good listener is hard work. Sometimes it takes more effort to be a good listener than it does to be a good speaker. If you put these suggestions into practice, they will pay you big dividends.[3]

[1] Sarah J. Ford, "The Power of Listening," *Communications Journal*, January 2001, p. 21.

[2] Earl T. Bickham and Christopher R. Lanham, *Communications for Daily Living*, Mid-Continent Associates Press, Houston, Tex., 2003, p. 56.

[3] Regina Land, "Technological Communication," *BusinessWeek*, November 22, 2002, p. 68.

F. LONG QUOTATIONS

A paragraph of 4 or more lines that is quoted or considered essential to a report may be highlighted or displayed by using single-spacing and indenting the paragraph 0.5 inch from both the left and the right margins to make it stand out from the rest of the report.

Word Processing Manual

G. WORD PROCESSING: FOOTNOTES

Study Lesson 41 in your word processing manual. Complete all of the shaded steps while at your computer. Then format the jobs that follow.

Report 41-13

Business Report

" direct quotation

SHOPPING FOR A HOME

Luisa Rodriguez

¶ Buying a home is a proces that many of us will go through in our life time. If we are like many prospective buyers, we will experience this decision three or four major times in our working years. A home is typically the largest purchase we will make, and it deserves therefore our careful attention. ~~We must be certain to look carefully at all the information available to us.~~

¶ "Most people think that the important criteria in shopping for a home is its site,"[1] ~~says John Calendar.~~ The site should be on land that is well drained and free from ~~from~~ flooding ~~that can cause extensive damage~~. Check the ~~area~~ city zoning plan to determine if you have choosen a site that is free from flooding and highwater levels ~~that can cause extensive damage~~. You should also check to see if the ground is stable. Ground that shifts can cause cracks in foundations and walls.

¶ Moreau suggests that a ~~home~~ survey be undertaken in the early stages:

> Key problems are encroachments such as tees, buildings, or additions to the house that overlap the property line or may violate zoning regulations. The solution can be as simple as moving or removing trees or bushes ~~from the front or back of your house.~~[2]

¶ The buying of a house is a major under taking with a long list of items that must be investigated. To ensure that the building is structurally sound, many prospective buyers use the services of a building inspector.

¶ The walls, ceiling, and floors need to be checked for proper insulation. "Both depth and 'r' factor need to be checked for proper levels."[3] In addition, crossbraces should have been used between the beams supporting a floor.

(Continued on next page)

¶ Carefully check the roof. Walk around the entire house so that you have a clear view of all roof lines and angles. Are there any shingles missing or is there water damage?[4]

" title — [1] James Nelson, "A New Home for the Millennium," *home planning magazine*, April 27, 2003, pp. 19-24.

title — [2] Eva Bartlett, "Settlement Issues when Buying a New Home," *Home Finances*, 2002 July, p. 68.

" title — [3] "Home Construction in the 21st Century," *Family Living*, October 9, 2002, p. 75

title — [4] Karen Ostrowski, "A Short Course in Buying a Home," *Homebuilders' Guide*, Kramer Publishing Company, Boston, 2004, p. 37.

Report 41-14

Business Report

Open the file for Report 41-13 and make the following changes:

1. Add these lines to the end of the final paragraph in the report:

    Finally, a thorough check should be made of the heating, cooling, and electrical systems in the home. "These features are as critical as any others to be examined."[5]

    ---

    [5] Maria Gonzalez, *Home Facilities Planning*, Bradshaw Publishing, Salt Lake City, Utah, 2003, p. 64.

2. Insert the footnote as indicated.
3. Remember to italicize book and magazine titles.

Keyboarding Connection

Inedible Cookies

Is that cookie good for you? A cookie is a short text entry stored on your computer that identifies your preferences to the server of the Web site you are viewing.

Certain Web sites use cookies to customize pages for return visitors. Only the information you provide or the selections you make while visiting a Web site are stored in a cookie. You can control how your browser uses cookies.

Use the Help feature in your browser to find out how to control cookies. Try using the keywords "cookie" or "security" when you search the Help index. You will probably find some great tips on how to increase security when working on the Internet.

YOUR TURN Access your browser's cookie policy defaults. Decide if you want to change them.

Reports in APA Style

Goals

- Type at least 36wpm/3′/3e
- Format reports in APA style
- Format author/year citations

A. Type 2 times.

A. WARMUP

The giant-size trucks, all carrying over 600 bushels, 11
were operating "around the clock"; quite a few of them had 23
dumped their boxes at Joe's during the last 18 to 20 hours. 35
| 1 | 2 | 3 | 4 | 5 | 6 | 7 | 8 | 9 | 10 | 11 | 12

SKILLBUILDING

B. PROGRESSIVE PRACTICE: ALPHABET

If you are not using the GDP software, turn to page SB-7 and follow the directions for this activity.

C. Type the paragraph 2 times, using your right thumb to press the SPACE BAR in the center.

C. TECHNIQUE PRACTICE: SPACE BAR

Dale is it. Adam is there. Mark is home. Eve was lost.
Helen can see. Faith can knit. Gayle can fly. Hal can type.
Fly the kite. Swim a mile. Close the door. Lift the weight.

D. Take two 3-minute timed writings. Review your speed and errors.

Goal: At least 36wpm/3′/3e

D. 3-MINUTE TIMED WRITING

The size of their first paycheck after they finish 10
college seems quite high to a few young men and women. They 22
rent a place to live that is just too much to pay, or they 34
may buy a car with a huge monthly payment. For some, it 45
takes a while to learn that there are other items in the 57
monthly budget. 60

Some other budget items are food, student loans, car 71
insurance, renters' insurance, credit card debt, health 82
insurance, utilities, and miscellaneous expenses. A good 93
goal is to put a regular amount from each paycheck into a 105
savings account. 108
| 1 | 2 | 3 | 4 | 5 | 6 | 7 | 8 | 9 | 10 | 11 | 12

Refer to page R-10A of the Reference Manual for additional guidance.

E. REPORTS FORMATTED IN APA STYLE

In addition to the traditional academic style, academic reports may also be formatted in APA (American Psychological Association) style. In the APA style, format the report as follows:

1. Use the default 1-inch top and bottom margins and change the left and right margins to 1 inch.
2. Double-space the entire report.
3. Insert a header for all pages; type a shortened title and insert an automatic page number that continues the page-numbering sequence from the previous page right-aligned inside the header.
4. Center and type the title and byline using upper- and lowercase letters. (Do not bold either the title or the byline.)
5. Indent all paragraphs 0.5 inch.
6. Type main headings centered, using upper- and lowercase letters. Press ENTER 1 time before and after the main heading.
7. Type subheadings at the left margin in italics using upper- and lowercase letters. Press ENTER 1 time before and after the subheading.

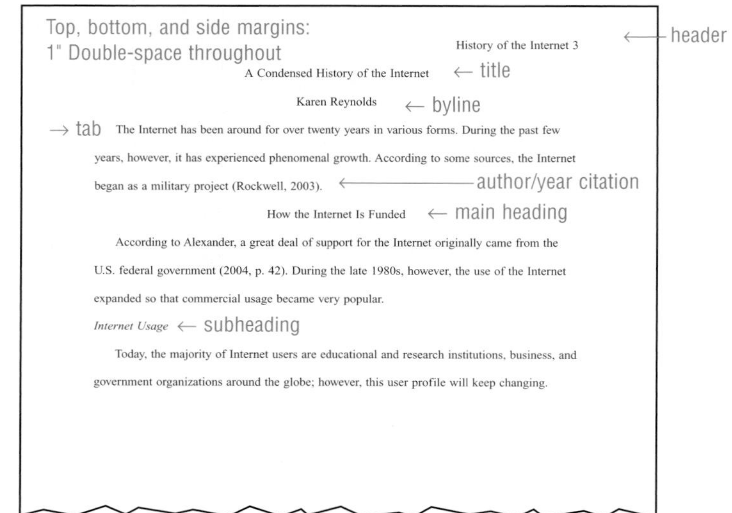

History of the Internet 3

A Condensed History of the Internet

Karen Reynolds

The Internet has been around for over twenty years in various forms. During the past few years, however, it has experienced phenomenal growth. According to some sources, the Internet began as a military project (Rockwell, 2003).

How the Internet Is Funded

According to Alexander, a great deal of support for the Internet originally came from the U.S. federal government (2004, p. 42). During the late 1980s, however, the use of the Internet expanded so that commercial usage became very popular.

Internet Usage

Today, the majority of Internet users are educational and research institutions, business, and government organizations around the globe; however, this user profile will keep changing.

F. AUTHOR/YEAR CITATIONS

Any information based on other sources and used in a report must be documented or cited. The author/year method of citation includes the source information in parentheses at the appropriate point within the text. For more detailed information on APA citations, refer to the illustrations in this book or consult the current APA style guide.

L. 27: Page Numbering

G. WORD PROCESSING: MARGINS, HEADERS, AND FOOTERS

Study Lesson 42 in your word processing manual. Complete all of the shaded steps while at your computer. Then format the jobs that follow.

Report 42-15

Report in APA Style

Remember to add a short title and page number right-aligned in a header.

Computer Generations 3

A Brief History of Computer Generations

Joshua T. Reynolds

¶ The invention of the computer did not occur in the past two centuries; in fact, the first computer was probably the abacus, which was used about 5,000 years ago in Asia Minor. As we know them today, computers were first used just after the Second World War, around 1945. Since then, several computer advancements have occurred that make it possible to classify computer power by one of the significant advancements that can be associated with particular time periods or generations. The following paragraphs summarize the major developments that occurred in each of these generations.

First-Generation Computers

¶ The first generation of computers generally runs from 1945 to 1956. During this time, the first vacuum tube computer, the ENIAC, was invented. The first commercial computer was called the UNIVAC, and it was used by the U.S. Census Bureau. It was also used to predict President Eisenhower's victory in the 1952 presidential election (Baker, 2003).

Second-Generation Computers

¶ During this period, 1956 to 1963, computers were run by transistors. These computers were known for their ability to accept instructions for a specific function that could be stored within the computer's memory. This is also the period when COBOL and FORTRAN were used for computer operations. The entire software industry began in this generation.

Third-Generation Computers

¶ This computer generation ran from 1964 to 1971, and it is characterized by the use of integrated circuits to replace the transistors from the previous generation. As a result of this invention, computers became smaller, faster, and more powerful (Diaz & Moore, 2004).

(Continued on next page)

Fourth-Generation Computers

¶ This generation is placed in the 1971 to 1999 time category. Again, computers became smaller and faster, and the Intel chip was responsible for most of the changes taking place in this 29-year period. Because of the rapid miniaturization that took place with the chip, the CPU, memory, and input/output controls could now be placed on a single chip. Computers were becoming faster and faster; and they were being used in everyday items such as microwave ovens, televisions, and automobiles.

Fifth-Generation Computers

¶ According to Allen, the turn of the century marks this generation, and it will be associated with artificial intelligence, spoken word instructions, and superconductor technology, which allows electricity to flow with little or no resistance (2005, p. 130).

Report 42-16

Report in APA Style

Open the file for Report 42-15 and make the following changes:

1. Place the insertion point at the end of the second sentence in the Fourth-Generation Computers paragraph, and press ENTER 1 time.
2. Type the subheading `Enhancements in Speed` in italics at the left margin; press ENTER 1 time.
3. Press TAB to indent the paragraph.
4. Move the insertion point to the end of the last sentence just above the Fifth-Generation Computers heading; press ENTER 1 time.
5. Type the subheading `Commercial Applications` in italics at the left margin; press ENTER 1 time.
6. Press TAB and type the following text as a paragraph under the new subheading:

```
Word processing and
spreadsheet applications
made their debut in this
generation, as did home
and video game systems.
Names such as Pac-Man and
Atari were very popular
with computer users.
```

Reports in MLA Style

Goals

- Improve speed and accuracy
- Refine language arts skills in composing sentences
- Format reports in MLA style

A. Type 2 times.

A. WARMUP

```
     "Baxter & Heimark, Inc., sold 82 new vehicles (47 cars  11
and 35 trucks) during June," the sales manager reported.     23
This is 16.9% of quarterly sales, an amazing achievement!    34
|  1  |  2  |  3  |  4  |  5  |  6  |  7  |  8  |  9  |  10  |  11  |  12
```

SKILLBUILDING

B. PROGRESSIVE PRACTICE: NUMBERS

If you are not using the GDP software, turn to page SB-11 and follow the directions for this activity.

C. Take a 1-minute timed writing on the first paragraph to establish your base speed. Then take four 1-minute timed writings on the remaining paragraphs. As soon as you equal or exceed your base speed on one paragraph, advance to the next, more difficult paragraph.

C. SUSTAINED PRACTICE: SYLLABIC INTENSITY

```
     Taking care of aging parents is not a new trend. This  11
issue has arisen more and more, since we are now living     22
longer. Companies are now trying to help out in many ways.  34
     Help may come in many ways, ranging from financial aid 12
to sponsoring hospice or in-home respite care. Workers may  24
find it difficult to work and care for aging parents.       35
     Why are employers so interested in elder care? Rising  11
interest is the result of a combination of several things.  23
The most notable is a marked increase in life expectancy.   34
     Another trend is the increased participation of women, 11
the primary caregivers, in the workforce. Businesses are    22
recognizing that work and family life are intertwined.      33
|  1  |  2  |  3  |  4  |  5  |  6  |  7  |  8  |  9  |  10  |  11  |  12
```

D. Answer each question with a complete sentence.

D. COMPOSING SENTENCES

16 What are your best traits that you will bring to your job when you graduate?
17 Would you like to work for a small company or a large company?
18 How much money will you expect to earn each month in your first job?
19 Would you like that first job to be in a small town or a large city?
20 As you begin your first job, what career goal will you have in mind?

Refer to page R-10C of the Reference Manual for additional guidance.

E. REPORTS FORMATTED IN MLA STYLE

In addition to the traditional academic style and APA style, academic reports may also be formatted in MLA (Modern Language Association) style. If citations are used, usually the author's last name and page number are cited inside parentheses. For more detailed information on MLA style, refer to the illustrations in this book or consult the current MLA style guide.

In the MLA style, format the report as follows:

1. Use the default 1-inch top and bottom margins and change the left and right margins to 1 inch.
2. Double-space the entire report.
3. Insert a header for all pages; type the author's last name and the page number right-aligned inside the header and positioned 0.5 inch from the top of the page.
4. Type each element of the heading information (your name, your instructor's name, the class name, and the date) on a separate line at the left margin.
5. Type the date day-month-year style (15 April 20--).
6. Center and type the title using upper- and lowercase letters.
7. Indent all paragraphs 0.5 inch.

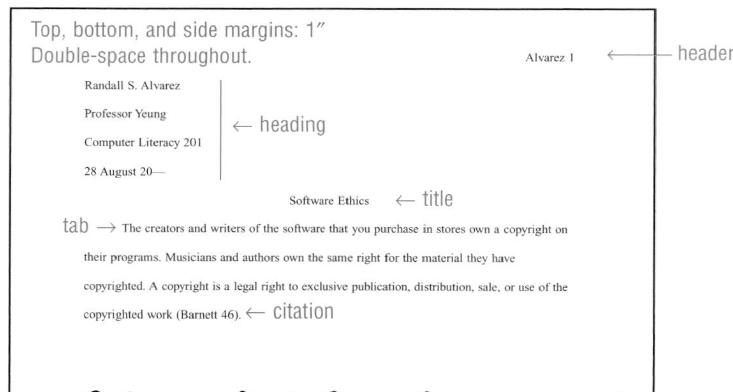
Top, bottom, and side margins: 1″
Double-space throughout.

Alvarez 1 ← header

Randall S. Alvarez
Professor Yeung
Computer Literacy 201
28 August 20— ← heading

Software Ethics ← title

tab → The creators and writers of the software that you purchase in stores own a copyright on their programs. Musicians and authors own the same right for the material they have copyrighted. A copyright is a legal right to exclusive publication, distribution, sale, or use of the copyrighted work (Barnett 46). ← citation

Report 43-17

Report in MLA Style

Remember to type the author's last name and page number right-aligned 0.5 inch from the top as a header. Remember to double-space the entire report.

Lee 1

Youn Suk Lee
Dr. Gloria Hernandez
Telecommunications 315
14 September 20--

Judging a Computer System

¶ Judging the effectiveness of a computer system has taken on a new dimension in the past few years, if for no other reason than the wide range of computer systems from which the user can select. It is, therefore, important that we investigate the criteria that should be considered in making this important decision.

¶ Probably the most obvious criterion to be considered when one purchases a computer system is speed. The value of a computer is directly related to its speed, and a computer's speed is typically measured in gigahertz (GHz). A gigahertz is one billion cycles per second, and many of today's microcomputers run in the range of 2 to 5 GHz (Kramer 173).

¶ Flexibility is especially important because of the rapid turnover of hardware and software in the computer industry. The flexibility of a computer system is important for two general reasons: to accommodate a variety of programs and to permit expandability. Hundreds and possibly thousands of software packages are available today to meet the needs of computer users. The computer you purchase must be able to accommodate this variety of software and be flexible enough to change with the increasing sophistication of software packages. Because of the substantial investment you make in a computer, you do not want to commit your resources to a computer that cannot be expanded to handle (1) newer, more powerful operating systems; (2) "memory-hungry" software packages; (3) network interfaces; and (4) additional users (Hartung and Kallock 239).

¶ A third consideration is convenience. Is it easy to learn how to operate your computer? Does the manufacturer stand by its warranty, and is it difficult to obtain repairs? How convenient is it to buy parts for your computer (such as memory boards and drives) if you want to expand your system? These questions need to be answered, and the answers should be weighed carefully before you purchase a new computer system.

Report 43-18

Report in MLA Style

Christina Espinoza

Professor Sakata

Introduction to E-commerce

9 April 20--

¶ The Internet is dramatically changing the way we shop. In years past, our shopping practices consisted of driving to a local mall or department store, walking through the aisles until we found an item we wished to purchase, and then making the purchase and driving home. Today, it is becoming more common to find shoppers doing their shopping via the Internet. Shopping on the Internet brings with it some cautions that we should observe when we shop. Here are some basic rules to follow when shopping on the Internet.

¶ When you are asked to enter information on your order, do not disclose personal information unless it is needed for shipping your order to you. Be sure you know who is collecting this information, why it is needed, and how it is going to be used. Be certain that the information asked for is actually necessary for the purchase. For example, there are few instances when your password should be disclosed.

¶ You should always verify that the company from whom you are purchasing has secured the purchasing procedures. You will often be asked to enter your credit card number to complete the purchase. Be certain that the transfer of this information is made in a secure environment. Also, be certain that you know the exact cost of the item for which you are being charged. The company from which you are purchasing the item should have a built-in calculator so that you know at all times how much your purchase will cost you, including all necessary shipping and handling charges.

¶ Understand exactly what you should do if you encounter a problem with your purchase online. Is there an easy way to contact the company? Does the company have an e-mail address you can use to contact a customer relations representative? Does the company's order page include a telephone number that you can call if you have questions about your order?

Report Citations

Goals

- Type at least 37wpm/3′/3e
- Format bibliographies, references, and works-cited pages

A. Type 2 times.

A. WARMUP

```
     The prize troops received the following extra gifts:     11
$20 from Larson's Bakery; $19 from Calsun, Ltd.;* $50 from    23
some judges; and quite a number of $5 gift certificates.      34
|  1  |  2  |  3  |  4  |  5  |  6  |  7  |  8  |  9  |  10  |  11  |  12
```

SKILLBUILDING

PPP PRETEST → PRACTICE → POSTTEST

PRETEST
Take a 1-minute timed writing. Review your speed and errors.

B. PRETEST: Vertical Reaches

```
     Kim knew that her skills at the keyboard made her a      11
top rival for that job. About six persons had seen her race   23
home to see if the mail showed the company was aware of it.   34
|  1  |  2  |  3  |  4  |  5  |  6  |  7  |  8  |  9  |  10  |  11  |  12
```

PRACTICE
Speed Emphasis:
If you made 2 or fewer errors on the Pretest, type each *individual* line 2 times.
Accuracy Emphasis:
If you made 3 or more errors, type each *group* of lines (as though it were a paragraph) 2 times.

C. PRACTICE: Up Reaches

```
se seven reset seams sedan loses eases serve used seed dose
ki skids kings kinks skill kitty kites kilts kite kids kick
rd board horde wards sword award beard third cord hard lard
```

D. PRACTICE: Down Reaches

```
ac races pacer backs ached acute laced facts each acre lace
kn knave knack knife knows knoll knots knelt knew knee knit
ab about abide label above abode sable abbey drab able cabs
```

POSTTEST
Repeat the Pretest timed writing and compare performance.

E. POSTTEST: Vertical Reaches

F. Take two 3-minute timed writings. Review your speed and errors.

Goal: At least 37wpm/3′/3e

F. 3-MINUTE TIMED WRITING

```
     Every business should have its code of ethics. A code   11
contains rules of conduct and moral guidelines that serve    23
the company and its employees. Some general ethics that may  35
be recognized in the code are equal and fair treatment,      46
truth, and zeal on the job.                                  51
     Companies may include a few rules in the code that      62
relate to their type of work. For example, if some laws      73
govern how they conduct business, an owner just might ask    85
employees to conduct all activities in a just and lawful     96
process. The code of business ethics should be equal for    107
all these workers.                                          111
| 1 | 2 | 3 | 4 | 5 | 6 | 7 | 8 | 9 | 10 | 11 | 12
```

FORMATTING

Reference Manual

Refer to page R-9B of the Reference Manual for additional guidance.

G. BIBLIOGRAPHIES

A bibliography is an alphabetic listing of all sources of facts or ideas used or cited in a report. The bibliography is typed on a separate page at the end of a report. In general, titles of major works like books or magazine titles are italicized, and titles of minor works like articles from magazines are typed in quotation marks. For more detailed information on entries in a bibliography, refer to the illustrations in this book or consult a current style guide.

To format a bibliography:

1. Press Enter 6 times to begin the first line approximately 2 inches from the top of the page.
2. Center and type BIBLIOGRAPHY in all-caps, 14-point font, and bold; then press Enter 2 times.
3. Set a hanging indent and type the first line. Each entry will begin at the left margin, and the carryover lines will automatically be indented 0.5 inch by the hanging indent.
4. Single-space each entry in the bibliography, and press Enter 2 times between each entry.

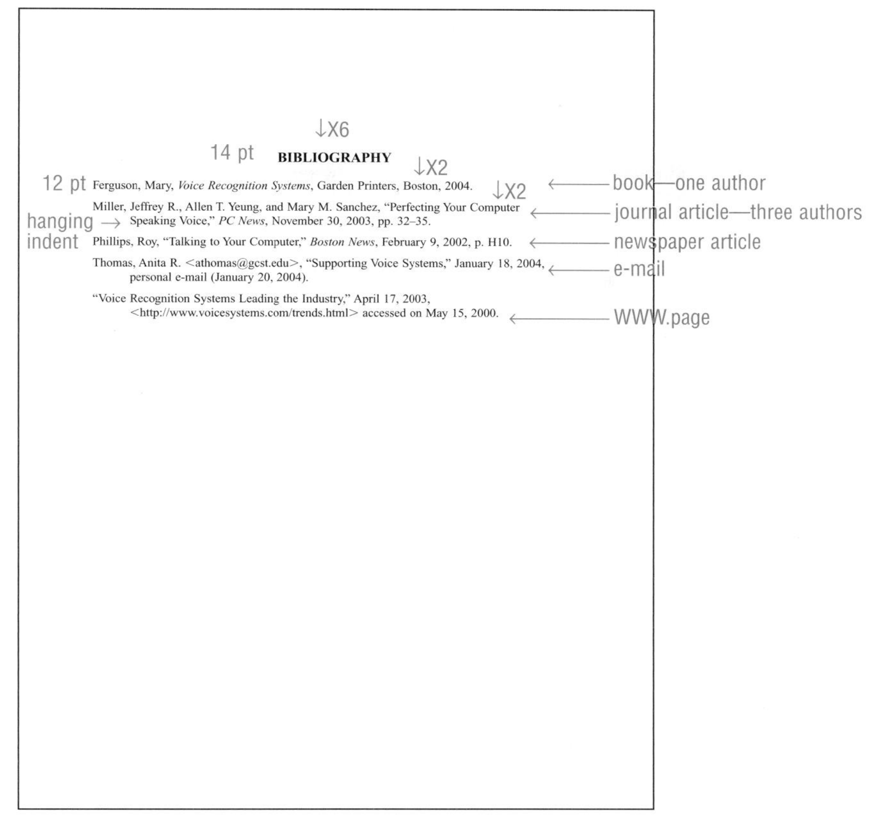

BIBLIOGRAPHY

Ferguson, Mary, *Voice Recognition Systems*, Garden Printers, Boston, 2004.

Miller, Jeffrey R., Allen T. Yeung, and Mary M. Sanchez, "Perfecting Your Computer Speaking Voice," *PC News*, November 30, 2003, pp. 32–35.

Phillips, Roy, "Talking to Your Computer," *Boston News*, February 9, 2002, p. H10.

Thomas, Anita R. <athomas@gcst.edu>, "Supporting Voice Systems," January 18, 2004, personal e-mail (January 20, 2004).

"Voice Recognition Systems Leading the Industry," April 17, 2003, <http://www.voicesystems.com/trends.html> accessed on May 15, 2000.

Refer to page R-10B of the Reference Manual for additional guidance.

H. REFERENCE LIST PAGES IN APA STYLE

A reference list is an alphabetic listing of all sources of facts or ideas used or cited in a report formatted in APA style. The reference list is typed on a separate page at the end of a report. For more detailed information on reference list entries, refer to the illustrations in this book or consult a current APA style guide.

To format an APA reference list page:

1. Use the default 1-inch top and bottom margins and change the left and right margins to 1 inch.
2. Double-space the entire page.
3. Insert a header, type a shortened title, and insert an automatic page number that continues the page-numbering sequence from the previous page right-aligned inside the header.
4. Center and type `References` at the top of the page; then press ENTER 1 time.
5. Set a hanging indent and type the first line. Each reference will begin at the left margin, and the carryover lines will automatically be indented 0.5 inch by the hanging indent.

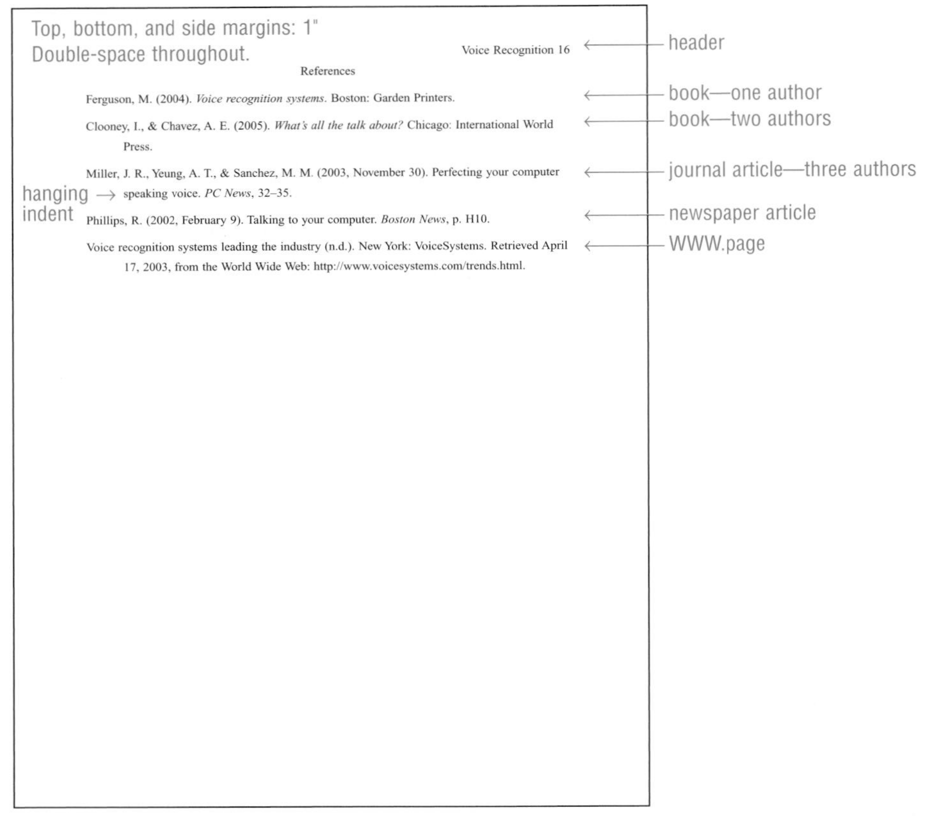
Voice Recognition 16

References

Ferguson, M. (2004). *Voice recognition systems*. Boston: Garden Printers.

Clooney, I., & Chavez, A. E. (2005). *What's all the talk about?* Chicago: International World Press.

Miller, J. R., Yeung, A. T., & Sanchez, M. M. (2003, November 30). Perfecting your computer speaking voice. *PC News*, 32–35.

Phillips, R. (2002, February 9). Talking to your computer. *Boston News*, p. H10.

Voice recognition systems leading the industry (n.d.). New York: VoiceSystems. Retrieved April 17, 2003, from the World Wide Web: http://www.voicesystems.com/trends.html.

Refer to page R-10D of the Reference Manual for additional guidance.

I. WORKS-CITED PAGES IN MLA STYLE

A works-cited page is an alphabetic listing of all sources of facts or ideas used or cited in a report formatted in MLA style. This reference list is typed on a separate page at the end of a report. For more detailed information on reference list entries, refer to the illustrations in this book or consult a current MLA style guide.

To format a works-cited page:

1. Use the default 1-inch top and bottom margins and change the left and right margins to 1 inch.
2. Double-space the entire page.
3. Insert a header, type the author's last name, insert an automatic page number that continues the page-numbering sequence from the previous page right-aligned inside the header positioned 0.5 inch from the top of the page, and close the header.
4. Type `Works Cited` centered at the top of the page; then press ENTER 1 time.
5. Set a hanging indent and type the first line at the left margin; the carryover lines will automatically be indented 0.5 inch by the hanging indent.

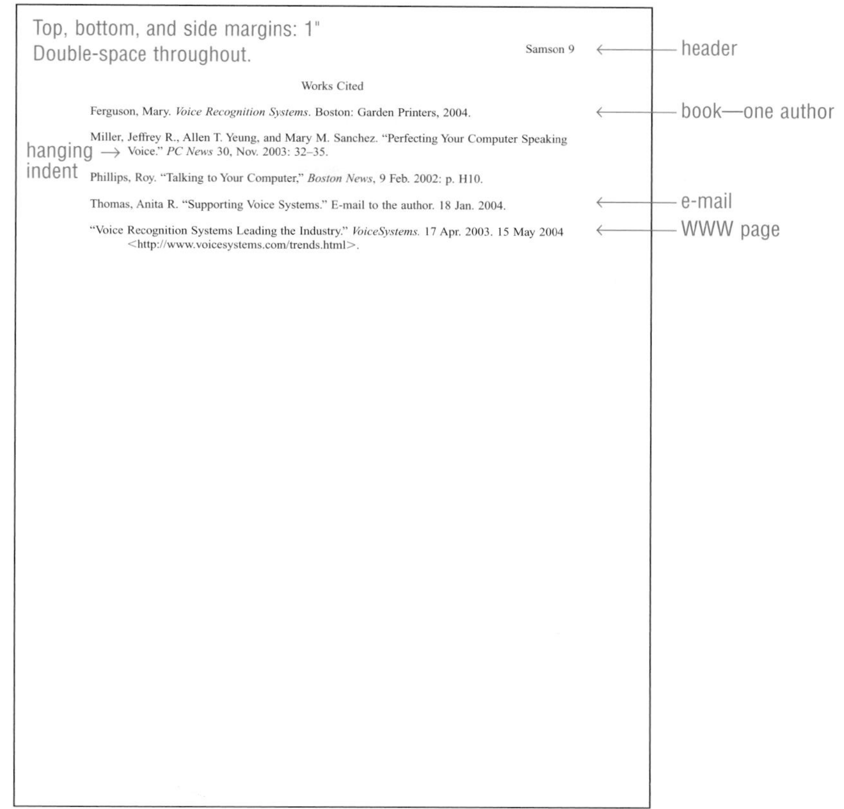

Samson 9

Works Cited

Ferguson, Mary. *Voice Recognition Systems*. Boston: Garden Printers, 2004.

Miller, Jeffrey R., Allen T. Yeung, and Mary M. Sanchez. "Perfecting Your Computer Speaking Voice." *PC News* 30, Nov. 2003: 32–35.

Phillips, Roy. "Talking to Your Computer," *Boston News*, 9 Feb. 2002: p. H10.

Thomas, Anita R. "Supporting Voice Systems." E-mail to the author. 18 Jan. 2004.

"Voice Recognition Systems Leading the Industry." *VoiceSystems*. 17 Apr. 2003. 15 May 2004 <http://www.voicesystems.com/trends.html>.

Word Processing Manual

J. WORD PROCESSING: HANGING INDENT

Study Lesson 44 in your word processing manual. Complete all the shaded steps while at your computer. Then format the jobs that follow.

DOCUMENT PROCESSING

Report 44-19

Bibliography

Italicize publication titles rather than underlining them.

BIBLIOGRAPHY

Bilanski, Charles R., "Corporate Structures in the New Millennium," Modern Management, Vol. 43, June 2003, pp. 43-46.

Calhoun, Josten C., Stockholders' Guide, Missouri Valley Press, St. Louis, 2003.

Dahlman, Leland, and Joyce C. Mahler, Trends for Boards of Directors, Vineyard Press, Boston, 2003.

Hammersmith Institute, Bold Positions of the New Administration, Hammersmith Institute Press, Baltimore, Md., 1999.

"Investing in the Corporate World," March 27, 2003, <http://www.efinance.com/invest/today'sworld.htm>, accessed on May 18, 2003.

Polaski, James S., "Summary of Investment Guide," e-mail message, October 10, 2003.

Report 44-20

References in APA Style

References

Chandler, R. D., & Thompson, A. S. (2002). *The evolution of America's economy in the late 1800's*. Westerville, OH: Glencoe/ McGraw-Hill. ~~Chapter 24, pp. 130-145.~~

Deming, W. H. (2003). Economists' guide to economic indicators. *The Economic Review, XVI*, 42-44.

Fortenberry, J. E., Kingston, A.E., & Worthington, S. O. (2004). *The environment of business*. Los Angeles: The University Press.

Meier, T. D., & Hovey, D. H. (2002). *economics on the world wide web*. Toronto: The Northern Press.

Tetrault, G. M. (2003). A guide for selecting economic indicators for the business entrepreneur. ~~*The Southern Economic Forecaster*, 23.~~

Zysmanski, R. J. (2004). *American capitalism and its impact on society*. San Francisco: Bay Press Area.

Report 44-21

Works Cited in MLA Style

Works Cited

Abernathy, Thomas R. "Welcome to the Internet." E-mail to the author. 19 Mar. 2005.

Benson, Lisa, et al. "E-commerce on the Net." *Online Observer*. Vol. 17. Sept. 2004: 144–146.

Cooper, Stanley. *Trends for the New Millennium*. Denver: Mountain Press, 2003.

Lawrence, Donna, and Becky Silversmith. *Surfer's Guide to the Internet*. Atlanta: Southern Publishers, 2005.

"Starting a Business on the Internet." *Entrepreneur*. 19 Dec. 2003. 12 June 2005 <http://www.entrepreneur.com/startups.htm>.

Tidwell, Joel, and Jean Swanson. "Things You Don't Know About the Internet." *New York Ledger*, 13 May 2004: C2.

Preliminary Report Pages

Goals

- Improve speed and accuracy
- Refine language arts skills in proofreading
- Format title pages and tables of contents

A. Type 2 times.

A. WARMUP

Did Kenny and Hazel see the first Sox ball game? I've 11
heard there were 57,268 people there (a new record). Your 23
home crowd was quiet when the game ended with a 4-9 loss. 34
| 1 | 2 | 3 | 4 | 5 | 6 | 7 | 8 | 9 | 10 | 11 | 12

SKILLBUILDING

B. PACED PRACTICE

If you are not using the GDP software, turn to page SB-14 and follow the directions for this activity.

C. DIAGNOSTIC PRACTICE: SYMBOLS AND PUNCTUATION

If you are not using the GDP software, turn to page SB-2 and follow the directions for this activity.

LANGUAGE ARTS

D. Study the proofreading techniques at the right.

D. PROOFREADING YOUR DOCUMENTS

Proofreading and correcting errors are essential parts of document processing. To become an expert proofreader:

1. Use the spelling feature of your word processing software to check for spelling errors; then read the copy aloud to see if it makes sense.
2. Proofread for all kinds of errors, especially repeated, missing, or transposed words; grammar and punctuation; and numbers and names.
3. Use the appropriate software command to see an entire page of your document to check for formatting errors such as line spacing, tabs, margins, and bold.

E. Compare this paragraph with the Pretest on page 137. Edit the paragraph to correct any errors.

E. PROOFREADING

Kim new that her skills at the key board made her a top rivel for the job. About six persons had scene her race home to see if the male showd the company was awarre of it.

Refer to page R-7B of the Reference Manual for additional guidance.

F. TITLE PAGE

Reports may have a title page, which includes information such as the report title, to whom the report is submitted, the writer's name and identification, and the date. To format a title page, follow these steps:

1. Center the page vertically.
2. Center the title in all caps and bold, using a 14-point font.
3. Press ENTER 2 times; then center the subtitle in upper- and lowercase and bold, using a 12-point font.
4. Press ENTER 12 times; then center the words `Submitted to`.
5. Press ENTER 2 times; then center the recipient's name and identification on separate lines, single-spaced.
6. Press ENTER 12 times; then center `Prepared by`.
7. Press ENTER 2 times; then center the writer's name and identification on separate lines, single-spaced.
8. Press ENTER 2 times; then center the date.

center page↓

14 pt **A TECHNOLOGY ASSESSMENT OF THE GRANTLAND CORPORATION** ↓2X

12 pt↓ **The Status of Technology in the New Millennium** ↓12X

Submitted to ↓2X

Marcia Abernathy
Regional Manager
Grantland Corporation ↓12X

Prepared by ↓2X

Timothy R. Rassmussen
District V Manager
Grantland Corporation ↓2X

March 20, 20—

Refer to page R-7D of the Reference Manual for additional guidance.

G. TABLE OF CONTENTS

A table of contents is usually included in a long report. The table of contents identifies the major and minor sections of a report and includes page numbers preceded by dot leaders. Dot leaders are a series of periods that guide the reader's eye across the page to the page number at the right. To format a table of contents:

1. Press ENTER 6 times to begin the first line approximately 2 inches from the top of the page.
2. Center and type `CONTENTS` in all-caps, 14-point font, and bold; then press ENTER 2 times.
3. Set a left tab at 0.5 inch; then set a right tab at 6 inches with dot leaders.
4. Change to 12-point font and type the main heading in all-caps.
5. Press TAB 1 or 2 times as needed to insert dot leaders and to move to the right margin; then type the page number, and press ENTER 2 times.
6. Type the next main heading in a similar fashion. If the next item is a subheading, press TAB 1 time to indent the subheading 0.5 inch.
7. Type the subheading, and then press TAB to insert dot leaders and to move to the right margin; then type the page number, and press ENTER 1 time to type the next subheading or 2 times to type a new main heading.
8. Continue in like fashion until the table of contents is complete.

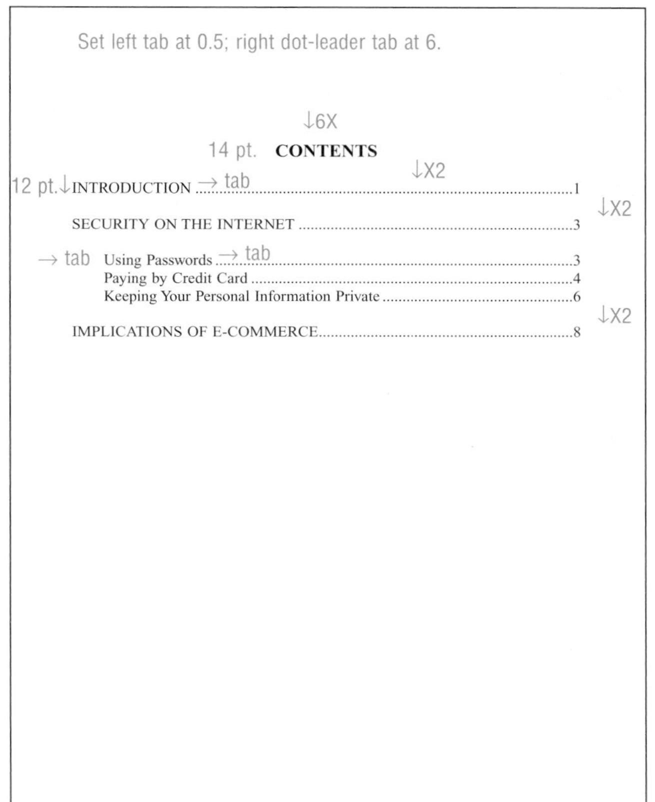

H. WORD PROCESSING: TAB SET—DOT LEADERS

Study Lesson 45 in your word processing manual. Complete all of the shaded steps while at your computer. Then format the jobs that follow.

Report 45-22

Title Page

↓center page

14 pt. **DISTANCE LEARNING CLASSROOMS** ↓2X

12 pt.↓ **Using Technology to Reach Students at a Distance** ↓12X

Prepared by ↓2X

Alicia T. Gonzalez
Technology Coordinator
T-Systems Media, Inc. ↓12X

February 19, 20--

Report 45-23

Table of Contents

Set left tab at 0.5; right dot-leader tab at 6.

↓6X

14 pt. **CONTENTS**

↓X2

Report 45-24

Title Page

Create a title page for the report below entitled LOOKING INTO THE 21ST CENTURY and a subtitle that reads Some Predictions for the New Millennium. The report is to be submitted to Alfredo Sanchez, District Manager, Millennium Concepts, Inc. The report is being prepared by Richard P. Morgan, Computer Consultant, Millennium Concepts, Inc. Use a date of May 18, 20--.

Report 45-25

Table of Contents

CONTENTS

Report 45-26

Business Report

Progress and Proofreading Check

Documents designated as Proofreading Checks serve as a check of your proofreading skill. Your goal is to have zero typographical errors when the GDP software first scores the document.

Do not indent paragraphs in a business report.

LOOKING INTO THE 21ST CENTURY

Some Predictions for the New Millennium

Evelyn Hasagawa

¶ It is predicted that computers will alter almost every activity of our lives in the first ten years of this millennium. There is strong evidence to suggest that this prediction will soon become a reality. This report will summarize the changes we will experience in the areas of artificial intelligence and the Internet.

ARTIFICIAL INTELLIGENCE

¶ Artificial intelligence is generally described as a computer's ability to assume an intelligence similar to that of the human brain—thus, its ability to reason and make decisions based on a preassigned set of facts or data.[1] But many experts predict that the computer's power will not stop there. They predict that the computer will soon become much smarter than humans by a process in which "intelligent" computers create even more intelligent computers. What we learn from these computers will have a far greater impact than the combined discoveries of the microscope, telescope, and X-ray machines.

¶ It is also predicted that the power of computers will double every 18 months through the year 2010.[2] With these enhancements, robots will displace humans from farms and factories; we will travel in cars, planes, and trains that are operated solely by computers; and traveling on the interstate highways will be as safe as watching television at home.

(Continued on next page)

COMPUTERS AND THE INTERNET

¶ The Internet will continue to expand and proliferate around the world. The speed at which information is transmitted on today's Internet will be considered a "snail's pace" on tomorrow's telemetric system. Most computers will transmit information at gigabit speeds and higher.[3] Computer security will be "foolproof," and most business transactions will be conducted on the Net. Fewer people will travel to foreign countries to vacation since "virtual vacations" will be commonplace.

---

[1] Peter F. Boyd, "Artificial Intelligence," *Journal of Computer Trends*, January 2004, pp. 23–24, 36.

[2] Toshida Doi, "Is Computer Intelligence Better Than the Human Brain?" *Power PC Magazine*, April 2003, pp. 14–17.

[3] Melanie T. Reynolds, "Tomorrow's Brainpower," March 17, 2004, <http://www.businessweek.com/2004/brainpower.htm>, accessed on August 19, 2005.

Strategies for Career Success

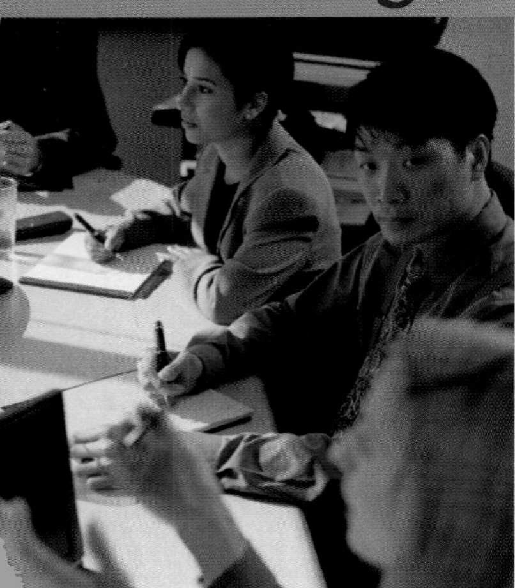

Letter of Transmittal

A letter or memo of transmittal introduces a report or proposal. Such letters provide an overview of the report in an informal, conversational writing style.

Let the recipient know what you are sending; for example, "Enclosed is the proposal you requested." If you're submitting an unsolicited report, explain why you've written the report. Include the report topic and identify the person or persons who authorized the report. Recap the main points. Cite any specific information that would help your audience comprehend the material. Is it a draft?

Conclude with a note of appreciation, a willingness to discuss the report, and intended follow-up action. Will you do something? Do you want feedback? If you want the reader to act, explain what you need and provide a deadline; for example, "Please provide your comments by July 15."

YOUR TURN List some ways that a letter of transmittal can promote goodwill between the sender and recipient.

Unit 10

Correspondence

LESSON 46
Personal Titles and Complimentary Closings in Letters

LESSON 47
Personal-Business Letters

LESSON 48
Memos With Lists

LESSON 49
Letters With Copy Notations

LESSON 50
Letters in Modified-Block Style

January 10, 20--

Mrs. Connie Filstad
4034 Kennedy Lane
Mount Vernon, WA 98274-2340

Dear Mrs. Filstad:

We at Mirror Lake Homes believe that your selection of a SunCity townhouse is just the right choice for you. The SunCity model received three national awards the 12th of last month. You have selected one of the most popular of our six models. As you requested, a brochure of the SunCity model is enclosed. Fifty-four units in the Creekwood site in Mount Vernon, Washington, have been built since December 2000.

I am certain you will agree that the $500 earnest money you put down was a wise decision on your part, and the 6.5 percent loan you received was the best available through our lending agency.

Thank you, Mrs. Filstad, for the opportunity to work with you these past few days. If you have any questions, please let us know.

Sincerely,

(Mrs.) Maria Martinez
Sales Director

urs
Enclosure

November 30, 20--

Sales Manager
Bachmann's Nursery and Landscaping
6823 Oneta Avenue
Youngstown, OH 44500-2175

Dear Sales Manager:

As you requested on the telephone, I am providing the following list of events relating to my tree problem.

1. On April 15, I purchased at your branch in Warren four silver maples for the atrium outside our Riverdale office. We also purchased four Japanese red maples at your branch in Niles later that afternoon.
2. After about six months, one silver maple and one red maple had died. I phoned both the Warren and Niles branches several times on November 1, but no one returned my messages.
3. On November 8, I phoned your nursery in an attempt to have these trees replaced. Again, there was no response.

As these trees were expensive, I expect that you will either replace them or reimburse me for the cost of the trees. I shall look forward to hearing from you.

Sincerely,

Marvin L. Norgaard
Grounds Manager

urs

MEMO TO: Charles A. Cornelius, President

FROM: Alfred A. Long, Convention Director

DATE: September 8, 20--

SUBJECT: Convention Locations

As you know, this year's convention will meet in Jacksonville, Florida. It is the Executive Board's decision to rotate the convention site to each of the districts in our region. Our next three conventions will be held in the following locations:

- Mobile, Alabama
- Atlanta, Georgia
- Myrtle Beach, South Carolina

In May the Board will travel to Mobile to visit the location of our next convention site. When we return, we will draft our convention site proposal for you.

urs

Personal Titles and Complimentary Closings in Letters

Goals

- Type at least 37wpm/3′/3e
- Format personal titles in letters
- Format complimentary closings in letters

A. Type 2 times.

A. WARMUP

     B & Z requested 14 boxes at $37/box. The items they 11
wanted were #6 and #17. A discount of 20% would bring the 22
total to approximately $950. Will you verify that order? 33

| 1 | 2 | 3 | 4 | 5 | 6 | 7 | 8 | 9 | 10 | 11 | 12

SKILLBUILDING

B. DIAGNOSTIC PRACTICE: NUMBERS

If you are not using the GDP software, turn to page SB-5 and follow the directions for this activity.

C. Take three 12-second timed writings on each line. The scale below the last line shows your wpm speed for a 12-second timed writing.

C. 12-SECOND SPEED SPRINTS

Nine of those new women were on time for the first session.
She could see that many of those old memos should be filed.
Forty of the men were at the game when that siren went off.
The line at the main hall was so long that I did not go in.

5 10 15 20 25 30 35 40 45 50 55 60

Keyboarding Connection

Evaluating Internet Sources

Are you sure your Internet source has valid information? Because of the broad availability of the Internet and the lack of careful review stages like the ones built into print publishing, you must be cautious about the dependability of information you find on the Internet. Evaluate information on the Internet by the same standards you use to evaluate other sources of information.

The best way to assure that information is valid is to get it from a reputable source. The Internet versions of established, reputable journals in medicine (for example, *Journal of the American Medical Association*), business (for example, *Harvard Business Review*), engineering, computer science, and so forth, warrant the same level of trust as the printed versions.

When you do not use established, reputable Web sites, use caution. Keep in mind that anyone can publish on the Internet. For many sources, there are no editorial review safeguards in place.

YOUR TURN Search the Web for more assessment methods.

D. Take two 3-minute timed writings. Review your speed and errors.

Goal: At least 37wpm/3′/3e

D. 3-MINUTE TIMED WRITING

Now is a great time for you to look for a job. Most 11
employers look for people who have mastered a few office 22
skills. For example, if you have acquired good computer 33
skills and are capable of working with people around you 45
and are steadfast, you can find a good job. There are some 56
who will pay top dollar to find and keep good workers. 67
Your first impression on a prospective employer will 78
be a lasting one. Your resume should list your job skills, 90
your experience, and your personal information. Your zeal 102
when you interview for a job must come through. 111

| 1 | 2 | 3 | 4 | 5 | 6 | 7 | 8 | 9 | 10 | 11 | 12

FORMATTING

E. PERSONAL TITLES IN CORRESPONDENCE

Inside Addresses
Always use a courtesy title before a person's name in the inside address of a letter; for example, *Mr., Mrs.,* or *Dr.*

Type a person's title on the same line with the name (separated by a comma), if the title is short, or on the line below. The title and business name may be typed on the same line (separated by a comma) if they are both short.

Personal Titles in Inside Addresses

Mr. Frank R. Yashiro, Manager
Landmark Security Systems

Mrs. Joyce Mansfield
Executive Director
Tanner Hospital

Dr. Carlotta Torres
Manager, Duke Oil Co.

Salutations
When possible, use a person's name in the salutation. The correct form for the salutation is the courtesy title and the last name. If you do not know the name of the person, use a job title or *Ladies and Gentlemen*. A colon is used after the salutation in standard punctuation.

Personal Titles in Salutations

Dear Ms. North:

Dear Dr. Chapman:

Dear Mr. Wagner:

Dear Sales Manager:

Ladies and Gentlemen:

F. COMPLIMENTARY CLOSINGS IN CORRESPONDENCE

Every letter should end with a complimentary closing. Some frequently used complimentary closings are *Sincerely, Sincerely yours, Yours truly, Cordially*, and *Respectfully yours*.

In the closing lines, do not use a courtesy title before a man's name. A courtesy title may be included in a woman's typed name or her signature. A comma is used after the complimentary closing in standard punctuation.

Closing Lines

Sincerely yours,

Gretchen Day

Miss Gretchen Day
Account Manager

Cordially,

(Ms.) Juanita Ponce

Juanita Ponce
Marketing Director

Yours truly,

Ben R. Cameron

Ben R. Cameron
Regional Supervisor

DOCUMENT PROCESSING

Correspondence 46-22

Business Letter in Block Style

January 10, 20-- | Mrs. Connie Filstad | 4034 Kennedy Lane | Mount Vernon, WA 98274-2340 | Dear Mrs. Filstad:

¶ We at Mirror Lake Homes believe that your selection of a SunCity townhouse is just the right choice for you. The SunCity model received three national awards last month. You have selected one of the most popular of our six models. As you requested, a brochure of the SunCity model is enclosed. Fifty-four units in the Creekwood site in Mount Vernon, Washington, have been built since December 2002.

¶ I am certain you will agree that the $500 earnest money you put down was a wise decision on your part, and the 6.5 percent loan you received was the best available through our lending agency.

¶ Thank you, Mrs. Filstad, for the opportunity to work with you these past few days. If you have any questions, please let us know.

Sincerely, | (Mrs.) Maria Martinez | Sales Director | urs | Enclosure

Correspondence 46-23

Business Letter in Block Style

May 20, 20-- | Mr. Lawrence S. Alwich | 1800 East Hollywood Avenue | Salt Lake City, UT 84108 | Dear Mr. Alwich:

¶ Our radio station would like you to reply to our editorial about the proposed airport site that aired from Provo, Utah, on May 15. Actually, you are 1 of over 27 listeners who indicated your desire for us to air your rebuttal.

¶ Of the more than 100 request letters for equal time, we selected yours because you touched on most of the relevant points of this topic.

¶ We will contact you further about taping your rebuttal on June 4. Please read the enclosed disclaimer that we would like you to sign before airing the rebuttal.

Yours truly, | Peng T. Lim | General Manager | urs | Enclosure

Lesson 47

Personal-Business Letters

Goals

- Improve speed and accuracy
- Refine language arts skills in number expression
- Format personal-business letters

A. Type 2 times.

A. WARMUP

```
     "Rex analyzed the supply," Margie said. Based on the     11
results, a purchase request for 7# @ $140 (23% of what we     22
needed) was issued. Was Jackie surprised by this? Vi was!     34
|  1  |  2  |  3  |  4  |  5  |  6  |  7  |  8  |  9  |  10  |  11  |  12
```

SKILLBUILDING

B. PACED PRACTICE

If you are not using the GDP software, turn to page SB-14 and follow the directions for this activity.

C. PROGRESSIVE PRACTICE: ALPHABET

If you are not using the GDP software, turn to page SB-7 and follow the directions for this activity.

LANGUAGE ARTS

D. Study the rules at the right.

D. NUMBER EXPRESSION

RULE ▶ # general

In general, spell out numbers zero through ten, and use numerals for numbers above ten.

We rented two movies for tonight.
The decision was reached after 27 precincts sent in their results.

RULE ▶ # figures

Use numerals for

- **Dates. (Use *st, d,* or *th* only if the day comes before the month.)**
  The tax report is due on April 15 (*not* April $15^{\underline{th}}$).
  We will drive to the camp on the 23d (or *23rd* or 23rd) of May.
- **All numbers if two or more *related* numbers both above and below ten are used in the same sentence.**
  Mr. Carter sent in 7 receipts, and Ms. Cantrell sent in 22.
  But: The 13 accountants owned three computers each.
- **Measurements (time, money, distance, weight, and percent).**
  The $500 statue we delivered at 7 a.m. weighed 6 pounds.
- **Mixed numbers.**
  Our sales are up 9½ (or *9 1/2* or *9.5*) percent over last year.

(Continued on next page)

Edit the sentences to correct any errors in number expression.

On the 3d of June, when she turns 60, 2 of her annuities will have earned an average of 10 3/4 percent.

All seven investors were interested in buying 14 condos if they were located within fifteen miles of each other.

The credit fee is fifteen dollars, and the interest is set at 8 percent; escrow will close on March 23rd before five p.m.

The parcel weighed two pounds. She also mailed three large packages and twelve small packages on June 4.

They paid 2.5 points on the loan amount.

FORMATTING

E. PERSONAL-BUSINESS LETTERS

Personal-business letters are prepared by individuals to conduct their personal business. To format a personal-business letter:

1. Type the letter on plain paper or personal stationery, not letterhead.
2. Include the writer's address in the letter directly below the writer's name in the closing lines.
3. Since the writer of the letter usually types the letter, reference initials are not used.

DOCUMENT PROCESSING

Correspondence 47-24

Personal-Business Letter in Block Style

Refer to page R-3D of the Reference Manual for an illustration of a personal-business letter.

↓6X
October 1, 20-- ↓4X

Ms. Valarie Bledsoe, Director
City Parks and Recreation Department
7034 Renwick Avenue
Syracuse, NY 13210-0475 ↓2X

Dear Ms. Bledsoe: ↓2X

\# general
\# figures

Thank you for the excellent manner in which your department accommodated our family last summer. About 120 Turners attended the reunion at Rosedale Park on August 21.

\# general
\# figures

I would like to again request that Shelter 5 be reserved for our next year's family reunion on August 20. A confirmation of the date from your office will be appreciated. ↓2X

Sincerely, ↓4X

Blair R. Turner
2410 Farnham Road
Syracuse, NY 13219

Correspondence 47-25

Personal-Business Letter in Block Style

This personal-business letter is from Roberto G. Trujillo, who lives at 482 22d Street East, Lawrence, KS 66049. Use July 13, 20--, as the date, and supply the appropriate salutation and closing using standard punctuation. The letter is to be sent to Mr. Robert A. Sotherden, Administrator | Glencrest Nursing Home | 2807 Crossgate Circle | Lawrence, KS 66047.

¶ Thanks to you and dozens of other people, the fall crafts sale at Glencrest was highly successful. I am very appreciative of the ways in which you helped.
¶ I particularly wish to thank you for transporting the display tables and chairs to Glencrest and back to the community center. Many people from the community center attended the sale and commented about how nice it was of you and your staff to support such an activity.
¶ Having a parent who is a resident of the home, I am grateful that over 20 people from the Lawrence area volunteer their services to help make life more pleasant for the residents. Please accept my special thanks to you and your staff for supporting the many activities that benefit all Glencrest residents.

general

Correspondence 47-26

Personal-Business Letter in Block Style

June 4, 20-- | Mr. Karl E. Davis | 5270 Rosecrans Avenue | Topeka, KS 67284 | Dear Mr. Davis:

¶ Your presentation at the Sand Hills Country Club was one of the most enjoyable our members have ever observed. It is always a pleasure to have professionals like you speak on ways college graduates can prepare themselves for future employment. I especially enjoyed the question-and-answer session at the conclusion of your ~~wonderful~~ presentation, and I received many favorable comments from other attendees as well.

¶ Our professor has suggested that we take the information you gave us and prepare a web site that focuses on the key points 6 you mentioned in your speech. That way, many of our class mates can take advantage of your excellent advice when preparing for their 1st search job. We have also found at least 20 ~~several~~ other sources to use on the world wide web that we plan to include on ~~in~~ our web site.

general

figure

(Continued on next page)

¶ I believe this is one of the most interesting assignments I have ever been assigned, thank to the excellent information you provided. Members of my project team are excited to see there information on our web site. The project has given other students an incentive to construct their own web sites pertaining to job searches and interviewing techniques.

¶ If you would like to view our Web site, you can do so at the following URL which will be posted by the 10th of the month: www.tamu.edu/comm/abed3600/interview.html. Again, thank you for all your excellent ideas.

Sincerely, | Tamika Yamemoto | 3421 Carlisle Avenue | Topeka, KS 67209

figure

Memos With Lists

Goals

- Type at least 38 wpm/3′/3e
- Format lists in correspondence

A. Type 2 times.

A. WARMUP

Three travel agencies (Jepster & Vilani, Quin & Bott, 11
and Zeplin & Wexter) sold the most travel tickets for the 23
past 12 months. They sold 785, 834, and 960 total tickets. 34
| 1 | 2 | 3 | 4 | 5 | 6 | 7 | 8 | 9 | 10 | 11 | 12

SKILLBUILDING

B. DIAGNOSTIC PRACTICE: SYMBOLS AND PUNCTUATION

If you are not using the GDP software, turn to page SB-2 and follow the directions for this activity.

C. Type each sentence on a separate line by pressing ENTER after each sentence.

C. TECHNIQUE PRACTICE: ENTER KEY

Debit the accounts. Balance your checkbook. Add the assets.
Take the discount. Send the statements. Compute the ratios.
Review the accounts. Credit the amounts. Figure the totals.
Prepare the statements. Send the catalog. Call the clients.

D. Take two 3-minute timed writings. Review your speed and errors.

Goal: At least 38wpm/3′/3e

D. 3-MINUTE TIMED WRITING

Some of us like to use the Internet for shopping. With 11
just a simple click of the mouse, you can shop for almost 23
any type of product. You can purchase books, cars, food, 34
games, toys, zippers, boxes, and even golf clubs by using 46
the computer to shop online. 52
The advantages of using the Web to shop with such ease 63
are many. First, you can shop from any place that has some 75
access to the Internet. Second, you can compare all prices 86
with other places before you make any purchase. Third, you 98
can have your purchases shipped directly to you. All the 110
savings mount quickly. 114
| 1 | 2 | 3 | 4 | 5 | 6 | 7 | 8 | 9 | 10 | 11 | 12

FORMATTING

Refer to pages R-3B, R-3C, and R-5B of the Reference Manual for examples of lists in correspondence. Refer to page R-12C of the Reference Manual for an overview of formatting lists.

E. LISTS IN CORRESPONDENCE

Numbers or bullets may be used in correspondence to call attention to items in a list. If the sequence of the items is important, use numbers rather than bullets.

1. Begin the number or bullet at the left margin for blocked paragraphs.
2. Press ENTER 2 times to insert 1 blank line before and after the list.
3. Within the list, use single spacing as is used in the rest of the document.
4. If all items require no more than 1 line, single-space between the items in the list. If any item requires more than 1 line, single-space each item but press ENTER 2 times to insert 1 blank line between each item.

To format a list in correspondence:

1. Type the list unformatted. (**Note:** If you apply the number or bullet feature at the start of the list, any paragraphs that might follow will usually be indented incorrectly.)
2. Select the items in the list.
3. Apply the number or bullet feature.
4. Decrease the indent to move the position of bullets or numbers to the left margin.

DOCUMENT PROCESSING

Correspondence 48-27

Memo

Refer to page R-12C of the Reference Manual for an overview of formatting lists.

↓6X → tab

MEMO TO: Charles A. Cornelius, President ↓2X

FROM: Alfred A. Long, Convention Director ↓2X

DATE: September 8, 20-- ↓2X

SUBJECT: Convention Locations ↓2X

As you know, this year's convention will meet in Jacksonville, Florida. It is the Executive Board's decision to rotate the convention site to each of the districts in our region. Our next three conventions will be held in the following locations: ↓2X

- Mobile, Alabama
- Atlanta, Georgia
- Myrtle Beach, South Carolina ↓2X

In May the Board will travel to Mobile to visit the location of our next convention site. When we return, we will draft our convention site proposal for you. ↓2X

urs

Correspondence 48-28

Memo

MEMO TO: Marcia Davis | **FROM:** Alex Pera | **DATE:** April 9, 20-- | **SUBJECT:** Program Descriptions

¶As you requested, I have contacted the speakers for our afternoon session discussions. All three speakers have sent me a brief description of their sessions, and they are listed in the order of presentation as follows:

1. Salon A. This session will discuss the advantages of e-commerce and its influence on the economy of the United States.
2. Salon B. This session will introduce several suggestions for enhancing your Web site.
3. Salon C. This session will discuss changes occurring in Internet access and its impact on entrepreneurial ventures.

¶By next Monday I will send you an introduction for each speaker.

urs

Correspondence 48-29

Memo

Open the file for Correspondence 48–27 and make the following changes:

1. Change the three convention sites to Miami, Florida; Raleigh, North Carolina; and Montgomery, Alabama.
2. Change the final paragraph to indicate that the Board will travel to Miami.

Strategies for Career Success

Reducing Bias in Business Communication

Everything we do in business communication attempts to build goodwill. Bias-free language and visuals help maintain the goodwill we work so hard to create.

Bias-free language does not discriminate against people on the basis of sex, physical condition, race, age, or any other characteristic. Do not emphasize gender-specific words in your business vocabulary. Instead, incorporate gender-neutral words (for example, chairman is chairperson) into your business communication.

Organizations that treat people fairly should also use language that treats people fairly. The law is increasingly intolerant of biased documents and hostile work environments. Practice nondiscriminatory behavior by focusing on individual merits, accomplishments, skills, and what you might share in common rather than illustrating differences. Treating every group with respect and understanding is essential to gaining loyalty and future business while cultivating harmonious relationships.

YOUR TURN Review a document that you have recently written. Is the document bias-free?

Letters With Copy Notations

Goals

- Improve speed and accuracy
- Refine language arts skills in spelling
- Format letters with copy notations

A. Type 2 times.

A. WARMUP

"Look at them! Have you ever seen such large birds?" 11
When questioned later on an exam, about 80% to 90% of the 22
junior girls were amazed to learn that they were ospreys. 34
| 1 | 2 | 3 | 4 | 5 | 6 | 7 | 8 | 9 | 10 | 11 | 12

SKILLBUILDING

B. MAP

Follow the GDP software directions for this exercise in improving keystroking accuracy.

C. Take a 1-minute timed writing on the first paragraph to establish your base speed. Then take four 1-minute timed writings on the remaining paragraphs. As soon as you equal or exceed your base speed on one paragraph, advance to the next, more difficult paragraph.

C. SUSTAINED PRACTICE: NUMBERS AND SYMBOLS

The proposed road improvement program was approved 10
by the county commissioners at their last meeting. There 22
were about ten citizens who spoke on behalf of the project. 34

The plan calls for blacktopping a 14-mile stretch on 11
County Road #2356. This is the road that is commonly called 23
the "roller coaster" because of all the curves and hills. 34

There will be 116 miles blacktopped by J & J, Inc. 10
(commonly referred to as the Jeremy Brothers*). J & J's 22
office is at 1798 30th Avenue past the 22d Street bridge. 33

Minor road repair costs range from $10,784 to a high 11
of $163,450 (39% of the total program costs). The "county 23
inspector" is to hold the project costs to 105% of budget! 34
| 1 | 2 | 3 | 4 | 5 | 6 | 7 | 8 | 9 | 10 | 11 | 12

LANGUAGE ARTS

D. Type this list of frequently misspelled words, paying special attention to any spelling problems in each word.

D. SPELLING

```
16 per other receipt present provided commission international
17 service position questions following industrial maintenance
18 well absence support proposal mortgage corporate management
19 upon balance approval experience facilities recommendations
20 paid because premium procedure addition directors currently
```

Edit the sentences to correct any misspellings.

```
21 The international comission provided a list of proceedures.
22 That industrial maintainance proposal is curently in place.
23 The directers and management supported the recomendations.
24 Those present raised a question about a corperate morgage.
25 Six of the folowing persons have now given their aproval.
26 In adition, Kris has premium experience at the facilitys.
```

FORMATTING

E. COPY NOTATIONS

Making file copies of all documents you prepare is a good business practice. At times you may also need copies to send to people other than the addressee of the original document.

A copy notation is typed on a document to indicate that someone else besides the addressee is receiving a copy.

1. Type the copy notation on the line below the reference initials or below the attachment or enclosure notation.
2. At the left margin, type a lowercase *c* followed by a colon.
3. Press the SPACE BAR 1 time and type the name of the person receiving the copy.
4. If more than one person is receiving a copy, type the names on one line separated by a comma and space between each name.

Sincerely, ↓4X

Lester A. Fagerlie
Branch Manager ↓2X

jlt
Enclosure
c: Mrs. Coretta D. Rice, Dr. Thomas Moore

DOCUMENT PROCESSING

Correspondence 49-30

Business Letter in Block Style

Highlighted words are spelling words from the language arts activities.

May 11, 20-- | Mr. and Mrs. Richard Belson | 783 Wellcourt Lane | Mount Vernon, WA 98273-4156 | Dear Mr. and Mrs. Belson:

¶ Marian Dickenson has informed me that you have several questions pertaining to the maintenance proposal that was submitted by the directors and approved by management. It is our position, based upon the procedures we provided following last week's meeting, that the proposal was submitted to corporate headquarters prior to your inquiry. Therefore, your questions should be directed to Alfred A. Long in our Seattle office.

¶ It has been our experience that inquiries such as yours will receive an immediate response because of the support you have demonstrated during other maintenance negotiations. I would recommend that you call me if you have not heard from Mr. Long by the 13th of the month. In the absence of Mr. Long's response, I am sending you a copy of other materials related to your inquiry.

¶ Thank you for your interest in this matter.

Sincerely, | Theodore A. Gardner | Sales Director | urs | c: Marian Dickenson

Correspondence 49-31

Business Letter in Block Style

Open the file for Correspondence 49-30 and make the following changes:

1. Send the letter to Mr. and Mrs. George Tanner | 105 Royal Lane | Commerce, TX 75428
2. Add the following sentence to the end of the second paragraph:

```
These materials are
enclosed for your review.
```

3. Include an enclosure notation.
4. Send a copy of this letter to Marian Dickenson and also to Carla Orellano.

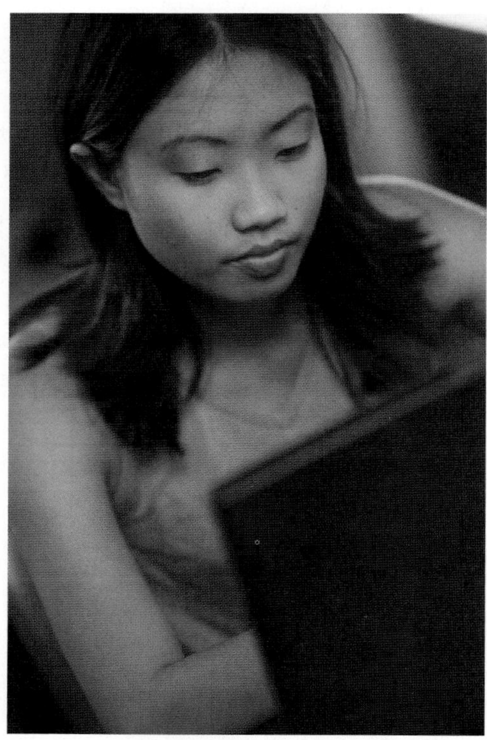

Letters in Modified-Block Style

Goals

- Type at least 38wpm/3′/3e
- Format letters in modified-block style

A. Type 2 times.

A. WARMUP

1 Mark Kara's quilts down by 25%: #489, #378, and #460. 11
2 Leave the prices as they are for the remainder of the sizes 23
3 in that section. Eleven adjoining sections will be next. 34
| 1 | 2 | 3 | 4 | 5 | 6 | 7 | 8 | 9 | 10 | 11 | 12

SKILLBUILDING

PPP PRETEST → PRACTICE → POSTTEST

PRETEST
Take a 1-minute timed writing. Review your speed and errors.

B. PRETEST: Alternate- and One-Hand Words

4 The chair of the trade committee served notice that 11
5 the endowment grant exceeded the budget. A million dollars 23
6 was the exact amount. The greater part might be deferred. 35
| 1 | 2 | 3 | 4 | 5 | 6 | 7 | 8 | 9 | 10 | 11 | 12

PRACTICE
Speed Emphasis:
If you made 2 or fewer errors on the Pretest, type each *indivdual* line 2 times.
Accuracy Emphasis:
If you made 3 or more errors, type each *group* of lines (as though it were a paragraph) 2 times.

C. PRACTICE: Alternate-Hand Words

7 amendment turndown visible suspend visual height signs maps
8 authentic clemency dormant figment island emblem usual snap
9 shamrocks blandish problem penalty profit thrown chair form

D. PRACTICE: One-Hand Words

10 pumpkin eastward plumply barrage greater poplin trade holly
11 minikin cassette opinion seaweed created kimono union exact
12 minimum attracts reserve million scatter unhook plump defer

POSTTEST
Repeat the Pretest timed writing and compare performance.

E. POSTTEST: Alternate- and One-Hand Words

F. Take two 3-minute timed writings. Review your speed and errors.

Goal: At least 38wpm/3′/3e

F. 3-MINUTE TIMED WRITING

```
     The Web is a vast source of facts and data on many          10
topics. You can view many newspapers, zip through weather        22
reports, find a tax form and learn how to complete it, and       34
search for a job. You can find answers to health questions       46
and learn about world events almost as soon as they occur.       57
     E-mail is another part of the Internet that people are      69
using more often. They use e-mail to keep in touch with          80
friends and family in a quick and efficient way that costs       92
very little. They can write down their thoughts and send        103
messages just as if they were writing a letter or memo.         114
|  1  |  2  |  3  |  4  |  5  |  6  |  7  |  8  |  9  |  10  |  11  |  12
```

FORMATTING

G. MODIFIED-BLOCK STYLE LETTERS

Modified-block style is a commonly used format for business letters. The date, the complimentary closing, and the writer's identification line(s) are typed at the horizontal centerpoint for each of these lines. Begin the document by first setting a left tab at the centerpoint (usually at 3 inches), and then press TAB 1 time to move to the centerpoint before typing each of these lines. (**Note:** These lines are *not* centered horizontally.)

1. Clear all tabs and set a left tab at the centerpoint (usually at 3 inches).
2. Press ENTER 6 times to begin the letter about 2 inches from the top of the page.
3. Press TAB 1 time to move to the centerpoint, and type the date of the letter.
4. Press ENTER 4 times, and type the inside address at the left margin.
5. Press ENTER 2 times, type the salutation at the left margin, and press ENTER 2 times again.
6. Type the paragraphs blocked at the left margin, and press ENTER 2 times after all paragraphs.
7. After typing the final paragraph, press ENTER 2 times and press TAB 1 time to move to the centerpoint.
8. Type the complimentary closing, and then press ENTER 4 times.
9. Press TAB 1 time to move to the centerpoint, and type the writer's identification. If the writer's identification is to be typed on 2 lines, press TAB 1 time again for any additional line.
10. Press ENTER 2 times, and type the reference initials and remaining letter parts at the left margin.

(Continued on next page)

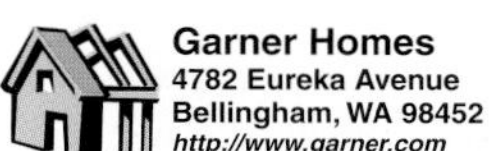

Garner Homes
4782 Eureka Avenue
Bellingham, WA 98452
http://www.garner.com

"Putting a Roof on America"

↓6X

→ tab to centerpoint November 29, 20-- ↓4X

Mr. and Mrs. Arvey Gates
2308 Hannegan Road
Bellingham, WA 98226 ↓2X

Dear Mr. and Mrs. Gates: ↓2X

Val Osugi, who hosted our Ridgeway open house last Saturday, has referred your unanswered questions to me. We are pleased that you are interested in a Garner home.

The usual down payment is 20 percent of the total selling price, but some lending agencies require a smaller amount in certain situations. Garner Homes is not itself involved in home financing, but we work with the financial institutions shown on the enclosed list.

Yes, the lot you prefer can accommodate a walkout basement. Val will be in touch with you soon. We can have your new Ridgeway ready for occupancy within 90 days. ↓2X

→ tab to centerpoint Sincerely, ↓4X

Alfred A. Long

→ tab to centerpoint Alfred A. Long
Sales Director ↓2X

azk
Enclosure
c: Loan Processing Dept.

Word Processing Manual

H. WORD PROCESSING: RULER TABS AND TAB SET

Study Lesson 50 in your word processing manual. Complete all of the shaded steps while at your computer. Then format the jobs that follow.

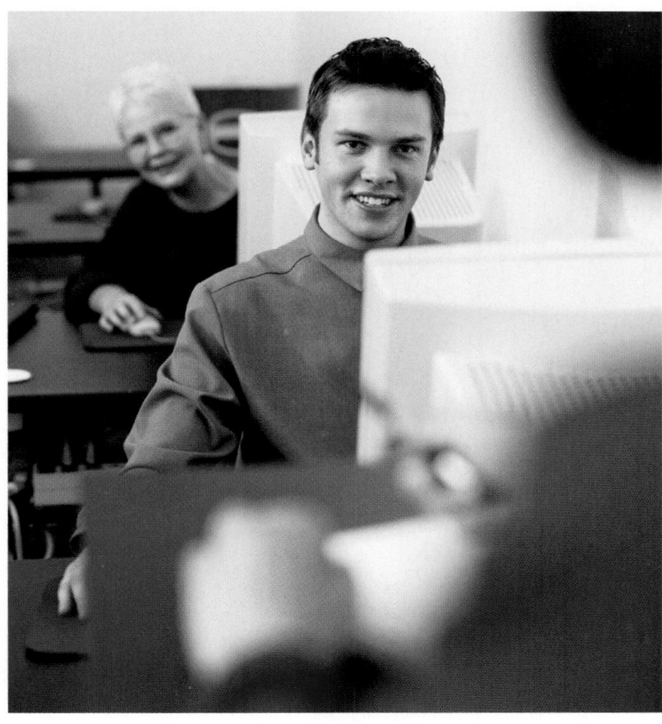

DOCUMENT PROCESSING

Correspondence 50-32

Business Letter in Modified-Block Style

Refer to page R-3B of the Reference Manual for additional guidance.

↓6X

→ tab to centerpoint November 29, 20-- ↓4X

Mr. and Mrs. Arvey Gates
2308 Hannegan Road
Bellingham, WA 98226 ↓2X

Dear Mr. and Mrs. Gates: ↓2X

Val Osugi, who hosted our Ridgeway open house last Saturday, has referred your unanswered questions to me. We are pleased that you are interested in a Garner home.

The usual down payment is 20 percent of the total selling price, but some lending agencies require a smaller amount in certain situations. Garner Homes is not itself involved in home financing, but we work with the financial institutions shown on the enclosed list.

Yes, the lot you prefer can accommodate a walkout basement. Val will be in touch with you soon. We can have your new Ridgeway ready for occupancy within 90 days. ↓2X

→ tab to centerpoint Sincerely, ↓4X

Alfred A. Long

→ tab to centerpoint Alfred A. Long
Sales Director ↓2X

urs
Enclosure
c: Loan Processing Dept.

Correspondence 50-33

Business Letter in Modified-Block Style

Refer to page R-12C of the Reference Manual for information on formatting lists and an illustration.

Use November 30, 20--, as the date as you format this modified-block style letter to be sent to the sales manager at Bachmann's Nursery and Landscaping | 6823 Oneta Avenue | Youngstown, OH 44500-2175

Dear Sales Manager:
¶ As you requested on the telephone, I am providing the following list of events relating to my tree problem.

1. On April 15, I purchased at your branch in Warren four silver maples for the atrium outside our Riverdale office. We also purchased four Japanese red maples at your branch in Niles later that afternoon.
2. After about six months, one silver maple and one red maple had died. I phoned both the Warren and Niles branches several times on November 1, but no one returned my messages.
3. On November 8, I phoned your nursery in an attempt to have these trees replaced. Again, there was no response.

¶ As these trees were expensive, I expect that you will either replace them or reimburse me for the cost of the trees. I shall look forward to hearing from you.
Sincerely, | Marvin L. Norgaard | Grounds Manager | urs

Correspondence 50-34

Business Letter in Modified-Block Style

December 10, 20-- | Mr. Marvin L. Norgaard | 4782 Saranac Avenue | Youngstown, OH 44505-6207 | Dear Mr. Norgaard:
¶ This is in response to your recent letter.
¶ Your trees will be replaced without cost to you. We will make sure that the replacement trees will match the others you purchased in both size and color. I am enclosing a warranty for these new trees so that you can feel confident that we stand behind our product.
¶ The survival rate for trees cannot be perfect; however, we are indeed sorry that you have had to have this temporary setback.
¶ The communication breakdown with our two branch offices should not have occurred. We will take steps to ensure that this will not happen in the future. You can be confident that the appearance of your atrium will be restored and that the beauty of the new trees will add to your property's value. Thank you for shopping at Bachmann's.
Sincerely, | Mrs. Alice G. Schmidt | Co-owner | urs | Enclosure | c: Mr. Raul Cornejo, Co-owner

Correspondence 50-35

Personal-Business Letter in Modified-Block Style

Progress and Proofreading Check

Documents designated as Proofreading Checks serve as a check of your proofreading skill. Your goal is to have zero typographical errors when the GDP software first scores the document.

March 11, 20-- | Ms. Karen Shalicky | Lincoln Travel Center | 2384 Longdale Avenue | Suite 4113 | Boston, MA 02134-3489 | Dear Ms. Shalicky:
¶ I am interested in taking a cruise in one of the following regions:

- Alaska Inland Passageway
- Caribbean Islands
- Greek Isles

¶ Could you please send me some promotional materials for these cruises? My financial resources are such that I would like to limit my cruise package to $5,000 and would prefer a cruise no longer than ten days in length. I will be accompanied by my friend Bonnie Davis, and I assume that any quotes you give me could apply to both of us.
¶ We would like to do sightseeing in some of these locations. Do you have special excursions available to passengers? I am enclosing a list of the sites we would like to visit in each of these regions.
¶ The best time for us to travel is between June 1 and June 20, and we would like you to schedule our trip around those dates. I hope to hear from you soon.
Yours truly, | Rita Wright | 678 Ardale Avenue | Milton, MA 02186-2190 | Enclosure | c: Bonnie Davis

Keyboarding Connection

Avoid E-Mail Flame Wars

Don't fan the flames! A flame is an offensive e-mail that expresses anger, criticism, or insults. If flames are transmitted to a mailing list, they can produce a long list of flames and counter flames known as flame wars.

You may be tempted to join in, but this is a waste of everyone's time. Often the initial offense was merely a poorly worded e-mail that a reader interpreted as an insult. There are those who intentionally send inflammatory e-mails called flame bait. Resist the urge to send a cutting response, and consider whether the writer's intent was to provoke you.

If your reader misjudges something you wrote and becomes offended, just apologize. A timely apology can thwart a potential fire. Avoid miscommunication by watching how you word your e-mails.

YOUR TURN Have you ever been insulted by an e-mail? What was your response?

Unit 11

Employment Documents

LESSON 51
Traditional Resumes

LESSON 52
Electronic Resumes

LESSON 53
Letters of Application

LESSON 54
Follow-Up Letters

LESSON 55
Integrated Employment Project

PATSY R. ROTHEL

2525 Hickory Ridge Drive, Plant City, FL 33567
Phone: 813-555-0704; e-mail: prothel@netmail.com

OBJECTIVE To continue my career in computer graphics by securing a position related to graphic design.

EDUCATION Central Florida Business College, Valrico, Florida
Two years of related courses in graphic design

Plant City High School, Plant C
Graduated: May 2005

EXPERIENCE *Graphic Designer, NetView, Inc.*
Orlando, Florida
October 2004–Present
Designed Web pages for
central Florida. Edited p
database for Web-based

Copy Editor, The Plant City Pre
Plant City, Florida
May 2000–September 2004
Assisted the news editor
editing copy for daily ne
from local businesses. C
the Week forum.

ACTIVITIES
- Spanish Honor Society, 2001
- Member, Phi Beta Lambda, 2
- Newsletter Editor, *CFBC Ne*
- President, FBLA Chapter, 19
- Treasurer, FBLA Chapter, 19

REFERENCES References available upon requ

August 10, 20--

Personnel Director
Arlington Communications
2403 Sunset Lane
Arlington, TX 76015-3148

Dear Personnel Director:

Please consider me as an applicant for a position with Arlington Communications. My strengths have always been in the communication arts, as you can see on the enclosed resume, which lists a number of courses in English, speech, and communication technology. The two part-time jobs I held during the summer months at your company convinced me that Arlington Communications is the place where I want to work.

If you would like to interview me for any possible openings this summer or fall, please
d to hearing from you.

April 7, 20--

Ms. Kay Brewer, Personnel Director
Blanchard Computer Systems
2189 Dace Avenue
Sioux City, IA 51107

Dear Ms. Brewer:

Thank you for the opportunity of interviewing yesterday with Blanchard Computer Systems. Please express my appreciation to all of those who were involved.

The interview gave me a good feeling about the company. The positive description that you shared with me convinced me that Blanchard is indeed a company at which I would like to work. I was greatly impressed with the summary of social service programs that are sponsored by Blanchard for citizens throughout the community.

You may recall that I have had experience with all of the equipment that is used. It appears to me that my strengths in computer application software and office systems would blend in well with your company profile.

I look forward to hearing from you soon regarding your decision on the position of data records operator.

Sincerely,

Arlene F. Jefferson
1842 Amber Road
Wayne, NE 68787

Traditional Resumes

Goals

- Improve speed and accuracy
- Refine language arts skills in the use of commas
- Format traditional resumes

A. Type 2 times.

A. WARMUP

```
     Janice had sales of over $23,000; Kathy's sales were     11
only $17,368 for the same quiet period. Craig agreed that     22
some inventory sizes were wrong and should be exchanged.      34
| 1 | 2 | 3 | 4 | 5 | 6 | 7 | 8 | 9 | 10 | 11 | 12
```

SKILLBUILDING

B. MAP

Follow the GDP software directions for this exercise in improving keystroking accuracy.

C. Take a 1-minute timed writing on the first paragraph to establish your base speed. Then take four 1-minute timed writings on the remaining paragraphs. As soon as you equal or exceed your base speed on one paragraph, advance to the next, more difficult paragraph.

C. SUSTAINED PRACTICE: CAPITALIZATION

```
     There are several different approaches that one can      11
take when considering a major purchase. Some people make      22
the mistake of simply going to a store and making a choice.   34

     When one couple decided to buy a chest-type freezer,     11
they looked at a consumer magazine in the library. The        22
Sears, Amana, and General Electric were shown as best buys.   34

     That same issue of their magazine compared electric      11
ranges. Jonathan and Mary Anne found that the Maytag, Magic   23
Chef, Amana, and Gibson were determined to be best buys.      34

     Best buys for full-size microwave ovens were the Sharp   11
Carousel, Panasonic, and GoldStar Multiwave. Good midsize     23
models were the Frigidaire, Panasonic, and Sears Kenmore.     34
| 1 | 2 | 3 | 4 | 5 | 6 | 7 | 8 | 9 | 10 | 11 | 12
```

LANGUAGE ARTS

D. Study the rules at the right.

D. COMMAS

RULE ▶ , date

Use a comma before and after the year in a complete date.

We will arrive on June 2, 2005, for the conference.

But: We will arrive on June 2 for the conference.

But: Work should be submitted between November 2005 and December 2005.

RULE ▶ , place

Use a comma before and after a state or country that follows a city (but not before a ZIP Code).

Joan moved to Vancouver, British Columbia, in May.

Send the package to Douglasville, GA 30135, by Express Mail.

But: Send the package to Georgia by Express Mail

Edit the sentences to correct any errors in the use of commas.

16 The warehouse building will be ready in September, 2004.
17 The attorney told a clerk to use June 30, 2005 as the date.
18 The books were sent to Los Angeles, CA, 90029 on July 13, 2005 and will arrive soon.
19 The move to Toledo, Ohio, was scheduled for November, 2004.

FORMATTING

E. TRADITIONAL RESUMES

When you apply for a job, you may be asked to submit a resume. The purpose of a resume is to convey your qualifications for the position you are seeking. A resume should include the following:

- Personal information (name, address, telephone number, and e-mail address).
- Your career objective (optional).
- A summary of your educational background and special training.
- Previous work experience.
- Any activities or personal achievements that relate to the position for which you are applying.
- References (optional). If an employer requests references, you should have at least three people who can tell a prospective employer what kind of worker you are.

Often, your resume creates the first impression you make on a prospective employer; be sure it is free of errors.

Various styles are acceptable for formatting a resume. Choose a style (or design one) that is attractive and that enables you to get all the needed information on one or two pages. The first page of a resume should start about 2 inches from the top of the page.

To format a traditional resume:

1. Press ENTER 6 times.
2. Insert an open table with 2 columns and 1 row for each section of the resume. **Note:** In the example that follows, you would use 6 rows.
3. Merge the cells in Row 1.
4. Change to center alignment.
5. Type your name in all caps in Arial Bold 14 pt. in Row 1, and press ENTER 2 times.
6. Change to Arial Bold 12 pt; then type your street address followed by a comma and 1 space; type your city followed by a comma and 1 space; then type your state followed by 1 space and your ZIP Code; press ENTER 1 time.

(Continued on next page)

7. Type `Phone:` followed by 1 space; then type your area code and phone number followed by a semicolon and 1 space.
8. Type `e-mail:` followed by 1 space and your e-mail address.
9. Press ENTER 1 time.
10. Apply a bottom border to Row 1.
11. Move to Row 2, Column A; and press ENTER 1 time.
12. Type the entry in Column A in all caps and bold in Times New Roman 12 pt., and press TAB to move to Column B.
13. Press ENTER 1 time, and type the information related to the Column A heading in Column B.
14. Press ENTER as needed in each section to insert 1 blank line between sections. **Note:** Type job titles and business names in italics.
15. Continue typing all entries until you are finished. **Note:** For any job descriptions, increase the indent to reposition the information. For any lists, decrease the indent until the list is positioned at the left of the column.
16. Decrease the width of Column A to about 1.25 inch to accommodate the longest entry and provide a small amount of space after the longest entry.

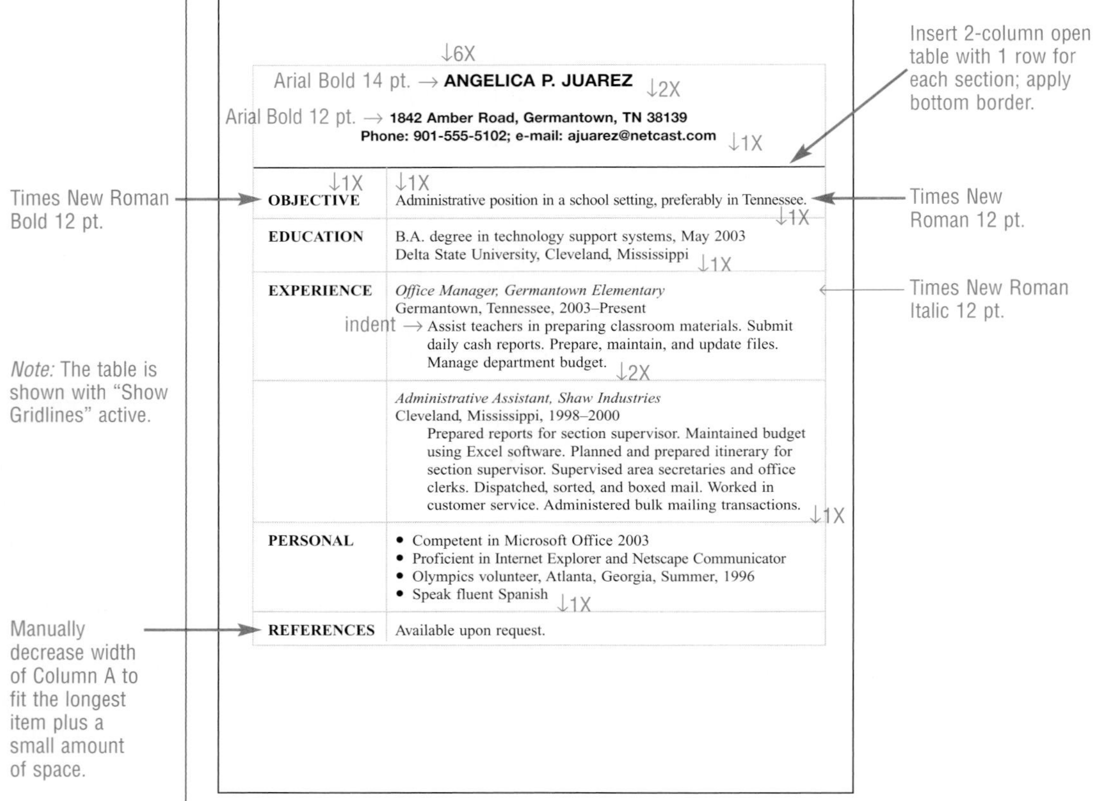

↓6X
Arial Bold 14 pt. → ANGELICA P. JUAREZ ↓2X
Arial Bold 12 pt. → 1842 Amber Road, Germantown, TN 38139
Phone: 901-555-5102; e-mail: ajuarez@netcast.com ↓1X
Insert 2-column open table with 1 row for each section; apply bottom border.
Times New Roman Bold 12 pt.
↓1X OBJECTIVE
↓1X Administrative position in a school setting, preferably in Tennessee. ↓1X
Times New Roman 12 pt.
EDUCATION
B.A. degree in technology support systems, May 2003
Delta State University, Cleveland, Mississippi ↓1X
EXPERIENCE
Office Manager, Germantown Elementary
Times New Roman Italic 12 pt.
Germantown, Tennessee, 2003–Present
indent → Assist teachers in preparing classroom materials. Submit daily cash reports. Prepare, maintain, and update files. Manage department budget. ↓2X
Note: The table is shown with "Show Gridlines" active.
Administrative Assistant, Shaw Industries
Cleveland, Mississippi, 1998–2000
Prepared reports for section supervisor. Maintained budget using Excel software. Planned and prepared itinerary for section supervisor. Supervised area secretaries and office clerks. Dispatched, sorted, and boxed mail. Worked in customer service. Administered bulk mailing transactions. ↓1X
PERSONAL
• Competent in Microsoft Office 2003
• Proficient in Internet Explorer and Netscape Communicator
• Olympics volunteer, Atlanta, Georgia, Summer, 1996
• Speak fluent Spanish ↓1X
Manually decrease width of Column A to fit the longest item plus a small amount of space.
REFERENCES
Available upon request.

Go To

Word Processing Manual

F. WORD PROCESSING: FONTS AND TABLES—CHANGING COLUMN WIDTH

Study Lesson 51 in your word processing manual. Complete all of the shaded steps while at your computer. Then format the jobs that follow.

Report 51-27

Resume in Traditional Style

Insert 2-column open table with 1 row for each section; apply top border.

Note: The table is shown with "Show Gridlines" active.

↓6X

Arial Bold 14 pt. → **PATSY R. ROTHEL** ↓2X

Arial Bold 12 pt. → **2525 Hickory Ridge Drive, Plant City, FL 33567**
Phone: 813-555-0704; e-mail: prothel@netmail.com ↓1X

Times New Roman Bold 12 pt.

↓1X **OBJECTIVE**	↓1X To continue my career in computer graphics by securing a position related to graphic design. ↓1X (Times New Roman 12 pt.)
EDUCATION	Central Florida Business College, Valrico, Florida A.A. degree in graphics design Graduated: May 2005 ↓2X Plant City High School, Plant City, Florida Graduated: May 2003 ↓1X
EXPERIENCE	*Graphic Designer, NetView, Inc.* ← Times New Roman Italic 12 pt. Orlando, Florida October 2005–Present indent → Designed Web pages for Internet-connected companies in central Florida. Edited page copy for Web sites. Created a database for Web-based users. ↓2X *Copy Editor, The Plant City Press* Plant City, Florida May 2003–September 2005 Assisted the news editor with typing, proofreading, and editing copy for daily newspaper. Solicited subscriptions from local businesses. Conducted interviews for Citizens of the Week forum. ↓1X
ACTIVITIES	• Member, Phi Beta Lambda, 2004–2005 • Newsletter Editor, *CFBC News*, 2004 • President, FBLA Chapter, 2002 • Treasurer, FBLA Chapter, 2001 ↓1X
REFERENCES	References available upon request.

Manually decrease width of Column A to fit longest item.

Report 51-28

Resume in Traditional Style

Open the file for Report 51-27 and make the following changes:

1. Change the name to JOYCE K. LEE.
2. Change the address to 10234 Wood Sorrell Lane, Burke, VA 22015.
3. Change the phone number to 703-555-4902 and the e-mail address to jklee@netlink.net.
4. Replace the OBJECTIVE entry with the following:

   To gain experience in retail sales as a foundation for a retail management position.
5. Replace both of the EDUCATION entries with the following:

   Central High School, Burke, Virginia | Graduated: May 2003.
6. Change the first EXPERIENCE entry to the following:

   Computer Systems Technician, Kramer & Kramer, Inc. | Harrisburg, Virginia | June 2004-Present | Duties include reviewing, installing, and updating software programs used for processing legal documents.
7. Change the second EXPERIENCE entry to the following:

   Salesclerk, Blanchard's Department Store | Richmond, Virginia | May 2002-May 2004 (part-time) | Duties included selling sporting goods and operating Panasonic cash register. Assisted sales manager in completing monthly sales reports.
8. Change the entries for ACTIVITIES to the following:

   Volunteer for Habitat for Humanity, 2000-Present | Member, Computer Technicians Association, 2000-Present | Senior Class President, 2002-2003 | Member, Intramural Soccer Team, 2001-2003 | Member, Beta Club, 2001-2003.

Strategies for Career Success

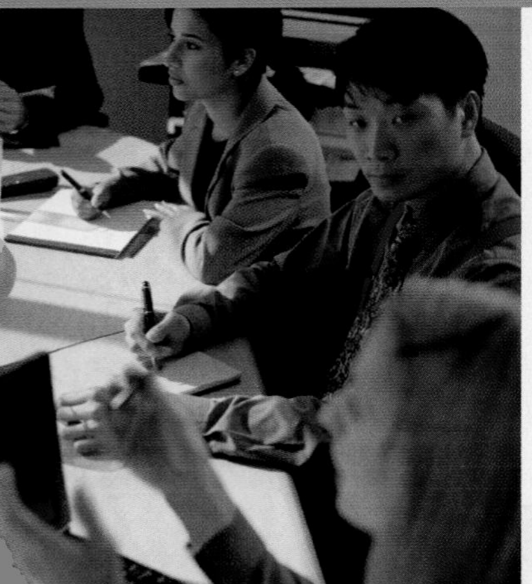

Formatting Your Resume

The format of your resume communicates important skills—neatness and the ability to organize. Make a good first impression by following these guidelines.

Watch the spacing on your resume. A crowded resume implies that you cannot summarize. Leave adequate white space between the section headings of your resume. Use different font sizes, boldface, and italics to separate and emphasize information. Font sizes should be between 10 and 14.

Print your resume on good-quality 8½" × 11" white or off-white bond paper (for example, 20-pound stock). Colored paper doesn't provide enough contrast when your resume is copied or faxed.

Proofread your resume for spelling errors and consistency of format. Ask a few friends to review it and provide feedback.

YOUR TURN Print one copy of your resume on a dark-colored paper and print one copy on white paper. Photocopy each resume. Which provides the better contrast for readability?

Electronic Resumes

Goals

- Type at least 39wpm/5′/5e
- Format an electronic resume

A. Type 2 times.

A. WARMUP

```
     The new firm, Kulver & Zweidel, will be equipped to        11
handle from 1/6 to 1/4 of Martin's tax needs after they         22
move to the new location at 1970 Gansby, just east of Main.     34
|  1  |  2  |  3  |  4  |  5  |  6  |  7  |  8  |  9  |  10  |  11  |  12
```

SKILLBUILDING

B. Take three 12-second timed writings on each line. The scale below the last line shows your wpm speed for a 12-second timed writing.

B. 12-SECOND SPEED SPRINTS

```
Pat went back to the store where she had seen the red book.
The good girl was sure that she had not seen that old door.
There was a huge change when he walked into the same class.
Pat was met at the door with one red rose and a giant cake.
    5    10    15    20    25    30    35    40    45    50    55    60
```

C. PROGRESSIVE PRACTICE: ALPHABET

If you are not using the GDP software, turn to page SB-7 and follow the directions for this activity.

D. Take two 5-minute timed writings. Review your speed and errors.

Goal: At least 39wpm/5′/5e

D. 5-MINUTE TIMED WRITING

```
     Have you completed your education when you graduate    11
from high school or finish your college work? Most people   22
look forward to reaching milestones, such as graduation or  34
completing a course. Have they learned everything they will 46
need to know to be successful in the real world? The answer 58
is not so simple.                                           62
     Learning continues to occur long after you leave the   72
classroom. No matter what job or career you pursue, you     84
will learn something new every day. When you investigate    95
new ideas, ask questions, or find a different way to do a   107
job, you are continuing to learn. In the process, you gain  118
additional experience, develop new skills, and become a     130
better worker.                                              133
     Getting along with your peers, for example, is not     143
something that you learn from studying books. You learn to  155
be a team player when you listen to your coworkers and      166
share your ideas with them. Do not hesitate to acquire new  178
skills or to initiate new ideas. Be zealous in your efforts 190
to continue your education.                                 195
|  1  |  2  |  3  |  4  |  5  |  6  |  7  |  8  |  9  |  10  |  11  |  12
```

FORMATTING

E. ELECTRONIC RESUMES

An electronic resume is a resume that has been formatted for display on the Internet and for electronic transmission via e-mail. Format an electronic resume as follows:

1. Use a monospaced font like Courier New, and use the default font size.
2. Use left alignment.
3. Use a line length of 60 characters maximum.
4. Do not hyphenate words at the end of a line.
5. Do not press TAB to indent lines. Instead, space 5 times.
6. If any lines wrap to a second line, press ENTER immediately after the last word of the first line, space 5 times if the turnover line should be indented, and continue typing the lines in this way until all lines for a section are completed.
7. Do not use any special formatting features (bold, italic, or underline) or graphic features (rules, bullets, pictures, boxes, tables, or columns).
8. Use all-caps as a substitute for bold or underline.
9. To create a bulleted list, space 5 times, and type an asterisk; space 1 time and type the line. On the wraparound line, space 7 times and continue typing in this way until all lines for the bulleted list are completed.
10. Save the resume as a text-only file (one that has a .txt extension).

Word Processing Manual

F. WORD PROCESSING: SAVING IN TEXT-ONLY FORMAT

Study Lesson 52 in your word processing manual. Complete all of the shaded steps while at your computer. Then format the jobs that follow.

DOCUMENT PROCESSING

Report 52-29

Resume in Electronic Style

Type the electronic resume as shown in the illustration below according to these guidelines:

- Change to 12 pt. Courier New.
- Press the SPACE BAR 5 times to indent lines.
- Press the SPACE BAR 5 times, type an asterisk, and type a space, as shown, to create a bulleted list.
- If any lines wrap to a second line, press ENTER immediately after the last word of the first line, space 5 times if the turnover line should be indented or 7 times if the turnover line is part of a bulleted list, and continue typing the lines in this way until all lines for a section are completed.
- Save the resume as a text-only file.

```
BRENDA COTTON ↓2X

→5 spaces 1611 Amherst Way
     Emporia, KS 66801
     Phone: 316-555-1384
     E-mail: bcotton@plains.net
     Home page: http://www.esc.org/staff/cotton.htm ↓2X

OBJECTIVE

→5 spaces Staff-level accounting position in an educational
→5 spaces institution or public accounting firm. ↓1X

EDUCATION

→5 spaces, *, 1 space * B.B.A. degree in accounting from Emporia State
→7 spaces University, Emporia, Kansas, May 2004 ↓1X ↓2X

     * High school diploma from Central High School,
       Wichita, Kansas, June 2000

EXPERIENCE

     * STAFF ACCOUNTANT, Gateway Properties
       Emporia, Kansas
       December 2003-Present
       Responsible for budget control. Prepare variance
       report and annual business plan. Generate fixed-
       asset inventory. Prepare consolidated monthly
       financials.

     * ACCOUNTS RECEIVABLE CLERK, Aris Corporation
       Salina, Kansas
       January 2002-December 2003
       Posted cash receipts, prepared bank deposits, and
       processed tax requests.

PERSONAL

     *  Proficient in Microsoft Office desktop tools
     *  Member of AICPA
     *  Graduated summa cum laude from Emporia State

REFERENCES

     Available upon request.
```

Report 52-30

Resume in Electronic Style

Type an electronic resume in correct format for ALLEN P. HUNTER, 10234 Wood Sorrell Lane, Burke, VA 22015; Phone: 703-555-4902; E-mail, aphunter@netlink.net.

1. Type this OBJECTIVE entry: Retail management entry-level position with a midsize | department store.
2. Type these two EDUCATION entries as a bulleted list:
   * Central Virginia Business College, Burke, Virginia, | December 2004
   * High school diploma from Central High School, Burke, | Virginia, May 2002
3. Type these EXPERIENCE entries as a bulleted list:
   * COMPUTER SYSTEMS TECHNICIAN, Kramer & Kramer, Inc. | Harrisburg, Virginia | June 1999-Present | Duties include reviewing, installing, and updating | software programs used for processing legal | documents and monitoring computer network system for | branch offices.
   * SALESCLERK, Blanchard's Department Store | Richmond, Virginia | May 2000-May 2002 (part-time) | Duties included selling sporting goods and operating | Panasonic cash register. Assisted sales manager in | completing monthly sales reports generated by Word | and Excel software programs.
4. Type PERSONAL entries as a bulleted list:
   * Volunteer for Habitat for Humanity, 2000-Present |
   * Senior Class President, 1999 |
   * Member, Intramural Soccer Team, 1997-1999
5. Type this REFERENCES entry: Available upon request.
6. Save the resume as a text-only file.

```
ALLEN P. HUNTER

     10234 Wood Sorrell Lane
     Burke, VA 22015
     Phone: 703-555-4902
     E-mail: aphunter@netlink.net

OBJECTIVE

     Retail management entry-level position with a midsize
     department store.

EDUCATION

     * Central Virginia Business College, Burke, Virginia,
       December 2004

     * High school diploma from Central High School, Burke,
       Virginia, May 2002

EXPERIENCE

     * COMPUTER SYSTEMS TECHNICIAN, Kramer & Kramer, Inc.
       Harrisburg, Virginia
       June 1999-Present
       Duties include reviewing, installing, and updating
       software programs used for processing legal
       documents and monitoring computer network system for
       branch offices.

     * SALESCLERK, Blanchard's Department Store
       Richmond, Virginia
       May 2000-May 2002 (part-time)
       Duties included selling sporting goods and operating
       Panasonic cash register. Assisted sales manager in
       completing monthly sales reports generated by Word
       and Excel software programs.

PERSONAL

     * Volunteer for Habitat for Humanity, 2000-Present
     * Senior Class President, 1999
     * Member, Intramural Soccer Team, 1997-1999

REFERENCES

     Available upon request.
```

Letters of Application

Goals

- Improve speed and accuracy
- Refine language arts skills in composing paragraphs
- Format letters of application

A. Type 2 times.

A. WARMUP

```
     Prices were quickly lowered (some by as much as 50%) @  11
Julia's garage sale. She could see that extra sales would    24
not be over the 9%* she had projected to finance the prize.  36
|  1  |  2  |  3  |  4  |  5  |  6  |  7  |  8  |  9  |  10  |  11  |  12
```

SKILLBUILDING

PPP PRETEST → PRACTICE → POSTTEST

PRETEST
Take a 1-minute timed writing. Review your speed and errors.

B. PRETEST: Common Letter Combinations

```
     They formed an action committee to force a motion for   11
a ruling on your contract case. This enabled them to comply  24
within the lawful time period and convey a common message.   36
|  1  |  2  |  3  |  4  |  5  |  6  |  7  |  8  |  9  |  10  |  11  |  12
```

PRACTICE
Speed Emphasis:
If you made 2 or fewer errors on the Pretest, type each *individual* line 2 times.
Accuracy Emphasis:
If you made 3 or more errors, type each *group* of lines (as though it were a paragraph) 2 times.

C. PRACTICE: Word Beginnings

```
for forget formal format forces forums forked forest formed
per perils period perish permit person peruse perked pertly
com combat comedy coming commit common compel comply comets
```

D. PRACTICE: Word Endings

```
ing acting aiding boring buying ruling saving hiding dating
ble bubble dabble double enable feeble fumble tumble usable
ion action vision lesion nation bunion lotion motion legion
```

POSTTEST
Repeat the Pretest timed writing and compare performance.

E. POSTTEST: Common Letter Combinations

F. PROGRESSIVE PRACTICE: NUMBERS

If you are not using the GDP software, turn to page SB-11 and follow the directions for this activity.

LANGUAGE ARTS

G. Choose one of the phrases at the right; then compose a paragraph of three to four sentences on that topic.

G. COMPOSING PARAGRAPHS

13 My computer was working fine until it . . .
14 The Internet has helped me complete my class assignments by . . .
15 Several of us decided to take the cruise because . . .
16 I have several skills, but my best skill is . . . .

FORMATTING

Refer to page R-12B of the Reference Manual for additional guidance.

H. LETTERS OF APPLICATION

A letter of application is sent along with a resume to a prospective employer. Together, the letter and the resume serve to introduce a person to the organization.

The letter of application should be no longer than one page and should include (1) the job you are applying for and how you learned of the job, (2) the highlights of your enclosed resume, and (3) a request for an interview.

DOCUMENT PROCESSING

Correspondence 53-36

Personal-Business Letter in Modified-Block Style

September 15, 20-- | Ms. Kay Brewer, Personel Director | Blanchard Computer Systems | 2189 Dace Ave. | Sioux City, IA 51107 | Dear Ms. Brewer:

¶ Please consider me as an applicant for the position of Data Records Operator advertized in the September 13th edition of the Sioux City Press.

¶ In May I will graduate with an A.A. degree in Systems Office from West Iowa Business College. My enclosed resume shows that I have completed courses in Excel, Access, and Microsoft word. I also have significant experience in working on the internet. The skills I gained using these software packages and accessing the Internet will be extremely useful to your branch office in Sioux City.

¶ The position with your company is appealing to me. If you wish to interview me for the position, please call me at 402-555-7265.

Sincerely, | Arlene Jefferson | 1842 Amber Road | Wayne, Ne 68787 | Enclosure

Correspondence 53-37

Personal-Business Letter in Block Style

August 10, 20-- | Personnel Director | Arlington Communications | 2403 Sunset Lane | Arlington, TX 76015-3148 | Dear Personnel Director:
¶ Please consider me as an applicant for a position with Arlington Communications. My strengths have always been in the communication arts, as you can see on the enclosed resume, which lists a number of courses in English, speech, and communication technology. The two part-time jobs I held during the summer months at your company convinced me that Arlington Communications is the place where I want to work.
¶ If you would like to interview me for any possible openings this summer or fall, please call me at 903-555-2340. I look forward to hearing from you.
Sincerely, | Kenneth R. Diaz | 105 Royal Lane | Commerce, TX 75428 | Enclosure

Strategies for Career Success

Writing a Job Application Letter

What's the goal of the letter that accompanies your resume? The goal is to get the interview. No two letters of application are alike.

In the opening paragraph, state your purpose (for example, the position applied for, how you became aware of it).

In the middle section, sell yourself. Convince the reader that you are the best match for the job. If you respond to a job posting, match your qualifications to the job description. If you send an unsolicited letter, specify how the employer will benefit from your qualifications. Also, refer to your resume.

In the closing paragraph, show confidence in your abilities (for example, "I'm certain I can meet your needs for a . . ."). Then state a specific time you will call to schedule an interview.

YOUR TURN Obtain a job description for which you believe you are qualified. List the job requirements, and then list your qualifications that match.

Follow-Up Letters

Goals

- Type at least 39wpm/5'/5e
- Format follow-up letters

A. Type 2 times.

A. WARMUP

```
     Quite a night! All sixty senior citizens (including       11
the handicapped) really enjoyed that play. Over 3/4 of the     22
tickets were sold; most had been sold by Frank's workers.      34
| 1 | 2 | 3 | 4 | 5 | 6 | 7 | 8 | 9 | 10 | 11 | 12
```

SKILLBUILDING

B. DIAGNOSTIC PRACTICE: SYMBOLS AND PUNCTUATION

If you are not using the GDP software, turn to page SB-2 and follow the directions for this activity.

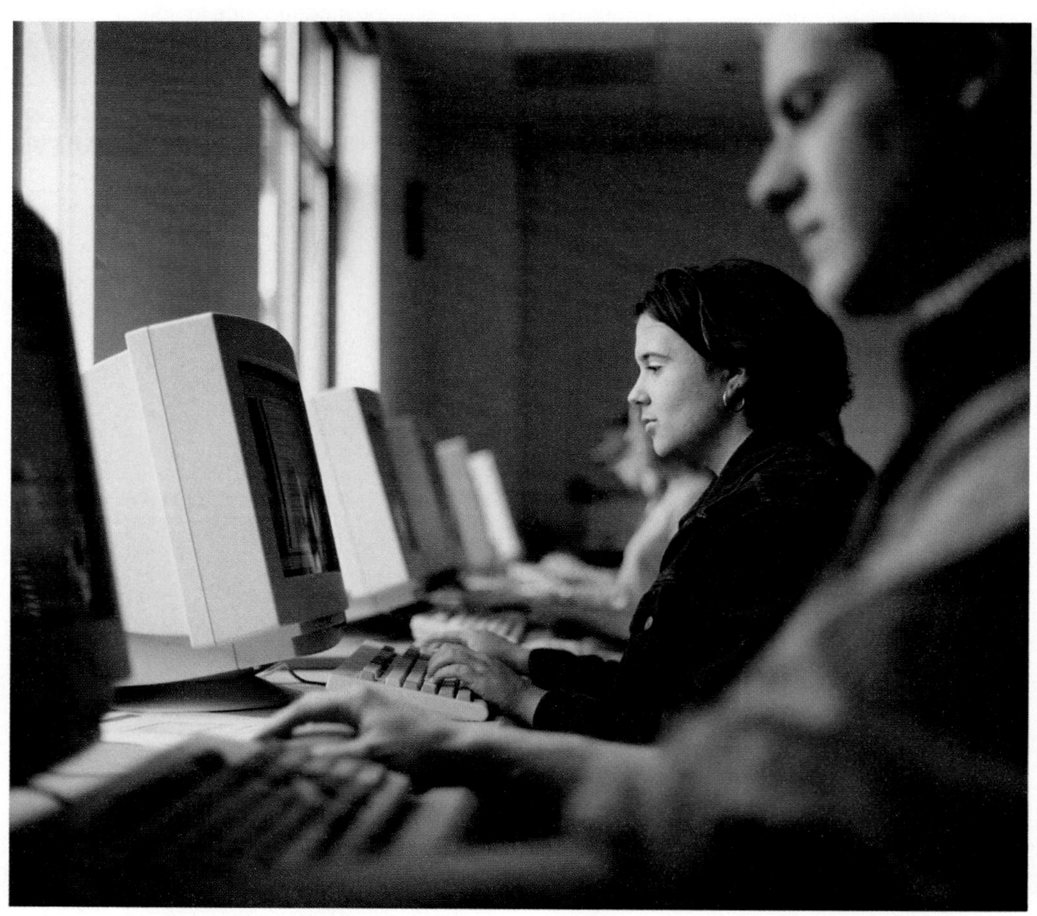

C. Take two 5-minute timed writings. Review your speed and errors.

Goal: At least 39wpm/5'/5e

C. 5-MINUTE TIMED WRITING

In the past, typing was a skill that was used only by 11
those who were secretaries, students, and office workers. 23
High school students who were in school with plans for 34
going on took a typing class so that they could type their 45
work with ease and skill. Often students who wanted to be 57
hired for office jobs would make a plan to take advanced 68
courses in typing. 72

As prices drop and as we have more and more advances 83
in technology of all types, people are recognizing that 94
they need keyboarding skills. From the top executive to the 106
customer service representative, everyone needs to be able 118
to use a computer keyboard. Workers in almost any kind of 130
business use their keyboarding skills to perform their 141
daily tasks. 143

Employers are looking for skilled workers who type 154
with consistent speed and accuracy. People who can type 165
documents accurately and enter data quickly are needed for 177
many types of careers. Skills in keyboarding are important 188
assets for several types of jobs. 195

| 1 | 2 | 3 | 4 | 5 | 6 | 7 | 8 | 9 | 10 | 11 | 12

FORMATTING

D. FOLLOW-UP LETTERS

As soon as possible after your interview (preferably the next day), you should send a follow-up letter to the person who conducted your interview. In the letter you should:

- Use a positive tone.
- Thank the person who conducted the interview.
- Mention some specific information you learned during the interview.
- Highlight your particular strengths.
- Restate your interest in working for that organization and mention that you look forward to a favorable decision.

DOCUMENT PROCESSING

Correspondence 54-38

Personal-Business Letter in Block Style

September 12, 20-- | Ms. Carole Rothchild | Personnel Director | Arlington Communications | 2403 Sunset Lane | Arlington, TX 76015-3148 | Dear Ms. Rothchild:
¶ It was a real pleasure meeting with you yesterday and learning of the wonderful career opportunities at Arlington Communications. I enjoyed meeting all the people, especially those working in the Publications Division. Thank you for taking the time to tell me about the interesting start-up history of the company and its location in Arlington.
¶ I believe my experience and job skills match nicely with those you are seeking for a desktop publishing individual, and this position is exactly what I have been looking for. You may recall that I have had experience with all of the equipment and software that are used in your office.
¶ Please let me hear from you when you have made your decision on this position. I am very much interested in joining the professional staff at Arlington Communications.
Sincerely yours, | Kenneth R. Diaz | 105 Royal Lane | Commerce, TX 75428

Correspondence 54-39

Personal-Business Letter in Modified-Block Style

April 7, 20-- | Ms. Kay Brewer, Personnel Director | Blanchard Computer Systems | 2189 Dace Avenue | Sioux City, IA 51107 | Dear Ms. Brewer:

¶ Thanks you for the opportunity of interviewing with Blanchard computer Systems yesterday. Please express my appreciation to all of those who were involved.

¶ The interview gave me a very good feeling about the company. The positive description that you shared me with convinced me that blanchard is in deed a company at which I would like to work. I was greatly impressed with the summary of social service programs for citizens throughout the community that are sponsored by Blanchard.

(Continued on next page)

¶ You may recall that I have had experience with all of the equipment that is used. It appears to me that ^my strengths in ~~software~~ ^computer application soft ware ^and office systems would blend in well with your ~~company~~ profile.

¶ I look forward to hearing you from soon regarding you^r decision on the position of data records operator.

Sincerely, | Arlene F. Jefferson | 1842 Amber Road | Wayne, NE 68787

Correspondence 54-40

Personal-Business Letter in Modified-Block Style

Open the file for Correspondence 54-39, and make the following changes:

- Change the date of the letter to `August 7, 20--.`
- Send the letter to `Mr. William E. Takashi | Personnel Director | Hawkeye Computers, Inc. | 5604 Melrose Avenue | Sioux City, IA 51105.`
- Replace "Blanchard Computer Systems" with `Hawkeye Computers` in both the first and the second paragraphs.
- Change "yesterday" in the first paragraph to `August 5.`
- Change the complimentary closing to `Yours truly.`
- Change "data records operator" to `technology support assistant` in the final paragraph.

Strategies for Career Success

Interview Thank-You Letter

Expressing your appreciation is a very important follow-up step in your job search. Send a thank-you letter or e-mail within 24 hours after your interview.

In the opening paragraph, thank the interviewer for taking time to meet with you. Make a positive statement about the company or interview feature (for example, meeting potential coworkers).

In the middle paragraph, close the sale. Address any qualifications you neglected to mention. Turn around an interview weakness (for example, reconsider your statement that you wouldn't travel). Strengthen your relationship with the interviewer (for example, refer the interviewer to a good article on a topic in which he or she expressed interest).

In the closing paragraph, ask to be notified when the decision is made. A thank-you letter ensures that your last impression is a positive one.

YOUR TURN After your next interview, send a thank-you letter that effectively closes the sale.

Lesson 55

Integrated Employment Project

Goals

- Improve speed and accuracy
- Refine language arts skills in proofreading
- Format employment documents

A. Type 2 times.

A. WARMUP

Lex was quite pleased with his travel plans; the trip 11
to Bozeman was on Flight #578 on July 30, and the return is 23
on August 12 on Flight #643. The ticket will cost $1,090. 34

| 1 | 2 | 3 | 4 | 5 | 6 | 7 | 8 | 9 | 10 | 11 | 12

SKILLBUILDING

B. Type the columns 2 times. Press TAB to move from column to column.

B. TECHNIQUE PRACTICE: TAB

J. Barnes	P. Varanth	S. Childers	M. Christenson
F. Gilsrud	J. Benson	D. Bates	M. Jordan
B. Harringer	J. Suksi	J. Lee	P. North
V. Hill	A. Budinger	T. Gonyer	S. Kravolec

C. PACED PRACTICE

If you are not using the GDP software, turn to page SB-14 and follow the directions for this activity.

LANGUAGE ARTS

D. Edit this paragraph to correct any typing or formatting errors.

D. PROOFREADING

The Smith were please to learn from their insurance
agent that the covrage ona $50,000 life insurance policy
policy would be increased by $ 20,000 at no extra cost.

The continued to pay the same premum, not knowing that the
cash value of there original policy was being taped each
month to pay an addition premium for hte new coverage.

In this unit you have learned how to prepare a resume, an application letter, and a follow-up letter—all of which are frequently used by job applicants. You will now use these skills in preparing the documents necessary to apply for the job described in the newspaper ad illustrated below.

Desktop Publisher

NetJobs, a worldwide leader in employment and job searches, has an immediate opening for a desktop publisher. This person will work in the ad production and Web page design office.

This is an entry-level position within the Advertising Department in our San Francisco office. Applicant must have experience in using Word, FrontPage, and PageMaker. Creative ability and typing skills are a must. Candidate must be able to work in a fast-paced team environment and be highly self-motivated.

Excellent company benefits are available, and they include a comprehensive medical and dental program, disability insurance, and a credit union.

If interested, send a letter of application and resume to:

Ms. Danielle E. Rose
HRM Department
NetJobs, Inc.
9350 Kramer Avenue
San Francisco, CA 94101

NetJobs Is an Equal Opportunity Employer

Report 55-31

Resume in Traditional Style

Prepare a resume for yourself as though you are applying for the job described in the ad above. Use actual data in the resume. Assume that you have just graduated from a postsecondary program. Include school-related activities, courses you have completed, and any part-time or full-time work experience you may have acquired. Make the resume as realistic as possible, and provide as much information as you can about your background.

Correspondence 55-41

Personal-Business Letter in Block Style

Prepare an application letter to apply for the position described in the ad. Date your letter March 10. Emphasize the skills you have acquired during your years in school and while working in any part-time or full-time positions. Use Correspondence 53-37 as a guide for your letter.

Correspondence 55-42

Personal-Business Letter in Modified-Block Style

Assume that your interview was held on March 25 and that you would very much like to work for NetJobs. It is now the day after your interview. Prepare a follow-up letter expressing your positive thoughts about working for NetJobs. Use Correspondence 54-39 as a guide for your letter.

Correspondence 55-43

Personal-Business Letter in Block Style

April 15, 20-- | Mr. Blair N. Scarborough | Wyatt Insurance Agency | 2834 International Blvd. | Fort Worth, TX 76390 | Dear Mr. Scarborough:

¶ My adviser, Dr. Bonnie Allworth, mentioned to me that you have an opening for a computer specialist in your Denton office. I would like to be considered as an applicant for that position.

¶ My extensive training and experience in using various software programs are ideal for the position you have open. As a student at Texas State University, I won two national awards in computer programming competition. Also, as my enclosed resume indicates, I have completed several computer courses that uniquely qualify me for the computer specialist position at Wyatt Insurance Agency.

¶ At Texas State University I took an active leadership role as president of the local chapter of Phi Beta Lambda. In my junior year I was treasurer of my campus fraternity, and during my senior year I was elected class president. These activities have provided me with valuable leadership and teamwork skills that I hope to demonstrate at Wyatt.

¶ I am very interested in working for Wyatt Insurance Company. I will telephone your office later this week to arrange an interview with you at your convenience. If you would like to speak to me prior to that time, please telephone me at my home number, 901-555-3203, after 5 p.m. or e-mail me at pmcclean@stu.edu.

Sincerely, | Pat R. McClean | 894 Cremans Avenue | Fort Worth, TX 76384 | Enclosure

Correspondence 55-44

Personal-Business Letter in Modified-Block Style

Progress and Proofreading Check

Documents designated as Proofreading Checks serve as a check of your proofreading skill. Your goal is to have zero typographical errors when the GDP software first scores the document.

Assume that you have interviewed for the position mentioned in the previous letter and that you would now like to send a follow-up letter dated June 15, 20--, to Mr. Blair N. Scarborough, thanking him for the interview. Use the inside address, salutation, and closing lines shown in Correspondence 55-43 to create the follow-up letter below:

¶ Thank you for the time you spent with me, [yesterday] telling me about the Computer Specialist position with Wyatt. My interview with you reafirmed [f] my interest in working for Wyatt.

¶ I was very impresed [s] with work done in your Information Processing department. The hardware and software you use for writing computer code and the people working in that department are very apealing [p] to me.

¶ I believe my particular background and skills blend perfectly with ~~the~~ [this] position. I hope to hear from you by the end of next week for a positive decision on my employment. Thank you [again] for bringing me in for the interview.

Strategies for Career Success

Looking for a Job

Don't waste time! Start your job search early. Scan the Help Wanted section in major Sunday newspapers for job descriptions and salaries. The Internet provides electronic access to worldwide job listings. If you are interested in a particular company, access its home page.

Ask a reference librarian for handbooks (for example, *Occupational Outlook Handbook*), government publications (for example, *Federal Career Opportunities*), and journals or magazines in your field. Visit your college placement office. Sign up for interviews with companies that visit your campus.

Talk with people in your field to get advice. Look for an internship or join a professional organization in your field. Attend local chapter meetings to network with people in your chosen profession.

Taking the initiative in your job search will pay off!

YOUR TURN Visit the Internet site for the *National Business Employment Weekly* at http://www.employmentguide.com, which provides more than 45,000 national and international job listings online.

Unit 12

Skillbuilding and In-Basket Review

LESSON 56
In-Basket Review (Insurance)

LESSON 57
In-Basket Review (Hospitality)

LESSON 58
In-Basket Review (Retail)

LESSON 59
In-Basket Review (Nonprofit)

LESSON 60
In-Basket Review (Manufacturing)

MEMO TO: Blanche O. Pruitt

FROM: Kevin Hite

DATE: January 11, 20--

SUBJECT: District Meetings

As you know, each year we rotate the location of our district meetings to one of our regional offices. This year our meeting will be held in your region, preferably in Albuquerque. Would you please contact the hotels in Albuquerque and select a suitable site for this year's meeting, which will be held on March 7 and 8.

October 16, 20--

Mr. Brandon T. Wright
District Manager
206 South Rock Road
Wichita, KS 67210

Dear Mr. Wright:

Ellen B. Boldt
Executive Vice President

lcm

September 15, 20--

Ms. Rolanda L. Farmer
203 Grand Avenue
Bozeman, MT 59715

Dear Ms. Farmer:

Your order for Internet service has been processed, and you can enjoy surfing the Web immediately! As a customer of Global Communications, a subsidiary of Disk Drives, Etc., you will enjoy several benefits:

1. You will receive 24/7 customer service when using our service hotline at 1-800-555-3888.
2. You will be protected by E-Protect, Global's virus protection software. This software is updated weekly, and you can download weekly updates at www.global.net.
3. You will receive 10 Mbytes of Web page space.
4. You will receive automated credit card billing, as requested.

A complete listing of all our services is enclosed for your perusal.

Thank you for joining Global Communications. Please e-mail us at support@gc.net if you have any questions, or call us on our service hotline. We expect the coming months of providing Internet service to you to be a very enjoyable experience for both of us.

Sincerely,

Nancy Mendez
Sales and Marketing Director

jrt
Enclosure

In-Basket Review (Insurance)

Goals

- Type at least 40wpm/5′/5e
- Format insurance documents

A. Type 2 times.

A. WARMUP

```
     Kyu Choi jumped at the opportunity to assume 40% of        11
the ownership of your restaurant. Alverox & Choi Chinese        22
Cuisine will be opening quite soon at 1528 Waysata Street.      34
|  1  |  2  |  3  |  4  |  5  |  6  |  7  |  8  |  9  |  10  |  11  |  12
```

SKILLBUILDING

B. DIAGNOSTIC PRACTICE: NUMBERS

If you are not using the GDP software, turn to page SB-5 and follow the directions for this activity.

C. Take three 12-second timed writings on each line. The scale below the last line shows your wpm speed for a 12-second timed writing.

C. 12-SECOND SPEED SPRINTS

```
Kay Sue is on her way to that new show to take some photos.
Most of the ones who go may not be able to make it on time.
When they got to their seats, they were glad they had come.
Both men and women might take some of their pets with them.
||||5||||10||||15||||20||||25||||30||||35||||40||||45||||50||||55||||60
```

Keyboarding Connection

Creating an E-Mail Signature File

Creating a signature file saves you time and adds a personal touch to your e-mail messages! A signature file is a tag of information at the end of your e-mail. It may include your signature, a small graphic, your address, your phone number, or a quotation. The signature file appears on every e-mail message you send. Use the following guidelines to create a signature file.

Open your e-mail software. Open the menu item that allows you to create a signature file. Type the information you want to include in your signature file. Close the file.

YOUR TURN Create a signature file. Then address an e-mail to yourself. Type "Test" in the Subject box. In the body, type "This is a test of the signature file." Send the e-mail. Open the test e-mail and locate your signature file at the bottom of the e-mail message.

D. Take two 5-minute timed writings. Review your speed and errors.

Goal: At least 40wpm/5′/5e

D. 5-MINUTE TIMED WRITING

```
     When you begin to think about a career, you should        10
assess your personal abilities and interests. Do you have a   22
natural aptitude in a certain area? Do you have special       34
interests or hobbies that you would like to develop into a    45
career? Do you enjoy working with other people, or do you     57
like to work on your own? Would you like to work in a large   69
office, or do you prefer to work outdoors? These questions    81
are important to consider when you think about your career.   93
     Your quest to find the perfect career will be more      103
successful if you try to maximize the opportunities that     115
are available. For example, you might consider working with  127
an organization that offers you career counseling. A career  139
counselor is trained to help you determine your aptitudes    150
and interests. You may contact people who work in a career   162
that interests you and ask to shadow them on their jobs and  174
ask them questions. You might find an online service to      185
help you find a very interesting career that will meet each  197
of your goals.                                               200
| 1 | 2 | 3 | 4 | 5 | 6 | 7 | 8 | 9 | 10 | 11 | 12
```

DOCUMENT PROCESSING

Correspondence 56-45

Business Letter in Block Style

Situation: You are employed in the office of All-City Insurance of Columbia, Missouri. Their offices are located at 17 North Eighth Street, Columbia, MO 65201-7272. All-City handles auto, home, and life insurance coverage in Iowa, Kansas, and Missouri. You work for Ellen B. Boldt, executive vice president. Ms. Boldt prefers the letter in block style and *Sincerely* as the complimentary closing. Add your reference initials as appropriate.

October 16, 20-- | Mr. Brandon T. Wright | District Manager | 206 South Rock Road | Wichita, KS 67210 | Dear Mr. Wright:

¶ Several of our service representatives have indicated on our Web site chat room that new clients are becoming increasingly interested in the criteria to consider when evaluating their insurance carriers. All-City has prided itself in years past on its reputable service record with its policyholders, and the service representatives have undoubtedly shared this record with prospective customers. However, we want to be certain that other characteristics about

(Continued on next page)

All-City are also shared with these potential policyholders.

¶ Please be sure that your representatives share the following service characteristics with potential customers:

Refer to page R-12C of the Reference Manual for information on formatting lists.

- Our claims are handled quickly and with a minimum of "red tape."
- Our ratio of number of policies to number of complaints is the highest in the industry.
- No disciplinary actions have been taken against All-City in the past 50 years.

Provide suitable closing lines.

¶ Please share this information with your service representatives and inform them that updated information on our services is provided on our home page for their use or for their policyholders' use.

Correspondence 56-46

Memo

Ms. Boldt has dictated the following memo for you to transcribe. As you can see, there are several rough-draft changes that you will have to make to the memo.

MEMO TO: Sheila Parsons, Training Director

FROM: Ellen B. Boldt, Executive Vice President

DATE: October 17, 20--

SUBJECT: Training seminar

¶ Our new agent training seminar will be held on December 10, and we plan again this year as we have in the past to conduct separate sessions for auto and life insurance policies. You will be in charge of the auto insurance seminars, and Victor Samuels will conduct the life insurance seminars.

¶ I expect that this years' auto insurance seminars will present our 6 basic coverage areas using the latest presentation demo software for the following:

(Continued on next page)

Refer to page R-12C of the Reference Manual for information on formatting lists.

- Bodily injury liability
- Medical payments or personal injury protection
- Property damage liability
- Collision
- Comprehensive
- Uninsured Motorist

We are the market leaders in bodily injury liability and property damage liability coverages. Therefore you should plan to spend at least one-half of your presentation discussing our strengths in these coverages. You might want to include in your presentation the fact that our coverages in these areas have more than surpaed those of our competitors for the past 7 years or so.

¶ Use Table 1, which is enclosed, to be sure that we explain the variety of discounts offered for Iowa, Kansas, and missouri.

urs | Enclosure

Table 56-17

Boxed Table

Prepare Table 56-17 on a full sheet of paper in correct table format as an enclosure for the memo to Ms. Parsons. Press ENTER to create the 1- and 2-line column headings, as shown, before automatically adjusting the table width.

DISCOUNT PROGRAMS (For Selected States)	
Available Discounts	**Discount Amount (%)**
Air Bag	Up to 8.5
Antitheft Device	Up to 18
Claims Cost Reduction	Up to 1.8
Driving Course	Up to 4.5
Good Driver	20
Good Student	Up to 16
Mature Driver	Up to 1.8
Multipolicy	2 up to 7
Multivehicle	Up to 25
New Driver	Up to 10
Select Professionals Program	4.5 up to 14

In-Basket Review (Hospitality)

Goals

- Improve speed and accuracy
- Refine language arts skills in number expression and in the use of the hyphen
- Format hospitality documents

A. Type 2 times.

A. WARMUP

```
     Dexter gave an ultimatum: Quit driving on the lawn or   11
I will call the police. A fine of $100 (or even more) may    23
be levied against Kyle, who lives at 2469 Zaine in Joplin.   34
| 1 | 2 | 3 | 4 | 5 | 6 | 7 | 8 | 9 | 10 | 11 | 12
```

SKILLBUILDING

B. PROGRESSIVE PRACTICE: ALPHABET

If you are not using the GDP software, turn to page SB-7 and follow the directions for this activity.

C. PACED PRACTICE

If you are not using the GDP software, turn to page SB-14 and follow the directions for this activity.

LANGUAGE ARTS

D. Study the rules at the right.

D. NUMBER EXPRESSION AND HYPHENATION

RULE ▶ # word

Spell out

- **A number used as the first word of a sentence.**
  Seventy-five people attended the conference in San Diego.
- **The shorter of two adjacent numbers.**
  We have ordered 3 two-pound cakes and one 5-pound cake for the reception.
- **The words *million* and *billion* in round numbers (do not use decimals with round numbers).**
  Not: A $5.00 ticket can win $28,000,000 in this month's lottery.
  But: A $5 ticket can win $28 million in this month's lottery.
- **Fractions.**
  Almost one-half of the audience responded to the question.

Note: When fractions and the numbers twenty-one through ninety-nine are spelled out, they should be hyphenated.

(Continued on next page)

RULE ▶
- number

Hyphenate compound numbers between twenty-one and ninety-nine and fractions that are expressed as words.

Twenty-nine recommendations were approved by at least three-fourths of the members.

Edit the sentences to correct any errors in number expression.

4 Seven investors were interested in buying 2 15-unit condos.

5 The purchase price for the buildings will be $3,000,000.00 each, which is 1/2 the total.

6 The computers were mailed in 5 40-pound boxes for 2/3 of the price paid yesterday.

7 Our food chain sold hamburgers for $3.00 each last year.

8 I can sell nearly one-half of all the tickets at the gate on November 13.

9 59 parking spaces are located within 1/2 mile of the city center.

10 We must place our mailing pieces in 8 twenty-pound bags for the mail clerk.

11 I don't believe more than 1/5 of the drivers have insurance.

DOCUMENT PROCESSING

Situation: Today is August 21, and you are employed in the office of Suite Retreat, a group of vacation resorts in Naples, Florida. Your employer, the general manager, is Mr. Aaron Hynes. Mr. Hynes is attending a meeting in Miami and has left the following jobs for you to complete. Press ENTER to create the 1- and 2-line column headings as displayed before automatically adjusting the table width.

Table 57-18

Open Table

SUITE RETREAT PROPERTIES
Selected Beach Rentals

Property	Rooms	Rental Rate In Season	Rental Rate Off Season
Carriage House	4	$3,500	$2,400
Naples Hideaway	5	2,750	2,100
Ocean Breeze	5	3,850	2,700
Princeton Palace	4	3,200	2,550
Seville Landings	6	4,250	3,100
The Vanderbilt	5	3,475	2,575
Westover Estates	6	5,250	4,150

Correspondence 57-47

Business Letter in Modified-Block Style

August 21, 20-- | Mr. Leland Mott | 243 Worth Street | Raleigh, NC 27603 | Dear Mr. Mott:

¶ We were pleased to hear of your interest in renting one of our prime beach units in Naples, Florida. I have enclosed a listing of all our current properties in the Naples area. We have 14 two-bedroom rentals, 15 three-bedroom rentals, and 11 four-bedroom rentals. Five of our three-bedroom units have already been rented for this season; one-half of the other thirty-four units are still available.

word

word

≡ number

¶ Let me review a few of the particulars of each unit with you. Our Carriage House and Naples Hideaway have Gulf Coast views and garage facilities. The Ocean Breeze and Princeton have lake views and tennis courts. The Seville, Vanderbilt, and Westover have a Gulf Coast view and a private golf course.

¶ If you plan to rent one of our units, please be sure to notify us by writing or by calling our toll-free number at 1-800-555-1348.

Sincerely, | Aaron Hynes | General Manager | urs | Enclosure | c: Theresa McDonald, Celeste Binghamton

Keyboarding Connection

Finding Business Information on the Internet

To begin research on a business-related topic, try one of the following sites:

Business Resources on the Web at www.cio.com/bookmark provides links to Cable News Network (CNN) Business News, the Wall Street Journal Money and Investing Update, and other news sources. It includes information about careers, Electronic Data Interchange (EDI) and the Internet, general business sources, training, marketing, and resources for entrepreneurs.

Business Administration Internet Resources at www.acad.sunytccc.edu/library/busman.htm provides links to news and financial market updates, the Securities and Exchange Commission (SEC), Thomas Register, U.S. Census Bureau, U.S. Economic and Labor Statistics, and World Bank reports.

Selected Business Resources on the Web at www.bls.gov provides information about marketing, finance, small business, business law, international business, stock markets, and a link to the Small Business Administration.

YOUR TURN Access one of the business information sites listed above and explore its offerings.

Mr. Hynes has recently purchased a fishing resort on Lake Okeechobee, Florida, and plans to open it on September 1. Type the following report and send it to the *Naples Press* so that it will appear in this Sunday's special *Travel and Tourism* section. Use a standard business format to prepare the report.

Report 57-32

Business Report

FISHING PARADISE SCHEDULED TO OPEN | Suite Retreat | Naples, Florida

¶ Suite Retreat is celebrating the grand opening of its newest fishing resort, Kamp Kellogg, located on the northwest corner of Lake Okeechobee, on the banks of the Kissimmee River.

GENERAL INFORMATION

¶ The following information will give you an overview of our policies and accommodations:

¶ **Reservations**. The reservation desk will open on September 1 to reserve your cabin at our beautiful resort. You can reach reservations via the Internet by logging on to our Web site at http://www.kampkellogg.com.

¶ **Accommodations.** Whether you're looking for deluxe accommodations or rustic surroundings, Kamp Kellogg has it all. You have a choice of rustic cabins nestled in the woods or large chalets overlooking Lake Okeechobee.
If you enjoy an evening of relaxation, each cabin includes a gazebo, out near the water's edge, that is screened in for a perfect evening of comfort.

¶ **Amenities.** Your lodging choice includes full kitchens for those who want to do their own cooking, or you can order a full meal through our catering service. Each unit has a game room with a large-screen television, VCR, videotapes, and computer workstation with Internet connection. Outside the sliding glass door is a covered deck, equipped with a barbecue grill and hot tub.

LAKE OKEECHOBEE

¶ Lake Okeechobee lies geographically in the center of the state of Florida. The name "Okeechobee" was given to the lake by the Seminole Indians, and it means "big water." Lake Okeechobee is the largest freshwater lake in the United States occurring in one state. It is approximately 37 miles long and 30 miles wide, with an average depth of almost 10 feet. The lake produces more bass over 8 pounds than any other lake in the United States. It is famous for bass, crappie, and bluegill fishing. Several species of wildlife also thrive around the lake, such as the bald eagle, blue heron, egret, white ibis, sand hill crane, turkey, vulture, owl, alligator, bobcat, turkey, and panther.

Refer to page R-12C of the Reference Manual for information on formatting lists.

PRICING INFORMATION

¶ We are offering a special introductory rate of $250 through November 1. This rate includes the following:

- Two-night stay for a family of four (# word)
- Two half days of fishing (# word)
- One USCG-licensed fishing guide (# word)
- Tackle and bait

¶ A full refund will be made if the fishing excursion is canceled because of inclement weather or failure of equipment (boat, trailer, or vehicle). If only a partial day of fishing is completed, one-half of the charges will be refunded. (- number)

Lesson 58

In-Basket Review (Retail)

Goals

- Type at least 40wpm/5′/5e
- Format retail documents

A. Type 2 times.

A. WARMUP

1 Do you think 1/3 of the contents of the five quart- 11
2 sized boxes would be about right? I do! If not, they can 22
3 adjust the portions by adding 6 or 7 gallons of warm water. 34

| 1 | 2 | 3 | 4 | 5 | 6 | 7 | 8 | 9 | 10 | 11 | 12

SKILLBUILDING

B. DIAGNOSTIC PRACTICE: SYMBOLS AND PUNCTUATION

If you are not using the GDP software, turn to page SB-2 and follow the directions for this activity.

C. Type each line 2 times. Change every singular noun to a plural noun, and change every plural noun to a singular noun.

C. TECHNIQUE PRACTICE: CONCENTRATION

4 Debit the accounts. Balance your checkbook. Add the assets.
5 Take the discount. Send the statements. Compute the ratios.
6 Review the accounts. Credit the amounts. Figure the totals.
7 Prepare the statements. Send the catalog. Call the clients.

D. Take two 5-minute timed writings. Review your speed and errors.

Goal: At least 40wpm/5′/5e

D. 5-MINUTE TIMED WRITING

```
     Most workers will learn about their success on the job  11
at least once a year. The person in charge will be the one   23
to conduct these reviews. Even though the job review is      34
important, either party might not look forward to such a     46
meeting. Frequently, an employee and a boss can view these   57
meetings as a time to discuss everything that this person    69
has done wrong in the last year. Such a negative approach    81
can add a lot of stress and tension between the employee     92
and management. In the long run, work performance suffers.  104
     A good manager must learn a new way to conduct more    114
positive job reviews. Such a meeting might start by sizing  126
up what the employee has done to help improve things in the 138
past year. Positive comments may include coming to work on  150
time, working well with others, and being willing to pitch  162
in whenever needed. Next, the areas for improvement may be  174
discussed. Then the employee should be given the chance to  185
ask questions, write a response to the appraisal, and get   197
other feedback.                                             200
 |  1  |  2  |  3  |  4  |  5  |  6  |  7  |  8  |  9  |  10  |  11  |  12
```

DOCUMENT PROCESSING

Situation: You are employed as an administrative assistant for Good Sports, a retailer for sports equipment and clothing in Denver, Colorado. Your employer is Mr. Kevin Hite, marketing director for Good Sports. Upon arriving at your office on Monday morning, you notice that Mr. Hite has left several jobs that need to be completed for his signature. He prefers a letter in block style in his correspondence and uses *Sincerely* as the complimentary closing.

Correspondence 58-48

Business Letter in Block Style

January 10, 20-- | Mr. Alex R. Chaney, Principal | Madison Heights High School | 1839 East Colfax Avenue | Denver, CO 80212 | Dear Mr. Chaney:

¶ Thank you for your invitation to advertise on your school's Web site. We were delighted to have the opportunity to sponsor last week's Marathon Mile at Madison Heights High School and hope that all the participants enjoyed the competition and spectator activities.

¶ This week my office staff will be putting together a Web page that we would like to display on the Web space you have so generously provided. It is my understanding that the Web site will remain online throughout this school year. We will be certain to maintain it on a regular basis so that our products and prices always remain current.

(Continued on next page)

Add the closing lines to Mr. Hite's letter. Send copies of this letter to Ardele Stevens, Jennifer Smits, and Randall Campbellton.

¶ The Marathon Mile has certainly become one of the county's most popular school events. We look forward to the opportunity of cosponsoring next year's Marathon Mile at Madison Heights.

Correspondence 58-49

Memo

MEMO TO: Blanche O. Pruitt | **FROM:** Kevin Hite | **DATE:** January 11, 20-- | **SUBJECT:** District Meetings

¶ As you know, each year we rotate the location of our district meetings to one of our regional offices. This year our meeting will be held in your region, preferably in Albuquerque. Would you please contact the hotels in Albuquerque and select a suitable site for this year's meeting, which will be held on March 7 and 8.

¶ We decided at our last regional managers' meeting that this year's meeting would highlight our Internet sales campaign. Specifically, we want to focus on the following issues:

1. How can we improve our Web page design to attract a higher percentage of the market?
2. How can we improve our e-commerce procedures so that our order-processing routine is easier and faster for the average Web visitor?
3. What links can we add to our home page to encourage visitors to view a greater percentage of our product line?

¶ Please let me know when you have made arrangements for our meeting site. I look forward to meeting with all of you in March. | urs

Refer to Reference Manual

Refer to page R-12C of the Reference Manual for information on formatting lists.

Table 58-19

Boxed Table

WEEKLY BICYCLE SPECIALS
January 13, 20--

Model	**Price**	**Special Features**
Comanche	$270	15" Y-frame; 18-speed drivetrain; adjustable seat
Cyclone	375	Our lightest bike; preassembled; wired blue color
Duster	480	Front suspension fork; semislick tires; 24-speed
Trail Blazer	725	Titanium frame; aluminum seat post; two bottle mounts

Lesson 59

In-Basket Review (Nonprofit)

Goals

- Improve speed and accuracy
- Refine language arts skills in spelling
- Format government documents

A. Type 2 times.

A. WARMUP

```
     Crowne and Metzner, Inc., employees* joined with 68        11
youngsters to repair the brick homes of 13 elderly persons;     23
several became very well acquainted with six of the owners.     35
|  1  |  2  |  3  |  4  |  5  |  6  |  7  |  8  |  9  |  10  |  11  |  12
```

SKILLBUILDING

B. MAP

Follow the GDP software directions for this exercise in improving keystroking accuracy.

C. Take a 1-minute timed writing on the first paragraph to establish your base speed. Then take four 1-minute timed writings on the remaining paragraphs. As soon as you equal or exceed your base speed on one paragraph, advance to the next, more difficult paragraph.

C. SUSTAINED PRACTICE: PUNCTUATION

```
     The men in the warehouse were having a very difficult      11
time keeping track of that inventory. Things began to go        22
much more smoothly for them when they got the new computer.     34

     Whenever something was shipped out, a computer entry       11
was made to show the changes. They always knew exactly what     23
merchandise was in stock; they also knew what to order.         34

     Management was pleased with that improvement. "We          10
should have made the change years ago," said the supervisor     22
to the plant manager, who was in full agreement with him.       34

     This is just one example (among many) of how the work      11
areas can be improved. Workers' suggestions are listened        22
to by alert, expert managers. Their jobs are better, too.       34
|  1  |  2  |  3  |  4  |  5  |  6  |  7  |  8  |  9  |  10  |  11  |  12
```

LANGUAGE ARTS

D. Type this list of frequently misspelled words, paying special attention to any spelling problems in each word.

D. SPELLING

16 development determine enclosed complete members recent site
17 permanent personal facility medical library however purpose
18 representative implementation electrical discussed eligible
19 organization performance minimum discuss expense areas next
20 professional arrangements separate changes reason field pay

Edit the sentences to correct any misspellings.

21 Members of the medicle and profesional group discussed it.
22 The development of the seperate cite will be completed.
23 A recent representive said the libary facility may be next.
24 A perpose of the electricle organization is to get changes.
25 However, the implimentation of changes will be permenant.
26 Arrangments for the enclosed eligable expenses are listed.

DOCUMENT PROCESSING

Situation: Today is October 10. You work for Quick Trip, a ride-share company located in Windsor, Connecticut.

Your company is a nonprofit commuter company that provides the following services: move people to and from work, conduct parking studies, match people with available rides, and publish a commuter ride-share weekly report.

Your job responsibilities include preparing reports that summarize weekly commuter news, typing correspondence to advertise and promote Quick Trip's services, and communicating with area commuters who subscribe to Quick Trip's services.

Today, you must (1) prepare a report that summarizes services offered by Quick Trip, and (2) create a table that lists new additions to the weekly report.

Report 59-33

Business Report

QUICK TRIP

Windsor's Premier Ride- Share

¶ If you're tired of driving that one- to two hour commute into Connecticuts' busy metropolitan areas, then let us take that burden ~~on for you.~~ off your shoulders. Quick Trip, the metro's premier ride-share company, is a convenient, economical way to get to & from work. All you have to do is get on board!

(Continued on next page)

Costs of Commuting

¶ A recent article showed that commuting just 15 miles each way can cost a minimum of 1,200 per year; sharing the ride with some one else can cut your comuting expenses in half.[1] In addition to the cost of gas, you must also figure in other costs of transportation such as maintenance on your vehicle, insurance premiums, depreciation, and finance charges.[2] When you consider all these costs, ride-sharing takes on a whole new significance. You should also consider how you are helping the trafic congestion and air pollution problems by ride-sharing. And don't forget about the possibility of being involved in an accident. Finally you can reduce stress by ride-sharing because you can choose to leave the driving to someone else.

RESERVATIONS AND BENEFITS

¶ If you want to reserve a seat on a Quick Trip route, just call one of our professional service representatives at 1-800-555-Trip. Our representatives in the field have information on routes, schedules, rides availability, and other benefits. For example, we have an E-ride available for you if there is an emergency that requires you to get home. Here are some special benefits with Quick Trip:

Refer to page R-12C of the Reference Manual for information on formatting lists.

- A free commute for every 500 comuting miles.
- Separate insurance and medical coverage.
- Flexible payment policies.
- A free commute for every 500 commuting miles.
- Full insurance coverage.
- Flexible payment policies.
- 4 free taxi rides home per year in the event of illness or personal emergency.

SERVICE AREAS

¶ Quick Trip serves the cities of Plainville, Rocky Hill, Manchester, Windsor, New Haven, and Sufield. Next month we open routes to Avon, Glastonbury,

(Continued on next page)

Durham, and Middletown. In all, we have over 300 regular routes state wide, and service is expanding monthly. Easy access is guaranteed with all our routes. To view our entire service area, go to our web site, http://www.qt.com, and link to the Quick Trip regional service map area. The map details all our routes, highlights specific pickup points, and identifies our regional service facilities. Visit our site today and become a ride-share enthusiast!

---

[1] Erica Sommers, "Ride-Sharing for the Environment," *Environmental Planning*, February 21, 2004, p. 18.

[2] Joshua R. Blake, *Cleaning Up America*, New Haven Publishing, Manchester, Connecticut, 2005, p. 138.

Table 59-20

Boxed Table

QUICK TRIP COMMUTER BULLETIN For October			
From	To	Name	Telephone
Manchester	Rocky Hill	S. Baskin	860-555-5581
Manchester	Windsor	E. Lindholm	203-555-4684
Manchester	Suffield	P. Mack	860-555-4322
New Haven	Plainville	T. Thompson	203-555-1249
Rocky Hill	Windsor	J. Kiczuk	860-555-1842
Suffield	Manchester	M. Duprey	203-555-9339
Suffield	New Haven	B. Huehner	203-555-0442
Suffield	New Haven	M. Mac	203-555-1844
Windsor	Manchester	L. Smith	203-555-8893
Windsor	Rocky Hill	R. McCaffrey	203-555-7782

In-Basket Review (Manufacturing)

Goals

- Type at least 40wpm/5'/5e
- Format manufacturing documents

A. Type 2 times.

A. WARMUP

"Fay's #6 report shows 26 pens @ .49 each and 37 pens 11
@ .79 each," the CEO announced. Mrs. Bailey's reaction was 23
quite amazing as 80 jobs were validated with checked boxes. 35
| 1 | 2 | 3 | 4 | 5 | 6 | 7 | 8 | 9 | 10 | 11 | 12

SKILLBUILDING

PPP PRETEST → PRACTICE → POSTTEST

PRETEST
Take a 1-minute timed writing. Review your speed and errors.

B. PRETEST: Close Reaches

Sally took the coins from the pocket of her blouse 10
and traded them for seventy different coins. Anyone could 22
see that Myrtle looked funny when extra coins were traded. 34
| 1 | 2 | 3 | 4 | 5 | 6 | 7 | 8 | 9 | 10 | 11 | 12

PRACTICE
Speed Emphasis:
If you made 2 or fewer errors on the Pretest, type each *individual* line 2 times.
Accuracy Emphasis:
If you made 3 or more errors, type each *group* of lines (as though it were a paragraph) 2 times.

C. PRACTICE: Adjacent Keys

as asked asset based basis class least visas ease fast mass
we weary wedge weigh towel jewel fewer dwell wear weed week
rt birth dirty earth heart north alert worth dart port tort

D. PRACTICE: Consecutive Fingers

sw swamp swift swoop sweet swear swank swirl swap sway swim
gr grade grace angry agree group gross gripe grow gram grab
ol older olive solid extol spool fools stole bolt cold cool

POSTTEST
Repeat the Pretest timed writing and compare performance.

E. POSTTEST: Close Reaches

F. Take two 5-minute timed writings. Review your speed and errors.

Goal: At least 40wpm/5'/5e

F. 5-MINUTE TIMED WRITING

Information technology is among the fastest-growing 11
job fields today and is also one of the fields to change 22
the quickest. The goal of many schools is to try to prepare 34
students to be specialists in a workplace that continues to 46
be challenging and will need to change quickly as advances 58
are made in technology. 63
Those who wish to work in a field that will not stand 74
still need to know all about the systems with which they 85
labor. Network administrators, for example, will often take 97
courses to certify that they have a sound knowledge of any 109
of the new hardware. They must also learn about specific 120
equipment and have an understanding of how new software 131
will function with hardware. 137
Those who wish to pass certification exams must have 148
the zeal, determination, and drive to complete all of the 160
requirements. They know that it will not be long before the 172
current systems will be upgraded or new software will be 183
released. They need to learn the latest systems and review 195
their certification again. 200

| 1 | 2 | 3 | 4 | 5 | 6 | 7 | 8 | 9 | 10 | 11 | 12

DOCUMENT PROCESSING

Situation: You are an administrative assistant, and you work for Disk Drives, Etc., in Phoenix, Arizona. Your supervisor is Ms. Nancy Mendez, sales and marketing director. Ms. Mendez has asked you to prepare the following documents for her while she is in a staff meeting this morning. The letter is to be prepared for her signature, the table will be enclosed with the letter, and she will initial the memo before sending it out this afternoon.

Correspondence 60-50

Business Letter in Block Style

September 13, 20-- | Ms. Nancy Luo | 1387 Rim Drive | Flagstaff, AZ 86001-3111 | Dear Ms. Luo:

¶ We were pleased to see that you have used our Web site at www.tosabi.com to inquire about our online catalog. We specialize in computer drives of all types: CD-ROM, DVD, Zip, Jaz, floppy, and hard drives. I have enclosed a listing of our most popular CD-ROM writers that will appear online next week in our catalog. As a new customer, you are invited to visit our catalog and place your order at these special prices.

(Continued on next page)

¶ Our online customers receive the same privileges as our hard-copy catalog shoppers. These online privileges include:

- No shipping charges.
- Toll-free customer support line.
- Discounts on 10 or more purchases.
- Ninety-day warranties (parts and labor) on all purchases.

¶ We look forward to many years of doing business with you. Please e-mail me at nmendez@tosabi.net if you have any questions or would like additional information.
Sincerely, | Nancy Mendez | Sales and Marketing Director | urs | Enclosure | c: S. Choi, W. Matson

Table 60-21

Boxed Table

Your finished table will have different line endings for Column D when you resize the column widths to fit the contents.

CD-ROM WRITERS (Effective Dates September 18-23)			
Model No.	**Part No.**	**Price**	**Specifications**
460RW	841120	$199	4x speed write, 16x speed read, CD recording software
2600E	841111	235	4x speed write, 24x speed read, 4x speed rewrite, stores up to 650 MB per disk
9282E	841415	415	Rewritable. 4x speed write, 8x speed read, Direct CD software
8428S	842013	595	Rewritable. 8x speed write, 24x speed read, 2x speed erase, Direct CD software
93422R	841712	658	Rewritable. 4x speed write, 6x speed read, 2x speed rewrite, Direct CD software, CDR-DJ

Correspondence 60-51

Memo

MEMO TO: Claudia Crenshaw | Publications Department | **FROM:** Nancy Mendez | Sales and Marketing Director | **DATE:** September 13, 20-- | **SUBJECT:** Ad in the *Arizona Daily Sun*
¶ Claudia, please include the following criteria in our ad that will run in the *Arizona Daily Sun* this Sunday:

1. Quarter-page ad
2. Run-time: 2 weeks
3. Location: Business Section as well as Classified Section
4. Contact: Include telephone, fax, and e-mail numbers

¶ This is our first ad piece in the *Sun* since we ran that special promotion last March. Let's add some graphics to make this one an "eye-catcher." | urs

Correspondence 60-52

Business Letter in Modified-Block Style

September 15, 20-- | Ms. Rolanda L. Farmer | 203 Grand Avenue | Bozeman, MT 59715 | Dear Ms. Farmer:
¶ Your order for Internet service has been processed, and you can enjoy surfing the Web immediately! As a customer of Global Communications, a subsidiary of Disk Drives, Etc., you will enjoy several benefits:
1. You will receive 24/7 customer service when using our service hotline at 1-800-555-3888.
2. You will be protected by E-Protect, Global's virus protection software. This software is updated weekly, and you can download weekly updates at www.gc.net.
3. You will receive 10 Mbytes of Web page space.
4. You will receive automated credit card billing, as requested.

¶ A complete listing of all our services is enclosed for your perusal.
¶ Thank you for joining Global Communications. Please e-mail us at support@gc.net if you have any questions, or call us on our service hotline. We expect the coming months of providing Internet service to you to be a very enjoyable experience for both of us.
Sincerely, | Nancy Mendez | Sales and Marketing Director | urs | Enclosure

Reference Manual

Refer to page R-12C of the Reference Manual for information on formatting lists.

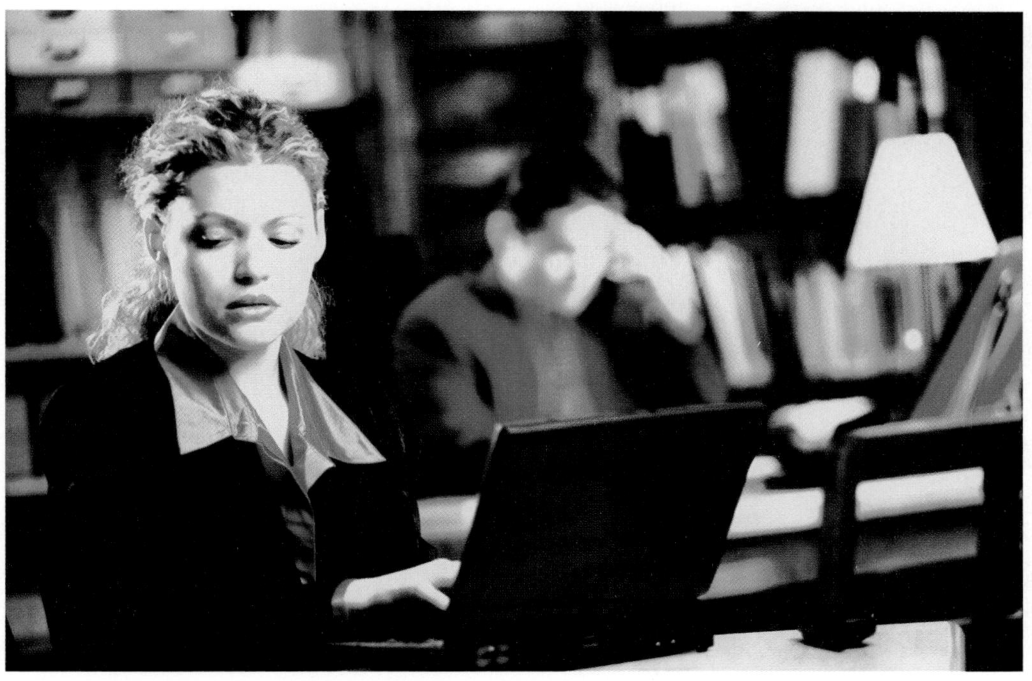

Table 60-22

Boxed Table

Progress and Proofreading Check

Documents designated as Proofreading Checks serve as a check of your proofreading skill. Your goal is to have zero typographical errors when the GDP software first scores the document.

Your finished table will have different line endings for all columns when you resize the column widths to fit the contents.

CUSTOMER SERVICES (Effective October 1, 20--)		
Service	**Description/Comments**	**Representative**
24/7 Service	Call 1-800-555-3888; wait time is usually less than 1 minute.	M. R. Osumi, mrosumi@global.net
Virus-Protection Service	E-Protect software is down-loaded automatically to your computer when service is installed.	W. N. Gauthier, wngauth@global.net
Web Space	10 MB of Web page space is standard; an additional 10 MB can be obtained on an as-needed basis.	M. J. Martinez, mjmartinez@global.net
Credit Card Billing	When requested by the customer, we automatically send your monthly bill to a credit card of your choice.	L. T. Matthews, ltmatt@global.net

Strategies for Career Success

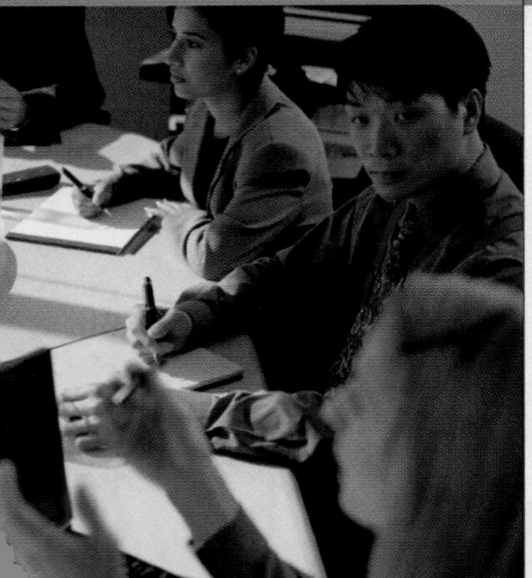

Successful Interviewing Techniques

The interview is a useful tool for researching information. Here are some steps to effective interviewing.

Conduct preliminary research so you can ask intelligent questions and make efficient use of the interview time. Prepare a list of questions (for example, an interview script) to use in the interview. Make sure the questions are open-ended, unbiased, and geared toward gathering insights you can't gain through reading. Be prepared to take notes, listen actively, and ask follow-up questions, as needed.

Greet the interviewee by name and thank him or her for taking time to talk with you. Explain why you are interested in interviewing him or her. Stay within the scheduled time limits. In closing the interview, thank the interviewee again, and ask if you can get in touch if other questions come to mind.

YOUR TURN Prepare a list of questions you might use in interviewing someone concerning the current U.S. immigration policies.

Skills Assessment on Part 3

5-Minute Timed Writing

People are often the most prized assets in a business. 11
Excellent firms know that having well-qualified workers is 23
an important step to ensure the success of the company. The 35
people in charge can play a huge part in how much success a 47
firm will have when they provide a workplace that is meant 59
to support teams of people who can work together to achieve 71
a common goal. When people know they are being encouraged 82
to work toward achieving their own goals as well as the 94
goals of the company, they will respond by working to their 106
highest potential with ardor and zeal. 113
Managers need to show that they value the hard work 124
and long hours that employees put in to ensure the success 136
of the business. People thrive on compliments that show 147
their work is appreciated. They like to be rewarded in some 159
way when they have done an exceptional job. When those in 171
charge are successful in motivating the employees to work 182
to their full potential, their company will prosper. The 194
result is that each person wins. 200

| 1 | 2 | 3 | 4 | 5 | 6 | 7 | 8 | 9 | 10 | 11 | 12

Correspondence Test 3-53

Business Letter in Block Style

Add an envelope to the letter, and omit the return address.

July 13, 20-- | Mr. Anthony Gillespie | Goddard Properties | 1808 Augusta Court | Lexington, KY 40505-2838 | Dear Mr. Gillespie:

¶ Let me introduce myself. I am committee chair of a group that monitors development projects in Lexington, Kentucky. It was brought to my attention that your proposal to construct 100 three- and four-bedroom homes was approved by the city council last night. As a resident in a neighboring community, I wish to share with you the stipulations

(Continued on next page)

we would like you to incorporate into your development project:

- The new homes should have no less than 2,700 square feet of living space.
- All structures should have brick frontage.
- No external, unattached buildings should be constructed.

¶ Following these stipulations will ensure that your homes adhere to our community building codes. Sincerely, | Dora H. Hayes | Committee Chair | urs | c: S. Benefield, T. Grace

Correspondence Test 3-54

Memo

MEMO TO: Ana Pacheco
FROM: Liang Quan
DATE: June 26, 20--
SUBJECT: Desktop Publishing Certificate
¶ Our DTP certificate seminar will be held in St. Louis on August 14. Upon request of last year's participants, we want to be sure to include the following topics:

- Integrated Computer Applications
- Advanced Desktop Publishing
- Introduction to Computer Graphics
- Graphic Design A and B

¶ These were the four most popular topics at last year's seminar. Let's use a brochure design similar to the one we used at the Denver meeting last year. A copy of that brochure is attached for you to review. | urs | Attachment

Report Test 3-34

Business Report

AIR POLLUTION

¶ When we hear about pollution, we tend to think of smog, traffic congestion, acid rain, and other pollutant-related terms. However, we also need to consider the air we breathe as we work.

AIR QUALITY AND POLLUTANTS

¶ We need to be concerned about indoor air because it can affect the health, comfort, and productivity of workers.[1]

¶ **Strategies to Improve Air Quality.** The three basic approaches to improving air quality include the use of air pressure to keep the pollutants "at bay," the use of ventilation systems to remove the pollutants, and the use of filters to clean the air. The pollutants can appear in various forms but are typically biological contaminants, chemical pollutants, or particles.

¶ **Pollutant Descriptions.** Biological contaminants can include viruses, molds, bacteria, dust mites, pollen, and water spills. These contaminants cause allergic reactions that trigger asthma attacks for an estimated 16 million Americans.[2] Chemical pollutants include tobacco smoke and accidental chemical spills. Particles include such pollutants as dust and dirt from drywall, carpets, copying machines, and printing operations.[3]

MANAGERS' RESPONSIBILITIES

¶ Office managers should help by reviewing records pertaining to air conditioning and ventilation systems. They should also provide training sessions for employees to learn about maintaining clean air. Finally, they should keep a record of reported health complaints related to polluted air and aid in resolving these complaints.

AIR QUALITY IS A TEAM EFFORT

¶ All workers can have a positive impact on improving the quality of the air they breathe. For example, simply making sure that air vents and grilles are not blocked will help improve the quality of air. People who smoke should do so only in areas designated as smoking areas for employees.

---

[1] Karen Scheid, "Pollution at Work," *Los Angeles Times*, May 4, 2004, p. C8.

[2] "Dirty Air in Today's Offices," March 12, 2004, <http://www.airamerica.com/dirty.htm>, accessed on May 13, 2004.

[3] Carlos Sanchez, *Pollutants in America*, Southwest Press, Albuquerque, 2003.

SKILLBUILDING

Diagnostic Practice: Symbols and Punctuation

The Diagnostic Practice: Symbols and Punctuation program is designed to diagnose and then correct your keystroking errors. You may use this program at any time throughout the course after completing Lesson 19.

Directions

1. Type one of the three Pretest/Posttest paragraphs 1 time, pushing *moderately* for speed. Review your errors.
2. Note your results—the number of errors you made on each symbol or punctuation key. For example, if you typed *75&* for *75%*, you would count 1 error on the % key.
3. For any symbol or punctuation key on which you made 2 or more errors, type the corresponding drill lines 2 times. If you made only 1 error, type the drill line 1 time.
4. If you made no errors on the Pretest/Posttest paragraph, type one set of the Practice: Symbols and Punctuation lines on page SB-4.
5. Finally, retype the same Pretest/Posttest, and compare your performance with your Pretest.

PRETEST/POSTTEST

Paragraph 1

```
Price & Joy stock closed @ 5 1/8 yesterday; it was up 13%
from yesterday. If we had sold our "high-demand" shares*
(*300 of them) before 3:30 p.m., we'd have made $15,000,
wouldn't we? Oh, well! I'll be in my office (#13C) crying.
```

Paragraph 2

```
The Time/CNN poll had the slate of Myers & Bassey ahead by
just 5%. Weren't you surprised? I was; after all, "they"*
(*meaning the crew) had ordered 60# of food @ $9.50 a pound
for a victory party at 3:30 p.m. today. What a sad mix-up!
```

Paragraph 3

```
Didn't my colleague* (*Elsa Jones-Salizar) send in $50 as a
10% deposit for reserving Room #5B on Friday and/or Monday?
Attached to her deposit was a note that said, "Call Tibby,
& me @ 10:30 a.m."; I was surprised. She sounded desperate!
```

PRACTICE: Individual Reaches

Ampersand

```
juj ju7j j7j j7&j j&&j j&&j juj ju7j j7j j7&j j&&j j&&j &&&
Alma & Bill & Carr & Dern & Epps & Farr & Gary & Horn & Ing
Jack & Kyle & Mann & Nash & Okum & Parr & Rand & Star & Tua
Uber & Vern & Will & Xang & Year & Zack & Sons & Bros & Inc
```

Apostrophe

```
;;; ;'; ;'; ';' ';' ''' Al's Bo's Di's it's Jo's Li's Moe's
you'd he'll she'd it'll she'll they'd aren't you're they're
we're we've we'll can't you've you'll hasn't didn't they've
she's don't isn't won't hadn't wasn't here's that's what'll
```

Asterisk

kik ki8k k8*k k8*k k**k k**k ki8k k8*k k8*k k**k k**k Note*
Ames* Beck* Carr* Dern* Epps* Farr* Gary* Horn* Iago* Jack*
Kyle* Mann* Nash* Okum* Parr* Rand* Star* Teri* Uber* Vern*
Will* Xang* Year* Zack* Note* Star* Also* List* Text* Cite*

At Sign

sws sw2s s2@s s2@s s@s s@@s and sws sw2s s2@s s2@s s@s s@@s
138 @ 34 and 89 @ 104 and 18 @ 458 and 89 @ 10 and 18 @ 340
162 & 31 and 48 & 606 and 81 @ 923 and 69 @ 42 and 54 @ 128
277 @ 89 and 57 & 369 and 70 @ 434 and 50 @ 15 and 37 @ 512

Colon

;;; ;:; ;:; :;: ::: and :/: and :?: and :p: and :-: and :::
From: Name: City: Madam: 4:30 Bill to: Address: To: cc: PS:
Date: Rank: Time: Dept.: 27:1 Subject: Time in: Hi: Re: Cf:
Sirs: Ext.: Apt.: State: 1:00 Ship to: Acts 4:2 FY: ID: OS:

Comma

kkk k,k k,k and ,k, and ,i, and ,8, and I,I and K,K and ,,,
Ava, ebb, lac, had, foe, elf, hug, ugh, poi, raj, ink, gal,
bum, Ben, ago, cop, req, far, has, dot, tau, env, wow, sax,
I am, you are, he is, we are, they are, Al, Ty, Hy, Jo, Ann

Diagonal

;;; ;/; /// and p/p and /p/ and 0/0 ;;; ;/; /// and p/p ///
a/c c/o B/L ft/s ac/dc and/or he/she cad/cam due/dew 1/2005
I/O n/a B/S n/30 AM/FM ob/gyn on/off lay/lie fir/fur 2/2006
p/e m/f w/o km/h d/b/a ad/add to/too set/sit him/her 3/2007

Dollar Sign

frf fr4 f4f f$f f$f f$f $40 $44 $44 f$f f4f $ff $45 $54 $$$
$40 and $82 and $90 and $13 and $33 and $56 and $86 and $25
$214 plus $882 plus $900 plus $718 plus $910 plus $112 plus
$1,937.53 plus $337.89 tax $3,985.43 minus $150.75 discount

Exclamation Mark

aqa aqla aq!a a!!a a!!a aqa aqla aq!a a!!a a!!a Go! Hi! Lo!
Oh! Wow! Gas! Dig! Yes! Sit! Rats! Darn! Well! Drat! Shoot!
So! Eat! Air! Out! Not! Aim! Whoa! Wait! Whee! Oops! Yahoo!
No! Yea! Eek! Run! Boo! Buy! Look! Help! Duck! Alas! There!

Hyphen

;;; ;p; ;-; -;- --- and -;- and -;- and -/- and -:- and -P-
add-on be-all F-stop H-bomb A-frame age-old all-day boo-boo
how-to in-out jam-up log-in come-on cop-out end-all fade-in
mix-up no-win say-so tie-up one-act pig-out rip-off T-shirt

Number/Pound

de3d de3#d d3#d d3#d d##d d##d #33 #33 #333 de3d de3#d d3#d
45# of #245 and 837# of #013 and 31# of #981 and 2# of #013
12# of #883 and 345# of #328 and 67# of #112 and 8# of #109
54# of #542 and 378# of #310 and 13# of #189 and 6# of #657

Parentheses

lo9l lo9l lo(l lo(l l((l l((l ;p0; ;p0; ;p); ;p); ;)); ;));
(a) (b) (c) (d) (e) (f) (g) (h) (i) (j) (k) (l) (m) (n) (o)
(p) (q) (r) (s) (t) (u) (v) (w) (x) (y) (z) (1) (2) (3) (4)
(5) (6) (7) (8) (9) (0) (@) (#) ($) (&) (*) (-) (;) (,) (:)

Percent

```
ftf ft5f f5f f5%f f%%f f%%f ftf ft5f f5f f5%f f%%f f%%f %%%
40% and 82% and 90% and 13% and 33% and 56% and 86% and 25%
21% and 48% and 82% and 90% and 70% and 18% and 91% and 10%
34.5% off 89% increase 12% credit 67% finished 10% discount
```

Period

```
1.1 ... and .1. and .o. and .9. and .(. and .O. and L.L ...
Jan. Feb. Mar. Apr. Jun. Jul. Aug. Sep. Oct. Nov. Dec. a.m.
Sun. Mon. Tue. Wed. Thu. Fri. Sat. Mrs. Esq. Mex. Can. D.C.
I am. I see. We do. He is. I can. Do not. Help me. Go slow.
```

Question Mark

```
;;; ;/; ;?; ??? ?;? and p?p and ?0? and ?)? and ?-? and ???
So? Who? What? Can I? Why not? Who does? Stop here? Is she?
Me? How? When? May I? Who, me? Says who? Do it now? For me?
Oh? Why? Am I? Do we? Am I up? How much? Who knows? Will I?
```

Quotation Mark

```
;'; ;"; ;"; ";" """ and ;'; ;"; ;"; ";" """ and ;"; ";" """
"Eat" "Sit" "Rest" "Stay" "Roll" "Hello" "Look" "Pet" "Dry"
"Yes" "Lie" "Halt" "Next" "Move" "Write" "Type" "Ink" "Sew"
"Beg" "See" "Walk" "Wave" "Stop" "Speak" "File" "Run" "Cry"
```

Semicolon

```
;;; ;:; and ;'; and ;"; and ;p; and ;-; and ;/; and ;?; ;;;
tea; ebb; Mac; mid; lie; arf; hug; nth; obi; Taj; ark; Hal;
dim; man; bio; hop; seq; our; Gus; let; you; Bev; row; lax;
do not cry; that is Liz; see to it; I am sad; we do; I can;
```

PRACTICE: SYMBOLS AND PUNCTUATION

```
Doe & Fry sued May & Ito; Ho & Fox sued Doe & Lee for M&Ms.
Ann's dad said he's happy she's out of school; she'd agree.
Yesterday* (*April 9), the rock star said **** right on TV.
E-mail them at glyden@sales.com to buy 3 @ $89 or 9 @ $250.

Hi, Ross: Place odds of 3:1 on the game at 10:30 and 11:15.
Tom gave Ava, Jo, Al, and Tyson a red, white, and blue car.
On 3/1/2008, he will receive a pension and/or a big buyout.
The $80 skirt was cut to $70 and then $55 for a $25 saving.

What! No ice! I'm mortified! Run, order some more. Quickly!
Jones-Lynch built an all-season add-on to her A-frame home.
Please order 500# of #684, 100# of #133, and 200# of #1341.
The answer is (a) 1, (b) 4, (c) 7, or (d) all of the above.

The car was cut 15% and then 25% for a final saving of 40%.
Mr. R. J. Dix ordered from L. L. Bean on Dec. 23 at 11 a.m.
Who? Me? Why me? Because I can type? Is that a good reason?
"Look," he said, "see that sign?" It says, "Beware of Dog."
Stop here; get out of your car; walk a foot; begin digging.
```

Diagnostic Practice: Numbers

The Diagnostic Practice: Numbers program is designed to diagnose and then correct your keystroking errors. You may use this program at any time throughout the course after completing Lesson 14.

Directions

1. Type one of the three Pretest/Posttest paragraphs 1 time, pushing *moderately* for speed. Review your errors.
2. Note your results—the number of errors you made on each key and your total number of errors. For example, if you type *24* for *25*, you would count 1 error on the number *5*.
3. For any number on which you made 2 or more errors, select the corresponding drill lines and type the drills 2 times. If you made only 1 error, type the drill 1 time.
4. If you made no errors on the Pretest/Posttest paragraph, type 1 set of the drills that contain all numbers on page SB-6.
5. Finally, retype the same Pretest/Posttest, and compare your performance with your Pretest.

PRETEST/POSTTEST

Paragraph 1

```
     The statement dated May 24, 2004, listed 56 clamps; 15
batteries; 169 hammers; 358 screwdrivers; 1,298 pliers; and
1,475 files. The invoice numbered 379 showed 387 hoes, 406
rakes, 92 lawn mowers, 63 tillers, and 807 more lawn items.
```

Paragraph 2

```
     My inventory records dated May 31, 2004, revealed that
we had 458 pints; 1,069 quarts; and 8,774 gallons of paint.
We had 2,953 brushes; 568 scrapers; 12,963 wallpaper rolls;
897 knives; 5,692 mixers; 480 ladders; and 371 step stools.
```

Paragraph 3

```
     Almost 179 hot meals were delivered to the 35 shut-ins
in April, 169 in May, and 389 in June. Several workers had
volunteered 7,564 hours in 2004; 9,348 hours in 2003; 5,468
in 2002; and 6,577 in 2001. About 80 people were involved.
```

PRACTICE: INDIVIDUAL REACHES

```
1 aq aq1 aq1qa 111 ants 101 aunts 131 apples 171 animals a1
They got 11 answers correct for the 11 questions in BE 121.
Those 11 adults loaded the 711 animals between 1 and 2 p.m.
All 111 agreed that 21 of those 31 are worthy of the honor.

2 sw sw2 sw2ws 222 sets 242 steps 226 salads 252 saddles s2
The 272 summer tourists saw the 22 soldiers and 32 sailors.
Your September 2 date was all right for 292 of 322 persons.
The 22 surgeons said 221 of those 225 operations went well.

3 de de3 de3ed 333 dots 303 drops 313 demons 393 dollars d3
Bus 333 departed at 3 p.m. with the 43 dentists and 5 boys.
She left 33 dolls and 73 decoys at 353 West Addison Street.
The 13 doctors helped some of the 33 druggists in Room 336.
```

```
4 fr fr4 fr4rf 444 fans 844 farms 444 fishes 644 fiddles f4
My 44 friends bought 84 farms and sold over 144 franchises.
She sold 44 fish and 440 beef dinners for $9.40 per dinner.
The 1954 Ford had only 40,434 fairly smooth miles by May 4.

5 fr fr5 fr5rf 555 furs 655 foxes 555 flares 455 fingers f5
They now own 155 restaurants, 45 food stores, and 55 farms.
They ordered 45, 55, 65, and 75 yards of that new material.
Flight 855 flew over Farmington at 5:50 p.m. on December 5.

6 jy jy6 jy6yj 666 jets 266 jeeps 666 jewels 866 jaguars j6
Purchase orders numbered 6667 and 6668 were sent yesterday.
Those 66 jazz players played for 46 juveniles in Room 6966.
The 6 judges reviewed the 66 journals on November 16 or 26.

7 ju ju7 ju7uj 777 jays 377 jokes 777 joists 577 juniors j7
The 17 jets carried 977 jocular passengers above 77 cities.
Those 277 jumping beans went to 77 junior scouts on May 17.
The 7 jockeys rode 77 jumpy horses between March 17 and 27.

8 ki ki8 ki8ik 888 keys 488 kites 888 knives 788 kittens k8
My 8 kennels housed 83 dogs, 28 kids, and 88 other animals.
The 18 kind ladies tied 88 knots in the 880 pieces of rope.
The 8 men saw 88 kelp bass, 38 kingfish, and 98 king crabs.

9 lo lo9 lo9ol 999 lads 599 larks 999 ladies 699 leaders 19
All 999 leaves fell from the 9 large oaks at 389 Largemont.
The 99 linemen put 399 large rolls of tape on for 19 games.
Those 99 lawyers put 899 legal-size sheets in the 19 limos.

0 ;p ;p0 ;p0p; 100 pens 900 pages 200 pandas 800 pencils ;0
There were 1,000 people who lived in the 300 private homes.
The 10 party stores are open from 1:00 p.m. until 9:00 p.m.
They edited 500 pages in 1 book and 1,000 pages in 2 books.
```

All numbers

```
a1a s2s d3d f4f f5f j6j j7j k8k l9l ;0; Add 6 and 8 and 29.
That 349-page script called for 10 actors and 18 actresses.
The check for $50 was sent to 705 Garfield Street, not 507.
The 14 researchers asked the 469 Californians 23 questions.
```

All numbers

```
a1a s2s d3d f4f f5f j6j j7j k8k l9l ;0; Add 3 and 4 and 70.
They built 1,299 houses on the 345-acre site by the canyon.
Her research showed that gold was at 397 in September 2004.
For $868 extra, they bought 15 new books and 61 used books.
```

All numbers

```
a1a s2s d3d f4f f5f j6j j7j k8k l9l ;0; Add 5 and 7 and 68.
A bank auditor arrived on May 26, 2004, and left on May 27.
The 4 owners open the stores from 9:30 a.m. until 6:00 p.m.
After 1,374 miles on the bus, she must then drive 185 more.
```

Progressive Practice: Alphabet

This skillbuilding routine contains a series of 30-second timed writings that range from 16wpm to 104wpm. The first time you use these timed writings, take a 1-minute timed writing on the Entry Timed Writing paragraph. Note your speed.

Select a passage that is 2wpm higher than your current speed. Then take six 30-second timed writings on the passage.

Your goal each time is to complete the passage within 30 seconds with no errors. When you have achieved your goal, move on to the next passage and repeat the procedure.

Entry Timed Writing

```
     Bev was very lucky when she found extra quality in the       11
home she was buying. She quietly told the builder that she        23
was extremely satisfied with the work done on her new home.       35
The builder said she can move into her new house next week.       47
|  1  |  2  |  3  |  4  |  5  |  6  |  7  |  8  |  9  |  10  |  11  |  12
```

16wpm The author is the creator of a document.

18wpm Open means to access a previously saved file.

20wpm A byte represents one character to every computer.

22wpm A mouse may be used when running Windows on a computer.

24wpm Soft copy is text that is displayed on your computer screen.

26wpm Memory is the part of the word processor that stores information.

28wpm A menu is a list of choices to direct the operator through a function.

30wpm A sheet feeder is a device that will insert sheets of paper into a printer.

32wpm An icon is a small picture that illustrates a function or an object in software.

34wpm A window is a rectangular area with borders that displays the contents of open files.

36wpm To execute means to perform an action specified by an operator or by the computer program.

38wpm Output is the result of a word processing operation. It can be either printed or magnetic form.

40wpm Format refers to the physical features which affect the appearance and arrangement of your document.

42wpm A font is a style of type of one size or kind which includes all letters, numbers, and punctuation marks.

44wpm Ergonomics is the science of adapting working conditions or equipment to meet the physical needs of employees.

46wpm Home position is the starting position of a document; it is typically the upper left corner of the display monitor.

48wpm The mouse may be used to change the size of a window and to move a window to a different location on the display screen.

50wpm An optical scanner is a device that can read text and enter it into a word processor without the need to type the data again.

52wpm Hardware refers to the physical equipment used, such as the central processing unit, display screen, keyboard, printer, or drives.

54wpm A peripheral device is any piece of equipment that will extend the capabilities of a computer system but is not required for operation.

56wpm A split screen displays two or more different images at the same time; it can, for example, display two different pages of a legal document.

58wpm When using Windows, it's possible to place several programs on a screen and to change the size of a window or to change its position on a screen.

60wpm With the click of a mouse, one can use a button bar or a toolbar for fast access to features that are frequently applied when using a Windows program.

62wpm An active window can be reduced to an icon when you use Windows, enabling you to double-click another icon to open a new window for formatting and editing.

64wpm Turnaround time is the length of time needed for a document to be keyboarded, edited, proofread, corrected if required, printed, and returned to the originator.

66wpm A local area network is a system that uses cable or another means to allow high-speed communication among many kinds of electronic equipment within particular areas.

68wpm To search and replace means to direct the word processor to locate a character, word, or group of words wherever it occurs in the document and replace it with newer text.

70wpm	Indexing is the ability of a word processor to accumulate a list of words that appear in a document, including page numbers, and then print a revised list in alphabetic order.
72wpm	When a program needs information from you, a dialog box will appear on the desktop. Once the dialog box appears, you must identify the option you desire and then choose that option.
74wpm	A facsimile is an exact copy of a document, and it is also a process by which images, such as typed letters, graphs, and signatures, are scanned, transmitted, and then printed on paper.
76wpm	Compatibility refers to the ability of a computer to share information with another computer or to communicate with some other apparatus. It can be accomplished by using hardware or software.
78wpm	Some operators like to personalize their desktops when they use Windows by making various changes. For example, they can change their screen colors and the pointer so that they will have more fun.
80wpm	Wraparound is the ability of a word processor to move words from one line to another line and from one page to the next page as a result of inserting and deleting text or changing the size of margins.
82wpm	It is possible when using Windows to evaluate the contents of different directories on the screen at the very same time. You can then choose to copy or move a particular file from one directory to another.
84wpm	List processing is a capability of a word processor to keep lists of data that can be updated and sorted in alphabetic or numeric order. A list can also be added to any document that is stored in one's computer.
86wpm	A computer is a wondrous device, which accepts data that are input and then processes the data and produces output. The computer performs its work by using one or more stored programs, which provide the instructions.
88wpm	The configuration is the components that make up your word processing system. Most systems include the keyboard that is used for entering data, a central processing unit, at least one disk drive, a monitor, and a printer.

90wpm Help for Windows can be used whenever you see a Help button in a dialog box or on a menu bar. Once you finish reading about a topic that you have selected, you will see a list of some related topics from which you can choose.

92wpm When you want to look at the contents of two windows when using Windows, you will want to reduce the window size. Do this by pointing to a border or a corner of a window and dragging it until the window is the size that you want.

94wpm Scrolling means to display a large quantity of text by rolling it horizontally or vertically past the display screen. As the text disappears from the top section of the monitor, new text will appear at the bottom section of the monitor.

96wpm The Windows Print Manager is used to install and configure printers, join network printers, and monitor the printing of documents. Windows requires that a default printer be identified, but you can change the designation of it at any point.

98wpm A stop code is a command that makes a printer pause while it is printing to permit an operator to insert text, change the font style, or change the kind of paper in the printer. To resume printing, the operator must use a special key or command.

100wpm A computerized message system is a class of electronic mail that enables any operator to key a message on any computer terminal and have the message stored for later retrieval by the recipient, who can then display the message on his or her terminal.

102wpm Many different graphics software programs have been brought on the market in recent years. These programs can be very powerful in helping with a business presentation. If there is any need to share data, using one of these programs could be quite helpful.

104wpm Voice mail has become an essential service that many people in the business world use. This enables anyone who places a call to your phone to leave a message if you cannot answer it at that time. This special feature helps lots of workers to be more productive.

Progressive Practice: Numbers

This skillbuilding routine contains a series of 30-second timed writings that range from 16wpm to 80wpm. The first time you use these timed writings, take a 1-minute timed writing on the Entry Timed Writing paragraph. Note your speed.

Select a passage that is 4 to 6wpm *lower* than your current alphabetic speed. (The reason for selecting a lower speed goal is that sentences with numbers are more difficult to type.) Take six 30-second timed writings on the passage.

Your goal each time is to complete the passage within 30 seconds with no errors. When you have achieved your goal, move on to the next passage and repeat the procedure.

Entry Timed Writing

Their bags were filled with 10 sets of jars, 23 cookie 11
cutters, 4 baking pans, 6 coffee mugs, 25 plates, 9 dessert 23
plates, 7 soup bowls, 125 recipe cards, and 8 recipe boxes. 35
They delivered these 217 items to 20487 Mountain Boulevard. 47

| 1 | 2 | 3 | 4 | 5 | 6 | 7 | 8 | 9 | 10 | 11 | 12

16wpm

There were now 21 children in Room 2110.

18wpm

Fewer than 12 of the 121 boxes arrived today.

20wpm

Maybe 12 of the 21 applicants met all 15 criteria.

22wpm

There were 34 letters addressed to 434 West Cranbrooke.

24wpm

Jane reported that there were 434 freshmen and 43 transfers.

26wpm

The principal assigned 3 of those 4 students to Room 343 at noon.

28wpm

Only 1 or 2 of the 34 latest invoices were more than 1 page in length.

30wpm

They met 11 of the 12 players who received awards from 3 of the 4 trainers.

32wpm

Those 5 vans carried 46 passengers on the first trip and 65 on the next 3 trips.

34wpm

We first saw 3 and then 4 beautiful eagles on Route 65 at 5 a.m. on Tuesday, June 12.

36wpm

The 16 companies produced 51 of the 62 records that received awards for 3 of 4 categories.

38wpm

The 12 trucks hauled the 87 cows and 65 horses to the farm, which was about 21 miles northeast.

40wpm	She moved from 87 Bayview Drive to 657 Cole Street and then 3 blocks south to 412 Gulbranson Avenue.
42wpm	My 7 or 8 buyers ordered 7 dozen in sizes 5 and 6 after the 14 to 32 percent discounts had been bestowed.
44wpm	There were 34 men and 121 women waiting in line at the gates for the 65 to 87 tickets to the Cape Cod concert.
46wpm	Steve had listed 5 or 6 items on Purchase Order 241 when he saw that Purchase Requisition 87 contained 3 or 4 more.
48wpm	Your items numbered 278 will sell for about 90 percent of the value of the 16 items that have code numbers shown as 435.
50wpm	The managers stated that 98 of those 750 randomly selected new valves had about 264 defects, far exceeding the usual 31 norm.
52wpm	Half of the 625 volunteers received over 90 percent of the charity pledges. Approximately 83 of the 147 agencies will have funds.
54wpm	Merico hired 94 part-time workers to help the 378 full-time employees during the 62-day period when sales go up by 150 percent or more.
56wpm	Kaye only hit 1 for 4 in the first 29 games after an 8-game streak in which she batted 3 for 4. She then hit at a .570 average for 6 games.
58wpm	The mail carrier delivered 98 letters during the week to 734 Oak Street and also took 52 letters to 610 Faulkner Road as he returned on Route 58.
60wpm	Pat said that about 1 in 5 of the 379 swimmers had a chance of being among the top 20. The best 6 of those 48 divers will receive the 16 best awards.
62wpm	It rained from 3 to 6 inches, and 18 of those 20 farmers were fearful that 4 to 7 inches more would flood about 95 acres along 3 miles of the new Route 78.

64wpm

Those 7 sacks weighed 48 pounds, more than the 30 pounds that I had thought. All 24 believe the 92-pound bag is at least 15 or 16 pounds above its true weight.

66wpm

They bought 7 of the 8 options for 54 of the 63 vehicles last month. They now own over 120 dump trucks for use in 9 of the 15 new regions in the big 20-county area.

68wpm

Andy was 8 or 9 years old when they moved to 632 Glendale Street away from the 1700 block of Horseshoe Lane, which is about 45 miles directly west of Boca Raton, FL 33434.

70wpm

Doug had read 575 pages in the 760-page book by March 30; Darlene had read only 468 pages. Darlene has read 29 of those optional books since October 19, and Doug has read 18.

72wpm

That school district has 985 elementary students, 507 middle school students, and 463 high school students; the total of 1,955 is 54, or 2.84 percent, over last year's grand total.

74wpm

Attendance at last year's meeting was 10,835. The goal for this year is to have 11,764 people. This will enable us to plan for an increase of 929 participants, a rise of 8.57 percent.

76wpm

John's firm has 158 stores, located in 109 cities in the West. The company employs 3,540 males and 2,624 females, a total of 6,164 employees. About 4,750 of those employees work part-time.

78wpm

Memberships were as follows: 98 members in the Drama Guild, 90 members in Zeta Tau, 82 members in Theta Phi, 75 in the Bowling Club, and 136 in the Ski Club. This meant that 481 joined a group.

80wpm

The association had 684 members from the South, 830 members from the North, 1,023 members from the East, and 751 from the West. The total membership was 3,288; these numbers increased by 9.8 percent.

Paced Practice

The Paced Practice skillbuilding routine builds speed and accuracy in short, easy steps by using individualized goals and immediate feedback. You may use this program at any time after completing Lesson 9.

This section contains a series of 2-minute timed writings for speeds ranging from 16wpm to 96wpm. The first time you use these timed writings, take the 1-minute Entry Timed Writing.

Select a passage that is 2wpm higher than your current typing speed. Then use this two-stage practice pattern to achieve each speed goal: (1) concentrate on speed, and (2) work on accuracy.

Speed Goal. To determine your speed goal, take three 2-minute timed writings in total. Your goal each time is to complete the passage in 2 minutes without regard to errors. When you have achieved your speed goal, work on accuracy.

Accuracy Goal. To type accurately, you need to slow down—just a bit. Therefore, to reach your accuracy goal, drop back 2wpm from the previous passage. Take consecutive timed writings on this passage until you can complete the passage in 2 minutes with no more than 2 errors.

For example, if you achieved a speed goal of 54wpm, you should then work on an accuracy goal of 52wpm. When you have achieved 52wpm for accuracy, move up 4wpm (for example, to the 56-wpm passage) and work for speed again.

Entry Timed Writing

```
     If you can dream it, you can live it. Follow your       10
heart. There are many careers, from the mundane to the       21
exotic to the sublime. Start your career planning now.       32
Prepare for the future by exploring your talents, skills,    44
and interests.                                               47
| 1 | 2 | 3 | 4 | 5 | 6 | 7 | 8 | 9 | 10 | 11 | 12
```

16wpm

Your future is now.[1] Seize each day. After[2] you have explored[3] your personal interests,[4] study the sixteen[5] career clusters[6] for a broad range of[7] job possibilities.[8]

18wpm

While exploring various[1] job options, think about[2] what a job means[3] to you. A job can mean[4] something you do simply[5] to earn money or something[6] you find more rewarding[7] and challenging.[8]

20wpm

If you have a job you enjoy,[1] work means more than[2] just receiving wages.[3] It means using your talents,[4] being among people[5] with like interests, making a[6] contribution, and gaining[7] a sense of satisfaction.[8]

22wpm

What is the difference between a job and a career? Think carefully. A job is work that people do for money. A career is a sequence of related jobs built on a foundation of interests, knowledge, training, and experiences.

24wpm

Learn more about the world of work by looking at the sixteen career clusters. Most jobs are included in one of the clusters that have been organized by the government. During your exploration of careers, list the clusters that interest you.

26wpm

Once you identify your career clusters of interest, look at the jobs within each cluster. Find out what skills and aptitudes are needed, what education and training are required, what the work environment is like, and what is the possibility for advancements.

28wpm

Use your career center and school or public libraries to research career choices. Search the Internet. Consult with professionals for another perspective of a specific career. As you gather information about career options, you may discover other interesting career possibilities.

30wpm

Gain insights into a career by becoming a volunteer, participating in an internship, or working a part-time or temporary job within a chosen field. You will become more familiar with a specific job while developing your skills. You'll gain valuable experience, whether you choose that career or not.

32wpm

Whichever path you choose, strive for a high level of pride in yourself and your work. Your image is affected by what you believe other people think of you as well as by how you view yourself. Evaluate your level of confidence in yourself. If you have self-doubts, begin to build up your self-confidence and self-esteem.

34wpm

Self-esteem is essential for a positive attitude, and a positive attitude is essential for success in the world of work. While you cannot control everything that happens at work, you can control how you react. Your attitude matters. Becoming more confident and cultivating positive thoughts can bring you power in your life and on the job.

36wpm

Several factors lead to success on the job. People who have studied the factors say that it is the personal traits that often determine who is promoted or who is not. One of the finest traits a person can possess is the trait of being likable. Being likable means a person is honest, courteous, loyal, thoughtful, pleasant, kind, and most assuredly, positive.

38wpm

If you are likable, probably you relate well with others. Your kindness serves you well in the workplace. Developing good interpersonal relationships with coworkers will make work more enjoyable. After all, think of all the hours you will spend together. By showing that you are willing to collaborate with your coworkers, most likely you will receive their cooperation in return.

40wpm

Cooperation begins on the first day of your new job. When you work for a company, you become part of the team. Meeting people and learning new skills can be exciting. For some people, however, any new situation can trigger anxiety. The best advice is to remain calm, do your job to the best of your ability, learn the workplace policies, be flexible, avoid being too critical, and always be positive.

42wpm

When you begin a new job, even if you have recently received your college diploma, chances are you will start at the bottom of the organizational chart. Each of us has to start somewhere. But don't despair. With hard work and determination, soon you will be climbing up the corporate ladder. If you are clever, you will embrace even the most tedious tasks, take everything in stride, and use every opportunity to learn.

44wpm

If you think learning is restricted to the confines of an academic institution, think again. You have plenty to learn on the job, even if it is a job for which you have been trained. As a new worker, you won't be expected to know everything. When necessary, do not hesitate to ask your employer questions. Learn all you can about your job and the company. Use the new information to enhance your job performance and to prepare for success.

46wpm

Begin every valuable workday by prioritizing all your tasks. Decide which tasks must be done immediately and which can wait. List the most important tasks first; then determine the order in which each task must be done. After you complete a task, triumphantly cross it off your priority list. Do not procrastinate; that is, don't put off work you should do. If a task needs to be done, do it. You will be on top of your task list if you use your time wisely.

48wpm

Prevent the telephone from controlling your time by learning to manage your business phone calls. Phone calls can be extremely distracting from necessary tasks. When making an outgoing call, organize the topics you want to discuss. Gather needed materials such as pencils, papers, and files. Set a time limit, and stick to business. Give concise answers, summarize the points discussed, and end the conversation politely. Efficient telephone usage will help you manage your time.

50wpm

As with anything, practice makes perfect, but along the way,[1] we all make mistakes. The difference between the successful peo[2]ple and those who are less successful is not that the successf[3]ul people make fewer mistakes. It's that they don't give up. In[4]stead of letting mistakes bring them down, they use their mist[5]akes as opportunities to grow. If you make a mistake, be patien[6]t with yourself. You might be able to fix your mistake. Look f[7]or more opportunities for success to be just around the corner.[8]

52wpm

Be patient with yourself when handling problems and accepting c[1]riticism. Handling criticism gracefully and maturely may be a cha[2]llenge. Still, it is vital in the workplace. Criticism presented [3]in a way that can help you learn and grow is constructive critici[4]sm . When you see criticism as helpful, it's easier to handle. Bel[5]ieve it or not, there are some employees who welcome criticism. It[6] teaches them better ways to succeed on the job. Strive to impro[7]ve how you accept constructive criticism, and embrace your growth.[8]

54wpm

People experience continuous growth during a career. Goal setting[1] is a helpful tool along any career path. Some people believe that g[2]oals provide the motivation needed to get to the place they want to[3] be. Setting goals encourages greater achievements. The higher we se[4]t our goals, the greater the effort we will need to reach these goa[5]ls. Each time we reach a target or come closer to a goal, we see an[6] increase in our confidence and our performance, leading to greater[7] accomplishments. And the cycle continues to spiral onward and upward.[8]

56wpm

One goal we should all strive for is punctuality. When employees are tardy or absent from the workplace, it costs the company money. If you are frequently tardy or absent, others have to do their own work and cover for you. If you are absent often, your peers will begin to resent you, causing everyone stress in the department. Being late and missing work can damage the relationship with your manager and have a negative effect on your career. To avoid these potential problems, develop a personal plan to assure that you arrive every day on time or early.

58wpm

Holding a job is a major part of being an adult. Some people begin their work careers as adolescents. From the beginning, various work habits are developed that are as crucial to success as the actual job skills and knowledge that a person brings to the job. What traits are expected of workers? What do employers look for when they evaluate their employees? Important personal traits include being confident, cooperative, positive, and dependable. If you are organized, enthusiastic, and understanding, you have many of the qualities that employers value most in their employees.

60wpm

Being dependable is a desirable trait. When a project must be completed by a specific time, a manager will be reassured to know that reliable workers are going to meet the deadline. Workers who are dependable learn to utilize their time to achieve maximum results. Dependable workers can always be counted on, have good attendance records, are well prepared, and arrive on time ready to work. If a company wants to meet its goals, it must have a team of responsible and dependable workers. You, your coworkers, your supervisors, and your managers are all team members, working to reach common goals.

62wpm

The ability to organize is an important quality for the employee who wishes[1] to display good work habits. The worker should have the ability to plan the work[2] that needs to be completed and then be able to execute the plan in a timely[3] manner. An employer requires a competent worker to be well organized. If an[4] office worker is efficient, he or she handles requests swiftly and deals with[5] correspondence without delay. The organized worker does not allow work to accumulate[6] on the desk. Also, the organized office worker returns all phone calls[7] immediately and makes lists of the activities that need to be done each day.[8]

64wpm

Efficiency is another work habit that is desired. An efficient worker completes[1] a task quickly and begins work on the next project eagerly. He or she thinks about[2] ways to save steps and time. For example, an efficient worker may plan a single[3] trip to the copier with several copying jobs rather than multiple trips to do[4] each separate job. Being efficient also means having the required supplies to[5] successfully complete each job. An efficient employee zips along on each project,[6] uses time wisely, and stays focused on the present task. With careful and thorough[7] planning, a worker who is efficient can accomplish more tasks in less time.[8]

66wpm

Cooperation is another ideal work habit. As previously mentioned, cooperation begins[1] on the first day on the job. Cooperation is thinking of all team members when making[2] a decision. A person who cooperates is willing to do what is necessary for the[3] good of the whole group. For you to be a team player, it is essential that you take[4] extra steps to cooperate. Cooperation may mean being a good sport if you are asked[5] to do something you would rather not do. It may mean you have to correct a mistake[6] made by another person in the office. If every employee has the interests of[7] the company at heart and works well as a team player, then cooperation is at work.[8]

68wpm

Enthusiasm is still another work trait that is eagerly sought after by employers. Being enthusiastic means that a person has lots of positive energy. This is reflected in actions toward your work, coworkers, and employer. It has been noted that eagerness can be catching. If workers show they are eager to attempt any project, they will not only achieve the highest praise but will also be considered for career advancement. How much enthusiasm do you show at the workplace? Do you encourage people or complain to people? There will always be plenty of good jobs for employees who are known to have a wealth of zeal and a positive approach to the projects that they are assigned.

70wpm

Understanding is also a preferred work habit for every excellent worker. In today's world, virtually all business includes both men and women of different religions, races, cultures, work ethic, abilities, aptitudes, and attitudes. You'll interact with various types of people as customers, coworkers, and owners. Treat everyone fairly, openly, and honestly. Any type of prejudice is hurtful, offensive, and unacceptable. Prejudice cannot be tolerated in the office. Each employee must try to understand and accept everyone's differences. Because so many diverse groups of people work side by side in the workplace, it is essential that all coworkers maintain a high degree of mutual understanding.

72wpm

It can be concluded that certain work habits or traits can play a major role in determining the success of an employee. Most managers would be quick to agree on the importance of these traits. It is most probable that these habits would be evaluated on performance appraisal forms. Promotions, pay increases, new responsibilities, and your future with the company may be based on these evaluations. You should request regular job performance evaluations even if your company does not conduct them. This feedback will improve your job performance and career development by helping you grow. If you continually look for ways to improve your work habits and skills, then you will enjoy success in the workplace and beyond.

74wpm

You can be certain that no matter where you work, you will use some form of computer technology.[1] Almost every business is dependent upon computers. Companies use such devices as voice[2] mail, fax machines, cellular phones, and electronic schedules. Technology helps to accomplish[3] work quickly and efficiently. A result of this rapidly changing technology is globalization,[4] which is the establishment of worldwide communication links between people. Our world is [5]becoming a smaller, global village. We must expand our thinking beyond the office walls. We must[6] become aware of what happens in other parts of the world. Those events may directly affect[7] you and your workplace. The more you know, the more valuable you will become to the company.[8]

76wpm

Technological advancements are affecting every aspect of our lives. For example, the advent of[1] the Internet has changed how we receive and send information. It is the world's largest information[2] network. The Internet is often called the information superhighway because it is a vast [3]network of computers that connect people and resources worldwide. It is an exciting medium to help[4] you access the latest information. You can even learn about companies by visiting their Web[5] sites. Without any doubt, we are all globally connected, and information technology services [6]support those necessary connections. This industry offers many different employment opportunities.[7] Keep in mind that proficiency in keyboarding is beneficial in this field and in other fields.[8]

78wpm

It is amazing to discover the many careers in which keyboarding skill is necessary today, and the[1] use of the computer keyboard by executive chefs is a prime example. The chefs in major restaurants[2] must prepare parts or all of the meals served while directing the work of a staff of chefs, cooks,[3] and other kitchen staff. The computer has become a necessary tool for a variety of tasks, including[4] tracking inventories of food supplies. By observing which items are favorites and which items[5] are not requested, the chef can calculate food requirements, order food, and supervise the food[6] purchases. Additionally, the computer has proven to be a very practical tool for such tasks as[7] planning budgets, preparing purchase orders for vendors, creating menus, and printing out reports.[8]

80wpm

Advanced technology has opened the doors to a wider variety of amazing new products and services to[1] sell. It seems the more complex the products, the higher the price of the products, or the greater[2] the sales commission, the stiffer the competition. Selling these technical products requires detailed[3] product knowledge, good verbal skills, smooth sales rapport, and proficient keyboarding skills. Business[4] favors people with special training. For example, a pharmacy company may prefer a person with[5] knowledge in chemistry to sell its products. Selling is for people who thrive on challenges and changes[6] in products and services. Sales is appealing to people who enjoy using their powers of persuasion[7] to make the sales. The potential for good earnings is very high for the well-trained salesperson.[8]

82wpm

As you travel about in your sales job or type a report at the office or create Friday night's pasta [1]special for your five-star restaurant, always remember to put safety first. Accidents happen, but they [2]don't have to happen regularly or to have such serious consequences. Accidents cost businesses billions[3] of dollars annually in medical expenses, lost wages, and insurance claims. A part of your job is to make[4] certain you're not one of the millions of people injured on the job every year. You may believe you[5] work in a safe place, but accidents occur in all types of businesses. A few careless people cause most[6] accidents, so ensure your safety on the job. Safety doesn't just happen. Safety is the result of the[7] careful awareness of many people who plan and put into action a safety program that benefits everyone.[8]

84wpm

In today's market, you need more than the necessary skill or the personal qualities described above to[1] succeed in the workplace. Employers also expect their employees to have ethics. Ethics are the principles[2] of conduct governing an individual or a group. Employees who work ethically do not lie, cheat, or steal.[3] They are honest and fair in their dealings with others. Employees who act ethically build a good reputation[4] for themselves and their company. They are known to be dependable and trustworthy. Unethical behavior[5] can have a spiraling effect. A single act can do a lot of damage. Even if you haven't held a job yet, you[6] have had experience with ethical problems. Life is full of many opportunities to behave ethically. Do the[7] right thing when faced with a decision. The ethics you practice today will carry over to your workplace.[8]

86wpm

Now that you know what is expected of you on the job, how do you make sure you will get the job? Almost everyone has experienced the interview process for a job. For some, the interview is a traumatic event, but it doesn't have to be stressful. Preparation is the key. Research the company with whom you are seeking employment. Formulate a list of questions. Your interview provides you the opportunity to interview the organization. Don't go empty-handed. Take a portfolio of items with you. Include copies of your resume with a list of three or more professional references, your academic transcript, and your certificates and licenses. Be sure to wear appropriate business attire. The outcome of the interview will be positive if you have enthusiasm for the job, match your qualifications to the company's needs, ask relevant questions, and listen clearly.

88wpm

How can you be the strongest candidate for the job? Be sure that your skills in reading, writing, mathematics, speaking, and listening are solid. These basic skills will help you listen well and communicate clearly, not only during a job interview, but also at your workplace. The exchange of information between senders and receivers is called communication. It doesn't matter which occupation you choose; you will spend most of your career using these basic skills to communicate with others. You will use the basic skills as tools to gain information, solve problems, and share ideas. You will use these skills to meet the needs of your customers. The majority of jobs available during the next decades will be in the industries that will require direct customer contacts. Your success will be based upon your ability to communicate effectively with customers and coworkers.

90wpm

Writing effectively can help you gain a competitive edge in your job search and throughout your career. Most of us have had occasion to write business letters whether to apply for a job, to comment on a product or service, or to place an order. Often it seems easy to sit and let our thoughts flow freely. In other cases, we seem to struggle to find the proper wording while trying to express our thoughts in exactly the right way. Writing skill can improve with practice. Implement the following principles to develop your writing skill. Try to use language that you would be comfortable using in person. Use words that are simple, direct, kind, confident, and professional. When possible, use words that emphasize the positive side. Remember to proofread your work. Well-organized thoughts and proper grammar, spelling, and punctuation show the reader that you care about the quality of your work.

92wpm

Listening is an essential skill of the communication process. It is crucial for learning, getting along, and forming relationships. Do you think you are an active or passive listener? Listening is not a passive activity. Conversely, active listening is hearing what is being said and interpreting its meaning. Active listening makes you a more effective communicator because you react to what you have heard. Study the following steps to increase your listening skills. Do not cut people off; let them develop their ideas before you speak. If a message is vague, write down your questions or comments, and wait for the entire presentation or discussion to be finished. Reduce personal and environmental distractions by focusing on the message. Keep an open mind. Be attentive and maintain eye contact whenever possible. By developing these basic communication skills, you will become more confident and more effective.

94wpm

Speaking is also a form of communication. In the world of work, speaking is an important way in which to share information. Regardless of whether you are speaking to an audience of one or one hundred, you will want to make sure that your listeners get your message. Be clear about your purpose, your audience, and your subject. A purpose is the overall goal or reason for speaking. An audience is anyone who receives information. The subject is the main topic or key idea. Research your subject. Using specific facts and examples will give you credibility. As you speak, be brief and direct. Progress logically from point to point. Speak slowly and pronounce clearly all your words. Do people understand what you say or ask you to repeat what you've said? Is the sound of your voice friendly and pleasant or shrill and off-putting? These factors influence how your message is received. A good idea is worthless if you can't communicate it.

96wpm

Developing a career is a process. You have looked at your interests, values, skills, aptitudes, and attitudes. Your exploration into the world of work has begun. The journey doesn't stop here, for the present is the perfect place to start thinking about the future. It's where you begin to take steps toward your goals. It's where you can really make a difference. As you set personal and career goals, remember the importance of small steps. Each step toward a personal goal or career goal is a small victory. That feeling of success encourages you to take other small steps. Each step builds onto the next. Continue exploring your personal world as well as the world you share with others. Expect the best as you go forward. Expect a happy life. Expect loving relationships. Expect success in life. Expect fulfilling and satisfying work in a job you truly love. Last but not least, expect that you have something special to offer the world, because you do.

Supplementary Timed Writings

Supplementary Timed Writing 1

All problem solving, whether personal or academic, 10
involves decision making. You make decisions in order to 21
solve problems. On occasion, problems occur as a result of 33
decisions you have made. For example, you may decide to 44
smoke, but later in life, you face the problem of nicotine 56
addiction. You may decide not to study mathematics and 67
science because you think that they are too difficult. 78
Because of this choice, many career opportunities will be 90
closed to you. There is a consequence for every action. Do 102
you see that events in your life do not just happen, but 113
that they are the result of your choices and decisions? 124

How can you prepare your mind for problem solving? A 135
positive attitude is a great start. Indeed, your attitude 147
affects the way in which you solve a problem or make a 158
decision. Approach your studies, such as science and math 170
courses, with a positive and inquisitive attitude. Try to 182
perceive academic problems as puzzles to solve rather than 192
homework to avoid. 198

Critical thinking is a method of problem solving that 209
involves decoding, analyzing, reasoning, evaluating, and 220
processing information. It is fundamental for successful 231
problem solving. Critical thinking is a willingness to 242
explore, probe, question, and search for answers. Problems 254
may not always be solved on the first try. Don't give up. 266
Try, try again. Finding a solution takes sustained effort. 278
Use critical thinking skills to achieve success in today's 290
fast-paced and highly competitive world of business. 300

| 1 | 2 | 3 | 4 | 5 | 6 | 7 | 8 | 9 | 10 | 11 | 12

Supplementary Timed Writing 2

For many, the Internet is an important resource in 10
their private and professional lives. The Internet provides 22
quick access to countless Web sites that contain news, 33
products, games, entertainment, and many other types of 44
information. The Web pages on these sites can be designed, 56
authored, and posted by anyone, anywhere around the world. 68
Utilize critical thinking when reviewing all Web sites. 79

Just because something is stated on the radio, printed 90
in the newspaper, or shown on television doesn't mean that 102
it's true, real, accurate, or correct. This applies to 113
information found on the Internet as well. Don't fall into 125
the trap of believing that if it's on the Net, it must be 137
true. A wise user of the Internet thinks critically about 149
data found on the Net and evaluates this material before 160
using it. 162

When evaluating a new Web site, think about who, what, 173
how, when, and where. Who refers to the author of the Web 185
site. The author may be a business, an organization, or a 197
person. What refers to the validity of the data. Can this 209
data be verified by a reputable source? How refers to the 221
viewpoint of the author. Is the data presented without 232
prejudice? When refers to the time frame of the data. Is 244
this recent data? Where refers to the source of the data. 256
Is this data from an accurate source? By answering these 267
critical questions, you will learn more about the accuracy 279
and dependability of a Web site. As you surf the Net, be 290
very cautious. Anyone can publish on the Internet. 300

| 1 | 2 | 3 | 4 | 5 | 6 | 7 | 8 | 9 | 10 | 11 | 12

Supplementary Timed Writing 3

Office employees perform a variety of tasks during 10
their workday. These tasks vary from handling telephone 21
calls to forwarding personal messages, from sending short 33
e-mail messages to compiling complex office reports, and 44
from writing simple letters to assembling detailed letters 56
with tables, graphics, and imported data. Office workers 67
are a fundamental part of a company's structure. 77

The office worker uses critical thinking in order to 88
accomplish a wide array of daily tasks. Some of the tasks 100
are more urgent than other tasks and should be completed 111
first. Some tasks take only a short time, while others take 123
a lot more time. Some tasks demand a quick response, while 135
others may be taken up as time permits or even postponed 147
until the future. Some of the tasks require input from 158
coworkers or managers. Whether a job is simple or complex, 170
big or small, the office worker must decide what is to be 182
tackled first by determining the priority of each task. 193

When setting priorities, critical thinking skills are 204
essential. The office worker evaluates each aspect of the 216
task. It is a good idea to identify the size of the task, 228
determine its complexity, estimate its effort, judge its 239
importance, and set its deadline. Once the office worker 250
assesses each task that is to be finished within a certain 262
period of time, then the priority for completing all tasks 274
can be set. Critical thinking skills, if applied well, 285
can save the employer money or, if executed poorly, can 296
cost the employer. 300

| 1 | 2 | 3 | 4 | 5 | 6 | 7 | 8 | 9 | 10 | 11 | 12

Supplementary Timed Writing 4

Each day business managers make choices that keep 10
businesses running smoothly, skillfully, and profitably. 21
Each decision regarding staff, finances, operations, and 32
resources often needs to be quick and precise. To develop 44
sound decisions, managers must use critical thinking. They 56
gather all the essential facts so that they can make good, 68
well-informed choices. After making a decision, skilled 79
managers review their thinking process. Over time, they 90
refine their critical thinking skills. When they encounter 102
similar problems, they use their prior experiences to help 114
them solve problems with ease and in less time. 124

What type of decisions do you think managers make that 135
involve critical thinking? Human resources managers decide 147
whom to employ, what to pay a new employee, and where to 158
place a new worker. In addition, human resources managers 170
should be unbiased negotiators, resolving conflict between 182
other employees. Office managers purchase copy machines, 194
computers, software, and office supplies. Finance officers 206
prepare precise, timely financial statements. Top managers 218
control business policies, appoint mid-level managers, and 230
assess the success of the business. Plant supervisors set 242
schedules, gauge work quality, and evaluate workers. Sales 254
managers study all of the new sales trends, as well as 265
provide sales training and promotion materials. 275

Most managers use critical thinking to make wise, well- 286
thought-out decisions. They carefully check their facts, 297
analyze these facts, and make a final judgment based upon 309
these facts. They should also be able to clearly discern 320
fact from fiction. Through trial and error, managers learn 332
their own ways of solving problems and finding the most 343
effective and creative solutions. 350

| 1 | 2 | 3 | 4 | 5 | 6 | 7 | 8 | 9 | 10 | 11 | 12

Supplementary Timed Writing 5

In most classes, teachers want students to analyze 10
situations, draw conclusions, and solve problems. Each 21
of these tasks requires students to use thinking skills. 32
How do students acquire these skills? What is the process 44
students follow to develop thinking skills? 53

During the early years of life, children learn words 63
and then combine these words into sentences. From there, 74
they learn to declare ideas, share thoughts, and express 85
feelings. Students learn numbers and simple math concepts. 97
They may learn to read musical notes, to keep rhythm, to 108
sing songs, and to recognize many popular and classical 119
pieces of music. Students learn colors, identify shapes, 130
and begin drawing. During the early years, students learn 142
the basic problem-solving models. 149

One way to solve problems and apply thinking skills 159
is to use the scientific approach. This approach requires 171
the student to state the problem to be solved, gather all 183
the facts about the problem, analyze the problem, and pose 195
viable solutions. Throughout this process, teachers ask 206
questions that force students to expand their thinking 217
skills. Teachers may ask questions such as these: Did you 229
clearly state the problem? Did you get all the facts? Did 241
you get the facts from the right place? Did you assume 252
anything? Did you pose other possible solutions? Did you 263
keep an open mind to all solutions? Did you let your bias 275
come into play? Did you listen to others who might have 286
insights? Did you dig deep enough? Does the solution make 298
sense to you? 301

This simple four-step process for solving problems 311
gives students a model to use for school, for work, and 322
for life. While the process may not be used to solve every 334
problem, it does provide a starting point to begin using 345
critical thinking skills. 350

| 1 | 2 | 3 | 4 | 5 | 6 | 7 | 8 | 9 | 10 | 11 | 12

Supplementary Timed Writing 6

A major goal for nearly all educators is to teach 10
critical thinking skills to a class. Critical thinking, 21
which is the process of reasonably or logically deciding 32
what to do or believe, involves the ability to compare and 44
contrast, resolve problems, make decisions, analyze and 55
evaluate, and combine and transfer knowledge. These skills 67
benefit the student who eventually becomes a part of the 78
workforce. Whether someone is in a corporate setting, is 89
in a small business, or is self-employed, the environment 101
of today is highly competitive and skilled employees are in 113
great demand. 116

One factor in achieving success in the workforce is 127
having the ability to deal with the varied demands of the 139
fast-paced business world. Required skills are insightful 150
decision making, creative problem solving, and earnest 162
communication among diverse groups. These groups could be 174
employees, management, employers, investors, customers, 185
or clients. 187

In school, we learn the details of critical thinking. 198
This knowledge extends far beyond the boundaries of the 209
classroom. It lasts a lifetime. We use critical thinking 220
throughout our daily lives. We constantly analyze and 231
evaluate music, movies, conversations, fashion, magazine 242
or newspaper articles, and television programs. We all had 254
experience using critical thinking skills before we even 265
knew what they were. So keep on learning, growing, and 276
experimenting. The classroom is the perfect setting for 287
exploration. Take this opportunity to see how others solve 299
problems, give each other feedback, and try out new ideas 311
in a safe environment. 316

A person who has learned critical thinking skills is 327
equipped with the essential skills for achieving success 338
in today's workforce. There are always new goals to reach. 350

| 1 | 2 | 3 | 4 | 5 | 6 | 7 | 8 | 9 | 10 | 11 | 12

Supplementary Timed Writing 7

Use your unique creativity when applying critical 10
thinking skills. One of the first steps in unlocking your 22
creativity is to realize that you have control over your 33
thinking; it doesn't control you. Creativity is using new 45
or different methods to solve problems. Many inventions 56
involved a breakthrough in traditional thinking, and the 67
result was an amazing experience. For example, Einstein 78
broke with tradition by trying lots of obscure formulas 89
that changed scientific thought. Your attitude can form 100
mental blocks that keep you from being creative. When you 112
free your mind, the rest will follow. 120

Do your best to unleash your mind's innate creativity. 131
Turn problems into puzzles. When you think of a task as a 143
puzzle, a challenge, or a game instead of a difficult 154
problem, you open your mind and encourage your creative 165
side to operate. Creative ideas often come when you are 176
having fun and are involved in an unrelated activity. 187
You will find that when your defenses are down, your brain 199
is relaxed and your subconscious is alive; then creative 210
thoughts can flow. 214

Habit often restricts you from trying new approaches 225
to problem solving. Remember, there is usually more than 237
one solution. Empty your mind of the idea of only one way 249
of looking at a problem and strive to see situations in a 261
fresh, new way. How many times have you told yourself that 273
you must follow the rules and perform tasks in a certain 284
way? If you want to be creative, look at things in a new 295
way, break the pattern, explore new options, and challenge 307
the rules. If you are facing a difficult problem and can't 319
seem to find a solution, take a quick walk or relax for 330
a few minutes; then go back to the problem renewed. When 341
working on homework or taking a test, always work the 352
easiest problems first. Success builds success. 362

A sense of humor is key to being creative. Silly and 373
irrelevant ideas can lead to inventive solutions. Humor 384
generates ideas, puts you in a creative state of mind, 395
and makes work exciting! 400

| 1 | 2 | 3 | 4 | 5 | 6 | 7 | 8 | 9 | 10 | 11 | 12

Supplementary Timed Writing 8

Keyboarding is a popular business course for many 10
students. The major objectives of a keyboarding course are 22
to develop touch control of the keyboard and proper typing 34
techniques, build basic speed and accuracy, and provide 45
practice in applying those basic skills to the formatting 57
of letters, reports, tables, memos, and other kinds of 68
personal and business communications. In the early part of 80
a keyboarding course, students learn to stroke by touch 91
using specific techniques. They learn to hit the keys in a 103
quick and accurate way. After the keys are learned and 114
practiced, students move into producing documents of all 125
sizes and types for personal and vocational use. 135

When you first learn keyboarding, there are certain 145
parameters, guidelines, and exercises to follow. There are 157
rules intended to help you learn and eventually master the 169
keyboard. Creating documents requires students to apply 180
critical thinking. What format or layout should be used? 191
What font and font size would be best? Are all the words 202
spelled correctly? Does the document look neat? Are the 213
figures accurate? Are punctuation and grammar correct? 224

There is a lot to learn in the world of keyboarding. 235
Be persistent, patient, and gentle with yourself. Allow 246
failure in class and on the job; that's how we learn. It's 258
okay to admit mistakes. Mistakes are stepping-stones for 269
growth and creativity. Being creative has a lot to do with 281
risk taking and courage. It takes courage to explore new 292
ways of thinking and to risk looking different, being 303
silly and impractical, and even being wrong. Your path to 315
creativity is such a vital component of your critical 326
thinking skills. Allow your creative thoughts to flow 337
freely when producing each of your keyboarding tasks. 348

Keyboarding skill and personal creativity are valuable 359
attributes for life and on the job. The worker who can see 371
situations and problems in a fresh way, reason logically, 383
explore options, and come up with inventive ideas is sure 395
to be a valuable employee. 400

| 1 | 2 | 3 | 4 | 5 | 6 | 7 | 8 | 9 | 10 | 11 | 12

Supplementary Timed Writing 9

One of the most important decisions we all have to 10
face is choosing a career. The possibilities can appear 21
overwhelming. Fear not! Your critical thinking skills will 33
save you! Start your career planning today. Begin with 44
self-assessment. What are your interests? Do you enjoy 55
working indoors or outdoors? Do you prefer working with 66
numbers or with words? Are you the independent type or 77
would you rather work with a group? What are your favorite 89
academic studies? Think about these questions and then 100
create a list of your interests, skills, aptitudes, and 111
values. What you discover about yourself will help you in 123
finding the career that is right for you. 131

After you have explored your personal interests, look 142
at the sixteen career clusters for a wide range of job 153
prospects. Most jobs are included in one of these clusters 165
that have been organized by the government. During your 176
exploration, make a note of the clusters that interest you 188
and investigate these clusters. 194

Gather as much information as possible by using all 205
available resources. Scan the Help Wanted section in the 216
major Sunday newspapers for job descriptions and salaries. 228
Search the Net. The Internet provides electronic access to 240
worldwide job listings. If you want to know more about a 251
specific company, access its home page. Go to your college 263
placement office. Sign up for interviews with companies 274
that visit your campus. Visit your local school or county 286
library and ask the reference librarian for occupational 297
handbooks. Talk with people in your field of interest to 308
ask questions and get advice. Attend chapter meetings of 319
professional organizations to network with people working 331
in your chosen profession. Volunteer, intern, or work a 342
part-time or temporary job within your career choice for 353
valuable, first-hand insight. Taking an initiative in your 365
job search will pay off. 370

A career search requires the use of critical thinking 381
skills. These skills will help you to choose the career 392
that will match your skills and talents. 400

| 1 | 2 | 3 | 4 | 5 | 6 | 7 | 8 | 9 | 10 | 11 | 12

Ten-Key Numeric Keypad

Goal

- To control the ten-key numeric keypad keys.

Some computer keyboards have a separate ten-key numeric keypad located to the right of the alphanumeric keyboard. The arrangement of the keypad enables you to type numbers more rapidly than you can when using the top row of the alphanumeric keyboard.

To input numbers using the ten-key numeric keypad, you must activate the Num Lock (Numeric Lock) key. Usually, an indicator light signals that the Num Lock is activated.

On the keypad, 4, 5, and 6 are the home keys. Place your fingers on the keypad home row as follows:

- First finger (J finger) on 4
- Second finger (K finger) on 5
- Third finger (L finger) on 6

The keypad keys are controlled as follows:

- First finger controls 1, 4, and 7
- Second finger controls 2, 5, and 8
- Third finger controls 3, 6, 9, and decimal point
- Right thumb controls 0
- Fourth finger controls ENTER

Since different computers have different arrangements of ten-key numeric keypads, study the arrangement of your keypad. The illustration shows the most common arrangement. If your keypad is arranged differently from the one shown in the illustration, check with your instructor for the correct placement of your fingers on the keypad.

NEW KEYS

A. Use the first finger to control the 4 key, the second finger to control the 5 key, and the third finger to control the 6 key.

Keep your eyes on the copy.

Before beginning, check to be sure the Num Lock key is activated.

Type the first column from top to bottom. Next, type the second column; then type the third column. Press ENTER after typing the final digit of each number.

A. THE 4, 5, AND 6 KEYS

444	456	454
555	654	464
666	445	546
455	446	564
466	554	654
544	556	645
566	664	666
644	665	555
655	456	444
456	654	456

B. Use the 4 finger to control the 7 key, the 5 finger to control the 8 key, and the 6 finger to control the 9 key.

Keep your eyes on the copy.

Press ENTER after typing the final digit of each number.

B. THE 7, 8, AND 9 KEYS

474	585	696
747	858	969
774	885	996
447	558	669
744	855	966
477	588	699
444	555	666
747	858	969
774	885	996
747	858	969

C. Use the 4 finger to control the 1 key, the 5 finger to control the 2 key, and the 6 finger to control the 3 key.

Keep your eyes on the copy.

Press ENTER after typing the final digit of each number.

C. THE 1, 2, AND 3 KEYS

444	555	666
111	222	333
144	225	336
441	552	663
144	255	366
411	522	633
444	555	666
414	525	636
141	252	363
411	525	636

D. Use the right thumb to control the 0 key.

Keep your eyes on the copy.

Press ENTER after typing the final digit of each number.

D. THE 0 KEY

404	470	502
505	580	603
606	690	140
707	410	250
808	520	360
909	630	701
101	407	802
202	508	903
303	609	405
505	401	506

E. Use the 6 finger to control the decimal key.

Keep your eyes on the copy.

Press ENTER after typing the final digit of each number.

E. THE . KEY

4.5	7.8	1.2
6.5	9.8	3.2
4.4	7.7	1.1
4.4	7.7	1.1
5.5	8.8	2.2
5.5	8.8	2.2
6.6	9.9	3.3
6.5	9.9	3.3
4.5	7.8	1.2
6.5	8.9	1.3

INDEX

NOTE: Page numbers preceded by A- indicate material in Appendix; page numbers preceded by R- indicate material in Reference Manual; page numbers preceded by SB- indicate material in Skillbuilding supplement.

A

B

C

D

E

F

G

H

I

J

K

L

M

N

O

P

Q

R

S

T

U

V

W

Y

McGraw-Hill/Irwin and the GDP author team would like to acknowledge the participants of the 2004 Focus Group for their efforts in making the 10th edition the best it can be:

Special thanks goes to Ken Baker for his work as the tech editor on GDP.

Kim Aylett
Branford Hall Career Institute
Southington, CT

Ken Baker
Sinclair Community College
Dayton, OH

Lenette Baker
Valencia Community College
Orlando, FL

Joyce Crawford
Central Piedmont Community College
Charlotte, NC

Martha Gwatney
Northern Virginia Community College
Annandale, VA

Marijean Harmonis
Community College of Philadelphia
Philadelphia, PA

Mary Hedberg
Johnson County Community College
Overland Park, KS

Kay Ono
Leeward Community College
Pearl City, HI

Marcia Polanis
Forsyth Tech Community College
Winston-Salem, NC

Photo Credits
Steve Cole/Getty Images 95; Adam Crowley/Getty Images 163; Jack Hollingsworth/Getty Images 66; Jeff Maloney/Getty Images 173; Ryan McVay/Getty Images iii, iv, R-23, 42, 56, 91, 154, 180; Royalty Free/Corbis vi, 120, 197, 207; Royalty Free/Getty Images R-2; Royalty Free/PhotoDisc 160; Jack Star/ Photo Link/Getty Images 117